Created and Directed by Hans Höfer

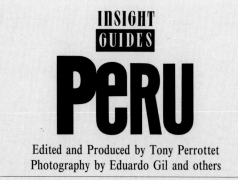

INSIGHT GUIDES

PERU

Edited and Produced by Tony Perrottet
Photography by Eduardo Gil and others

PERU

First Edition
© 1991 APA PUBLICATIONS (HK) LTD
All Rights Reserved
Printed in Singapore by Höfer Press Pte. Ltd

ABOUT THIS BOOK

With its combination of ancient ruins, magnificent scenery and vibrant Indian culture, Peru is the classic South American destination. Yet travelers have always been hampered by a lack of high quality, in-depth guide books to Peru, often being forced to choose between fanciful tourist brochures or dense academic works for information. Now *Insight Guide: Peru* ties the many strands of this huge and complex nation together into one accessible volume, making an impressive addition to Apa's rapidly growing list of South American titles.

Apa's Editor-in-Chief for the South American region, **Tony Perrottet**, used his years of experience as a foreign correspondent to put together an expert team for the project. Australian-born Perrottet studied history at Sydney University before embarking on a highly mobile career as a journalist. Lured by tales of relatives who had worked on the sheep farms in southern Patagonia, he ended up in South America in 1986 and first visited Peru as part of a journey exploring the continent from one tip to the other. Since then he has been back many times while working for magazines and newspapers in Australia, New Zealand, Britain and the United States.

For *Insight Guide: Peru*, project editor Perrottet made several more journeys from his current home in New York City to the colonial streets of Lima and Cuzco. Apart from editing the volume and providing some photographs, Perrottet also wrote the chapters on the Spanish Conquest and Amantaní.

Mary Dempsey, the writer for the Peru chapter of *Insight Guide: South America*, went straight on to compile a large chunk of this new volume. Dempsey, born in Toronto and brought up on the US Midwest, developed an "incurable case of wanderlust" before settling in Lima in the early 80s with her Peruvian-born husband. For *Insight Guide: Peru*, Dempsey used her experience to write on subjects as diverse as Peruvian cuisine and marlin fishing, as well as on the key tourist destinations of Cuzco, Arequipa, the North and Lake Titicaca.

Chosen to write the chapters on archaeology and colonial history was Peruvian journalist **Adriana von Hagen**. As the daughter of one of Peru's most famous archaeologists, Adriana's interest in these fields came fairly naturally – an enthusiasm that was backed by a degree in the field from the University of California. Today von Hagen lives in Lima and works for the prestigious *Andean Report*, a business journal on the area.

British-born journalist **Mike Reid** contributed the chapters on Peru Today, Mario Vargas Llosa, Lima and the coca trade. Reid, who has spent eight years as a correspondent in Lima for the Guardian and BBC, is the author of *Peru: Paths to Poverty* published by the Latin American Bureau in London.

Also well-known to Peru enthusiasts is **Peter Frost**, author of the highly-respected volume *Exploring Cuzco*. Having lived in the ancient Inca capital for many years, Forst was given the chapters on Inca Society and the mysterious ruins of Machu Picchu. He is currently writing a mythic novel about the last Incas and their modern descendents.

The key chapter on Peruvian Society entitled "An Andean Nation in the Making" was given to US-born journalist **Michael L. Smith**. A correspondent for the *Washington Post* in Lima from 1979 to 1990, Smith is also writing a book on the Sendero Luminoso.

Perrottet   *Dempsey*   *von Hagen*   *Reid*   *Frost*

Compiling the section on "Daily Life in the Andes" was US-born **Julia Meyerson**. An artist as well as writer, she has lived for several years in a remote Quechua village in the Peruvian Andes. Her book *Tambo: Life in an Andean Village* was published in 1990.

Anthropologist, jungle guide and freelance writer **Kim MacQuarrie** contributed the chapters on Amazon Indians and the jungle. Educated in France, the US and Peru, he has spent many months living with the recently-contacted Nahua Indians in the remote Manu National Park region of southeastern Peru. Having finished a thesis on the Nahua, he is writing a popular book based upon the tribe's sudden contact with the outside world.

Several other writers contributed to *Insight Guide: Peru* in their specialist fields. Journalist **Anne Kalosh** has written about the Norwegian Thor Heyerdahl's new dig in northern Peru. **Lynn Meisch**, anthropologist and author of *A Traveler's Guide to El Dorado and the Inca Empire*, contributed the section on Cuzco fiestas. Well-known naturalists **Barry Walker** and **Katherine Renton** contributed the sections on Sierra wildlife and Amazon birdwatching respectively.

The special sections on trekking and white water rafting in Peru were put together by **Betsy Wagenhauser**, head of the South American Explorer's Club in Lima and Quito. British journalist **Simon Strong** wrote on the Villa El Salvador in Lima, while Australian writer **Lesley Thelander** used her experience in the travel industry to put together the detailed Travel Tips section.

Finally, the section on the "Quest for Lost Cities" was written by the anthropologist and adventurer **Robert Randall**. US-born Randall ran a hotel in Ollantaytambo with his wife for many years and made annual expeditions into the Peruvian jungle with a group of friends calling themselves "the Ramblers" before his tragic death in 1990.

More than fifteen photographers contributed their work to *Insight Guide: Peru*. Most prolific amongst them is Argentine **Eduardo Gil**. Already well-known to Insight Guide readers for his work on the Buenos Aires, South America and Chile books, Gil studied sociology and trained as a commercial pilot before dedicating himself to photography. He is currently director of the prestigious Buenos Aires Cultural Center.

Peruvian-born photographer **Heinz Plenge** provides a selection of work from his photo library, gathered over a decade shooting his native land. Well-known within Peru for his magazine and newspaper work, Plenge also contributed to *National Geographic* and German *Geo* features on the recent archaeological discoveries at Sipán.

Based in Liechtenstein but specializing in Amazon nature photography is **Andre Bartschi**, whose work is well represented here. **John Maier**, a US photographer living in Rio de Janeiro and working for the Time-Life organization, added a series of shots from his latest assignment in Peru. Mountain photographer **Jim Bartle** provided shots from the magnificent Callejon de Huayllas area, while priest and photographer **Victor Campos Rios** sent work from his home city Cajamarca.

Meanwhile, special thanks must go to Ana Maria Arrarte de Aliaga, director of the Peruvian travel agency **Limatours** who helped in many ways to organize the traveling for *Insight Guides: Peru*; as well as Ada Garibaldi of the **Hotel Bolívar**, without doubt Lima's most charming hotel.

—APA Publications

Smith

Myerson

MacQuarrie

Wagenhauser

Gil

History

23 Welcome to Peru
—by Tony Perrottet

26 Geography
—by Mary Dempsey

35 Lost Empires: Peru Before the Incas
—by Adriana von Hagen

43 Discovery in the Desert
—by Mary Dempsey

47 Thor Heyerdahl Returns
—by Anne Kalosh

51 The Incas
—by Peter Frost

59 The Conquest
—by Tony Perrottet

69 Colony and Republic
—by Adriana von Hagen

72 *Las Tapadas*
—by Mary Dempsey

78 Democracy and Crisis
—by Mike Reid

Features

89 An Andean Nation in the Making
—by Michael L. Smith

99 Daily Life in the Andes
—by Julia Meyerson

106 Haunting Sounds of the Sierra
—by Julia Meyerson

111 Tribes of the Amazon
—by Kim MacQuarrie

117 Crafts of Peru
    —by Mary Dempsey

123 The Ancient Art of Peruvian Cuisine
    —by Mary Dempsey

131 Trekking in the Andes
    —by Betsy Wagenhauser

140 Wildlife of the Sierra
    —by Barry Walker

Places

151 Exploring Peru
    —by Tony Perrottet

159 Lima
    —by Mike Reid

171 *Peru's High-Profile Novelist*
    —by Mike Reid

172 *Lima's Oasis of Hope*
    —by Simon Strong

176 Railway to Huancayo
    —by Mary Dempsey

185 Cuzco and Valley of Incas
    —by Mary Dempsey

191 *Riding the Rapids*
    —by Betsy Wagenhauser

206 Fiestas in Cuzco
    —by Lynn A. Meisch

210 *The Quest for Lost Cities*
    —by Robert Randall

221 Machu Picchu
    —by Peter Frost

231 Lake Titicaca
    —by Mary Dempsey

241 *The Weaving Co-Ops of Taquile*
—by Mary Dempsey

242 *Amantaní Opens its Doors*
—by Tony Perrottet

247 **Arequipa**
—by Mary Dempsey

259 **The Peruvian Amazon**
—by Kim MacQuarrie

276 *Birdwatchers of the Amazon*
—by Katherine Renton

280 *The Valley of Coca*
—by Mike Reid

285 **Callejon De Huaylas**
—by Betsy Wagenhauser

297 **The North**
—by Mary Dempsey

306 *In Search of Hemingway's Marlin*
—by Mary Dempsey

317 **South Coast**
—by Mary Dempsey

329 *Guardian of the Nazca Lines*
—by Mary Dempsey

Maps

51 The Inca Empire
132 Inca Trail
150 Peru
156 Lima
174 South Peru
189 Cuzco
198 Urubamba Valley
218 Machu Picchu
232 Titicaca Lake
302 Northern Peru

Getting There

332 By Air
332 By Sea
332 By Land

Travel Essentials

332 Visas & Passports
332 Money Matters
333 Health
333 What to Wear
334 What to Bring

Getting Acquainted

334 Climate
334 Time Zones
334 Weights & Measures
335 Electricity
335 Business Hours
335 Festivals & Holidays

Communications

336 Newspapers
337 Postal Services
337 Telephone/Telegram/
Telex

Emergencies

337 Security & Crime
338 Medical Services

Getting Around

338 Orientation
338 Maps
338 From the Airport
339 Domestic Travel
340 Private Transport
340 Public Transport
341 On Foot

Where To Stay

341 Hotels

Food Digest

346 What To Eat
346 Where To Eat

Things To Do

349 General
349 Lima
350 Pisco
350 Ica
350 Nazca
350 Arequipa
351 Puno (Lake
Titicaca)
351 Cuzco
352 Huaráz
352 Trujillo
352 Chiclayo
352 Cajamarca
352 Iquitos

Culture Plus

352 Museums
354 Antique & Art
Galleries
355 Concerts
355 Theater & Music

Nightlife

356 Live Music
356 Nightclubs
357 Bars
357 Discos

Shopping

357 What To Buy
358 Shopping Areas

Sports

359 Participant
359 Spectator

Further Reading

359 General
360 Archaeology &
Pre-Inca Cultures
360 Inca Society
361 Colonial History
361 Machu Picchu
361 Other "Lost Cities"
361 Andean Wildlife
361 Amazon Jungle

Useful Addresses

362 Embassies &
Consulates
363 Airline Offices
364 Tourist Information
Offices (FOPTUR)

WELCOME TO PERU

Despite its rugged and often inhospitable landscape, Peru ranks amongst the world's great centers of ancient civilization. The sun-worshipping Incas are only the most famous in a long line of highly-developed cultures that thrived thousands of years before the arrival of Europeans. Their remains fascinate travelers and archaeologists alike. Along with the stunning Inca ruins near Cuzco and the "lost city" of Machu Picchu, Peru is home to the Nazca lines etched on its coastal deserts, Colla burial *chullpas* near Lake Titicaca, the enormous adobe city of Chan Chan and the recently-discovered Moche burial site of the Lord of Sipán. The fact that we know very little about these cultures – they left no written records, just mysterious works in gold, silver and stone – only seems to add to the fascination.

But ancient ruins are only a fraction of the story. Peru is the classic Andean republic, and, although the traditional American world was shattered by the bloody Spanish conquest in the 1530s, the legacy of ancient cultures is very much alive. Roughly half of Peru's 22-million population are of pure Indian origin: often living in remote mountain villages, they still speak the Quechua or Aymará tongue of their ancestors, and many of their beliefs and customs are a mixture of traditional Andean ways and the culture imposed by the *conquistadores*.

Peru is also one of the most spectacular countries on earth. Its variety is astonishing: scientists have ascertained that of 103 possible ecological zones, Peru has 83 crowded into its borders. As a result, the country has virtually every possible physical attraction. The Peruvian Andes have become a mecca for trekkers and mountain climbers, as well as those who want to enjoy dramatic mountain scenery in a more leisurely fashion. Over half of Peru is part of the Amazon jungle. And the coastal strip of Peru is one of the world's driest desert.

Meanwhile, Peru's often chaotic modern reality is an essential part of the experience. In Jean Renoir's classic film "The Golden Coach", a troupe of Italian actors arrives in 18th-century Lima to be greeted with the question: "What do you think of the New World?" The chief actor looks around at the provincial square and replies politely: "It will be nice when it's finished." Many people have a similar reaction today. Peru is a nation still in the process of being formed – coping not only with the demands of economic development in the 20th century, but also the cultural divisions that began with the Spanish Conquest over 450 years ago. For culturally sensitive travelers clued to the changes that are constantly underway, Peru remains one of the world's great travel destinations.

Preceding pages: expert horse rider of Trujillo (North); sumptuous tapestries from Cuzco; Mt. Huascarán in the Callejón de Huaylas; Machu Picchu, "Lost City of the Incas"; a slow afternoon on Taquile Island. Left, girl from Arequipa.

GEOGRAPHY

Ask Peruvians about their country and they will cut it into geographical slices – desert coast, highlands and jungle – proudly noting theirs is South America's only nation with all three. That geography, challenging to humans, sometimes even insurmountable, has given Peru its so varied legacy of ethnic cultures, foods, music and folklore.

Within that framework, Peruvians use the superlative to describe the country's offerings. They include Lake Titicaca, the world's highest navigable lake at 3,856 meters (12,725 feet) above sea level, and Mount Huascarán, Peru's highest Andean peak and South America's second tallest mountain at 6,768 meters (22,334 feet). The Amazon River, the world's mightiest, and its namesake rainforest make up much of Peru. Here, too, runs the world's highest single gauge rail line cutting over the Andes, the globe's deepest canyon (the Colca outside Arequipa) and Cuzco, capital of the Inca empire.

Settled among those wonders – both natural and manmade – are 22 million Peruvians, 6.5 million of whom are crowded into Lima. About 45 percent of the nation's residents are Indians, 37 percent are *mestizos* (mixed white and Indian), 15 percent are of European extract and 3 percent are descendants of black slaves brought to work the mines or Japanese and Chinese immigrants. Spanish and Quechua are the offical languages. An estimated 92 percent of the country's residents are Roman Catholic although the religious rites they practice still bear traces of the pre-Christian religions the Indians once followed.

Barren beaches: The Spanish conquistadors' first glimpse of what is now Peru was along its 2,500-km (1,500-mile) coastal desert – one of the world's driest in this, the continent's third largest country after Brazil and Argentina. Visitors familiar with South America's Caribbean coast find Peru's sandy beaches unsettling, with their harsh backdrop of dunes or cactus-covered cliffs. But when Pizarro arrived the coast was less desolate;

Preceding pages: the Amazon rainforest. Right, Mt. Alpamayo in the Cordillera Blanca near Huaráz.

the Indians had sophisticated irrigation systems and fields of vegetables and grains flourished in the desert. The northern desert where Pizarro landed with his men was, in part, mangrove swamps.

On the southern coast, Chile's appropriation of some of this desert land more than a century ago in the bloody War of the Pacific meant the loss of a hidden treasure – tracts rich in the nitrates sought for fertilizers. Still, the coast has brought wealth to Peru despite its inhospitable landscape and dearth of water. (Only a cup of measurable precipitation every two years is recorded in some areas.) And fish are plentiful in the coastal waters, making Peru one of the world's foremost exporters of anchovies.

In fact, it is this frigid fish-bearing current that keeps rain from the desert separating the ocean and the Andes. So little moisure accumulates above the cold Humboldt current running along the hot coast that ocean winds heading toward the mountains rarely carry condensation. What they do bring to the land, however, is a thick dense fog that causes havoc with air traffic and covers Lima for half the year with a gloomy mist known as *garua*. The exception to this rainless period are the freak showers when El Niño, a warm current traveling from the equator, comes too close to the coast.

Mountainous heart: But it is the highlands that are most associated with Peru. Here Quechua-speaking women weave, condors soar above the Andes and wild vegetation camouflages Inca ruins. Although breathtaking to look at, the Sierra seems brutally inhospitable: the thin, cold air here combines with rugged landscape to make the Andes an obstacle to transportation, communication and development.

Nevertheless, nearly half of Peru's population is scattered across the Sierra, on poor rocky land where alpacas and llamas graze while subsistence crops are eked out of terrace farms used since Inca times.

Although the Incas found a way to survive in the Andes, cutting terrace farms into steep hillsides, building aqueducts that astound modern hydraulic engineers and erecting massive forts and cities in isolated valleys, they met a formidable foe in the jungle – the region even they could not successfully pen-

Terraces in the lush Colca valley near Arequipa.

etrate. Three-fifths of Peru is jungle, divided into the hot, steamy low Amazon and the so-called high jungle, or *ceja de la selva* (eyebrow of the jungle). The latter is the area where the mountains meet the Amazon, a subtropical patch where Peru's coffee and 60 percent of the world's coca crop is grown.

Peru has set itself aside from its neighbors by aggressively protecting the rainforest through legislation and by designating virgin areas as national parks. Extending from the Andean foothills east of Cuzco into the low jungle is Manu National Park, boasting one of the world's most impressive concentrations of wildlife; more than 500 bird species alone have been spotted from the park's research station.

A few hours by river from Puerto Maldonado is another protected area, the Tambopata Wildlife Reserve with more than 1,110 butterfly species and a number of insects found only there.

Land of volcanoes: Nature as much as man has dealt this country cruel blows. Peru straddles the Cadena del Fuego, or Chain of Fire – a volcanic line over a geologic fault running the length of the continent. The line passes Peru along its coast, cutting directly through Arequipa which, over the centuries, has borne the brunt of the seismic damage.

In the Sierra, quake damage is aggravated by the breaching of highland lakes, pulling tons of water and mud onto small towns and burying their residents alive. The world's worst recorded disaster of this type occurred in 1970 in Yungay, near Huaráz. Tremors opened the banks of a lake over the city and 18,000 people were washed into a chasm. The ghastly site is marked by the tops of three palms trees – once on the city's Plaza de Armas – protruding from the earth.

The broad range of weather conditions from one part of the country to another leaves labels such as "winter" and "summer" of little practical use. Lima residents refer to summer as their hot sunny months (December to April) and winter as the rest of the year when the fog sets in. In the Sierra, winter is the months of rain (October to May). (Snow is uncommon in inhabited highland areas even though the highest of Peru's Andean peaks are snow covered year round.) The jungle, meanwhile, is hot and humid all year.

The barren coastal desert.

Civilization in the Andes has long been equated with the Incas. Impressive accounts by 16th-century Spanish chroniclers told of fabled Inca wealth and the architectural achievements of the Incas, inevitably compared to the feats of the Romans, featured in almost every account on Peru. But archaeologists working on the Peruvian coast and highlands have now shown that the origins of Peruvian civilization reach back 4 millennia, 3 thousand years before the Incas emerged from their highland realm to forge Tahuantinsuyu, their enormous empire of the four quarters.

It was not until the turn of this century when scientific archaeology was first carried out in Peru, that the true antiquity of Peruvian civilization began to emerge. No-one imagined at the time that civilization in the New World could be as ancient as that of the Old World. New data emerging from Peru, however, show that the earliest monumental architecture is roughly contemporary with the pyramids of Egypt and predates the large-scale constructions of the Olmec in Mesoamerica by over a thousand years.

The beginnings of civilization: Peru's harsh environment hardly seems the place to spawn such achievements. Along the coast, some 50 river valleys slice through the desert, creating fertile oases interspersed by arid expanses of sand. Between 2500-1800 B.C., a time known to archaeologists as the Cotton Preceramic, small communities thrived along the coast, harvesting the rich Pacific ocean for its bounty of shellfish, fish and marine mammals. On river floodplains they cultivated cotton and gourds and hunted for deer. In the *lomas*, lush belts of fog vegetation located a few miles inland, they gathered wild plants. Before the introduction of true weaving, they created twinned and looped textiles of cotton and sedge, some decorated with intricate designs that attest to technological and aesthetic skills.

Towards the end of the Cotton Preceramic, larger settlements, such as that of

Preceding pages: ancient weavings of the culture Nazca. Left, gold figurine at the Brüning Museum. Above right, Moche lord unearthed at Sipán.

Paraiso just north of Lima, covered 143 acres. Over 100,000 tons of quarried stone were used here to build monumental platforms. At the site of Aspero in the Supe valley, 145 km (90 miles) north of Lima, the largest mound, built of rubble and stone blocks, is 10 meters (33 feet) high and measures 30 by 40 meters (98 by 131 feet) at its base. Both these centers were surrounded by sprawling residential areas containing burials and thick midden, or refuse, deposits.

Some time around 1800 B.C., at the begin-

ning of what is known as the Initial Period, these fishing communities began to move inland. Although the majority of sites documented from this time only average 20 km (12 miles) from the coast, they were far enough up-valley to tap the rivers and construct irrigation canals, substantially increasing the ancient Peruvians' subsistence base. Evidence from the middens indicates that in addition to cotton and gourds they grew squash, peppers, lima and kidney beans, peanuts and avocado, supplementing their diet with marine products. Maize, which would become an Andean staple, was introduced somewhat later, possibly from

Mesoamerica where it was first domesticated.

Two further revolutionary inventions belong to this period: the introduction of simple weavings and pottery.

Sierra cultures: The emergence of complex society on the coast was paralleled by developments in the highlands, where archaeologists have documented the rise of ceremonial architecture at sites such as Huaricoto in the Callejon de Huaylas, 250 km (155 miles) northeast of Lima. Unfortunately, preservation of organic matter is not as good in the highlands as it is on the arid coast, and the archaeological record for this area is not as complete. Nonetheless, excavations at Hua-

Pampa de las Llamas. Located 18 km (11 miles) inland, the complex once covered an area of 2.5 square km (1 square mile) dominated by two mounds. The 27 meter (90 feet) high pyramid of Moxeke, excavated earlier this century, was decorated with awesome adobe friezes of snarling felines and human attendants, painted red, blue and white. The temple facade has been reconstructed at Lima's newly-opened Museo de la Nacíon. Facing Moxeke lies Huaca, or Mound A, which once stood almost 6 meters (20 feet) high and measured 135 by 135 meters (450 by 450 feet). Here, access to storage areas was controlled by wooden doorways and the images of two fanged felines guard one of

ricoto have unearthed ceremonial structures with firepits, where offerings were burned. Llamas were already domesticated by this time, serving as beasts of burden and providing an important food source. Llama caravans carried highland produce – potatoes and other Andean tubers and grains – to the coast in exchange for goods from the warm coastal valleys: dried fish and shellfish, seaweed, salt, cotton, peppers and coca leaves. The guinea pig, an Andean delicacy, was probably also domesticated about this time.

In the Casma Valley, 275 km (170 miles) north of Lima, large Initial Period settlements flourished at sites such as Moxeke-

two entrances to the complex.

Architectural monuments such as these, featuring U-shaped platforms and sunken circular courtyards, have been documented from sites just south of Lima to the Moche or Trujillo valley, 595 km (370 miles) north of Lima. Near Trujillo stands the Huaca de los Reyes, which also contained elaborate adobe friezes of felines, once painted red, yellow and cream. The arms of the U-shaped temple point upriver, towards the Andes and the source of water. Then, as now, water was a valuable commodity on the rainless coast, and a constant preoccupation of ancient, and modern, Peruvians.

Sometime toward the end of the Initial Period, around 900 B.C., archaeologists believe increasing warfare led to the construction of sites such as Cerro Sechin, also in the Casma Valley. Here a macabre procession of victorious warriors and their dismembered carved victims commemorate a battle on stone monoliths surrounding an earlier adobe temple.

The Early Horizon: In the highlands, construction began around 800 B.C. at the ceremonial center of Chavín de Huantar in the Callejon de Conchucos, southeast of the Callejon de Huaylas. Perhaps one of the most famous sites in ancient Peru, the site of Chavín was believed until recently to be the

Coastal sites contemporary with the florescence of the Chavín temple were perhaps branch shrines of a powerful Chavín oracle. Painted cotton textiles found at Karwa, near the Bay of Paracas on the south coast, for example, depict deities reminiscent of those carved on stone slabs at Chavín de Huantar. Located midway between the coast and the jungle lowlands, Chavín iconography even incorporated jungle fauna into its elaborate iconography. The Tello Obelisk, on view at Lima's National Museum of Anthropology and Archaeology, features a fierce caiman.

The spread of the Chavín cult brought with it innovations in textile and metallurgy technology. Weavings found buried with

inspiration for the related art style that spread throughout much of coastal and highland Peru. It is often referred to as the Early Horizon (800 B.C.-A.D. 0). Research over the past 20 years has shown that Initial Period developments on the coast (U-shaped temples, circular sunken courtyards, stirrup-spout ceramics, and an elaborate iconography featuring fanged felines and snarling gods) culminated at Chavín, and did not originate there.

Left, erotic Moche drinking vessel. **Above**, carved Moche gourd. **Above right**, drinking vessel of the Moche culture.

mummy bundles at Paracas and dated to about 400 B.C. are perhaps the finest cloth ever produced in ancient Peru. This was followed by the Necropolis phase, named after the hundreds of mummy bundles burried in stone-lined pits. Almost every technique known to the Andean weaver had been invented by this time. Evidence for a far-flung trade network is also visible at Paracas: obsidian from the highland region of Huancavelica to the southeast, cameloid fiber, probably alpaca, also from the highlands, and feathers of tropical birds used to adorn fans, which probably came from the jungle. Traces for the use of cameloid fiber in north coast weavings, again probably alpaca, also appear at this time.

Metalworking techniques such as soldering, sweat welding, repoussé and gold-silver alloys were first used by ancient Peruvians smiths during the Early Horizon. Only the Moche were to add to the repertoire of metalworking techniques a few centuries later.

Birth of new cultures: The decline of Chavín influence led to the emergence of regional culture in river valleys on the coast and in highland valleys during a time known as the Early Intermediate Period (A.D. 0-600). In the Nazca valley, weavers and potters followed the Paracas Necropolis tradition, but instead of producing painted and incised

Although there is plenty of evidence to tie these ancient markings to their Nazca creators, writers like Eric von Daniken would like to attribute their construction to visitors from outer space. Other theories, such as that they formed part of an astronomical calendar, have gained little acceptance among archaeologists. A more recent theory suggests that the geoglyphs were linked to mountain worship and fertility. Indeed, many of the animal images can be tied to Andean fertility concepts and some of the lines point to the mountains in the distance, the source of water.

The ancient Nazca lived in settlements dispersed around the Nazca drainage. They

pottery they began to make slip-decorated ceramics painted with a variety of mineral pigments.

On an arid plain north of the modern city of Nazca, the ancient Nazca people etched giant images on the desert by brushing away the surface soil and revealing the lighter colored soil beneath. Images of birds, some measuring 60 meters (200 feet) across, predominate, but they also drew killer whales, a monkey (90 meters/300 feet across), and a spider (45 meters/150 feet long). All these animals feature on Nasca ceramics. The straight lines and trapezoids were built a few hundred years later.

worshipped their gods at the ceremonial center of Cahuachi, downriver from the modern city of Nazca.

On Peru's north coast, the Moche people flourished in the Moche or Trujillo valley, known in ancient times as Chimor. From their early capital at the Pyramids of the Sun and the Moon, south of the modern city of Trujillo, the Moche held sway over 400 km (250 miles) of desert coast. The Pyramid of the Sun, one of the most imposing adobe structures ever built in the New World, was constructed of over 100 million bricks. They built irrigation canals, aqueducts and field systems that stretched for miles, even connecting neighboring valleys, and cultivated maize, beans, squash, peanuts and peppers. From their totora reed boats they fished and hunted for sea lions and captured deer along the rivers. They kept domesticated dogs and traded for luxury goods such as turquoise from northwestern Argentina, lapis lazuli from Chile and exotic seashells from the Gulf of Guayaquil, today Ecuador.

Masterful sculptors: Famed for their ceramics, Moche potters created realistic portrait heads and fine line drawings of gruesome blood-letting ceremonies. Perhaps the most imaginative and skilled metalsmiths in ancient Peru, they perfected an electro-chemical-plating technique that gilded cop-

Sometime between A.D. 650-700 the Moche kingdom came to an end. Torrential rains produced by the *El Niño* phenomenon, when the warm waters of the Ecuadorian current replace the cold waters of the Humboldt current, brought about massive destruction to irrigation canals, causing famine. In 1982-83 such rains flooded large areas and destroyed crops in much of northern Peru.

With the fall of Moche in the north and the decline of Nazca to the south, a powerful southern highland kingdom exerted its architectural and artistic influence over large areas of Peru between A.D. 600-1000. The capital of this empire was Wari, a large urban

per objects.

The discovery in 1987 of the tomb of a Moche lord at Sipán, near the modern city of Chiclayo almost 800 km (500 miles) north of Lima, has provided a wealth of new data on the ancient Moche, including evidence that most valleys under Moche influence had a powerful lord of their own. Discoveries at Sipán even link its metalwork to similar pieces looted from the site of Loma Negra near Piura, on Peru's far north coast.

Left, sun design in the Gold Museum of Lima. **Above**, mask found in the Lambayeque Valley of Northern Peru.

center near the modern city of Ayacucho. Archaeologists have excavated Wari sites near Cuzco at Piquillacta, Cajamarquilla near Lima and Marca Huamachuco in the highlands east of Trujillo.

The Wari style is strongly reminiscent of ceramics and sculpture from the Bolivian altiplano site of Tiahuanaco, which flourished between 200 B.C.-A.D. 1200. Situated at the southern end of Lake Titicaca at 3850 meters (12,600 feet) above sea level, Tiahuanaco was the highest urban settlement in the New World. The ancient people of Tiahuanaco employed an ingenious cultivation system that archaeologists estimate could have sustained a city of 40,000 people.

Tiahuanaco farmers cultivated potatoes, oca and olluco (Andean tubers) as well as quinoa and cañiwa (Andean grains) on raised fields known as *camellones*. They dug canals fed by the lake and heaped up the soil from the canals to construct raised fields some 10 meters wide. During the day the sun heated the water in the canals, and at night the water radiated its warmth to protect the crops from frost. Recent experiments revealed that crops grown on these raised fields produced harvests seven times higher than the average yield.

With the decline of Wari influence, regional cultures again flourished in the

coastal valleys. In the north the Lambayeque or Sican culture centered at Batan Grande, 48 km (30 miles) north of Chiclayo. Here, elaborate burials, some containing scores of gold and silver vessels, point to Batan Grande as an important metalworking center. But Batan Grande too appears to have been abandoned in about A.D. 1100, flooded by torrential rains caused by *El Niño*. The remnants of Batan Grande's population moved a few miles south to Tucume, a center of 26 large flat-topped adobe pyramids and numerous smaller structures. The largest complex of monumental adobe architecture in the New World, Tucume and the

Lambayeque valley were conquered by the Chimu a few centuries later.

Adobe City: In Trujillo construction had already begun at Chan Chan, the Chimu capital near the ancient Moche capital at the Pyramids of the Sun and the Moon. The earliest constructions at Chan Chan date back to A.D. 800 and the center was continuously occupied by the Chimu dynasty until it fell to the Inca armies in about 1464. The largest kingdom to rule Peru before the rise of the Incas, the Chimu realm stretched 965 km (600 miles) along the coast, from the Chillon Valley in the south to Tumbes on the Ecuadorian border to the north. This time is known archaeologically as the Late Intermediate Period (A.D. 1000-1476).

Seventeenth-century Spanish chroniclers recorded a Chimu origin myth that told of the Chimu dynasty's legendary founder Tacaynamu. It relates how he arrived on a balsa raft, but details of this life are largely mythical, although he probably existed. The legend spoke of ten Chimu kings, who ruled for about 140 years, placing the date of the founding to the first half of the 14th century.

Curiously, there are ten rectangular compounds at Chan Chan, each one corresponding to a Chimu monarch. Each compound served as the realm's administrative center as well as the reigning monarch's palace, royal storehouse, and on the king's death, his mausoleum. The succeeding monarch built a new compound and the deceased ruler's compound was kept up by his family and loyal retainers.

The surrounding population, estimated to have numbered 50,000 people, was composed almost entirely of weavers, potters and metalsmiths who supplied the royal storehouses. These craftsmen lived in and around the royal compounds in crowded, small-roomed dwellings.

Today the sprawling mudbrick capital of Chan Chan is a bewildering labyrinth of ruined adobe walls, some still standing 7.5 meters (25 feet) high and stretching for 60 meters (200 feet). At its height in 1450 the city covered 23 square kilometers. Remains of adobe friezes of fish and birds still adorn some of the compound walls.

Above left, mummy found in Paracas. **Right**, the Tello obelisk from the Chavín culture.

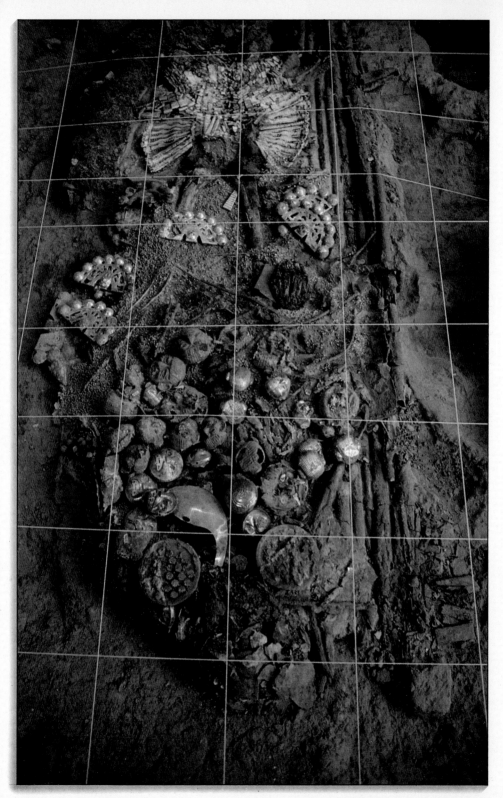

Hollywood couldn't have done it better.

A trail of thievery, tainted by a killing along the way, led archaeologists in northern Peru to the tomb of a Moche warrior lord and one of the archaeology world's most exciting finds in a half century. Now this excavation – the richest intact burial chamber ever uncovered in the Americas – is luring tourists and scientists alike. And it appears this tomb of the so-called "Lord of Sipán" may be just the beginning; at least one more pre-Inca burial chamber has been detected by scientists at the site.

Not since Harvard's Hiram Bingham stumbled onto Machu Picchu in 1911 and Peruvian Julio C. Tello uncovered the first Paracas funeral bundle on the Pacific coast some 18 years later have scientists been so enthusiastic about obtaining new information on the ancient Indian cultures that were sacked and vanquished by the Incas long before the Spanish conquistadors reached the New World 500 years ago. In fact, it wasn't until German archaeologist Max Uhle earlier this century investigated the long line of pre-Inca civilizations that modern scientists awakened to the sophistication of those cultures. Yale University archaeologists in the United States claim new discoveries may prompt scientists to reevaluate whether pyramids and architecture of Mesopotamia and the rest of the Old World actually predate the rise of advanced societies in the New World, or the Americas.

To that end, the continuing excavation at Sipán promises to provide anthropologists and archaeologists with crucial new evidence about the life of the Moches, the sophisticated Indian civilization that ruled the north coast between A.D. 100 and 700 and left no written word but whose ceramics have been used to unravel some of that society's secrets. It also offers tourists the unique opportunity to watch scientists literally digging up clues to Peru's mysterious pre-Inca past.

A lost world revealed: Until Sipán, the little

The old Lord of Sipán as he was found.

that was known about the Moches came from details in that Indian civilization's fine pottery. For tourists, it is most often the Moches' *huacos eroticos* – erotic ceramics – that shock and amuse with their graphic portrayals of sexual acts, birth, death and scenes from everyday life. Medical researchers have used the ceramics to conclude that ancient civilizations suffered from modern-day ills, including venereal disease, blindness and maybe even cancer. Sociologists have concluded that women's role in that culture, based on what is shown in the pottery, was one of submission.

Ceramics were found in the "Lord of Sipán" tomb along with a lavish treasure, beginning with four gold crowns, a breast plate and a copper mask and continuing – as the desecrated tomb was excavated – with larger-than-life size detailed peanuts of gold, beakers and body ornaments.

But scientists say it is not the monetary value alone of the excavation that is so astounding. Rather it is the information that the burial chamber reveals. Archaeologists have long theorized that the Moches were a patriarchal people. That theory stood up to scrutiny when the remains of three concubines – their feet cut off to symbolically prevent them from leaving their master's grave – were found in the Sipán tomb. Another footless body, believed to be the guard of the tomb, was also found outside the wooden sarcophagus containing the Moche lord.

A 10-year-old child and a jaguar found buried at the core of the tomb is still disputed by authorities, and scientists say that more detailed theories about the Moches will result from continued work at the excavation.

A second tomb: Archaeologists have already stumbled onto a second tomb, dubbed that of the "Old Lord of Sipán" or "Spiderman" because of the exquisite gold necklace of ten spiders that formed the top layer of the funerary offerings. While the second tomb is believed to be that of a person less important than the Lord of Sipán, owing to the fact he was buried in simple cane matting, the grave was littered with about 50 gold offerings and more than 100 gilded copper and silver artifacts. It is believed the Spiderman lived about 1,700 years ago.

One of the most striking items taken from this second grave is a silver nose ornament; attached to its silver backing is a golden warrior less than 1.5 inches high, wearing turquoise armor and holding a club and shield. On his head is a perched owl whose outspread wings form the warrior's headdress.

"The skill of the Moche metallurgists is remarkable," says Walter Alva, the Peruvian archaeologist in charge of the Sipán dig, financed in part by the National Geographic Society. "Although the Spiderman's tomb is not as elaborate as that of the Lord of Sipán, the iconography is richer and more complex."

"This is a very dynamic project. We are

tomed to the constant trafficking of archaeological artifacts but was shocked by the immense value of what the police would show him – copper masks, a gold face mask with silver and lapis lazuli eyes and elaborately detailed ornaments.

To halt the grave robbing, Alva and his assistants began holding all-night vigils at the Sipán ruins, discovering to their dismay that the looters would not be stopped. Police raided the homes of townspeople suspected of trafficking in the goods. It was during one of those surprise incursions that officers fatally shot a grave robber, shocking the tiny town of Lambayeque and leaving the archaeologists fearful that they would be attacked

still digging and it is very probable that we'll find other tombs," said Alva, who is director of the Brüning Gold Museum in Lambayeque, a tiny town north of Chiclayo and the closest village to the Sipán dig. Most of the Sipán finds are at the Brüning, which is Peru's best public gold museum.

A duel with the grave robbers: Alva knows there was one other sealed tomb at Sipán, at least as fabulous as the Lord of Sipán, but grave robbers reached it first. When the pre-Columbian treasures sacked from that burial chamber began to flood the local black market in 1987, police contacted the Brüning Museum director. Alva was wearily accus-

in revenge.

Although funds were eventually obtained to begin the excavation of the sight, the Sipán incident called attention to the seriousness of the looting problem at ancient Indian sites. It is a custom that began in Peru in the 1500s when the Spanish soldiers began sacking Inca burial grounds. Later, looting became so commonplace that it was a regular weekend activity for wealthy Limeños. So determined were the professional looters, or *huaqueros* as they are known in Peru, that they once diverted the Moche River so they could tunnel under a pyramid. That the Moche tomb escaped such pilfering for centuries is what made the Sipán tomb discovery so special.

Unique find: Until Sipán, scientists had examined a large number of ceramics, ornaments and even precious artifacts taken from minor graves or recovered from the black market. But this is the first time they stumbled upon an intact Moche leader's grave. The Moches preceded the Incas by some 1,200 years and irrigated a fertile but dry valley with such success that they were able to sustain a population estimated at about 50,000. But they never developed a system of writing, leaving later generations in the dark about their culture.

"Sipán is going to help us fill a vacuum in describe as a "cocoon of tribute" with precious metals adorning the body and placed above and below it. Fine ceramics near the body once held food and drink to sustain him on his journey to the next life. A dog and traces of two llamas were also discovered, likely sacrificed in the burial ritual.

Archaeologist Christopher Donner at the University of California at Los Angeles speculates from the presence of the concubines, guards and dog in the grave that the deceased was a warrior priest. Alva, on the other hand, has his own theories, although he predicts that further discoveries at Sipán will help establish the hierarchy of who was buried at the location.

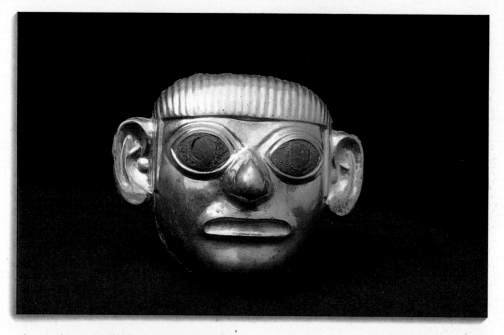

the continuum and help us know more about the life, the technology, the social structures and the interactions the Moches had with other Indian groups," Alva says.

At the Lord of Sipán grave, archaeologists armed with air-squeeze bulbs sifted through 13 layers of treasures, uncovering feathered headdresses, insignias, seashell necklaces, banners and jewelry of copper, gold, turquoise and silver. The man buried in the grave was interred in what his discoverers

Left, excavating at the Sipán dig. Above, gold mask found at Sipán.

An unusual aspect of the first grave is that the Moche lord was buried within a wooden coffin with copper ties – the first such burial box discovered by archaeologists in Peru. The "Lord of Sipán" was buried flat on his back, stretched out in the sarcophagus, far differently from the fetal position found in other ancient Peruvian graves.

"It is the first time that a funeral chamber with these characteristics has ever been found in Peru," Donner said.

Many of the items taken from the Sipán site are displayed at the Brüning Museum, where Alva is often available to answer questions about continuing work at the site.

THOR HEYERDAHL RETURNS

Norwegian explorer Thor Heyerdahl, who sailed from Peru to Polynesia on the balsa raft Kon-Tiki in 1947, is back in South America on a bold new quest.

Heyerdahl is in northern Peru, excavating a field of 26 pyramids which he hopes will hold clues to the prehistory of the continent. The adobe mounds, badly eroded but believed to be untouched by looters, lie near the village of Túcume, 800 km (500 miles) up the coast from Lima. They were built about 1,500 years ago by the elusive Moche people, who ruled centuries before the Incas. (See historical feature "Lost Empires" on page 35.)

The dig is bringing the 75-year-old adventurer full-circle. It was from the coast of Peru that Heyerdahl launched *Kon-Tiki* as a young man, a daredevil feat which catapulted him to international fame. He followed up that highly publicized voyage with more expeditions – all with the goal of lending credibility to his controversial ideas about prehistoric migration.

Unconventional theories: Heyerdahl has tried to establish links between the Near East and North Africa, Africa and the Americas, and Peru and Polynesia. He sailed from Iraq to northern Africa in 1977-78 on the Sumerian-style raft *Tigris* to show that navigators from Mesopotamia were capable of long-distance voyages. Earlier, in 1969 and 1970, he crossed the Atlantic on the papyrus *Ra I* and *Ra II* to prove that North Africans could have reached the New World.

Heyerdahl's first voyage on *Kon-Tiki* had attempted to support his theory that Polynesia was settled from the Americas instead of Asia, as conventional wisdom holds. Among his less disputed achievements, Heyerdahl introduced archaeology to the Maldives and Easter Island, and unlocked the mysteries of the monoliths. He has drawn global attention to pollution at sea and the international armaments race.

Yet he believes his finest hour is to come.

"This is the greatest and most exciting work I've ever done because of its dimen-

Thor Heyerdahl holds on oar found at Túcume.

sions and implications," Heyerdahl said of Túcume. At 550 acres it is reputedly the largest archaeological complex in the world.

Heyerdahl was lured there in 1987 by Walter Alva, a Peruvian archaeologist excavating the nearby Moche site of Sipán (see preceding feature "Discovery in the Desert" for more about this find). Alva has long crusaded to finance a scientific probe at Túcume, but the Peruvian government simply could not afford it.

Heyerdahl's Kon-Tiki Museum in Oslo agreed to bankroll the excavation to the tune of about $80,000 a year. Alva is heading up the international team of archaeologists. The world's eyes are on Túcume. Cambridge University prehistorian Peter Gathercole says the site is so significant it could change the murky prehistory of America.

Archaeological theory: The burden of scientific proof aside, Túcume is the sort of riproaring adventure that Heyerdahl fans have come to expect. The mission is replete with dangers like evil curses, witch doctors and demonic possession.

The complex of pyramids is known as *El Purgatorio*, and it is said to be haunted by the devil himself in the form of a giant rayfish called *El Rayo*. One night *El Rayo* swooped down on the dig's watchman. He was spooked so badly that a witch doctor with protective charms had to be rushed in.

As it turns out, the curse on *El Purgatorio* may be the site's blessing. Over the centuries the locals have superstitiously avoided it. Even the looters who have laid waste to nearly every archaeological site on the continent have steered clear.

An untouched site is the stuff of dreams for archaeologists, and the suspense is mounting as the related Moche complex at Sipán yields fabulous burials. Heyerdahl confirms the Túcume is also likely to have graves containing precious metals.

So far, simple pots and an unadorned female skeleton, about 1,000 years old, have been unearthed. "We are not rushing to open and see what we find inside the pyramids," Heyerdahl stresses. "We are not looking for gold; we are most interested in anything else – the sequence of cultures, evidence of long-distance contacts. This project is strictly archaeological."

Desert home: A life-long nomad, Heyerdahl settled right in to the Peruvian project. He bought land adjacent to the dig and built himself an oasis – a magnificent white-washed adobe house with parquet floors, christened *Casa Kon Tiki*.

He dug a well, raised a windmill, bought a white steed named *El Rayo* and set about the greatest challenge of all, being accepted by the local community.

Early on, he was put to the test. In a square off with the community's most influential witch doctor, Heyerdahl survived a moonlit ceremony at *El Purgatorio*. There was chanting, drinking and dancing, punctuated by snorting of a potent hallucinogen. By dawn, Heyerdahl and the *brujo* were amigos.

The Norwegian sees the move to Peru as logical: he believes the Moche pyramids will divulge much about early civilizations on the continent, their origins and their trade routes. He hopes they will even establish the link between Peru and Polynesia that he has been propounding for half a century.

Center of controversy: Over the years Heyerdahl has enraged colleagues by clinging to theories they claim have been discredited. Critics call him stubborn; some say he is not a legitimate scientist.

It all boils down to envy, said Bengt Danielsson, a Tahiti-based ethnologist and one of three surviving members of the *Kon-Tiki* crew. "Thor makes so much money on his books and films that he can pay to organize an expedition at any time. That, of course, can generate a little jealousy."

And then there's Heyerdahl's *modus operandi* – using a detective's approach to ethnographic problems. An early mentor warned him: "The task of science is investigation pure and simple. Not to try to prove this or that." It was one piece of advice Heyerdahl has ignored all his life.

And no matter what the scientific world thinks, the public loves this blue-eyed, modern-day Viking. For 40 years armchair adventurers around the world have thrilled to his exploits. He is the best-selling author of more than a dozen books, and the star of several major documentary films including the Academy Award winning *Kon-Tiki*.

Whether or not Túcume supports Heyerdahl's ideas, he vows to forge ahead. There is much to do, he said, more than a lifetime of work.

And there's a larger question. Heyerdahl is searching for something he considers to be more pressing than substantiating his migration theories. If the explorer had a crystal ball, he would look to the period just before 3000 B.C. At that time civilization suddenly blossomed along the Nile, the Tigris and Euphrates, and in the Indus Valley.

"We know today that man as a species existed for 2 million years or more," he said. "Then you think this blossoming wouldn't start in the same century and generation, all about 3100 B.C. And even more strange, it was at peak development. There was no background of evolution and no continued evolution after."

Crackpot visionaries: Such puzzles are why Erich von Däniken and his ilk have been liths at Easter Island were erected and in 1989 published the revelatory *Easter Islands: A Mystery Solved.*

"I feel confident that if we concentrate more efforts on our planet and not in our solar system, that somewhere, hidden by desert sand, jungle trees or ocean water, somewhere we will find the evolution that lay before 3000 B.C. To me, that is the most fascinating challenge to archaeology and prehistory studies."

Visitors are welcome to Túcume as long as they don't disturb the dig. Because it is difficult to reach, many opt for package tours or make arrangements through local travel agencies in Chiclayo, the nearest big city.

successful, Heyerdahl said. Von Däniken, author of the world best-seller *Chariots of the Gods* claims that advanced beings from outer space visited the Earth long ago, leaving evidence like the Egyptian pyramids and Peru's Nazca lines.

"It's so easy to fool the masses in a generation when we can fly to the moon," Heyerdahl mourned. "As long as science can't provide an explanation…people will be able to speculate in fairy tales." He himself has determined how the once enigmatic mono-

Above, one of the Túcume pyramids.

For those who wish to go it alone, Faucett and AeroPeru fly from Lima to Chiclayo daily. Mini-buses at the 200 block of San Jose go to Lambayeque, 6 miles north. In Lambayeque, it's sometimes possible to hitch a ride on to Túcume, about 12 miles. further north, with staff from the Brüning Museum.

The best hotel in Chiclayo, the choice of visiting archaeologists, is the Turistas at Villareal 115. It's nothing flashy, but offers a swimming pool, restaurant and all the standard basics. It makes a relaxing base for exploring a region where some of the most exciting finds in South American archaeology are being made.

ANDAS DEL INGA
PILLCORAUPA

guaynacapac

ynga ua ala conquista
delos cayanbis guancabil
ca canari cic chochacha
poya quito latauga

lleuan los yñs andamarcas y
soras lucanas parina cochas
alaguerray batalla deprico
sa lo lleuan

Andean scholars have painted Inca society in every imaginable color, from totalitarian nightmare to arcadian utopia. There are many reasons why we cannot get a firm historical grip on the nature of the Incas. They left no writing or codices for us to study, so almost all our contemporary information comes from the Spanish side. Even the most sympathetic Spanish lacked the mental openness to understand what they were seeing. Sixteenth-century Spain was a fanatical Christian nation, not noted for embracing different visions of the world.

Chroniclers were also grappling with the ambiguities of Quechua, the poor quality and distorting biases of native interpreters, and the questionable reliability of informants often desperate, for reasons of survival, to ingratiate themselves with their interrogators. And the Spanish arrived in the midst of a brutal civil war, when they would inevitably hear many conflicting versions of the Inca rulers. All our versions of the Incas fit into cultural frameworks familiar to "western" minds. But the Incas were uniquely Andean, and very different from other advanced civilizations of history. So modern accounts of the Incas must carry a disclaimer: if you want the unshakable truth, better invent time travel.

A strict world order: Inca society was clearly hierarchical and highly structured, but not necessarily tyrannical and repressive. Everyone had a place in the Inca world, and a part to play. Life wasn't easy, but food and resources were stored and distributed so that all were fed and clothed. There was no private property, and everything was communally organized. It may have been a society in which the majority accepted their role without feeling aggrieved or exploited.

The Inca polity was a pyramid, with the ruling Inca emperor and his *coya*, or queen, at the apex. Under him stood the Inca nobility, the "Capac Incas" supposedly the true descendants of Manco Capac, the founding Inca, and belonging to some ten or twelve *panacas*, or royal houses. Each Inca emperor

The Inca Huayna-Capac at war, from the chronicle of Waman Puma.

founded a panaca when he ascended to power, and the current ruler's was therefore the only panaca headed by a living man. The other panacas centered their lives and cult around the mummified remains of a former Inca emperor.

The city of Cuzco was filled with the huge palaces constructed by Inca rulers to house their panaca: that is, their personal retinue, their descendants via many wives and concubines, and, finally, their own mummy. This mummy was attended to as royally after

The Inca Empire

the death of the ruler, as during his lifetime. It was consulted through seers and mediums on all important matters. It received daily offerings of food and drink, and at certain festivals it was taken out on its royal litter, and paraded around Cuzco. Other nobility were also mummified after their deaths, and kept in lesser shrines. At one annual festival the royal mummies were carried about the countryside, revisiting the favorite places of their lifetimes.

The panacas of Cuzco existed together with a similar number of *ayllus* – large kinship groups – of lesser nobility, the so-called "Incas-by-privilege", who were early inhabitants of the Cuzco region, pre-dating the Incas. They held lands, ritual and economic functions, and many other aspects of life in common. The panacas and noble ayllus belonged to two moieties, Upper and Lower Cuzco, whose relationship was both competitive and complementary.

Below these groups stood the regional nobility, who were not Incas at all, but held aristocratic privileges along with intricate blood relationships and reciprocal obligations to the ruling caste. Everyone in the empire was bonded to the whole by these sorts of connections, except for one large, amorphous group called *yanakuna.* They were a domestic class, primarily serving the

panacas. They served without receiving formal reciprocal benefits, and although they could reach a high status, their loyalty was usually negotiable. Many of them defected to the Spaniards after Atahuallpa's capture.

The privileges of power: The Inca nobility reserved many privileges to themselves, granting them selectively to outsiders. Polygamy was common, but exclusively aristocratic. Likewise, chewing coca leaves and wearing vicuña wool were privileges of the ruling caste. Noble males wore huge, gold ornate ear plugs in their pierced ears. Their beautifully woven tunics carried heraldic symbols called *tokapu.* All citizens wore the

clothes and hairstyle fitting their station and ethnic group. The streets of Cuzco were colorful, for hundreds of groups were represented in the city, each with its own distinctive costume.

Scores of local languages existed, but the lingua franca of the empire was Quechua, a language spoken today from northern Ecuador to southern Bolivia. The origins of the language are obscure, but the Incas are believed to have acquired it from some other group. The nobles also used a private language, possibly a "high" chivalric dialect with elements of both Quechua and the Aymara language of the Titicaca region.

The ruling lords were fond of hunting. A royal hunt was a spectacular affair, involving thousands of beaters who encircled a vast area and drove all the animals into the center. The animals were not slaughtered indiscriminately, but culled. Young females of most species were released for future reproduction.

The myth of power within the Inca state held that the emperor was a divine being unlike ordinary mortals, descended from the Sun via his founding ancestor, Manco Capac. He gave voice to the desires and intentions of this powerful deity. Some Spanish chroniclers claimed that this was a cynical deception, foisted on the people.

The Sun may have become the supreme Inca deity after the rise of the ninth emperor, Pachacuti; before that, the supreme deity of the Incas was Viracocha, an almighty creator god also worshipped by other cultures.

Inca religion was not confined to the Sun and Viracocha. Cuzco's great temple, the Coricancha, or Court of Gold, contained shrines to the Moon, Lightning, the Pleiades, Venus, and the Rainbow. Moreover, there were shrines to scores of local deities – idols or sacred relics brought to Cuzco by the innumerable tribes and regions incorporated by the Incas. They did not attempt to erase local religions, they simply included them in an ever-expanding pantheon.

Besides the local and celestial deities there were the *apus* – usually the spirits of great mountains – and the *huacas.* These were stones, rock outcrops, caves, grottoes, springs, waterfalls, believed to contain spirit powers. More than three hundred huacas existed around Cuzco, many of them housing the mummies of lesser nobility, and all of them connected by imagined lines that radiated from Cuzco's Coricancha like the spokes of a wheel. This conceptual system of sacred geography, known as the *ceque* system, was closely linked to the ritual and economic life of Cuzco. The panacas and ayllus had care of individual huacas, and groups of ceque lines. Additionally, the ceques delimited landholdings, assigning rights and responsibilities to Cuzco's immensely complex irrigation and flood control system.

Holy concubines and astronomer-priestesses: Also important in Inca worship were the *acllas*, or chosen women. The Spanish drew a simplistic parallel between them and the Roman vestal virgins, labelling them Virgins

tion was the sacrificial fires of the Coricancha. It's also likely that some belonged to a caste of astronomer-priestesses associated with the cult of the Moon, whose divine incarnation was the *coya*, sister and principal wife of the emperor.

The young Inca nobles were educated by *amautas*, scholars who transmitted the knowledge of the culture, often in the form of mnemonic songs and verses. Music and poetry were respected arts among the nobility, and so perhaps was painting. There was an immense "national gallery" called Puquin Cancha, containing paintings of individuals and scenes from Inca history, which was destroyed either during Pizarro's conquest,

of the Sun. Some may have been virgin devotees of certain deities, but chastity was not a major preoccupation of the Incas, and young people were not expected to be sexually modest until they were married. The acllas were a motley group, selected from throughout the empire for their talents and beauty. Many were concubines of the Inca, some were destined to become wives of selected nobility, others served the main temple, producing weavings and foods whose destina-

Far left, Inca administrators cross a bridge (Waman Puma). **Above**, famous twelve-angled stone in Cuzco.

or the civil war that preceded it.

The Inca calendar featured an array of important festivals, which marked annual stages of life and the agricultural calendar. The summer and winter solstices were probably the two greatest celebrations, held with numerous sub-festivals. The Capac Raymi summer solstice, for example, also featured the coming of age celebrations for the new crop of young nobles. The males underwent severe trials, including ritual battles, and a death-defying foot race. Another great ceremony was *Sitwa*, in early September, when all foreigners had to leave Cuzco, and the Incas engaged in a huge ritual of purification, casting out sickness and bad spirits.

Cuzco itself was a holy city, as well as the administrative capital of the empire. It was the centre of *Tahuantinsuyu* – the four quarters of the world. The great royal roads to the four *suyus* began at the city's main square. Here all things came together. Here soil from every province was ritually mingled with the soil of Cuzco.

The four suyus corresponded roughly to the cardinal points. The northern quarter was the Chinchaysuyu – northern Peru and modern Ecuador. The south was the Collasuyu – Lake Titicaca, modern Bolivia and Chile. The Antisuyu was the wild Amazon forest to the east. The Contisuyu was the region west of Cuzco, much of it also wild and rugged country, but including the south and central Peruvian coast.

A rural empire: The Tahuantinsuyu was not significantly urbanized. There was the great complex of Chimú, on the north coast, and of course Cuzco. And there were a few large administrative centers along the spine of the Andes, housing a mainly transient population, which mustered and distributed the resources of entire regions. But most of the population lived in small rural communities scattered across the land.

The complex organization of the Inca state rested on a foundation of efficient agriculture. Everyone from the highest to the lowest was involved to some degree in working the land. Even the emperor ritually tilled the soil with a golden foot-plow, to inaugurate the new planting season, and it is notable that virtually any Inca ruin one visits, no matter what its original function, is surrounded and penetrated by agricultural terraces and irrigation channels. Fields of corn stood in the very heart of Cuzco.

Corn was their prestige crop. The great irrigated terracing systems whose ruins we see today were mainly devoted to its cultivation. Other Inca staples were potatoes and some other indigenous Andean root crops, plus beans, quinoa and amaranth. The tremendous altitude range of the tropical Andes allowed the Incas to enjoy a great variety of foods, but it also required them to develop many localized crop strains for particular microclimates. This they did, with typical thoroughness, at several experimental agriculture centers, whose ruins survive today.

The Incas' great food surpluses enabled them to divert labor to many other enterprises. They created a vast road network, so finely laid that much of it survives today, despite centuries of neglect. They built astonishing structures of stone so finely worked and of blocks so large that they required staggering amounts of time and effort. They used thousands of artisans to create ornaments of gold and silver, pottery and fine textiles. And they raised great armies, able to march thousands of miles without carrying provisions, so extensive was the network of storehouses.

The system which made these works possible was called *mit'a*. It was a kind of community tax, paid in labor. Every community

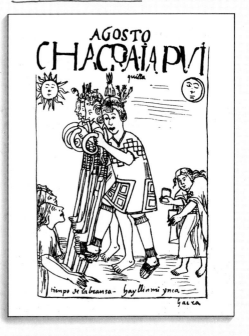

sent some of its able-bodied young men and women for a limited period into the service of the state. The period varied according to the hardship of the work – mines, for example, were a tough assignment, and accordingly brief. Working in a state pottery was easier, and correspondingly longer. Some communities – such as the famous one which rebuilt the Apurimac suspension bridge each year – rendered their *mit'a* in a specific task. One Inca-by-privilege ayllu provided the emperor with inspectors of roads, another with inspectors of bridges, and one ayllu even supplied the state with spies!

The life of a transient *mit'a* worker was

rewarded by institutional generosity and punctuated by public festivals of spectacular drunkenness. Peasants who were otherwise tied to their villages for life mingled with groups from exotic locations worlds away, and caught a glimpse of the dazzling world of the Inca nobility. It was probably the most exciting time of their lives. Later the Spanish took over this institution and turned it into a nightmare of slavery and early death.

Binding the Andes to Cuzco: Another, less benign institution was the *mitmaq*. Loyal Quechuas were sent to distant, newly incorporated provinces whose inhabitants were proving troublesome, in order to pacify and "Inca-ize" the region; the recalcitrant ones

displaced by the first group were moved to the Inca heartland where they were surrounded by loyal Quechuas.

About every 10 km (6 mile) along the great skein of roads that knit the empire together stood a *tambo*, a kind of lodge with storage facilities for goods in transit, and communal quarters for large groups of people. Closer together were the little huts which served as relay stations for the *Chasquis*, the message runners, who could allegedly cover the 2,400

km (1,500 miles) between Quito and Cuzco in five days.

Every major bridge and tambo had its *quipucamayoc*, an individual who recorded everything that moved along the road. Their instrument was the *quipu*, a strand of cord attached to color-coded strings, each carrying a series of knots tied so as to indicate a digital value. The *quipucamayocs* were the accountants of the empire. Quipus possibly served also as a cumbersome means of sending messages, certain types of knot being assigned a syllable value, so that a row of knots made a word.

Crimes of property were rare, and the Spanish "Viracocha" aura dimmed when it was learned that they not only stole from the Peruvians – which, though bizarre, made a kind of sense – but also from each other. Under the Incas, stealing was regarded as an aberration and dealt with ruthlessly when it occurred. Offenders suffered loss of privileges, with public humiliation and perhaps physical punishment. Serious or repeated crimes were punished by death, the victim being thrown off a cliff or imprisoned with poisonous snakes and dangerous animals.

A combination of techniques sustained the growth of the Inca empire. Military conquest played a part, but so did skillful diplomacy; some of the most important territories may have been allied confederates rather than subordinate domains. The glue holding the empire together was the practice of reciprocity: ritual generosity and favors to local rulers on a huge scale, in exchange for loyalty, labor and military levies, women for the Inca nobility, products special to the region, and so on. The emperor maintained fabulous stores of goods to meet his ritual obligations and create new alliances.

The Incas possibly were not imperialist in our usual sense, at the outset. There was an ancient Andean tradition of cultural influences, spreading out by means of trade and pilgrimage from important religious centers, such as Chavín, and later Tiahuanaco. It's likely Cuzco started this way, too; later the Incas extended their sway in southern Peru by means of reciprocal agreements and blood alliances.

The path to power: Then came the pivotal war of survival against the Chancas, a powerful group from the north. The historical existence of the Chancas has never been confirmed by archaeology, but the Inca version current at the time of the Conquest states that the man who would take the title Pachacuti – "transformer of the world" – defeated the invading Chancas at the very gates of Cuzco. Subsequently he transformed Inca culture from the roots up, and launched the career of expansion which would be continued by his son and grandson. As the Incas extended further from their center, they confronted groups with ideas and identities increasingly different from their own. Thus, continued expansion increasingly required force.

By the time of the Spanish invasion Pachacuti's grandson, Huayna-Capac, was far from his homeland, fighting almost continuously in the mountains along what is now the northern frontier of Ecuador with Colombia. Quito, the base from which these campaigns were launched, had become a de facto second capital, and a northern aristocracy without roots in Cuzco had formed. On the death of Huayna-Capac the two groups fell into conflict, and the disastrous civil war between Huascar and Atahuallpa was the result.

Many groups that the Incas had conquered, such as the Huanca from the Mantaro valley of Peru's central highlands, resented and resisted Inca domination. They had to be held in place by the threat of force, and later they happily deserted the Incas to fight alongside the Spanish.

When the Incas used military force they used it generously. Many an opponent surrendered without a fight when he saw the size of the army sent against him. If it came to a trial of arms, the Incas still preferred to cut off an enemy's water supply, or starve him into submission rather than confront him directly in battle. War and warriorhood was an important part of Andean life from early times. Yet it surely cannot have been of paramount value to the Incas. If it had, then military tactics and technology would have been at the peak of their achievements, whereas in fact their weapons and methods of warfare were extremely primitive – far inferior to their achievements in administration, architecture, agriculture and engineering – and had not evolved since the earliest times of Andean culture. They fought with clubs, stones and all-wooden spears. Even the bow and arrow, though known to them, was not widely used in battle. The gulf between their fighting capacity and that of the steely Spanish conquistadors was tragically wide.

Artists in stone: Like other peoples of the New World, the Incas had not discovered how to smelt iron ores. Their use of other metals was, however, quite sophisticated. They had mastered many techniques for working gold and silver, and created bronze alloys of varying types for different uses.

The finest bronze was too soft to be much use for working stone, however. Stoneworking was a major activity, involving staggering amounts of time and care. Modern research shows that their finely fitted

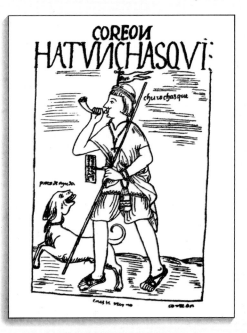

stones were primarily cut and shaped using hammer-stones of harder rock. This process was laborious, but not as slow as we might imagine. Their vast manpower and their evident reverence for stone, enabled them to persevere through the decades and even through the generations it took to complete such astounding structures as Machu Picchu and Sacsayhuaman.

How they moved and fitted the stones remains a mystery. Rollers and pulleys have been proposed, yet no theory explains how the combined efforts of 2,500 men – the number believed necessary to haul the largest stones up the ramp at Ollantaytambo –

were simultaneously applied to a single stone. As for fitting, a common suggestion is simply trial and error: stones were set and then removed; high spots were marked, as a dentist marks a filling; adjoining faces were then smoothed, and the process repeated, until the stones fitted together with astounding perfection. It sounds plausible – until one sees the stones; boulders so colossal that the mere thought of lifting them makes one nervous. A recent theory proposes that the cut stone profiles were matched by a large-scale version of the method we use today for duplicating door keys. Then again, some people explain the whole mystery in one word: extraterrestrials.

the distaff spindle for spinning thread, which has been used in the Andes for millennia.

Another invention the Incas lacked was the arch, an important engineering device in the Old World. Instead, to span great gaps they built sturdy suspension bridges. Their trademark workaday structural shape was the trapezoidal aperture. This shape – tapering upwards, with a stone or wooden lintel across the top – will take a fair amount of weight from above. All four walls of almost every Inca building also leaned slightly inwards, making them very stable. This technique, combined with the brilliantly interlocking joins of their stonework, made their buildings almost earthquake-proof – a useful

Whether or not the Incas had access to lasers and intergalactic travel, they evidently had not discovered the wheel, or a form of writing. Andean terrain is the most vertical on earth, and the Incas' only draft animal was the small, lightly built llama, who sinks to his knees under a load exceeding 45 kg. So the absence of a wheel is understandable. Lacking the first reasons to devise a wheel, the Incas never discovered other uses, such as the potter's wheel. They did, however, inherit

Left, a *Chasqui*, Inca message-runner (Waman Puma). **Above**, a *quipu*, used for records.

feature in Peru.

The absence of some form of writing is harder to explain. The tokapu textile symbols and the quipus were the closest they came. Quechua is full of ambiguities, puns, juxtapositions and multiple meanings, relying heavily on context for its true sense; it is the language style of an oral culture, but whether this is cause or effect of not having any written language is impossible to say. And although the Incas might have lacked certain things we would consider essential, this did not prevent their creating a sophisticated civilization, whose echoes still reverberate through the Andes.

CONQVISTA
EVBARCARŌSE ALAS ĨDIAS

qu dias. vsolis piloto

martin feronã del yngeso

uascones de ualboa

almagro pisaro

gatumi

la mar de nev seteis en mill leguas al vno dela plata

la mar

On September 24, 1532 a motley collection of Spanish *conquistadores* appeared at the fringes of the Inca empire, at that time the largest and most powerful that South America had ever known. In the months to come, these 62 horsemen and 106 footsoldiers commanded by an illiterate pig farmer named Francisco Pizarro would march to the heart of Peru and brutally seize control of the Inca throne. Within a decade, a glittering Andean world would be firmly in the grip of the Spaniards, its glories stripped and people virtually enslaved.

Few historical events are as dramatic or cruel as the conquest of Peru. Although only a handful in number, the invading Spaniards had on their side an astonishing streak of good luck, complete technological superiority and a lack of principle that would have made Machiavelli shudder. Apparently experiencing no other emotions than greed and fear, they were able to repeatedly trick their way into the confidence of the Incas only to betray them. By the time the Incas realized the ruthlessness of their foes, it was too late.

The invasion of America: Cautiously marching into Peru's coastal desert, Pizarro and his men were in the front ranks of Spain's explosion into the New World. It had been only four decades earlier, in 1492, that Christopher Columbus landed in the West Indies – the same year that Castile drove the last Moors from European soil. The violent energies of Spanish soldiers were soon directed across the Atlantic: in 1519, Hernando Cortes, with 500 men and 16 horses, conquered the fabulously wealthy Aztec Empire in Mexico. Panama was settled and conquistadors were soon looking at the newly-found Pacific Ocean as a route to further riches.

Although the existence of Peru was still no more than a rumor, three Spaniards in Panama formed a partnership to conquer it. Francisco Pizarro and Diego de Almagro were already relatively wealthy soldiers from Spain's barren Extremadura; the third was an ambi-

tious priest named Hernando de Luque. They led two expeditions down the west coast of South America before stumbling on the Inca city of Tumbez in modern-day Ecuador. Intoxicated by the prospect of conquering a new Mexico, Pizarro went back to Spain and recruited a band of adventurers and cutthroats from his home town Trujillo.

By the time Pizarro returned to Tumbez in 1532 with his 168 men, it was in ruins. In a stroke of fortune that would determine the fate of Peru, the Spaniards had found the Inca

empire in an unparalleled crisis, weakened for the first time by a bitter civil war. Several years earlier, a virulent disease – probably smallpox, spreading like wildfire from European settlements in the Caribbean amongst the Amerindians – had struck down the supreme Inca Huayna-Capac and his probable heir. Two sons had been left untouched by the plague: Huascar, in the capital city of Cuzco, and Atahualpa, heading the imperial army at Quito. In the civil war that followed, Atahualpa's troops were victorious, but the empire was rocked by the struggle.

When Pizarro landed, Atahualpa had only just learned that he was undisputed Inca. He

Left, the *conquistadores* leave Spain for the New world (Waman Puma). **Above**, portrait of Atahualpa.

was heading in triumph south from Quito to the capital when news arrived that a group of tall, bearded men had entered his lands. As luck would have it, Atahualpa was camped not far from the Spaniards' route of march. The Inca decided to meet the strangers himself.

Into the Andes: Pizarro and his force turned away from the barren coast to climb the rough road into the Andes. Although exhausted by the thin high-altitude air, the conquistadors marveled at the first signs of the Inca civilization: steep valleys were lined with rich terraces of maize; shepherds stood by with flocks of ungainly llamas; and powerful stone fortresses overlooked the Spaniards' path. But the Inca warriors watched the advancing strangers impassively: Atahualpa had given orders that they should not be hindered.

Finally Pizarro came to the town of Cajamarca. Stretching into the valley beyond were the tents of the Inca's army and entourage. One chronicler recorded the Spaniards' awe at the sight: "Nothing like this had been seen in the Indies up to then. It filled all us Spaniards with fear and confusion. But it was not appropriate to show any fear, far less to turn back. For had they sensed any weakness in us, the very Indians we were bringing with us would have killed us." Pizarro entered the near-deserted town and sent his brother Hernando with a group of horsemen to meet Atahualpa.

The Inca received the envoys with all the pomp and splendor of his magnificent court. When permitted to speak, the Spaniards used a translator to convey that Pizarro "loved (the Inca) dearly" and wished him to visit. Atahualpa agreed to meet in Cajamarca the following day.

Only that night did the Spaniards fully appreciate what they had got themselves into. Pizarro had no definite plan, and the conquistadors heatedly debated what should be done. They were several days march into an obviously huge empire. Outside, the camp fires of the Indian army lit up the surrounding hillsides "like a brilliantly star-studded sky". They were terrified, but the lust for gold was stronger than fear.

The capture of the Inca: Next morning, the Spaniards prepared an ambush. Hidden in Cajamarca's main square, the Spaniards waited tensely all morning without any sign of movement in Atahualpa's camp. Many began to suspect that their treacherous plan had been detected and they would all be slaughtered outright – one conquistador later recalled: "I saw many Spaniards urinate, without noticing it, out of sheer terror." It was not until nearly sundown, after Pizarro had once again sent envoys to promise that "no harm or insult would come to him," that the Inca decided to pay his visit.

The Incas arrived in full ceremonial regalia. "All the Indians wore large gold and silver discs like crowns on their heads," one observer wrote. Atahualpa himself wore a collar of heavy emeralds and was borne on a silver litter by eighty blue-clad nobles. Sur-

rounding him were "five or six thousand" men with battle axes and slings. But the Inca Atahualpa was to find no Spaniards in the square. He called out impatiently "Where are they?"

Friar Vicente de Valverde emerged from the darkness with a translator and copy of the Bible. What happens next is confused by the chroniclers, but has been pieced together by John Hemming in his classic *Conquest of the Incas*. It appears that Valverde began to explain his role as a priest. Atahualpa asked to look at the Bible, never having seen a book. "He leafed through (the Bible) admiring its form and layout. But after examining it he threw it angrily down amongst his men, his face a deep crimson." This "sacrilege" was all that the Spaniards needed to justify their actions. Valverde ran away from Atahualpa, screaming "Come out! Come out, Christians! Come at these enemy dogs who reject the things of God!"

Pizarro gave his signal. Cannons blasted and the Spanish spilled into the plaza with their battle cry of "Santiago!" Cavalry crashed into the horrified Indian ranks and began a wholesale slaughter: the Indians "were so filled with fear that they climbed on top of one another – to such an extent that they formed mounds and suffocated one another." Retreat had been blocked, and none of the

hardly believe their luck in capturing Atahualpa. The Inca empire, already divided by the civil war, was now without its absolute leader. Atahualpa issued orders from captivity on the instructions of the Spanish, and the stunned Incas could only obey.

The conquistadors took whatever they wanted from the surrounding camp. Inca soldiers looked on as Hernando de Soto demanded men as porters, women as slaves, llamas for food – and, naturally, as much gold, silver and jewelry as his squadron could carry. Atahualpa saw immediately that the Spaniards were interested in nothing but precious metal and assumed they must eat it. He offered a ransom for his freedom: a room

entourage escaped alive.

Pizarro himself hacked a path straight for the Inca and grabbed his arm. He suffered the only wound to befall the Spanish troops: a blood-crazed conquistador went to stab the Inca but Pizarro deflected the blow, cutting his hand. Atahualpa was rushed away from the carnage and locked, ironically enough, into the Temple of the Sun.

The royal prisoner: The Spanish could

Left, contemporary portrait of Francisco Pizarro. **Above**, the Spaniards surprise Atahualpa (Waman Puma). **Above right**, the Inca taken hostage (Waman Puma).

of 88 cubic meters in size would be filled once over with gold and twice with silver.

The Spaniards were amazed at the offer and Pizarro hastened to agree – summoning a secretary to record the details as a formal pledge and give a stamp of legality to the deal. In return, Pizarro promised to restore Atahualpa to Quito. It was a blatant lie, of course, one that served the conquistadors' purpose brilliantly: the whole Inca empire was mobilized to supply them with booty. Llama trains from Quito to Lake Titicaca were soon starting out, loaded down with precious statues, bowls, jugs and dishes.

Waiting for this treasure's arrival, the

Spaniards became impressed by their royal prisoner. One of Pizarro's men later wrote that "Atahualpa was a man of thirty years of age, of good appearance and manner, although somewhat thick-set … He spoke with much gravity, as a great ruler." The Inca possessed an incisive intellect, grasped Spanish customs quickly, learned the secrets of writing and rules of chess. During all this time, Atahualpa's servants and wives maintained the royal rituals, bringing the Inca his cloaks of vampire bat skin and burning everything he touched or wore.

Abuse and murder: Meanwhile, a small group of Spaniards went to Jauja, where Atahualpa's greatest general Chalcuchima was stationed. Unfortunately, the general obeyed Atahualpa's instructions that he should accompany the Spaniards back to Cajamarca, giving Pizarro the only other man that might have led a coordinated resistance to his invasion. Having treated the general well until his arrival at Cajamarca, they tortured him for information about gold and began to burn him at the stake. He was released "with his legs and arms burned and his tendons shrivelled."

Atahualpa began to realize that he had made a mistake in cooperating with the invaders and that they had no intention of releasing him or leaving his empire. In mid-April 1533, Pizarro's partner Diego de Almagro arrived from Panama with 150 Spanish reinforcements, before leaving again for Spain with news of the Conquest and booty for the King Charles V. The influx of treasure into Cajamarca turned it into a Wild West town and made the Spanish bolder. Pizarro put a chain around Atahualpa's neck to ensure that he would not escape, but rumors began that Inca forces were massing to rescue their leader.

Many Spaniards became convinced that they were in danger so long as Atahualpa remained alive. Others still saw the value of the Inca as a prisoner, and argued that it would be difficult to justify an execution. Chroniclers record that a Nicaraguan Indian was captured who claimed to have seen an Inca army marching on Cajamarca. Pizarro panicked and called an emergency council. It was obvious that the Inca could no longer be counted on to support Spanish rule. The council quickly decided that he should die. Pizarro's secretary coldly recorded the sordid proceedings. The Inca was "brought out of his prison…and was tied to a stake. The friar (Valverde) was, in the meantime, consoling and instructing him through an interpreter in the articles of our Christian faith… The Inca was moved by these arguments and requested baptism… His exhortations did him much good. For although he had been sentenced to be burned alive, he was in fact garrotted by a piece of rope that was tied around his neck."

News of the execution horrified Atahualpa's supporters, the Quitans, especially when it was learned that no Inca column was in fact advancing on the city. When news arrived in Europe, educated opinion was equally ap-

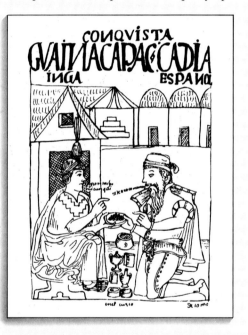

palled. Even Spain's Emperor Charles V was upset with the execution, realizing that it offended the divine right of kings upon which his own rule was based. But by then the Crown's share of booty was steadily arriving from Peru and such scruples would have to be overlooked. The priceless art and sculpture of the great Inca empire went straight to the smelters of Seville.

Onwards into the heartland: In August 1538, the Spaniards marched on to Cuzco. It seems an astonishingly audacious project, but it is important to realize that a large part of the Inca empire's population, especially around the southern sierra, openly welcomed the news of Atahualpa's death. To those who had backed his brother Huascar in the civil war, Atahualpa was a usurper and his Quitan troops an enemy occupying force. And many tribes still bore resentments at the Inca yoke. Pizarro was now ready to pose as the liberator of the Andes.

At Jauja, a contingent of Atahualpa's Quitan army tried to make a stand. The Spanish cavalry charged and routed them immediately. This first armed clash of the Conquest revealed a pattern that would be repeated: The native foot soldiers were no match for the mounted and well-armored Spaniards. Horses gave the conquistadors mobility and allowed them to strike down-

wards upon their opponents' heads and shoulders, while the strange animals also created fear and confusion amongst the Incas. The Spaniards' steel armor was almost impenetrable to the native's bronze hand-axes, clubs and maces. And Pizarro's conquistadors were some of the most experienced fighters Europe had to offer. Again and again the invaders would use their technological advantage to press home victories against apparently overwhelming odds.

Left, Atahualpa asks Pizarro whether the Spaniards eat gold (Waman Puma). **Above**, the Inca taken to execution.

Pizarro founded Jauja as the new Peruvian "capital" and pressed on. What followed was a desperate race to cross the several rope bridges spanning the Andean gorges before the Quitans could destroy them. On one occasion the Indians attempted an ambush, and managed to kill several Spaniards in hand-to-hand battle. Pizarro decided that the captured general Chalcuchima had planned the attack and ordered him finally burned alive. But the attack had been to no avail: there was a final pitched battle in the pass before Cuzco and the Quitans' morale broke. They slipped away from the Urubumba Valley under cover of night and left the Inca capital to the invaders.

Dividing up the spoils: Pizarro and his men marched unopposed into the nerve-center of the Inca world, the "navel of the universe", Cuzco. "The city is the greatest and finest ever seen in this country or anywhere in the Indies," Pizarro wrote back to Charles V. "We can assure Your Majesty that it is so beautiful and has such fine buildings that it would be remarkable even in Spain." But the invaders barely had time to marvel at the precise Inca masonry and channels of water running through every street before installing themselves in various Inca palaces and starting on the serious business of pillaging the city.

The historian Leon-Portilla describes the conquistadors' frenzy in the gold-laden Coricancha, the Temple of the Sun: "Struggling and fighting among each other, each trying to get his hands on the lion's share, the soldiers in their coats of mail trampled on jewels and images and pounded the gold utensils with hammers to reduce them to a more portable size... They tossed all the temple's gold into a melting pot to turn it into bars: the laminae that covered the walls, the marvelous representations of trees, birds, and other objects in the garden."

Pizarro realized that his small force would not survive a true popular uprising, and so attempted to keep the looting of Cuzco relatively orderly – at least until reinforcements arrived. He offered his men allotments of natives, called *encomiendas*, to induce them to stay on as colonists. After "founding" the city in the name of the Spanish king, Pizarro then rode back to the barren coast of Peru and created his colonial capital, facing the sea: modern-day Lima.

By this time Pizarro had also accepted the offer of a 20-year-old native prince named Manca, one of Huayna-Capac's sons, to become the new Inca. Manco wanted the Spaniards to restore him to his father's crown, and the conquistadors were happy to have him as a puppet leader in the southern sierra. He lived in Cuzco while two groups of Spaniards headed towards Quito to take on the retreating imperial army that remained loyal to Atahualpa's memory.

The reality of conquest: While Pizarro was founding Lima in 1534 and 1535, Cuzco under Manco's nominal rule seemed tranquil enough. But it wasn't long before the puppet Inca began to see the Spanish "liberators" in

tion to begin a rebellion. Unknown to the Spaniards, vast numbers of native soldiers were mobilized and Manco slipped from the Cuzco into the mountains. The great rebellion had begun.

Incas on the offensive: Manco's troops quickly took Sacsahuaman, the great fortress overlooking Cuzco whose massive stone blocks still awe visitors today. Chroniclers record that the Inca force was about 100,000 warriors against the Spaniards' 80 cavalry and 110 footsoldiers, commanded by Francisco Pizarro's brother, Hernando. The defences were bolstered by large contingents of native forces, but the outlook was grim: Cuzco was surrounded and, for all the de-

their true colors. The conquistadors' greed and brutality grew with their confidence: they were obviously in Peru to stay.

Manco was distressed to see the Inca world crumbling before his eyes. The natives of Cuzco refused to obey him, while many of his subject tribes began to assert their independence. The swelling ranks of Spaniards began forcing Indians into press-gangs, extorting gold from nobles and raping Inca women. They harassed Manco for treasure, took his wife and pillaged his house.

Finally Manco decided that he could tolerate no more: he summoned a secret meeting of loyal chiefs and announced his inten-

fenders knew, they may have been the last Spanish outpost in Peru.

The Inca attack finally began with slingshot stones, made red-hot in camp fires, hailing down onto Cuzco's thatched roofs, setting them alight. But the roof of the building where the main body of Spaniards was hiding remained untouched. Priests would later claim that the Virgin Mother herself had come down to douse the flames, but eyewitnesses suggest that Negro slaves stationed with buckets of water had a more practical hand in the job. Even so, Manco's forces had captured most of the city. The Spaniards decided on a desperate plan: to counterattack the strategic fortress of Sacsahuaman.

Another Pizarro brother, Pedro, led 50 horsemen in a charge straight at the native lines. Despite their overwhelmingly superior numbers, the Incas still did not have a weapon that could seriously injure the Spanish cavalry. Although Juan Pizarro was killed by a stone dropped onto his head, the conquistadors forced their way onto a safe position on the hill opposite Sacsahuaman. They prepared a night attack using medieval European siege tactics, and took the outer terrace of the fortress.

An Inca noble swore to fight to the death in defence of the inner towers. He is said to have knocked down any Spaniard who

extraordinary cruelty. Captured Spaniards had their heads and feet cut off. Indian prisoners were impaled or had their hands removed in Cuzco's main square.

The rebellion was more successful in other parts of the empire. Francisco Pizarro organized several relief expeditions from Lima, but by now the Incas had learned to use geography against the Spanish cavalry. One group of 70 mounted conquistadors were caught in a narrow gorge by a hail of rocks from above. Almost all were killed, and the remainder captured. Another force of 60 men under Diego Pizarro was trapped in a similar fashion: their heads were sent to Manco Inca. Now the victorious Indians

climbed onto the rampart and killed any Indian who attempted to retreat. Finally, when the Spanish attack was proving irresistible, the noble flung himself from the parapets in a spectacular suicide.

The Spanish hold on: The capture of Sacsahuaman was the key to Cuzco's defence. Although the city remained surrounded for another three months, the Incas found it impossible to take. Fighting continued with

Far left, the Incas rebel against the Spanish (Waman Puma). **Left**, the siege of Cuzco. **Above**, the fortress of Sacsayhuaman, where the greatest battle of the rebellion took place.

marched on to Lima.

The attack on the town came from three sides, but in these flat, open coastal plains, the Spanish cavalry proved invincible once again. A determined charge routed the main Indian force and the Inca's commanding general was cut down in his tracks.

Meanwhile the Spaniards went on to the offensive in Cuzco, with an attack on Manco in the terraced fortress of Ollantytambo. Archers from the Amazon jungle kept the conquistadors at bay, while Indians used weapons captured from the Spaniards to drive home an attack. Manco himself was seen at the crest of the fortress riding a captured horse and directing troops with a lance. The conquistadors beat a hasty retreat and the siege dragged on. But the tide had turned in the rebellion.

Reconquering Peru: Spanish governors from other parts of the Americas were quick to come to Pizarro's aid. Reinforcements soon arrived from Mexico and Nicaragua, while Diego de Almagro returned with troops from a failed expedition to Chile. When Almagro relieved Cuzco in April 1537, Manco Inca decided that his cause was lost and retreated with his forces into the remote Vilcabamba valley. The Spaniards chased him as far as the Vitcos, but became distracted by looting. The Inca escaped under cover of darkness,

had the Inca fled than the three surviving Pizarro brothers united against Diego de Almagro. Now Spaniard was pitted against Spaniard on Andean battlefields. The Pizarrist faction eventually defeated Almagro outside Cuzco and ordered the general garrotted.

Victory and revenge: At 63 years of age, Francisco Pizarro was at the peak of his bloodstained career. He was undisputed governor of a Peru which, although Manco Inca still occasionally harassed Spanish travelers from his jungle hideaway, was firmly under control. He possessed fabulous wealth and had been made a Marquis by the Spanish Crown. But on Sunday, June 26, 1541, Pizarro's past caught up with him: he

carried in the arms of 20 fast runners.

The Spaniards would have time to regret their greed: far inside the sub-tropical valley, behind an almost impenetrable series of narrow gorges and suspension bridges, Manco created an Inca court-in-exile that would survive in various forms for another 35 years.

But by now there was a new twist to the complicated politics of the Conquest that would distract the Spaniards: Almagro and Ferdinand Pizarro, the original partners who had arranged the invasion, had not agreed on how the empire should be divided between them. The plotting between the two former friends plunged Peru into civil war. No sooner

was surprised in his Lima palace by a group of 20 supporters of the murdered partner Diego de Almagro. The architect of the Conquest was able to kill one of his attackers before being hacked to death and his corpse thrown in a secret grave. Pizarro's ally Bishop Vicente de Valverde – who had first shown the Bible to Atahualpa – tried to escape to Panama, but the ship was wrecked off the island of Puna, where cannibilistic natives devoured the hypocritical cleric.

The wretched deaths of Pizarro and de Valverde seem a fitting end to the first stage of the Conquest. But the era that was born was no less brutal. Now that most of the easily grabbed Inca treasures had been taken and distributed, the Spanish began to exploit the population mercilessly. The 480 conquistadors who had been given natives as encomiendas became the new elite of the colony, extorting grain, livestock and labour. The rituals of conquest were becoming institutionalized, and the "black legend" of Spanish cruelty would mark Peru for centuries to come.

The last Incas: Manco Inca maintained his court in Vitcos for several years, teaching his troops Spanish fighting techniques to keep up a guerilla war. He escaped another Spanish attack led by Gonzalo Pizarro, this time by diving into a river, swimming across and disappearing into the jungle. (In frustration Pizarro took the Inca's wife, raped and beat her before having her shot to death by arrows. As a final touch, the corpse was floated down the Yucay River so that Manco could see it).

Manco's fatal mistake was to spare a group of pro-Almagro conquistadors who fled to Vilcabamba. The refugees grew bored and – with typical logic – realized that they would be pardoned if they murdered the Inca. The Spaniards were playing horseshoe quoits with their host Manco when they fell on him and stabbed him repeatedly. All paid with their lives for the treachery but the Inca leader was irreplaceable: with his death, resistance to the Spanish all but collapsed.

While Peru was sinking into colonial degradation, Manco Inca's son Titu Cusi maintained the court. The Spanish understood that, as long as any legitimate royal figure stayed free, there would always be some faint hope for the Indians. Long negotiations were aimed at drawing the Inca out to live in Cuzco, without avail.

Then, in 1569, two Augustinian friars entered the secret Inca nation and attempted to convert the Inca to Christianity. When Titu Cusi became ill, one friar prepared a healing potion to save him. Unfortunately, the Inca dropped dead as soon as he drank it. One friar was killed immediately by the horrified troops and the other dragged for three days by a rope, driven through a hole behind his jaw, before being dispatched with a mace to the skull.

Left, the Spaniards turn on one another. **Above right**, the capture of Tupac Amaru (Waman Puma).

This "martyrdom" gave the Spanish a pretext to invade Vilcabamba yet again. This time the conquistadors gathered an irresistible force. The new Inca Tupac Amaru put up a spirited defence against the invading column, but the Spaniards captured Vitcos and then Vilcabamba. Once again, the Inca tried to escape into the thick Amazon jungle, but this time progress was slowed by the Inca's wife on the verge of giving birth, and a local chief betrayed the party's movements. Finally a pursuing team of Spaniards saw a camp fire in the rainforest and pounced on the Inca, bringing him back to Cuzco with a golden chain behind his neck.

The final humiliation of the ancient Inca

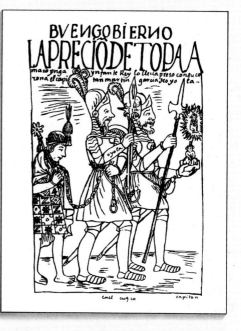

empire was at hand. Native generals were tried and hung. The Inca Tupac Amaru was put on trial for murdering the two Spanish priests. Despite appeals from Spanish liberals and native nobles, the Inca was condemned to be beheaded. On the scaffold, the Inca told his people that he had become a Christian and that the Inca religion was a sham. His head was placed on a pole, but because Indians gathered around it and seemed to be worshipping, it was removed and the Inca's body burned.

Four decades after the Spanish had arrived in Cajamarca, the last Inca had finally been killed.

The chaotic years of early colonial administration suddenly changed with the arrival in 1569 of Francisco de Toledo, Peru's fifth viceroy. A brutal but efficient ruler, Toledo consolidated Spain's command over the former Inca empire: After finally crushing the rebel bastion of Vilcabamba, he set about ordering every aspect of Indian Life.

Spain's iron fist: The effects of Toledo's decrees were to forever alter the face of the Andes. One of Toledo's most drastic measures was the establishment of *reducciones*, forced resettlements of peoples into Spanish-style towns complete with a central plaza, church, municipality and prison, the symbols of Spanish authority. *Reducciones* facilitated the collection of tribute from the Indians and their conversion to Christianity.

The new viceroy also secured the *encomienda* system, whereby Indians provided labor and tribute to an *encomendero*, their trustee. The premise of the *encomienda* was completely alien to the Andean way of life, a system based on reciprocity and redistribution. In addition, the large tracts of land that formed the *encomiendas* ignored the Andean concept of verticality, whereby an ethnic group living near say, Lake Titicaca, had access to land and produce – cotton, fish, hot peppers *(aji)* – from the warm coastal valleys. Under the colonial order, people were bound to tribute payments that went in only one direction: from tribute payer to local ethnic lord *(curaca)*, and thence to *encomendero*. Indians provided their Spanish masters with cloth, llamas, maize, wheat (introduced by the Spanish and cultivated almost exclusively for Spanish consumption), *aji*, dried fish, wild birds, beans, potatoes and coca leaves.

No longer did the state provide the necessary raw materials for people to carry out their tribute obligations. In Inca times, for example, a married woman had to provide the state with one woven garment per year. The fiber-cotton or alpaca was provided from the state storehouses. Under colonial administration, however, the textile tribute was

Indian nobles kept Inca trappings in the 17th century.

due every four months and weavers had to provide their own raw materials.

One group of tributaries serving an *encomienda* in Conchucos, near the city of Huanuco in the north-central highlands, had to provide their *encomendero* annually with 2,500 pesos of gold or its equivalent in silver; the harvest of over 1,500 hectares in wheat, maize, barley and potatoes; 30 sheep, 12 kilos of candle wax; and 15 pairs of grouse every four months. In addition, they also had to give their master 20 eggs every Friday throughout the year and 25 donkey-loads of salt annually, ten of which went to the Viceroy.

Because the *encomendero* lived in town and rarely traveled, the curacas were instrumental in the collection of tribute. Swept up by the colonial administration, the curacas, terrorized by the Spanish, in turn terrorized the Indians into fulfilling their tribute obligations. Some curacas also used their position of power to abuse the Indians. They quickly learned Spanish and borrowed the trappings of colonial nobility, dressing in Spanish-style clothing, carrying firearms and riding on horseback.

Squeezing Peru dry: Spanish colonial economy was essentially based on plunder. The treasures of Cuzco had already been distributed, but there were other sources. In the north coast city of Trujillo, named after Pizarro's birthplace in Spain, the Spanish crown granted licenses for the pillage of the ancient *huacas* (mud brick temples).

Once the Spanish had exhausted pre-Columbian tombs as a source of plunder, they turned to mines, a quest that led to the discovery in 1545 of Potosí. Today a bleak mining city in the Bolivian highlands at 4,070 meters (13,349 feet) above sea level, in its heyday Potosí was the richest and largest city in the world. At the time of Toledo, Potosí boasted a population of 150,000 people, more than that of contemporary Naples or Milan. Potosí's silver filled the coffers of Spanish royalty with the necessary cash to finance battles across Europe. Its coat of arms read: "I am rich Potosí, treasure of the world and envy of Kings."

But the discovery of Potosí brought with it

renewed hardship for the Indians. In 1574 Toledo legalized the mine *mita*, the traditional Inca system of enforced labor on a rotational basis. It was another example of an Andean institution twisted to suit Spanish needs: the Indians worked but received nothing in return. Although Toledo tried to limit the distance people had to travel and the amount of time they spent at Potosí, his ordinances were largely ignored.

Thousands died on the long, forced march to Potosí. The annual *mita* from Chucuito consisted of 2,200 Indians and their families, altogether more than 7,000 people. Each Indian took eight to ten llamas as pack animals and alpacas for food to nourish him and

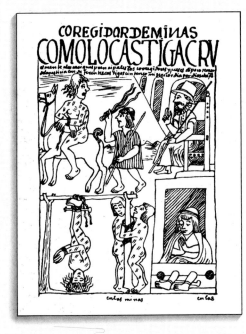

his family on the two-month, 480-km (300-mile) journey. Many would never return. Two out of every three Indians sent to Potosí died as a result of the appalling working conditions, where miners were forced to remain below ground for six-day stretches.

Even more horrific were the nearby mercury mines in Huancavelica – one of which, Santa Barbara, soon became known as the "mine of death". Thousands of Indians from neighboring provinces died in the mines, asphyxiated by lethal fumes of cinnabar (sulphide of mercury), arsenic, arsenic anhydride and mercury.

The coca leaf: Coca was initially condemned by the Spanish Church, until it realized that Indians could not survive the brutal mining *mita* without it. The leaf was soon touted by the Spanish as a cure-all to ward off hunger, thirst and fatigue. The trade was organized and controlled: thousands of highland Indians, unadapted to life in the torrid jungle, died working the coca fields. Llama caravans carried coca leaf from Cuzco, the center of production, to Potosí, 1,000 km (621 miles) away, where in only one year, 95,000 basketfuls of coca leaf were consumed. The church reaped the benefits of the lucrative trade, collecting a tithe on each full basket.

Because of coca's connections to Andean religion, some authorities tried to limit the production of this "diabolical herb". But too many fortunes were made from the trade. "There are those in Spain who became rich from this coca, buying it up and reselling it and trading it in the markets of the Indians," wrote Spanish chronicler and soldier Pedro de Cieza de Leon, who traveled throughout Peru in the 1540s. "Without coca there would be no Peru," noted another contemporary observer. This terse statement on 16th century coca production has a familiar if not sinister ring almost 500 years later, with the multi-billion dollar cocaine industry now threatening the stability of Andean nations.

Toledo also created the *mita de obrajes*, or textile workshops. Hundreds of Indians, working under factory conditions, wove for their Spanish masters, producing cloth for local consumption and export.

Toledo fought to limit the wealth of the *encomiendas* by ensuring that they reverted to the crown after a couple of generations and replacing them with *corregimientos*. By the mid-1600s, the similarly-run *corregimientos,* headed by crown-appointed *corregidores*, or co-regents, also collected tribute and provided Indians for the *obraje* and mine *mitas*. Poorly-paid *corregidores* supplemented their incomes by extorting the Indians.

Christians on the march: The early 1600s saw a far-flung campaign against idolatry, spurred on by a revival of native religion in 1565. The renewed religious zeal of the Spanish church led to a push to stamp out native religion once and for all. The church crusade also produced volumes of valuable dictionaries and accounts that are still being studied by historians today. Priests visited outlying provinces, collecting information on cults and torturing villagers to reveal the whereabouts of idols and *huacas*.

But in many ways, the Catholic campaign only served to entrench native beliefs even deeper. Rather than taking over, Christianity only formed a thin veneer over traditional cults and beliefs, many of which still exist today. This syncretism, in which traditional beliefs dominate, led to the replacement of Andean pilgrimage centers and festivals by other superficially Catholic ones. Many are still in use. Modern-day Copacabana on the Bolivían shores of Lake Titicaca, for example, is nothing more than a Catholic church built over an important Andean shrine venerated by peoples around the lake in Inca times.

By the early 1700s the colonial system was firmly established throughout the Andes. It was a system based on the exploitation of the Indian and marked by rampant corruption and extortion by Spanish officials.

At its height, the viceroyalty of Peru was 15 times the size of Spain and for two centuries ruled from Panama to Argentina. The South American mines, exhausted by almost two centuries of exploitation, eventually began to languish and output declined. But colonials in Peru flourished: Spain decreed that all trade from South America should pass through Lima first, ensuring a massive flow of taxes. Lima became the opulent "City of Kings", full of magnificent churches and mansions.

Spain, meanwhile, saw the replacement of the Hapsburg dynasty by the Bourbons, who reigned until Napoleon occupied Madrid in 1808. Efforts by various Bourbon monarchs to improve the colonial economy and stem corruption were to little avail. The colonial system, by now well-established, had acquired its own momentum.

Indian uprising: During the 18th century, unrestricted exploitation sparked off various Indian rebellions from Quito to La Paz. The most serious of these was the uprising instigated by José Gabriel Condorcanqui, also known as Tupac Amaru II.

Tupac Amaru claimed to be descended from Tupac Amaru I, the renegade Inca emperor killed by the Viceroy Toledo. Born

in Tinta, south of Cuzco, Tupac Amaru studied in Cuzco at a school for Indians of noble birth. After the death of his father, he inherited the title of curaca. It was never Tupac Amaru's intention to rid Peru of the Spanish yoke. Rather, he fought against the tyranny of the *corregidores*, and in his letters to crown officials spoke of the miserable conditions at the *haciendas*, mines, *obrajes* and coca plantations. Increasingly, he lobbied for Indian rights, demanding that the mine *mita* be lifted and the power of the *corregidores* limited.

One evening in 1780 he invited Tinta's hated *corregidor*, Antonio Arriaga, to dinner. After the meal, Arriga was taken pris-

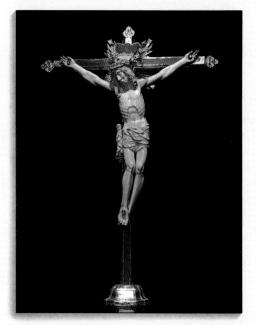

oner and later hanged in Tinta's public square. It was the start of a public revolt. The rebellion spread throughout the Peruvian highlands and Spanish reinforcements were sent from Lima to quell the uprising. At a decisive battle in Checacupe in 1781, the Spanish dispersed Tupac Amaru's men and captured the rebel leader and his wife.

The crown spared no one. First, Tupac Amaru was forced to witness the execution of his family. He was then drawn and quartered, like his ancestor, in Cuzco's public square. The survivors of Inca nobility were sent to Spain, where Charles III had them imprisoned.

<u>Left</u>, depradations of the Spanish (Waman Puma). <u>Above right</u>, colonial cross.

LAS TAPADAS

Friction between Peru's Spanish-born residents and its upper class *mestizos* did more than spark the independence revolution. It bred a rivalry between women from the two camps and gave Lima its most scandalous fashion.

The Spanish ladies enticed men with their tiny waists, by waving elaborate fans and by moving sveltely next to the shorter, darker and plumper Limeñas. Not to be outdone, the *mestizas* created a look of their own by covering their faces with an Arab veil – except for one eye that peeked out. They were the *tapadas* or "covered ones".

Although veiled, the *tapadas* were not modest. Their skirts were hiked to shamelessly show feet tinier than those of their Spanish counterparts. Simultaneously, the *tapadas* dropped their necklines, knowing the fair-skinned Spaniards would remain covered under Lima's strong sun. When the European women cinched their middles even more, the thick-waisted *mestizas* scrimped on the fabric encircling their ample hips. Skirts in the 1700s became so tight that the Limeñas could only take tiny steps as they promenaded down the street.

But one part of this costume remained constant – the veil hiding all but an eye.

Secret trysts: "This costume so alters a woman – even her voice since her mouth is covered – that unless she is very tall or very short, lame, hunchbacked or otherwise conspicuous, she is impossible to recognize," French feminist Flora Tristan wrote about the *tapadas*. "I am sure it needs little imagination to appreciate the consequences of this time-honored practice which is sanctioned or at least tolerated by law."

The *tapadas* spent their afternoons strolling and the "consequences" of their tantalizing fashion ranged from sinful trysts to playful flirting – sometimes with their own unknowing husbands. So scandalous was the costume that the archbishop attempted to condemn it, but the *tapadas* conspired and refused to serve their husbands, attend their families or carry out church duties while the sanction was in effect.

Conspiracy, in fact, was endemic at the time and many tapadas used their afternoon walks to anonymously pass notes and messages to organizers of the revolution. The site for this romantic and political intrigue was the Paseo de Aguas – a walkway of reflecting pools and gardens built for the woman who inspired one of South America's most famous romances.

By stealing a viceroy's heart, *mestiza* Micaela Villegas placed herself firmly in history and legend. Count Amat y Juniet built her Lima's finest house, bought her a gold and silver coach and, although in his 60s, fathered her only child. Their love inspired Jacques Offenbach's 1968 opera, *La Perichole*.

Villegas was known as "La Perrichola", Amat's mispronunciation of the "half breed bitch" epithet he threw her way during a heated argument. Despite the moniker, Amat adored the actress he first caught eye of on a Lima stage.

A Cristal beer factory now stands where La Perrichola's opulent mansion once was, but Paseo de Aguas – built so the couple would have a spot to stroll – survives in the Rimac district behind the presidential palace.

Inconsolable when her aged lover was ordered back to Spain (where, in his 80s, he married one of his nieces), La Perrichola vowed never to love again, gave her wealth to the poor and entered a convent.

As a result of the rebellion, French noble-man and Viceroy Teodoro de Croix (1784-90) began to institute long overdue reforms. He set up a special *audiencia*, or royal court, in Cuzco to deal with Indian legal claims. Meanwhile in Spain, Charles III ordered that trade and commerce be opened up, allowing other American ports to trade with Spain and foreigners. He banned the *repartimiento*, the forced sale of shabby goods to Indians at inflated prices, and ended the corrupt *corregimiento* system. In additional Charles III ordered that the viceroyalty be divided into seven intendencies under direct royal rule, paving the way for the regionalism that would break South America into its present

natural history and colonial life, Martinez de Compañon and his team of artists produced over 1,000 drawings, plans and maps in ink and watercolor bound in nine volumes and covering antiquities, flora and fauna, cus-toms, music, and costumes of northern Peru. The cleric is also considered by many to be the grandfather of Peruvian archaeology: he collected some 600 pre-Columbian textiles and ceramics for shipment to the King, who founded a "Cabinet of Natural History and of Antiquities" in Madrid.

The push for independence: On the eve of Napoleon's march on the Iberian peninsula, Spain's hold on its colonies was already waning. When Napoleon forced Charles IV

patchwork of republics.

Not all members of the Spanish govern-ment and clergy exploited the Indians. One clergyman of the time, Don Baltasar Jaime Martinez de Compañon y Bujanda, stands out. Appointed Bishop of Trujillo in 1779, Martinez de Compañon spent his years traveling around a vast diocese covering the northern third of Peru. In a letter to Charles III dated 1786 he described the "wretched-ness" he saw everywhere. Fascinated by

Left, scandalous fashion of "the covered ones".
Above, Simón Bolívar takes on Spanish forces in the Peruvian Sierra.

to abdicate in favor of Ferdinand VII, and then placed his brother on the Spanish throne, South America rebelled. Declarations of in-dependence in Upper Peru (Bolivía) and Quito in 1809 were followed by uprisings in the Peruvian cities of Huanuco and Cuzco. But freedom from Spain was not so easy: royalist troops regained control in many parts of the continent and bloody wars were waged for the next fifteen years. And many Peruvi-ans supported the colonial system, since Lima was still its wealthy administrative capital. Peru became the strongest bastion of pro-Spanish feeling, and other independent countries could not feel secure until it, too, was liberated.

After the Argentine general José de San Martín's successful invasion of Chile in 1818, a rebel navy commanded by British admiral Alfred Lord Cochrane sailed from the Chilean port of Valparaíso and landed in Paracas, on Peru's south coast. The following year the armada attacked Lima, dispersing royalist troops who fled to the central and southern highlands. Meanwhile, on Peru's north coast, the cities of Trujillo, Lambayeque, Piura and Cajamarca declared their independence. General San Martín entered Lima in 1821, proclaiming independence for all of Peru on July 28.

San Martín's first move was to abolish the

historians Henry E. Dobyns and Paul L. Doughty, "is one of those Latin American nations whose national politics have been plagued ever since independence by a futile quest for a functional substitute for a king."

In the tumultuous months following Peru's declaration of independence, the monarchical plan was scuttled following the election of a parliament. The seven viceregal intendencies became departments headed by a prefect, modelled on the French plan.

In 1822 San Martín sailed to Guayaquil, Ecuador where he met with Venezuelan statesman and fellow independence seeker Simón Bolívar. San Martín sought troops for Peru to rout out the last Spanish royalist

dreaded Indian tribute, the mine *mita* and *encomiendas*. The children of black slaves were freed. He even banned the term "Indian" and for the first time proclaimed the descendants of the Incas to be citizens of Peru.

But this was all too much for a conservative elite still immersed in its colonial ways. San Martín and the leaders of Lima opted for a monarchy to replace Spanish rule and at one stage actually searched for a prince in Europe to rule the former Spanish colony.

Peru was not prepared for self-rule. The descendants of the Spanish *conquistadores* and colonial administrators thrived in Peru, dependent on the motherland. "Peru", write

forces holed-up in the Andes and offered Peru's leadership to Bolívar.

Bolívar, however, advocated republicanism during his brief, two-year presidency of Peru between 1824-26. He commanded troops at the Battle of Junín in 1824, but it was not until the decisive Battle of Ayacucho later that year that rebel troops headed by Venezuelan general José de Sucre finally crushed royalist troops commanded by Viceroy José de la Serna while Arequipa, whose strong regional streak had sparked off uprisings before, advocated independence from Peru.

Freedom and chaos: Bolívar's departure for

Colombia in 1826 created a power vacuum and the congress elected José de la Mar president. Between 1821-26, eight men had governed Peru, establishing the pattern of coups d'etats and political instability that characterizes the country to this day.

San Martín's promises to abolish the Indian tribute, *mita,* servitude and even to recognize Quechua as an official language, were never followed through. The wars of independence had left the countryside ravaged, crops unattended and food scarce. Instead of granting Indians equal status as citizens of a republican Peru, an all-out assault began on Indian land-holdings. The next 50 years would set patterns for the mistreatment of

pick up bits of carrion."

By 1830 Peru discovered a new resource that replaced minerals as the country's main export: guano. The rich piles of bird droppings deposited on Peru's off-shore islands were much sought after in industrial Europe as fertilizer and fetched enormous prices. The first guano contract was negotiated with Britain in 1840. Indians worked in appalling conditions at the guano stations, where ammonia fumes shriveled the skin and often cause blindness. In 1854 traders even staged a raid on Easter Island off the coast of Chile, kidnapping hundreds of Easter Islanders to work the guano deposits. Most died, decimating the island's tiny population.

Indians that lasted well into the 20th century.

Between 1825 and 1865, 35 presidents governed Peru, many of whom were military officers. Chaos reigned in Lima and the countryside. Charles Darwin, a witness of early republican years, recalled "Lima, the city of Kings, must formerly have been a splendid town." But he found it in a "wretched state of decay; the streets are nearly unpaved, and heaps of filth are piled up in all directions, where the black *gallinazos* (vultures)

Left, missionaries head into the Amazon basin. **Above,** defending Lima from Chilean attack in the war of the Pacific.

The industry became so important that, by 1849, Peru's economy was almost entirely in the hands of the London-based firm of Anthony Gibbs and Sons and the Montane Company of Paris, who shared exclusive guano marketing rights. There were few other sources of income: large cotton and sugar estates developed on the coast and in 1849 Peru began to import Chinese labor to work the fields. At the same time, the government encouraged migration from Europe.

In 1865 Spain tried to gain a foothold in its former colony and occupied the Chincha guano islands, in response to what it considered unfair treatment of a group of Basque immigrants. A year later president Mariano Prado declared war on Spain and in 1866 the Spanish navy bombarded Callao, but were unable to capture it. As a result of the Spanish attack, Peru decided to revamp its fleet, buying up arms and munitions in Europe and borrowing heavily on its future guano income. Using the guano concession as a guarantee, Peru acquired the *Huascar* and *Independencia* warships in Britain, and owed its creditors the vast sum of 20 million pesos.

The guano boom also initiated an era of railroad construction. President Jose Balta signed contracts for eight major lines, including Arequipa-Puno, completed in 1876, Callao-La Oroya, completed in 1878, and

Meanwhile, Chile had obtained a Bolivian concession to nitrate of soda and borax deposits in the province of Tarapaca. Bolivía levied a tax on the concessionaires, but Chile refused to pay. Although Peru sought to resolve the conflict peacefully, Chile declared war on the two countries in 1879.

Despite some successes, Peru and Bolivía's armed forces proved to be woefully unprepared for the war. Chilean troops occupied southern Peru and then bombarded Callao, occupying Lima and cutting off the capital from the hinterland. The troops plundered Lima's national library, taking valuable books and manuscripts. When President Prado left for Europe in search of support, Nicolas de

Juliaca-Cuzco, completed in 1909. US railroad entrepreneur Henry Meiggs, nicknamed the "Yankee Pizarro", won the bid for the Callao-La Oroya line, a engineering feat of tunnels and bridges that began at sea level and rose over 5,000 meters (16,400 feet) to the mining town of La Oroya. Travelers can still take this spectacular route to Huancayo.

The bubble bursts: Peru financed its railroad construction with a 60 million soles loan from the French firm of Dreyfus, the leading guano trader. But in 1877 the second Mariano Prado regime was unable to pay back its British creditors and Peru was plunged into bankruptcy.

Piérola seized power. Following the peace treaty of 1883, Peru ceded Tarapaca to Chile. Bolivía remains landlocked to this day.

The war with Chile sent Peru into economic chaos. Desperate for funds, it reinstituted the Indian tribute and levied a tax on salt. Three years after the peace treaty, British bondholders started up debt negotiations. The negotiating team, headed by a son of W.R. Grace who had business interests in the country, cancelled Peru's debt in exchange for 66 years of control of the major railroads and 2 million tons of guano. The bondholders set up the Peruvian Corporation in 1890 to manage their Peruvian interests.

New century, old problems : By 1900, US interests were replacing British in controlling the Peruvian economy. Mining once again became pre-eminent. North American investors set up the Cerro de Pasco Mining Company, soon controlling all of the mines in the central sierra, and in 1922 a smelter at La Oroya began belching fumes of arsenic, lead and zinc into the atmosphere, ravaging the countryside. Fishmeal began being exported from Peru's abundant anchovy schools, while some industry grew in Lima and other urban centers.

These workers in the mines, coastal factories and urban sweatshops began hesitantly to form unions. But it was in the north coast, where laborers in the sugar haciendas began to organize, that a new class consciousness found political expression. In 1924, while exiled in Mexico, a popular activist named Victor Raul Haya de la Torre formed the Alianza Popular Revolucionaria Americana (APRA), with a loose platform based on anti-imperialism and nationalization that attracted members of the middle class feeling left out by the oligarchical rule.

Haya was allowed back into Peru to contest the 1931 elections, but was defeated in what Apristas denounced as a fraud. Party faithful rose up in rebellion in the northern city of Trujillo, killing some 60 military officers they had taken captive. The army retook the city and executed over 1,000 Apristas in the ancient ruins of Chan Chan.

For the next 50 years, APRA was kept out of power as Peru oscillated between conservative and military governments. (During one such rule in the late 40s, Haya was forced into hiding in the Colombian embassy in Lima for over eight years). In that time, Peru's manufacturing industry grew and hundreds of thousands left the countryside for Lima. Pressure for land reform and some redistribution of wealth grew. The first government of Fernando Belaunde (1963-68), who promised some cautious progressive measures, was a failure: after widespread disgust at tax concessions given to the International Petroleum Company (a subsidiary of Standard Oil of New Jersey), yet another military coup occurred. Belaunde was

marched out of the Presidential Palace in his pyjamas and on to an airplane and exile.

But General Juan Velasco, who headed the new junta, was not typical of military rulers. He went on to champion many of the most radical APRA reforms that Haya himself had given up as impossible. Velasco's measures drastically changed Peru. They included a sweeping agrarian reform, expropriating vast land-holdings and turning family-run estates into cooperatives overnight. The petrol, mining and fishing industries were nationalized at a stroke. Food for the urban population was subsidized by the state. And, in a profound symbolic gesture, Peru was recognized as a bilingual country,

with Quechua as the second language.

Unfortunately, the "Peruvian revolution" ran up against the 1973 oil crisis. The economy deteriorated and the military split into factions. In 1975, Morales Bermudez staged a bloodless coup against Velasco, who died of an illness soon afterwards. The coup provoked no popular protests, but Velasco's funeral train was followed by the largest crowd that Lima had ever seen.

Despite a series of economic plans, the new military government proved that it was incapable of running Peru. Debt was soaring, inflation out of control. Democratic elections were scheduled once again for 1980.

Left, the 1956 inauguration of President Manuel Prado. **Above right**, General Juan Velasco, who began wide-ranging reforms in the late 1960s.

Peru has remained a constitutional democracy since 1980, despite difficulties that hasty outside observers thought would inevitably precipitate a military intervention. The cold statistics of economic collapse and political violence conceal a deep-rooted and overdue process of social change. Though its eventual outcome is difficult to predict, it has already shaken up the rigid hierarchies of race and class that characterized Peru since the Spanish conquest.

Democracy returns: The last decade began

sor, General Francisco Morales Bermudez, had pushed Peru deep into debt.

A middle-of-the-road former architect with a reputation for personal honesty, Belaúnde was a close student of Peruvian geography and history. Aged 68 when his second term began, he seemed happiest poring over maps of the Amazon jungle, planning new roads and settlements. More complicated problems of economic management and social inequalities proved too much for a President who often appeared hesitant and passive.

hopefully for Peru with the restoration of constitutional rule and signs of economic progress. The election in 1980 was Peru's first with universal suffrage. Voters, by a comfortable margin, restored Fernando Belaúnde to a second term in power, twelve years after he had been ejected from the Presidential Palace by army tanks. He took over a country very different from the one he had hurriedly left. A program of radical reform under General Juan Velasco (1968-75) had included the expropriation of the old land-owning oligarchy and the nationalisation of many foreign-owned industries, utilities and banks. But Velasco and his succes-

Though Belaúnde was quick to restore democratic freedom, including freedom of the press and municipal elections, he neither moved to reverse Velasco's reforms nor attempted to extend them.

After two years of moderate economic growth and relative social peace, by 1983 his government faced serious problems. Some of the causes were external: after Mexico's default ushered in the Latin American debt crisis, foreign loans to Latin American dried up and Peru found itself thrust back into the arms of the International Monetary Fund and a new austerity program. A particularly strong *El Niño* (the rogue warm current that periodically disrupts Peru's climate) brought severe flooding to the north coast and drought to the southern Andes. The result of all this was rising inflation, a persistent budget deficit and a sharp recession with production falling by 13 percent in 1983.

Andean rebellion: But these largely familiar problems were compounded by a new development. The 1980 elections had seen the debut of the Maoist Sendero Luminoso (Shining Path) guerrilla movement. In its first armed action, Sendero had dynamited a polling station in the remote Andean village of Chuschi. As the decade wore on Sendero came to cast an ever-longer shadow over Peruvian democracy. Formed as a radical

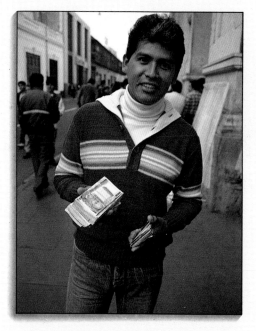

splinter party in the mid-1970s, Sendero was the brainchild of a group of obscure provincial intellectuals gathered at the University of San Cristóbal de Huamanga in Ayacucho. Under the leadership of Abimael Guzman (known to his followers as "President Gonzalo"), Sendero went underground and prepared for a Mao-style "prolonged popular war to surround the cities from the countryside" against the State and capitalist society. Its initial actions involved bomb

Far left, cross in Cuzco. **Left**, Apra offices in Lima. **Above**, wads of 5-million Inti notes as inflation runs riot.

attacks against state property and the killing of landlords and officials in and around Ayacucho, in the central-southern Andes at the center of the poorest and most neglected area of Peru.

The Belaúnde government made two serious mistakes in handling Sendero. The President began by ignoring it, allowing the guerrillas to consolidate a political presence in the Indian farming communities of Ayacucho. When he did send in a police counter-insurgency battalion and then, in December 1982, the armed forces, they acted with indiscriminate violence against the Quechua-speaking Indian population. Human rights organizations blamed the security forces for the "disappearance" of almost 2,000 people during this period. Hundreds more were killed in massacres in villages.

Youthful president: The 1985 elections gave Peruvians grounds for hope once again. Under the fresh and energetic leadership of Alan García, the populist-nationalist Apra (American Popular Revolutionary Alliance), Peru's oldest and best-organized political party with roots in the numerous lower middle class, had emerged from a period of decline. With outstanding campaign oratory and a populist promise to be "President of all Peruvians", the tall and good-looking García seized the middle-ground of politics, winning 47 percent of the vote (against 26 percent for Barrantes) to become, at age 35, South America's youngest President.

Apra had no clear policy agenda, much of its historic program having been implemented by General Velasco. And the mercurial García often chose to use his uncommon political skills for short-term advantage. But these problems were not immediately apparent. García made a swift and positive impact. He announced a unilateral cut in payments on Peru's foreign debt (then standing at US$14 billion) to the equivalent of 10 percent of the country's export earnings, and stopped payments to the IMF, whose policy prescriptions he denounced as "imperialist". García used the foreign exchange saved to pump money into the economy, which grew by a fifth in two years. But the boom stemmed from a consumption spree. With growth running out of steam and balance of payments difficulties looming in mid-1987, García made a crucial mistake. Without consulting his Ministers, he announced a state take-over of private banks and insurance companies. Though opinion polls showed the move to be marginally popular, it provoked a deep hatred and distrust of the President among business leaders and the powerful upper-middle classes. At one stroke, García's action revived the moribund right-of-center parties and precipitated a gradual swing in Peruvian opinion towards more free-market and outward-looking economic policies. The novelist Mario Vargas Llosa organized a public campaign against the nationalization, which was soon quietly dropped.

Sliding economy: One immediate consequence of the bank episode was to make an embittered García reluctant to court increased

national income. State investment shrank to zero, key state industries like the oil and electricity companies were bankrupted, and the maintenance of roads and other infrastructure was neglected. The government printed money to pay the wage bill for the state bureaucracy, swollen as Apra gave jobs to thousands of its supporters.

Meanwhile, the guerilla movement led by Sendero began to consolidate de facto control over much larger areas. These included the Upper Huallaga valley, where booming demand for cocaine in the United States and later in Western Europe, had created Peru's only growth industry of the 1980s – the cultivation of coca, the ancestral Andean

unpopularity by taking tough measures to tackle inflation. But his debt policy had cut Peru off from international credit and by September 1988, the Central Bank had run out of foreign exchange. The government slammed on the brakes, raising prices enough to provoke a deep recession that saw production fall by a fifth in two years. But García refused to follow this up with measures to cut the fiscal deficit. His government limped through to the end of its term amid mounting chaos. Inflation ranged between 30 percent and 60 percent a month. Living standards plunged and poverty increased. Government tax revenue slumped to less than 4 percent of

shrub from whose leaves cocaine is derived. By 1990, there were up to 200,000 hectares of coca in Peru, more than half the world's supply. A US-sponsored and designed anti-drug program focused on forcible eradication of coca crops, causing resentment among farmers that helped Sendero to gain control over the valley. But Sendero also made important mistakes: its killings of trade union, peasant and community leaders turned new sections of the population against it, for example, in shanty town districts of Lima and in Puno, where it faced organized opposition from the Church and the Left. Above all, it became apparent that Sendero had nothing to offer to a population weary of violence except further killings.

Under García a third of the country came to be under a permanent state of emergency and military control. Human rights violations continued, and a shadowy extreme right para-military group, apparently linked to the security forces, claimed responsibility for killings of students and leftist sympathisers. But a strengthened and better-equipped police force did score some successes against Sendero. Nevertheless, by then political violence had claimed more than 17,000 lives and guerrilla sabotage had cost the economy more than US$14 billion – the equivalent of two thirds of the annual production.

the last month of the campaign, a remarkable snowballing protest vote gathered behind Alberto Fujimori, a little-known former university rector of Japanese descent who was making his political debut as an independent. Fujimori surged into second place, cutting Vargas Llosa's vote to 27 percent. In a run-off ballot, Fujimori, strengthened by votes from Apra and the left, won easily.

Fujimori, a pragmatist of the center, acted swiftly to restore economic order, but at great social cost. Though he appears to have some chance of conquering inflation, achieving economic growth and prosperity, it is clearly going to be a long and difficult haul. He faces obvious political difficulties:

New directions: The 1990 election campaign was dominated by the economy. Mario Vargas Llosa stood as the candidate for a reorganized right-of-center alliance preaching a radical free-market program. With the left splitting in 1989, and Apra discredited by its record in government, he faced little opposition. But the poor majority appeared to see Vargas as a class warrior for the rich and they distrusted the politicians around him who had governed under Belaúnde. In

Left, moneychangers in central Lima. **Above**, Japanese-descended Alberto Fujimori, elected president in 1990.

he lacks both a parliamentary majority and the backing of an organized political party. In a potentially worrying development for Peru's democracy, he turned quickly to the armed forces for support, giving them control over the police.

Fujimori has taken charge of a country that had changed dramatically in ten years of economic decline. By 1990, four out of five Peruvians worked in the "informal economy" of back street workshops, street vendors, or subsistence farmers. Optimists see in the industry of these small businesses, and in the dense network of self-help community organizations, the future of the country.

In 1949 in Ayacucho, a forgotten corner of the Peruvian Central Sierra, several strangers from Lima walked into the workshop of a local craftsman. An impish little man, Don Joaquín Lopéz Antay looked up from his workbench. As an image-maker in a centuries-old tradition, he had often dealt with *hacienda* owners, judges and towns people. He repaired their statues of patron saints, refurbished their chapels or made an embellished cross for donation to a church. But these visitors did not behave with the swaggering arrogance of Creole notables. They chatted amicably about his craft, methods and the use of the articles that he fashioned from plaster, wood and glue.

These outsiders were artists, writers and academics. They had ventured from the capital into Peru's Andean provinces to uncover what really existed there, establish contact with peasants and traders and break out of the stereotypes prevailing in Lima about Peru's Indian interior.

Andean tradition meets the modern world: These intellectuals were intrigued by a piece of folk art that the Ayacucho elites rarely noticed. Don Joaquín made a piece called the *sanmarkos* for peasants. It was a simple wooden box containing miniature saints and livestock. A three-dimensional format with bright colors and Andean motifs, it served as the centerpiece in the magical religious branding rites in a traditional pastoral society. Its roots lay in the small portable shrines brought to Peru by the *conquistadores* as part of their evangelization mission. With time, the peasants assumed this artifact as a part of their own universe, combining the Christian God and his saints with Andean spirits.

The Lima visitors were impressed by the expressive potential of the form and wanted to commission something different. They asked him to break out of the strictures of the branding ceremony and use the figures to portray his own universe. Scratching the stubble on his chin, Don Joaquín set aside his

Preceding pages: riotous fiesta in Cuzco; rich Limeños in bar; skateboard riders in Lima. **Left**, flowers for sale in Chiclayo. **Above right**, Quechua *campesino* from Lake Titicaca.

May crosses, saints and *sanmarkos*. He transformed the format and content. He introduced the ebb and flow of life – the drunken fiestas in the streets, the bustle of markets and the repression of crowded jails. Other scenes showed the Nativity and Easter processions.

The Lima intellectuals called this new creation a *retablo*, meaning altarpiece. A new strain of folk art had been invented, one that would be taken up in textiles, ceramics and painting.

This chance encounter between the traditional Andean world and the modernizing influences of the 20th century was repeated up and down the Andes, in Cuzco, Puno, Huancayo, Cajamarca and even in Lima, over five decades. Some of these encounters resulted in new folk art forms, music and tales. Other encounters yielded new forms of organization, the demand for education and excursions into the alien coast through migration to gain a place in urban society. Each of these encounters was unique in the forging of Peruvian identity, of suffering and destruction, of joy and celebration.

What is striking about this process is that

the Andean realm drew on its tradition of cultural resistance against oppressive dominance. It avoided wholesale absorption into dominant white society, but created new ways of inserting itself into a broader world. Resistance and renewal, change and continuity are constants in Peruvian society. They became synonymous with modernization and breaking out of a rigid, backward, semifeudal society.

Two Worlds?: At first sight, Peruvian society may seem brutally divided. On one side, white creoles trace their bloodline back to the Spanish Conquest in 1536. Like the generations before them, most live in Lima – the old colonial capital that still boasts a

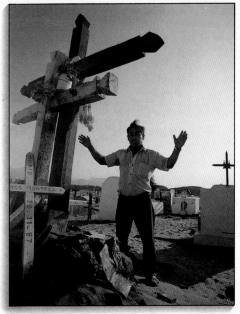

statue of Pizarro in its main square. They are products of industrialization, urbanization and the Age of Computers. And for cultural inspiration, their eyes are firmly fixed on Miami: every aspect of North American mass culture, from Reebok running shoes to Disneyland and *New Kids on the Block*, is part of their childrens' upbringing.

On the other side, according to this view, are the Andean Indians, subjected during the Spanish Conquest, yet heirs of an awe-inspiring pre-Columbian culture. Theirs can seem an archaic society, locked in a time warp: lost in their impoverished mountain villages, they still speak their ancient tongue

and listen to their haunting, melancholy music played on traditional wooden pipes.

But Peruvian society is a much more complex multicultural mixture. While it may be possible to pick out two extreme poles of cultural identity, there are many places for Peruvians to fit in between.

The Peruvian Indian cultures are a complex mix. The Andes has two large ethnic groups: one speaks Quechua, the language of the Inca Empire; the other speak Aymará and is settled around Lake Titicaca and neighboring Bolivia. (In fact, the Aymará people easily slip back and forth across the border to engage in commerce.) Even among the Quechua speakers, an Indian from Huancayo may not be able to make himself understood to an Indian from Cuzco because of regional differences in the dialects.

Beyond these global distinctions, there are other complexities that slip in. There are "white" ethnic groups, like the Morochucos of Pampa Cangallo (Ayacucho) who have light colored eyes and hair, speak Quechua and feel *campesino*. According to legend, the Morochucos are the descendants of a renegade band of *conquistadores* who held out in an isolate stretch of the Sierra. In other regions, like Cajamarca, peasants have lost their language and racial features but still think and act like peasants and feel bound to the earth. The *misti*, the dominant class in the Andes, may speak Quechua, share cultural traits and have Indian or *mestizo* (mixed blooded) physiological characteristics, but he falls on the other side of the racial-class divide. Meanwhile, in the Amazon jungle, there are 53 ethnolinguistic groups (see feature on "Tribes of the Amazon").

Complex mix: Other racial and ethnic distinctions were imported. Up to the 19th century, landowners brought in African blacks to serve as slaves on their *haciendas* and frequently used them to repress the Indians. Between 1850 and 1920, Chinese coolies and Japanese provided the hands and backs to build railways over the Andes or farm the

arrived to run foreign companies and stayed.

Over the past 400 years, there has been a long process of inter-marriage and mixing of bloods, creating the *mestizo*, of part Amerindian, part European heritage. Indeed, today the majority of Peruvians would fall into this category. (In this regard, it is important to note that in Peru, you can become a *mestizo* not only by birth but also by choice. Indians who renounce their culture and assume western dress are automatically *mestizo*, and are sometimes referred to as *cholos*. Peruvian social divisions are therefore not so much racially as *culturally* defined.)

Even among the elites, racial stock has not remained pure. Cross-ethinc marriages, while

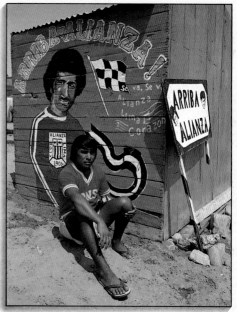

land when there was a scarcity of labor. Still today, the Nikei (as the Japanese community is called) are the largest ethnic migrant communities among Peru's 22 million inhabitants. They number about 60,000.

European immigrants, mainly Spaniards, Italians, Germans, Lebanese and Jews, arrived in the 19th and early 20th century to take a place in the caste system alongside the original Spaniards. Americans and English

Far left, young dancers in Trujillo (The North); **left**, praying before a grave. **Above**, pipe-playing on Taquile Island; **above right**, soccer player in the slums of Lima.

frowned on by the most recalcitrant, have occurred frequently. In fact, this permeability led many Peruvians to deny that there was a racial problem in the country until the late 1970s when Indians and *cholos* began to acquire rights and property and encroach on the privileges of *gente decente* ("decent people", as they called themselves).

From the oligarchy's stronghold on its landholdings in the Sierra and on the coast, which were crucial for its economic power and political leverage, it retreated to the cities in the first half of the 20th century. The Club Nacional, an exclusive private club located on San Martín plaza in downtown

Lima, was a symbol of this class. In its high-vaulted dining rooms and smoking parlors, the oligarchs and conservatives plotted military coups to get rid of uncomfortable reformist governments that did not serve their purposes between 1900 and 1962. Today, the sons of the plotters no longer frequent the Club Nacional, leaving it to dozing old men. Instead, they have shifted their headquarters to the Club de la Banca y Comercio in San Isidro. Businessmen and bankers do not scheme to overthrow a distasteful government, but how to make a profit in a topsy-turvy economy. They spend their summer weekends at beach resort towns, little colonies of comfort, within driving distance of

into its own, both in Lima and provincial cities. This growth was due to the diversification of the economy and to the expansion of the Peruvian state, both as a purveyor of public services and as an entrepreneur. It has brought political reform and change. Its composition is less defined by racial or ethnic characteristics, leaning more towards education and aspirations. As recent developments have shown however, the middle class is also precarious because it generally depends on salaries, which have been eroded by inflation. It has slide backwards into the hardship of survival.

A people coping with geography: One reason that it has been so difficult to unify Peru into

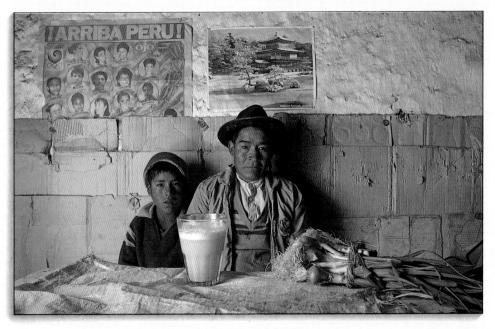

Lima, on the Pacific Ocean. They also congregate at bullfight and cockfights.

In all fairness, this same privileged class has produced the great intellectuals, progressive businessmen and political reformers of the 20th century. These were the men who believed in universal rights and progress and wanted to extend them to the hard-bitten Indians and *mestizos*.

The most difficult social terrain to define is the middle class. Up to the 1960s, it was the poor cousin of the oligarchy, providing clerks, merchants and civil servants to service the dominant class. Once modernization started in earnest in the 1970s, the middle class grew

a single society is the harsh, complex and hostile geography. Rising 6,000 meters (19,680 feet) above sea level, the Andes comprise about a third of Peru's territory, while the Amazon jungle and barren desert coast make up the rest. But precisely because of these demanding conditions, the Andean people have been challenged to come up with creative solutions. The Andes always have privileged organizations willing to work with labor-intensive methods, abnegation, patience, discipline and long-term strategies. The pre-Columbian cultures were admirably equipped to manage and prosper in these Andean micro-climates.

But for the modern nation-state of Peru, this mountain mass poses major problems for development and integration into a single society. It throws up huge physical barriers in providing basic services, like transport and communication. Some analysts have described Peru as an archipelago, small pockets of population scattered in isolated regions. This means that health, education and law enforcement programs must cover immense territories to be successful.

Even capitalism has found it difficult to put down firm roots in the Andes. Aside from mining and metallurgical enclaves and trading cities, the Andean version bears little resemblance to what Adam Smith had in

Sierra now. The communities in the Andes sustain themselves with a pastoral and farming economy, plus other secondary activities, like crafts, trading and services. Almost by definition, the zone is marginal and impoverished, removed from the modernizing influences of the national economy (see feature "Daily Life in the Andes"). The Andean peasants, however, do not want to remain poor, even if it makes for picturesque postcards. They are proud of their past, but also want a piece of the future.

Decade of change: In the 1970s, several trends began to break down the isolation of much of Peru. Roads penetrating into the Sierra and Amazon jungle started to link up

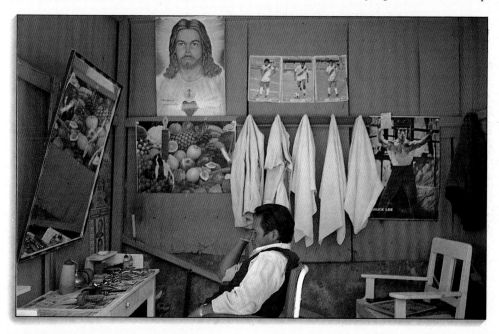

mind. Peru's elites forged alliances with international interests – for investments, manufacturing patents, technology and capital goods. But communities in large sections of the Andean Sierra existed with little or no contact with the money economy.

The Andes are still a refuge for Peru's underprivileged Quechua- and Aymará-speaking Indians. The Sierra region today holds 40 percent of the total population and 60 percent of the rural population. There are 5,000 peasant communities located in the

Left, enjoying a glass of *chicha*. **Above**, hairdresser waits for customers.

the hinterland with Lima and coastal markets. Mass communication reached out to new audiences. In 1970, the Peruvian football team's participation in the World Cup, which was broadcast nationally on radio and television, drove home to remote communities that they were Peruvians. Modern preventive health measures began to lower child mortality rates.

These social changes were matched by political changes. A military regime under Army General Juan Alvarado Velasco broke the stereotypes of Latin American strongarm governments. The military enacted progressive programs, expropriating large landholdings, nationalizing foreign companies, asserting a more independent foreign policy. This approach, at times demagogical, at times nationalistic, marked a change in attitudes. The peasants and shantytown residents began to raise their heads and challenge those who held power by virtue of birth.

The humble Ayacuchan artist, Don Joaquín Lopéz, might be seen as a symbol of the changes at work in Peru. In 1975, he was awarded a National Art Prize for his innovation and creativity in shaping folk art and the *retablo*. This award set off a bitter controversy in Lima. Mainstream art critics and artists were scandalized that folk artists were given the same status as the fine arts in the

dimensions. He started working themes that asked broader questions, like: where does the Andean peasant fit into national history and identity? He made massive *retablos* which portrayed national events, like the battles for political independence from Spain. He also narrated events from local history, like protest marches.

This shift in theme and content would not have been possible with the explosion of public education in the latter half of the 20th century. Peasants and their recently migrated cousins in the cities struggled and sacrificed to gain an education – not just the three R's, but even university degrees – so that they could gain access to status and income.

Western tradition. They claimed that the humble origins of the crafts disqualified them as a creative medium. The public debate, which was put in aesthetic terms, was in fact a racist slur, a denial of Peru's ancient Andean traditions.

But in Ayacucho, the *retablo* underwent even more changes. It was no longer Lima intellectuals who were buying them. The craftsmen of Ayacucho were gaining access to massive markets. Foreign buyers, tourists and even middle-class Peruvians now wanted a piece of the Andes on their mantlepieces.

A new generation of image-makers, like Florentino Jimenez, gave the *retablos* new

Thousands of peasant communities built one-room schools with dirt floors, benches and painted blackboards. They supported the teachers with their produce. The sharpest students were sent off to the cities to finish their schooling. Learning to read and write was equivalent to gaining full citizenship and a ticket to progress. It also meant opening new horizons beyond the outskirts of the small towns and villages scattered across the Andes. Meanwhile, the new *retablos* being made in the 1970s provided an alternative reading of Peruvian history, a view from below.

Growth of a monster: While these national

changes were taking place, Lima was growing into a metropolis. Today, the capital has come to represent all that went wrong with Peruvian development. One city now concentrates most of the country's capital, services and other resources, but they are grossly inadequate to sustain its 6 million inhabitants. Lima concentrates all the political power in its hands as well (though a belated attempt to decentralize power into the hands of novice regional governments began in 1990). Regional poles of development, like Trujillo on the northern coast, Cuzco in the Sierra, and Loreto in the Amazon basin, are dwarfed by Lima's overbearing gravity.

their first shelter. These settlements gradually changed into more permanent neighborhoods, with churches, schools and clinics. Deprived of water, electricity and paved streets, each neighborhood had to organize its own lobbying effort to press for attention. Frequently, more than petitions were required. Protest marches, sit-down strikes and rallies drove home the message that only those willing to take to the streets would win even the simplest skirmishes for survival.

Haphazard development: Westerners often take for granted the virtues of the 20th century. In Peru, democracy, urbanization, industrialization, consumer markets, the mass media and accelerated technological inno-

However, in the 1960s and 1970s, Lima seemed like the promised land to Peru's disadvantaged provincial resident. An invasion of migrants from places like Ayaviri, Bambamarca and Huaráz gradually turned Lima into an Andean city. Urban authorities were unable to create conditions in which they could satisfy their basic needs. For lack of adequate cheap housing, squatters seized idle lots in the surrounding wasteland. They threw up rustic huts made out of reed mats as

<u>Left</u>, enjoying a beer in Lima's Cordano bar and restaurant. <u>Above</u>, military parades in Lima for Independence Day (July 28).

vation are an inflammable mixture. The forced march of modernization has crammed huge behavioral changes into the span of a generation. In developed countries, these changes took place over 300 years. In Peru, the leap in expectations, frustrations and sensitivity to injustice has outrun the capacity of the government and other institutions to deliver. This lesson was driven home with a vengeance in the 1980s. That was when the Peruvian economy proved unable to sustain living standards acquired during the preceding three decades. The second presidential period of Fernando Belaúnde (1980-85) was an attempt to turn the political clock back to the times when the Creole, cosmopolitan faction was in control. But the old power elites did not have the same command of the system as they used to, nor was the country the same. Forces like the Shining Path guerilla insurgency in the Andes and drug trafficking in the Amazon began to threaten the state.

Even a pillar of the old order, the Catholic Church has changed tremendously in recent decades. The Peruvian hierarchy, at least the most socially sensitive clergy and the foreign religious, assumed the Vatican Council II's conclusions in 1965 with missionary zeal. The idea was to make the Church revelant to a temporal world, which in Peru

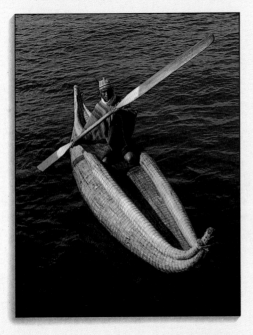

meant reaching outside the traditional pastures. The archbishop of Lima moved out of his palatial residence on the Plaza de Armas to a modest neighborhood. Not only were the masses said in Spanish, but also in Quecha, Aymará and other dialects. The National Bishops Conference issued communiques that challenged politicians to reduce poverty, injustice and inequality. Throughout the country, the parish house and chapel became a rallying point for the under-privileged and poor. Though not all of the hierarchy and faithful are convinced that the Church should play a political role in changing the country, its language and methods have been irrevocably transformed.

The Catholic Church's more socially active role was also spurred by the growing popularity of Protestant and Evangelical congregations in shantytowns and the countryside. Today, 5 percent of the population belong to non-Catholic denominations. The Evangelicals have also become an important political force since they tend to vote in block.

Responding to the new order: Just as the resourcefulness and creativity of Peruvians have allowed them to resist aggression, the challenge of a modern era has opened a window of opportunity to join the present. Over the past three decades, the rapid pace of change has created many new institutions and grassroots organization. Bootstrap capitalism has taken roots in the shantytowns. Small entrepreneurs have by-passed state barriers to build an "informal economy", accounting for 40 percent of all employment. Meanwhile, communal soup kitchens allow the poor to survive under the most severe conditions through solidarity in misery.

The ability of all Peruvians to vote is actually a very recent innovation. For instance, women did not get the vote until 1956 and the illiterate could not cast ballots until 1980. It could be argued that modern mass politics did not reach Peru until the 1980s. Representative institutions, like the Presidency, Congress and municipal government, are still tinged with the authoritarian traits of the past. Other institutions, like law enforcement agencies and the courts, have failed to modernize. All are prone to the abuse and misuse of power. The past decade has underlined the failings of the status quo. The government is incapable of meeting the needs of the population or generating the economic growth needed to sustain the burst of population and expectations.

An incipient liberation has also come to women in Peruvian society. In both the traditional realms of Creole and Andean society, women had fixed roles: In the former, women were confined to the kitchen, child bearing and rearing and tending to their husbands. On the Andean side, women may have had fuller roles, with rights and obligations in the productive cycles of farming and cattle-raising. One of the women's losses in the shift to Western acculturation was the spreading of *machismo*. It oppressed women into a stereotype of subservience to men. Even when feminism was at its peak worldwide, it found little receptive ground in Peru.

Advances have come more silently. Middle and upper class women acquired university education and professional careers and began to venture into business on their own. In the working class, the upheaval of the 1980s has intensified the struggle for survival. Women had to supplement their spouses' income by working part-time or setting up street vendor's stalls. To make meager budgets stretch, they set up communal soup kitchens and took leadership roles in the community. Though far from having equal standing with men, women have con-

matter, there is little that separates migrants or their offspring from the Andes from a migrant from Japan. As president, Fujimori is an outsider who has not been locked into the power network that has kept large portions of Peruvians from gaining access to the system. They saw him as an impartial arbiter who left open the prospect of a fairer shake in government. For many, voting for Fujimori was an exercise in ironic wit and even a bit of inverse racism. Despite their powerlessness before the entrenched interests that control banks and factories, they could take revenge by voting for an underdog candidate who would most offend the powerful.

One of the crucial questions being asked at

quered cornerstones of self-esteem that would have been undreamed of a decade ago.

This decade of social and political change came to a head in the 1990 general elections. The Peruvian electorate rejected a presidential candidate like novelist Mario Vargas Llosa – cosmopolitan, plugged into the fashionable intellectual circles and well-financed. Instead, Peruvians picked the son of a Japanese immigrant, Alberto Fujimori.

For many poor Peruvians, it's easier to vote for a Japanese than for a white. For that

Far left, managing a reed boat on Lake Titicaca.
Above, Lima's crowded beaches in summer.

the start of the 1990s is whether Peru is a viable society. But despite the social upheaval, the economic crisis, the squandered opportunities, many see Peru on the threshold of a new era, close to resolving its centuries old social problem – not by overt design, but by the sheer weight of the dynamics set loose by the 20th century. The resources are to found in the Peruvians themselves, the unique capacity to resist and renew themselves under adverse conditions. Like the image-makers of Ayacucho, they can take humble materials – earth, water and their experience – and turn them into a lively and living creation.

DAILY LIFE IN THE ANDES

The route to most villages in the Andes is a narrow, graded-earth road, in the winter baked concrete-solid under the fierce dry-season sun, in the summer awash with torrents of rain, slick with mud, narrowed or closed by rock-slides. These roads wind tortuously through the mountains, making complicated switchbacks up and down their flanks or following deep river valleys. The vehicles that ply them, the means of transportation readily available and affordable to most of the inhabitants of those villages, are sometimes small, rattle-trap buses, retired from service on proper roads somewhere else and consigned to end their days traveling perilous mountain routes; or, more often, heavy, several-ton trucks with wooden sides and a gate and ladder at the back, which carry everything from grains and potatoes destined for markets in the cities, to livestock and people.

The villages at the ends of these roads of the Peruvian Andes are inhabited for the most part by the Quechua, descendants of the population once ruled by the Inca, whose empire encompassed at its height an area from which is now Ecuador south to Chile and east to Bolivia. In the ensuing centuries, the resilient Quechua have adapted to the cultures superimposed upon their own, adopting elements that were forced upon them, like the ardent though shrewdly flexible Catholicism of their conquerors, and also those that were useful to them, like the Old World livestock and crops the Spanish introduced to the Americas. They took the European dress of the period of the Conquest which, in most places and in a derivative form, is still worn to this day. And more recently they have accepted such amenities as running water (in some places) and aluminium pots and pans, radios, record players, and flashlights. Nevertheless, today, although the accoutrements are different, the fundamental outlines of Quechua life remain remarkably as they were in the 16th century, resembling life in a medieval European village more than any contemporary way of life

Colorful *campesino* market.

we might be familiar with.

Harsh agricultural world: Life in the village is simple and hard, based on subsistence agriculture and pastoralism. Most villages are only marginally connected to the national cash economy through the production of some crops for sale in city markets, and so, as they have since the inception of agriculture in the Andes, each family must produce during the growing season the food it will live on for the entire year – hopefully, enough to sustain it through a bad year if the crops should ever fail. Amenities are few. Only the larger towns have electricity or even generators. Some villages now have a system of drinkable water, so that there may be taps earthern benches built against the walls of the house. The family's possessions consist of their clothing, their pots and pans and cooking and eating utensils, simple agricultural implements and a few other tools, their house and land and animals and usually, and most prized, a radio. The radio is their sole connection to the rest of the world, a connection perhaps most valued in years when the World Cup Soccer Tournament is played.

The Quechua inhabit the entire range of altitudes in the complex vertical ecology of the Andes that will sustain human life, from the lushest, sub-tropical river valleys to the high, desolate *puna*. Each village exists within a sort of micro-climate that affords it

outside houses or at selected points throughout the village where cold mountain water can be drawn (sparing people a several-times-daily trek to a spring or stream to fetch water). The houses are of adobe bricks or, in some places, of stone, with packed earth floors and thatched or tiled roofs, the open rafters inside always blackened and sooty from years of smoke from the cooking fire in a hearth in the corner. There is no furniture save perhaps a couple of rudimentary stools, though a more affluent family may have a bed, or a table; women sit, or more often, squat, on the floor – a characteristic posture for a Quechua woman – and men sit on a certain range of crops – from tropical fruits like lemons, limes, oranges, avocados and chilis and a variety of vegetables both familiar and exotic.

High-altitude living: The character of each village is in large part determined by the potential of the land it controls. For a village in the high *puna*, the economy consists mainly of the cultivation of potatoes and high-altitude grains and of herding – mainly of llamas, sheep, a few goats and perhaps a few cattle. There is little arable land to be conserved and it might be widely dispersed amongst various settlements of small houses of one or two joined or detached rooms, sometimes with a second-story storeroom, built often of stone and roofed with a heavy thatch of *puna* grasses. Among the houses might be corrals for the animals, ringed by fences of stacked stone. Around the perimeter of the village will be small potato fields, their ridges and furrows giving them the appearance of corduroy patches on the smooth fabric of short tough *puna* grasses.

Other towns in this range reveal a markedly different plan. These were the *reducciones* ("reductions") created by the Spanish in the 1570s as they gathered together the native population living in scattered settlements throughout a particular region, for purposes of control and taxation, forced conversion to Catholicism, and, in general, "civilization". The *reducciones* were laid out according to a plan prescribed by Viceroy Francisco de Toledo, the Spanish king's representative in Peru, after a four-year tour of the highlands to determine what means would be necessary to govern the new country: they were to be founded in this most temperate zone – deemed to be the most healthy – neither too high nor too low in altitude, near a good source of water; they were to have perpendicular streets laid out on an orderly grid, a town plaza, prison, house for the local governor, and, of course, a church. Finally, each family's house or compound was to have a door on to the street, so that they could be easily seen and policed.

The populations of many *reducciones* are today much smaller than they were at the time of their initial settlement, for many of the inhabitants have drifted back to their native communities and land, a migration which began in some cases soon after the towns were created and has continued for four hundred years. But the straight, roughly-cobbled streets remain, and the broad public plazas, and, sometimes, in some little town in the middle of nowhere, you will find a magnificent old rambling adobe church, its tiled roof sagging, its gloomy interior still brightened by a great altar of tarnished silver or flaking gilt, its walls still adorned by enormous paintings, their ornate frames warped and their images darkened to obscurity by the years.

The Andean cycle: The activities of nearly every member of nearly every family are determined throughout the year, and indeed, throughout their lives, by the needs of the crops. The agricultural cycle begins, in villages in this middle range, in August and September, when the Andean winter – a succession of warm, cloudless days and stunningly clear and frigid nights – just begins to draw to a close. The crops are planted generally from low altitude to high altitude, and harvested in reverse order.

Summer, the growing season, is also the rainy season. During these months, the fields are hoed and weeded, and the earth of fallowed fields is turned in preparation for the coming year's crops, often under most

unpleasant conditions – in rain, hail and mud. In May, when the rains have ended, the potatoes are harvested. The village's communally-held potato lands lie in the *puna*, often two or three hours' walk from the village, and the harvest is a tedious and time-consuming labor, so each family packs up the essentials of its household – food and pots and serving and eating utensils, bedding and perhaps even the chicken – and, leaving behind someone, an older child perhaps, to pasture the sheep and cows, moves to the fields until the harvest is completed. They live during that time in a tiny, temporary hut, much like a form of camping. The grains and

<u>Left</u>, drinking up at a fiesta. <u>Above</u>, woman with llamas.

beans are then cut and allowed to dry for threshing; the corn is harvested in June. After the grains are threshed, the community turns to the dry-season activities of weaving and building and repairing the damage done by the rain, and to the wholehearted celebration of the numerous Catholic religious festivals that fall during these months.

Twenty-four hours in the village: The day begins when, in the darkness well before the first cock's crow, someone stirs and perhaps turns on the radio. In the south central highlands around Cuzco, it will be tuned to Radio Tawantinsuyu, a station based in that city whose disc-jockeys broadcast their programs in Quechua and Quechua-Spanish. In the

corn, one of the elemental dishes of Quechua cuisine. As her sleepy family eats this simple meal, she begins to prepare the next: *almuerzo*, or "lunch", which will be taken at an hour when most of *us* would be having breakfast…

Almuerzo – usually a rich soup of potatoes and other vegetables, served with boiled potatoes and perhaps a hot pepper sauce and hearty glass of *chicha*, a homemade corn beer – is served before the men set out for their day's work. The man of the household is assisted in his work by his sons and grandsons, and by other men – often *compadres*, the godfathers of his children – who owe him a day's work in exchange for a day he has

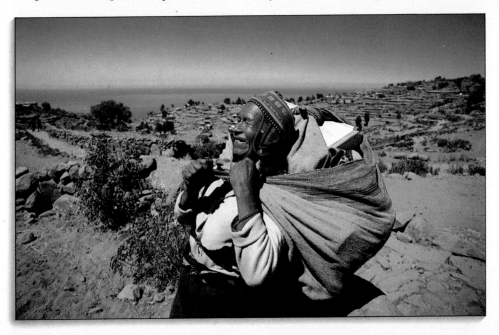

dark the day's first strains of *wayno* and *marinera*, the "country music" of Peru, are heard. The woman of the family rises from her bed, a pallet of heavy, handwoven woolen blankets laid over a pile of sheepskins on the earthen floor of the adobe hut, or, in more fortunate households, on a spare wooden bed-frame with a mattress fashioned of bundles of spilt reeds. She moves over to the hearth and stirs up the embers of yesterday's fire, adds a few sticks of firewood, fetches water and puts on a kettle for *mate*, which here means a heavily-sugared herbal infusion like tea. Breakfast, at or before dawn, consists of *mate* with bread or with *mote* – boiled dried

spent helping them in their fields. The entire complement of laborers gathers in the woman's kitchen to be fortified with as many bowls of soup and glasses of *chicha* as they can be persuaded to consume. They will work steadily all day, pausing only occasionally for *chicha* and once for a meal, which the woman will bring later, in the hope of completing the job in one day.

As they leave the house, the woman begins cooking her third meal of the day, a bountiful meal, considerably more complex in its preparation, of two or three dishes, with meat and potatoes and *mote*, because this meal is a gesture of gratitude toward the men assisting her husband. At the same time, she tends to the children and animals, feeding children, chickens and pigs, and milking the cow before it is led to pasture by one of the children, along with the sheep. Depending on the task being performed in her husband's fields, she may be assisted in her kitchen by the wives of the men working with her husband, or only by her daughters and small children, sometimes a dubious benefit. By midday, she packs the meal into a carrying cloth with plates and spoons, and sometimes a bottle or two of cane liquor for the men, and sets out herself for the fields, sometimes accompanied by another woman or two who carry a share of the burden, sometimes trailing small

the *trago*, everything is gathered up and they begin the walk home. The group meets up in the deepening shadows with the children driving home the cattle and herds of sheep and goats. At home, the small children drowse in their parents' or their siblings' laps as the adults have another cup of *chicha* warmed over the fire, perhaps another class of *trago*, maybe only a cup of *mate*; and eventually the fire is allowed to die, the pallets are laid out, and everyone settles for the night into well-earned sleep.

Days of rest and celebration: But on other days, the villagers' primary obligation will be not work but the hearty celebration of one of the numerous Catholic religious festivals

children if she hasn't left them in the care of an older child, her mother, a sister, or a *comadre*.

At the side of the field, she will serve the fruits of her efforts. The men pause in their work to eat, to drink *chicha* and a few tiny glasses of cane liquor, called *trago*. As the men plow or hoe the last rows of the field, the women may help, though more often they sit and watch, talking among themselves and sipping *chicha*. At the end of the day, after another cup or two of *chicha* and the last of

<u>Left</u>, a heavy load, Taquile island. <u>Above</u>, grinding maize on the Uros islands.

that fall throughout the year. Each village celebrates a series of Catholic saints' days – that of its patron saint certainly, and those of other saints significant to the village for one reason or another – and certain other signal dates in the religious calendar: Christmas and Carnival and Easter, the Day of the Holy Cross, and All Souls Day, the Day of the Dead. Those which fall during the months of the dry season, when the most critical and urgent work of the year – the work upon which simple survival depends – is done, are approached with special abandon.

While the basic religious formulas pertaining to at least the most significant of these holidays are generally observed in some fashion – masses spoken and attended, vigils kept, the processions of the images of saints followed piously through the plaza or streets of the village – each of these festivals has taken on, in the Andes, a distinctly Quechua flavor. Around each there has developed a whole separate complex of ceremony which seems to have little to do with Spanish Catholicism, and much more to do, perhaps, with Andean traditions of worship and religious observance which long pre-date the Spanish Conquest.

Every festival – as well as birthdays and anniversaries of various events, weddings, baptisms and christenings – is also celebrated

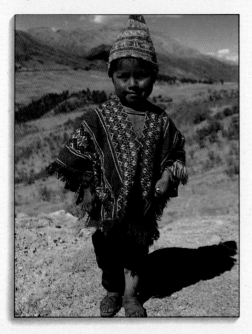

by the sometimes overwhelming exercise of the characteristic, near-compulsive, Andean hospitality, resulting in the serving of great quantities of food and copious drink. The point here is to serve your guests more and richer food than they would normally eat, and to literally force them to get very drunk and to dance (much to the consternation of any representative of the official church hierarchy who may be present).

Cultural mix: In short, contemporary Quechua culture is a result of syncretism, a thorough blending of the ideologies of two very different cultures – Quechua and Spanish. While pictures of Saints may adorn the walls of adobe huts, and nearly everyone in the villages has learned and may remember at least some of the words to common Catholic prayers in Quechua, people pay homage and turn as often or more often for guidance and healing to the traditional powers of the Andes – the mountains and the earth.

One ironic example of the intimate coexistence of Quechua and Catholic custom exists in the contemporary Quechua rituals of marriage. The ultimate goal of the process is a proper Catholic wedding in a church, registered in the parish log-books, but the Quechua take a distinctly un-Catholic route to get there. An alliance between a young couple is arranged by their parents, based on the expressed interest of the two young people. From this point, the couple enters into a period called *sirvinakuy* – the word means, in Quechua, "to serve each other" – during which each helps his or her potential in-laws with the work of their households, the young woman her mother-in-law, the young man his father-in-law, a test of their suitability and readiness for marriage. During this time also, the young couple sleeps together under the roof of one set of parents or the other.

The couple will not marry until a child is conceived, demonstrating the reproductive viability of the union, and may not even then – a wedding, to be sponsored (and paid for) by the parents and godparents of the couple, is an elaborate and expensive affair, and may be put off for years, though the couple must be officially married before their children can be baptised. And though the Quechua practice of this system of trial marriage is commonly known, among the clergy as well as everyone else, the issue is generally studiously avoided when the couple arrives at the church, often with children in tow, to be married.

How to celebrate: A festival such as the Day of the Virgin of the Nativity, in one village, might include an array of events: playing host to the visiting images of patron saints from the churches and chapels of other villages, daily masses and processions, led by a priest, throughout the week-long celebration – some holidays are celebrated until the *octava*, the "eighth day", though sometimes the celebration wanes before then as the will to drink and dance falters from simple exhaustion. There may be bullfights, and soccer tournaments between regional village teams, all performed in the shadows of enormous altars the men of the village have erected in the plaza, of eucalyptus poles adorned with complex configurations of painted wooden panels, banners and small mirrored boxes containing miniature images of saints.

For other festivals, there are bands of musicians, local or hired from the nearest city, playing instruments ranging from brass and accordions and drums to native flutes, violins, the little Andean mandolin, the *charango*, the body of which is the shell of an armadillo, and the Andean harp with its great half-conical sounding box.

sanitario, a rural doctor. At night there might be bonfires in front of the altars in the plaza, tended all night long as people dance in their light, with music giving the night an unaccustomed life and *chicha* flowing freely until the celebrants stagger home to collapse into bed. The festival might also attract vendors from the cities and other towns who come to offer for sale everything from clothing to candy to small manufactured goods like barrettes, sewing needles, toys and balloons. The villagers themselves may claim a space among the vendors at the edges of the plaza to sell *chicha* and prepared food and produce, so that the village enjoys for the duration of the festivities the benefits of its own open-air

Or the music may be provided by scratchy 45-rpm records of *waynos* and *marineras*, played on little, portable, battery-operated phonographs, the kind you find now only in nursery schools, turned up to full volume, the words of the songs and even the tunes rendered unrecognizable by distortion. There may be troupes of dancers in costumes which transform their wearers into entities and personages from every era of Andean history – characters ranging from the *ukuku* or Andean spectacled bear, to the soldier and the

market.

Feasting, drinking and dancing also goes on in the households – especially those of the *carguyugs,* the men who have accepted and fulfilled the responsibility, for some element of the public celebrations, there is feasting and drinking and dancing. The hospitality and generosity of the host family is another ritual gesture of gratitude for whatever small or large part another has played. The village is transformed. Everywhere, the holiday reigns: work is temporarily abandoned, and everyone revels in the respite from the weighty responsibilities of everyday life and survival.

Far left, boy in the Sierra. **Above**, typical village near Arequipa.

How many times have I told you, my heart
"Do not want, do not love!"
But always you answer me,
"I can't, I can't"

One day, oppressed by sorrow,
Alone, I asked my heart,
"Why are you so sad and dejected,
finding no happiness in anything?"

"Don't you hear the laughter of the mountains,
and smell the perfume of the flowers?
The song of the rivers,
the play of the fishes?"

Again, it cries,
"Happiness no longer exists for me,
I lost all feeling long ago,
My dead heart is already buried."

(Peruvian *Wayno* from *Huaynos del Cuzco*.)

Many of us became acquainted with Andean music (whether to this day we are aware of it or not) in the late 1960s when Paul Simon and Art Garfunkel released a recording called *El Condor Pasa*, accompanied by a group called Los Incas. Its English lyrics were new to the song, but the melody was ancient, a traditional Andean folksong of haunting native tonalities. Los Incas, who later called themselves Urubamba, were among the vanguard of a movement to preserve this element of the indigenous culture of the Andes, to present it proudly to the world beyond the borders of its native countries. And so now, this music is played by the *conjuntos folklóricos* who perform, in settings – dimly lit restaurants in fine hotels or on a stage in Paris – which the indigenous people, for whom this music is a part of daily life, can probably scarcely conceive.

It can also be heard on the street corners played by native musicians who, often because of some disability, must depend on their talents – sometimes extraordinary – and other people's appreciation of them to gain themselves a meagre living. And it can be heard far from the nightlife of the cities, in the villages where a less well-rehearsed group of musicians may gather to accompany the private celebration of a wedding or the public performance of a costumed dance during a festival, or where a lone shepherd, perhaps a young boy, might play a melancholy song on his *quena* on the mountainside where he pastures his family's animals.

Ancient musical tradition: The instruments, forms of the songs, and lyrics have constituted a linked tradition of oral poetry in a culture which until recently has had no written language. Its roots lie deep in Peru's pre-

Columbian history. In the ruins and ancient graveyards on the Peruvian coast you can still find small broken clay panpipes and whistle-like flutes which play pentatonic or diatonic scales, and sometimes other exotic scales which defy description by western musical notation, tossed aside by *huaqueros* (robbers) in search of the fine textiles and pottery which were buried in the graves. The Incas inherited from the cultures before them an astonishing variety of wind instruments, including flutes and panpipes of all types and sizes. Inca musicians also played conch shell trumpets and drums made from the skin of the Andean puma.

To this ensemble the Spanish introduced strings, which native musicians readily adopted, inventing new, uniquely Andean instruments like the *charango* (a tiny guitar scarcely the size of a violin, the body of which is the shell of an armadillo) and the Andean harp with its great, boat-like, half-conical sounding box. These, essentially, are the instruments which are played today – joined occasionally by a violin or accordion – though the drums now are more likely covered with goat skin than puma skin, and the eerie wind-like call of the conch shell trumpet may only be heard in the most traditional villages, deep in the mountains, at certain times of the year.

tion, has a distinctly melancholy tone. *Quenas* vary in size and thus in pitch, so that each has its own reedy voice. The panpipes, called *antaras* or *zamponas*, vary also, from a few inches long to several feet, from one set of four or five pipes to three or four joined sets of eight or ten pipes each, each of a different octave, to be played of course by a single musician with an astonishing dexterity. *Antaras* and *zamponas* are played by blowing across the end of the pipes, a technique which gives a breathy sound, which may be as high-pitched as a bird call or almost as deep as the voice of a bassoon. They are often played in a kind of complex duet, with musicians alternating single notes of a quick,

The effect is magical, utterly characteristic of the Andes, evocative of high, windy passes, of the breeze blowing through the reeds of Lake Titicaca, of the dwarfing immensity of the mountains on a clear bright winter day. The *quenas* are notched, end-blown flutes with a fingering style similar to that of a recorder. *Quenas* were often made of llama bone, but are now most often carved of wood. They play a pentatonic scale which, to ears trained to a European musical tradi-

smooth-flowing melody, never missing a beat.

An ensemble of *quenas* and *zamponas* weaves a rich tapestry of windy pentatonic harmony. Into this fabric is woven, like golden threads, the bright, quick sound of the *charango* – which may be strummed or plucked, but is most often strummed in an intricate rhythm of inconceivable velocity – and the voice of the harp. The Andean harp has thirty-six strings spanning five octaves of the diatonic scale, though it too is usually played in a pentatonic mode. Its deep sounding box gives it a full, rich sound and a powerful bass voice, so that a bass line is

Left and above, musicians play Andean tunes in the Hotel Bolívar, Lima.

usually played by the left hand while a melody or harmony is plucked by the right. Percussion is provided by a simple, deep-voiced frame drum – a *tambor* or a *bombo* – played with a stick with a soft, hide-covered head, or by an even simpler instrument called the *caja*, which is, as its name implies, a wooden box with a sound hole for reverberation, upon which one sits to thump out a rhythm with the hands. The instrument is actually a little more sophisticated than it may appear, and a skilfull *caja* player can elicit a remarkable range of tone.

This is the basic ensemble, though, of course, infinite variations occur offstage – in the villages, for example, where the group

characters or activities – like the shepherd's song, or songs for victory in war or a successful harvest or for working in the fields. Of these names only that of the *yaravi* or *haravi* seems to have survived in common usage, but nevertheless the lineage of contemporary Andean music can be traced back to at least the 17th century, and probably to pre-Columbian origins, perhaps the songs named by Waman Puma. The traditional music, which has survived in relatively pristine form among native musicians and in the past few decades enjoyed its renaissance as folklore, has also evolved, naturally, a parallel, popular form, which is today not only performed in the *chicherias* or cantinas

may consist of whatever instruments are played by whatever musicians are available and willing and able to play.

Range of forms: The native Peruvian chronicler, Felipe Waman Puma de Ayala, in his massive descriptive history of life under Inca and then Spanish rule (*Nueva Cronica y Buen Gobierno*, which he began about 1576 and completed in 1615), listed the names of a number of song forms, which are the ancestors of contemporary Andean music: the *yaravi*, the *taqui*, the *llamaya* – a shepherd's song: the *pachaca harahuayo*, the *aimarana*, the *huanca*, the *cachiva*, and the *huauco*. Many of these he attributed to particular

frequented by both urban and rural Quechua speakers, but is recorded in sound studios on phonograph records and cassette tapes, and played on the radio. The recording artists, like North American or European musicians and vocalists, are known to everyone – at least to everyone of a certain social stratum – and their careers followed attentively; they come into and fall out of fashion much like the groups one hears on "Top 40" radio.

The primary form of popular music which has evolved from those traditional forms is the *wayno* (or *huayno* in its Spanish spelling, and pronounced "wino"), which constitutes a rich complex of poetry, music and dance.

The *wayno* is a rural music, like bluegrass, for example in the United States, and each region has developed its own characteristic variations. Music has always accompanied nearly all aspects of Quechua life – as Waman Puma's list suggests – from the most mundane activities to the most solemn ritual and the most abandoned celebration. The Quechua people live, in a way, to dance: all new clothing – new shoes, a new skirt – is said to be "for dancing"; and the *wayno* is fundamentally music for dancing. It is typically played in 2/4 time with an insistent and infectious rhythm; the dance is usually performed by couples, their hands joined, with much stamping of the feet to cries of "*Más*

sion, like everything which is reflected in the waters…Perhaps, if God approves, we shall one day meet and be together forever. Remembering your smiling eyes, I feel faint; remembering your playful eyes, I am near death… (translated by Christopher Dilke in *Letter to a King*, E.P. Dutton, 1978) Waman Puma's example of the *yaravi* reveals much the same themes.

The contemporary *wayno* is clearly a direct descendant of the songs of Waman Puma's day. Melodramatic as they may be, however, anthologies of lyrics disclose a sophistication of poetic form and of poetic voice, ranging from tragic to ironic to comic, which is remarkable in a completely un-

fuerza! Más fuerza!" ("Harder! Harder!").

But the *wayno* is also a literary form, representative of a tradition of oral poetry which goes back at least to the time of the Incas. The *wayno* is essentially a love song, but a melancholy and melodramatic one: a song of love found and lost or rejected, a song of rivalry and abandonment and separation and wandering in strange lands far from home. Waman Puma offered the words of a song he called a *huanca. You were a lie and an illu-*

written, completely oral, tradition. *Waynos* to this day are learned and preserved in the social context itself, transmitted informally and most often anonymously, from musician to musician, in the context of private celebrations or great religious festivals in every village of the Peruvian *sierra*. Certainly, they will continue to evolve: today, an urbanized form of this fundamentally rural music is developing, in which the traditional naturalistic motifs are being replaced by abstract terms more universally understood. But, in light of its history, it seems safe to guess that this music will survive nearly as long as the Andes themselves.

Left, an Andean ensemble. **Above**, Andean harp.

"I say truly to Your Highness that these people are the most insolent that I have seen in all the time that I have traveled in the Indies and engaged in their conquest."
– Captain Hernando de Benavente on the Jivaro Indians, March 25, 1550, to the Royal Audiencia of Spain.

It was Francisco Orellana, a Spanish conquistador in Gonzalo Pizarro's expedition, who first got close up looks at Peru's Amazon Indians and ultimately became the first European to float 3,500 km (2,200 miles) down the Amazon river.

Four years after Francisco Pizarro had brought the Inca empire to its knees, in 1540 the elder Pizarro dispatched his younger brother Gonzalo to seek out rumors of an empire of gold to the east – the legend of El Dorado. Leaving what is now Quito, Ecuador with a vast expedition that included over 200 Spaniards, 4,000 Indian slaves, horses and flocks of llamas and pigs, the conquistadors headed over the Andes and down through the cloud forest before constructing a boat and floating down what is now the Napo river. It wasn't long before they came upon the inhabitants of this mysterious, dripping world. He later recalled:

"…we saw coming up the river a great many canoes, all equipped for fighting, gaily colored, and the men with their shields on, which are made out of the shell-like skins of lizards and the hides of manatees and of tapirs…they were coming on with a great yell, playing on many drums and wooden trumpets, threatening us as if they were going to devour us."

Unlike the younger Pizarro, Orellana was anthropologically astute. Separating from Gonzalo's party which would later return to Quito, Orellana learned several Indian dialects as he descended, kept his men from killing them, and questioned the Indians at length. Eventually, after a voyage of nine months, Orellana and his men sailed from the mouth of the Amazon and returned to

Yagua Indian near Iquitos.

Peru via Panama. One and a half years after the expedition had begun, Gonzalo Pizarro and a ragged crew stumbled into Quito. Only 80 of the original 4,200 men had survived.

Feared jungle warriors: The Amazon Indians have long played a part in Peruvian history. According to Inca oral history, hordes of fierce jungle Indians were said to have climbed into the Andes and to have sacked the Inca capital of Cuzco several times. Indeed, the Inca fortress of Pisac is thought to have been an outpost protecting the capital from the attack of the feared jungle tribes to the east. The Incas themselves referred to the eastern quarter of their 4,500-km long empire as *Antisuyo*, and to the Indians who lived in its jungles as the *Antis*; it is from the latter word that the name Andes derives.

When not warring, trade was routinely carried out between the Incas and the Antis, the former trading cloths, manufactured goods and bronze axes in return for gold, feathers, exotic fruits, woods and other jungle products. After the empire was sacked by the Spaniards one of the last Inca kings, Manco Capac, fled from Cuzco and established a new capital deep in the jungle in Vilcabamba (the lost capital was rediscovered in 1964 by the American explorer Gene Savoy). Manco Capac was aided by legions of loyal jungle warriors who were deadly with bow and arrow.

After the collapse of the Incas, the jungle was largely abandoned by the Spaniards who concentrated on mining wealth from the more tractable peasants in the Andes and on the coast. The few expeditions mounted into the jungle generally met with disaster. In a few cases, such as among the fierce, head-shrinking Jivaro Indians living in northern Peru, the Spaniards did establish jungle towns and attempted to tax the Indians' increasing quantities of gold. In 1599, however, the Jivaros staged a massive revolt, burning and sacking the cities and slaughtering an estimated 20-30,000 men, women and children. They then captured the Spanish governor who happened to be on a tax-collecting mission at the time.

"They stripped him naked, tied his hands and feet; and while some amused themselves with him, delivering a thousand castigations and jests, the others set up a large forge in the courtyard, where they melted the gold. When it was ready in the crucibles, they opened his mouth with a bone, saying that they wanted to see if for once he had enough gold. They poured it little by little, and then forced it down with another bone; and bursting his bowels with the torture, all raised a clamor and laughter."

In southern Peru, the Spaniards didn't fare much better. An expedition mounted to explore the Madre de Dios and Manu rivers encountered numerous hostile Indians. A second Spanish expedition was launched, after convincing the authorities that the first

to have had about 7 million Indians at the time of the Spanish contract, had less than 2 million fifty years later. The same pattern was repeated in the jungle, beginning in the zone of greatest contact – the Amazon and its major tributaries – and gradually working its way into deeper parts of the forest. Slave raiding, which started on Brazil's coast in the 16th century, gradually worked its way further and further into the Upper Amazon and Peru. Within a hundred years of Orellana's descent, the "teeming Indians" that had once infested the Amazon's banks were nowhere to be seen. Indian tribes that hadn't been captured or wiped out by disease simply retreated further and further into the jungle's

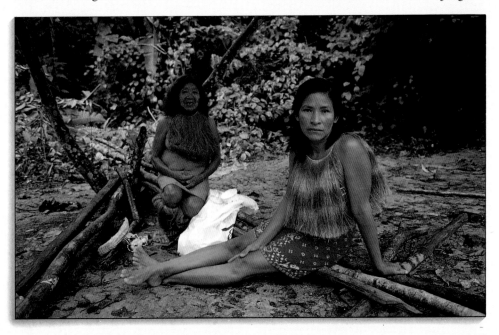

had no legal right to conquer new empires. When they met, the two groups nearly annihilated each other, whereupon the ever watchful Indians massacred all but two of the survivors.

Decimated by disease: From then on for Peru's Indians, however, it was all downhill. As elsewhere, their greatest nemesis was not so much the Spaniards as it was the introduction of European diseases. Having crossed the Bering Straight out of Asia anywhere from 10-40,000 years ago, the New World Indians' immunological systems were totally unprepared for European pathogens. The Inca empire, for example, which is thought

interior.

The biggest incursion into Peru's Amazon, however, didn't occur until the rubber boom exploded in the late 19th century. Almost overnight, the most isolated jungle rivers and streams were overrun by rubber tappers who carried the latest Winchester carbines. Rubber trees were few and far between – hence rubber tapping demanded intensive labor. Entire Indian villages were therefore sacked to capture Indian slaves. In the case of especially hostile tribes, *correrias*, or armed raids, were carried out in which villages and Indians were surrounded and slaughtered by the employees of the great rubber barons. Whole areas of the Amazon were thus wiped clear of native populations in a matter of decades.

In 1912, however, the rubber market began to collapse and this time, almost overnight the rubber tappers withdrew. Haltingly, the remaining tribes were left alone except for occasional missionaries. In the 1960's, as the peasants in the Andes became more numerous, Peru's government – burdened by hordes of peasants moving into the coastal cities and unwilling to enact land reform in the *sierra* – chose the easier alternative and began encouraging these peasants to move into the vast, unsettled Amazon which makes up two-thirds of the country. A north-south

there were some forty uncontacted tribes in the Peruvian Amazon at the turn of this century, today there are only two or three of these tribes left (all in the southeastern jungle). Today the majority of Peru's 200,000 Amazon Indians exist in varying stages of acculturation.

Indian cultures: Although in the 16th century there was considerable discussion in Europe as to whether the New World Indians were indeed "the sons of Adam and Eve" and hence deserving of the rights of real human beings, in 1512 a Papal Bull decreed that Amazonian Indians possessed souls. In later centuries scientists such as Wallace, Bates, Humboldt and Agassiz visited the Amazon

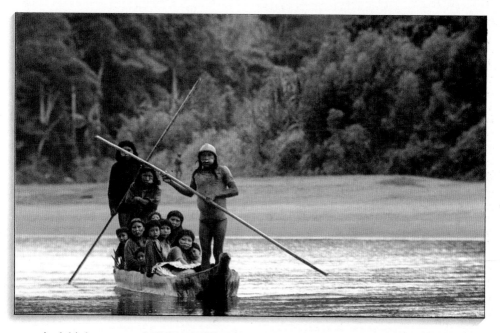

marginal highway was bulldozed through the jungle to encourage settlement and soon impoverished Peruvians began to pour in. The extraction of hardwood trees – mahogany, cedar and caoba – repeated the pattern of the rubber boom as peons bankrolled by wealthy patrons once again moved into the virgin forest looking for quick extractable wealth. Gradually, one by one, isolated Indian tribes were contacted by missionaries, woodworkers and/or oil drillers. Although

Left, two generations. **Above**, Yaminahua Indians in Manu National Park.

and eventually anthropologists began living with different tribes and recording a bewildering variety of cultures. Today it is generally recognized that the culture of any human group is strongly influenced by its environment. Thus, while incredibly diverse, because of their unique environment Amazon tribes have many features in common.

While certain areas on the Peruvian coast and mountains encouraged and supported permanent settlement and later statehood by virtue of stream valleys that renewed their soil (much as the Nile river did in Egypt), the Amazon jungle is characterized in contrast as having extremely poor soils and game animals that, while diverse, are few and far between.

As a result, the typical Amazon village on the *terra firme* – the immense lands between the large rivers – are typically small (25-100 people), mobile and widely spaced out due to the jungle's low bioproductivity and to the quick exhaustion of the land. In addition, *terra firme* tribes almost universally practiced warfare and contraception or infanticide techniques in order to keep their populations down. Thus the Jivaro Indians' penchant for head-shrinking was simply a variation on trophy-head taking and warfare patterns widely practiced throughout the Amazon.

But tribes on the *varzea* – the more limited floodplain areas where the soil is renewed annually – did not fight among themselves and instead had permanent villages ranging into the thousands of inhabitants. Although battles were sometimes fought with the *terra firme* tribes in order to take slaves to work in *varzea* fields, population control did not exist. The necessity of carefully monitoring seasonal planting patterns and river flunctuations gave rise to temples, priests, complex rule and food storage. And although the *varzea* tribes were the first hit by contact and disease, Orellana's men reported numerous *varzea* tribes and towns with temples and roads that led off into the the interior.

Given their similar habitat, the Amazon tribes had other features in common. Almost invariably, they viewed their forest and the animals in it as sacred and imbued with spirits. Most Peruvian tribes took one or more hallucinogenic drugs such as *Ayahuasca*, the "Vine of Death", which allowed them to see and interact with the powerful spiritual world. The forest was their provider – their mother – and was not to be abused. Even today, most scientists concede that no one understands the jungle better than the remaining Indians. For thousands of years they have lived in the jungle harmoniously, and while they do not possess our own overwhelmingly more powerful technology, they also do not possess our almost complete lack of understanding and irreverence for this most complex habitat on earth.

A people left in limbo: Currently there are some 200,000 native Indians in the Peruvian Amazon divided into 53 different ethnic groups and speaking languages from 12 different linguistic families. Some groups, such as the Toyeri in southern Peru are composed of only a handful of surviving families. Others, such as the Machiguenga and Campa, living in the jungles east of Machu Picchu and who are thought to have been the allies of the Incas, number in the tens of thousands.

Unlike Brazil, which has a governmental entity (FUNAI) to regulate Indian affairs, jungle Indians in Peru have little governmental support. Legislation allowing Indian communities to possess land was only passed in 1974. Over 30 native organizations have sprung up in the last two decades as different Indian groups have gradually realized that only by putting aside historical enmities and organizing can their rights be defended or

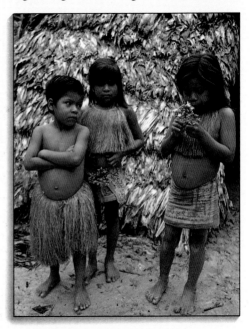

secured.

Despite increasing organization, however, Peru's Amazon Indians continue to exist in a social and legal limbo. At best they are seen as a hindrance to a government whose goal is to "develop" the Amazon. Enormous pressure on the part of the national society, missionaries and the education system encourages Indians to reject their own culture and become deracinated Peruvian citizens. The US protestant missionary group, the Summer Institute of Linguistics (SIL) has a large airbase just outside of the jungle town of Pucallpa and has worked with dozens of tribes since 1946. Although the SIL has nursed a number of recently-contacted tribes through contact-induced epidemics, they and a host of other missionaries have had an enormous acculturative impact. In a very real sense, because of the Peruvian government's historical lack of interest, foreign missionary groups have been relegated the job of contacting and integrating Peru's jungle Indians into the national culture.

Some cultures, however, seem to withstand or assimilate acculturation better than others. The numerous Shipibo Indians living in central Peru along the Ucayali river have – despite long historical contact – maintained much of their traditional culture. They even operate a Shipibo-owned cooperative

in a very few generations.

Meeting the outside world: Tourism can have an adverse effect on native cultures, especially if poorly handled. Certain tour groups in Iquitos advertising visits to "wild Amazon Indians", for instance, use completely acculturated tribes which strip down and don costumes to play the part of "savages". Other companies have been known to actually fly tourists out to relatively unacculturated Indians. The latter's lack of immunity to common colds and other diseases, along with their culture's relatively fragile nature, however, make such practices questionable. When visiting any native community, therefore, the tourist should always ask first before

store (Moroti Shobo in Yarinacocha, just outside of Pucallpa), where they sell and export their exceptionally high-quality weavings and pottery to museums and collectors all over the world. In 1990 the Ashanika Indians, living on the Ene river, went on the warpath when the Maoist Shining Path guerrillas killed their chief, shooting and expelling all guerrillas from their territory. Other tribes, however, have less resistance to change and have lost their cultures

Left, Yagua children. **Above**, preparing for a ritual in the south-east.

taking photos, should offer small presents such as fishing hooks or fishing line in return, and should when buying, pay a good price directly to the Indians themselves for their handmade traditional crafts.

For most Indians, however, culture change is inevitable. As one anthropologist working in Peru's Amazon phrased it, "The Indians cannot be expected to remain 'pristine' and thus live somewhere where they are caged in by 'white' wardens in parks. They are very curious about our world and it is inevitable that they will change. Their culture doesn't die, however, rather it reformulates itself so that it can better deal with the outside world."

Long before the Incas, Peru was a land of craftspeople. Fine weaving found in the funeral bundles at Paracas, gold pieces worked by the Chimu Indians in northern Peru and startlingly realistic Moche ceramics pay testimony to a people for whom work done with the hands was always important. Specially chosen women in the Inca empire dedicated their lives to such tasks as weaving delicate capes from exotic bird feathers. And metallurgy was a high-status job before the Spanish arrived in the New World.

Fortunately, those artistic traditions did not die with the European conquest and today there are few places in Peru where handicrafts – some little changed from those done hundreds of years ago, others modified for the tourists – cannot be found.

Ancient artefacts: For Indian cultures with no written word, handicrafts played multiple roles. Moche ceremonial cups were not simply for drinking, they told stories – depicting everything from festivities to daily events. Through these finely detailed ceramics archaeologists have identified the diseases afflicting the Moches, discovered the Indians punished thieves by amputating their hands (then fitted the reformed criminals with prosthetic limbs) and determined that they practiced rudimentary birth control. Likewise, the patterns on clothes woven in the highlands have unraveled some of the secrets of how the Aymará Indians lived. Designs in some clothes told the status of the wearer, others were used only for special fiestas and still others had woven into them motifs that were important to the community. (Nowadays those designs carry airplanes and other modern inventions that have changed the lives of the Indians.) After the Spanish conquest, handicrafts began to fuse the old and new ways as Indian wood carvers whittled statues of virgins dressed like *campesinos* or angels with Indian faces.

Some handicrafts are found all over the country, but in different colors and designs, such as the popular wall hangings found in

outdoor markets. Other items come from only one community or region. The decorative gilt-edged mirrors sold in Peru generally originate in Cajamarca. Authentic Pucara bulls come only from Pupuja, near Puno. Real Yagua Indian jewelry comes only from the jungle area near Iquitos. But, like Peru's residents who migrate from all parts of the nation to the capital, so too artisan work from all over the country can be picked up in Lima.

The biggest selection of handicrafts in Lima is available at the **Mercado Artesanal,**

a group of Indian markets in the 10th block of Avenida La Marina between downtown and the airport. Some of these goods, especially the Christmas tree ornaments and *arpilleras* – embroidery and appliqued scenes – are produced by Mothers Clubs cooperatives in Lima's shantytowns. At these markets, visitors can find gold and silver trimmed wine glasses, carved leather bookbags, handknit wools of all kinds, blowguns from the jungle, ceramics carrying both modern and antique designs and jewelry. At the Mercado Artesanal, bargaining is expected on prices and the final bill may be comparable to what one would pay in Cuzco, Pisac or

Left, ancient craft, modern view. **Right**, traditional weaving technique.

the jungle.

At the cooperatively run **Artesanías del Peru**, Avenida Jorge Basadre 610 in San Isidro, the selection is smaller but the items are all of highest quality. Almost as intriguing as the finely displayed collection of everything from woven pillow covers and colorful wood carvings of toucans to pewter mugs and delicate silver and turquoise jewelry is the neo-colonial style house in which the shop is located. Artesanias del Peru, which has handicrafts from all over the country, has sister stores in Arequipa at Avenida General Moran 120, and in Iquitos at Putumayo 128. Arrangements can be made here for shipping articles to the United States or Europe and

century chronicles by Garcilaso de la Vega tell of the Europeans' first glimpse into the courtyard of Koricancha, the Temple of the Sun in Cuzco. Before them was a lifesized scene, in blindingly brilliant gold, perfect in detail down to the tiniest butterfly perched on a plant. Worked in gold were objects and animals common to the Indian life: llamas, corn stalks, flowers, birds. What remains in the Mujica Gold Museum in Lima and the Bruning Museum in Lambayeque are but a fraction of the gold, silver and copper work that once existed.

Today, gold and silver items, ranging from silver trimmed crystal glasses to fruit bowls and candelabras, are available from a number

the prices – although not negotiable – are quite attractive.

Another good selection of handicraft work – both in variety and price – is found in the small shops in the defunct Tambo de Oro restaurant building where the National Tourism Office is located in Lima (Belén 1066). **Artesanías Huamanqaqa** across the street from the tourism office has one of the city's finest quality collection of crafts, although the variety is limited.

Sweat of the sun: Just as Chile has its lapis lazuli and Colombia its emeralds, the items most associated with Peru is gold, with silver and copper running close seconds. The 16th

of boutiques in Lima. The oldest and best known stores are on Jirón de la Union: **Casa Welsch** at Jiron de la Union 498, **Murguia** a block down at number 553 and **Johari** at 851. A fine selection of gold and silver is also available at **Cabuchon** on Libertadores 532 in the suburb of San Isidro. For the best in gold and silver jewelry in both stylized and traditional Inca designs, stop by H. Stern. This outlet for fine quality jewelry has stores in most of the South American capitals; in Peru its locations are in the Hotel Sheraton, Hotel Bolívar, Hotel Cesar's Miraflores, Jorge Chavez Airport in Lima and the Museo de Oro (Gold Museum) in Lima.

Jewelry made from out-of-circulation Peruvian coins is sold at Plaza San Martín in Lima and around the Plaza de Armas in Cuzco; the most popular are earrings, necklaces and bracelets made from leather and sol coins bearing the image of a llama. These informal jewelry makers also sell necklaces and earrings made from Peruvian turquoise and handpainted ceramic. But Peru's best quality handpainted ceramic jewelry is designed by the Association of Artisans of **Pisac Virgen del Carmen** in Pisac, about an hour outside Cuzco.

Woven tales: Although much of today's artesanía is more practical than illustrative and is geared toward tourists, some still tell

ing. Some colors are used only on certain holidays. Legend has it that the rainbow Kuyichi, angered by the Taquile Indians, took away their color and left them in a world of grays and browns. But the Indians used their fingers to weave color back into their lives. (See section on "Taquile".)

The Taquile items can be purchased from the cooperative on the island. Knit items are available from a number of shops in Cuzco and some of the best bargains (although the quality is hit and miss) come from the women selling their wares in the arcade around the Plaza de Armas in that city. Be wary of assurances by these unlicensed vendors about whether the item is wool, llama or alpaca as

stories. Delicately woven belts sold in the Sunday market at Huancayo carry designs of trains, a tribute to the metal monster that connected that isolated highland city to the rest of the country. (The wide belts are worn for decoration and to give back support to the women who trudge the highlands with their children on their backs.) Colors in the textiles and knit goods on Taquile, the weavers' island in Lake Titicaca, can indicate the wearer's marital status or community stand-

Left, tapestries for sale at Pisac (near Cuzco). **Above,** elaborate carving.

they are likely to upgrade the fiber to assure a sale; stop at some of the upscale shops and feel the difference between the wools from the three animals before starting your shopping. Also beware of the rare unscrupulous merchants who claim to be selling anything made from vicuñas. It is nearly certain to be untrue and, if the item actually does contain vicuña fibers, then it has been made in violation of the law.

Wool cloth purported to be "antique" usually is not. The damp highland's climate does not allow wool to last indefinitely and many weavers now intentionally use dark colors and ancient designs to give the impression the textile has been around for centuries. These cloths are no more antique than are the rustic-looking dolls that some sellers claim come from ancient graves.

Market bargains: Without a doubt, knits and weaves are the most popular purchases of visitors. Highland markets – including the weekend market in Pisac outside Cuzco – abound with alpaca sweaters, llama rugs, small woolen bags called chuspas used to carry coca for chewing, blankets and cotton cloth. In Cajamarca, Indian women in layered skirts called *polleras* walk down the streets with drop spindles dangling from their fingers. And in some communities even the men weave.

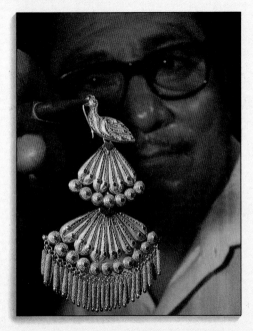

Tourists find that the quality of woven items ranges from crude wools still embedded with flecks of thistle to fine contemporary designs found in Lima's upscale boutiques. Often they use brilliant dyes made from seeds, herbs and vegetables. When an agreement can be worked out with the United Nations, Peru may even begin marketing vicuña fabric, under strict guidelines to limit the amount of fur shaven from the protected animals. Cloths can come from the Andean highlands, particularly Cuzco, Puno and Cajamarca, or as far away as the jungle where Conibo and Shipibo Indians weave cotton with designs of serpents and, since

missionaries entered the rainforest, Christian crosses.

For those who do not visit the jungle, crafts from that region of the country can still be obtained. In the Lima suburb of Miraflores, the **Antisuyo** store on Tacna 460 specializes in rainforest handicrafts. The South American Explorers Club (Av. Republica de Portugal 146) also sells items from the jungle.

Not all weavers handle cloth; from frigid Puno to the hot desert enar Chiclayo, Peru is proud of its basket weavers. On Lake Titicaca, tortora reed baskets and miniature boat souvenirs are produced by the Indians who themselves live in reed huts on reed islands. In the north, basket weaving started in fishing communities where the finished baskets stored fish, rice and fruits. In the port of Huanchaco, the fishing boats themselves are woven from reed; in the Amazon, Indians weave hammocks. The northern coastal region is also known for its finely woven straw hats, similar to Panama hats, known as *jipijapas*. These hats and white cotton ponchos make up the traditional dress of the northern cowboys, or *chalanes.*

Erotic pottery: Contemporary ceramics in Peru, while plentiful, do not live up to the tradition of ancient cultures such as the Moche, whose erotic *huacos* – or pottery – still startle observers by graphically depicting marital relations, contraceptive methods and death allegories. The finest pottery techniques died with the Spanish conquest, but ceramics are still an important craft. Contemporary pottery ranges from simple baked clay dishes found at open air markets to the stylized work produced at the Aylambo workshops outside Cajamarca (See "Northern Peru".) Shipibo women in the Amazon jungle mix tree ash with clay to form their thin pottery decorated with delicate lines and glazed with tree resin, which they bake in rudimentary ovens dug in the earth, while *naíf* clay churches painted with designs of corn and flowers come from Ayachucho (boasting the greatest number of churches per city block than anywhere else in the country). Tawaq, a workshop started by a group of ceramics artisans in Quinua outside Ayacucho, has expanded and now involves most of the residents of that small village. Their pottery is polished with river stones and painted with hen feathers.

Pucara bulls, actually made down the road

from Pucara in the town of Pupuja, have changed over the years to accommodate tourists' tastes. These clay bulls from near Lake Titicaca are now colorful and ornate, unlike the dull pink and brown clay bulls first used in annual branding festivals; those bulls had small hollows where oils were burned in offerings to the gods. The bulls are an example of how a legacy of the Spanish – the fearful bull that awed the Indians – has been incorporated into native crafts. The best of these can be purchased in Cuzco and Puno.

When the Spanish reached Peru, they found skilled craftsmen working gold and silver into finely turned jewelry and adornments. This tradition has not been lost, as evidenced

Religious scenes: Nearly as detailed as the filigree are the colorful *retablos*, originally small portable altars. Smaller nowadays and tucked into a decorated wooden box or the hollow of a reed, these are busy scenes – often religious in nature – that may be solemn or comical depending on the artist's mood. The figures in wood, plaster or clay overflow from the scenes showing religious processions, rollicking fiestas complete with a snoozing drunk, disruptive children and wayward animals or even artisans making hats or weaving cloth. Wooden retablos may be found in most outdoor markets but the most delicate *retablos* – carved from the white and gray Huamanga stone some call Peru's

by the intricate gold filigree produced in Catacaos outside Piura in the northern desert. These complicated pieces, which try an artist's patience and imagination, dangle from the ears of the townswomen who claim gold shines even brighter under the desert sun. These are the big, drooping earrings that women dancing the Marinera wear. In San Jeronimo, near Huancayo in the central highlands, silver filigree is tooled into peacocks, fighting cocks and doves.

Far left, master goldworkers. **Above**, a selection of silver jewelry.

marble – are found only in boutiques and cooperatives, such as Artesanias del Peru. Actually a type of soapstone, Huamanga stone is carved into anything from matchbook sized Nativity scenes to oversized chess sets – with figures of Incas and llamas replacing the traditional kings and knights. Much of what appears to be marble in Peru's churches is actually Huamanga stone.

Outside of Lima and Cuzco, the best places to purchase crafts are usually cooperatives or outdoor markets. Depending on the town, the markets may last only from predawn to mid-morning once a week, or they may go on for days.

An Indian tale describes the dismemberment of the god Pachacamac. His teeth were changed into grains of corn and his genitals into yucca and sweet potatoes, providing the earth with food. Another legend tells of an Inca noble who fell into a well while walking. His father, the sun god, looked down sadly on his imprisoned son. The tears of gold that fell from the father's eyes reached the earth, irrigated it and made the fields flourish. The grains of corn that grew were said to be the golden tears of the sun god.

Food and its importance are intrinsic parts of Peruvian culture and history. The legends of the ancient Indian civilizations highlight the food products that were most important in the diet of their time – especially corn and potatoes, which still show up with amazing regularity in contemporary cuisine. In fact, many visitors to Peru are stunned by the number of ways potatoes can be prepared. At the same time, the range of geography and climates in Peru, from the cold highlands and hot, wet jungle to the arid coast and the Pacific waters rich with fish, have handed this South American nation what may be the continent's most extensive and varied menu.

The food not only shows up on the dining table, but it is immortalized in pre-Hispanic pottery, in the centuries-old weavings found in burial grounds and in paintings. In fact, on the arid coast where food was available only after painstaking irrigation and planning by pre-Inca cultures, the priests in those societies had elevated status in the community because they were the ones who studied astral movements and declared when crop planting should occur. Pre-Colombian cultures buried foodstuffs with their dead to sustain them on the journey to the next life. Then, as today, cuisine was based around three main elements – potatoes, corn and hot peppers.

Powerful spices: Hot peppers are found in a number of varieties and are used to add pizzazz to everything from soup to fish. Hot peppers are also the one element that trans-

gresses geography. On the northern coast where fish is an important part of the diet, sauces of hot peppers and onions are usually heaped on top of the main dish or at least offered in small bowls as self-service condiments. In the jungle, however, food in general tends to be less spicy although Amazon residents routinely dip jungle vegetables and yucca into fiery sauces. But it is the highland area where *picante* (as the hot spiciness is known), reaches an art form. Dishes are elaborated in a range of degrees of spiciness depending on the type of chile pepper – or *aji* – used. They start with the biting edge that bland food eaters can tolerate and increases to the screamingly torried rocoto peppers whose fire engine red color is not only decorative but illustrative as a danger signal.

It is believed that South American Indians originally grew about five species of hot peppers which were gradually transported to Central America, the Caribbean and Mexico. Christopher Columbus may be responsible for its misnomer: pepper. He was searching for the black pepper (genus Piper) of the East Indies when he stumbled upon hot chiles. "There is much *axi*, which is their pepper and it is stronger than pepper, and the people won't eat without it for they find it very wholesome," Columbus wrote in his journal in 1493. His cargoes of hot peppers spread like wildfire in Europe, Africa and Asia. In India in particular, they were adopted as irreplaceable in cooking.

Contrary to popular belief, researchers have found that hot spices are not all that hard on the stomach. And, ounce for ounce, they contain double the vitamin C of oranges. However, those unaccustomed to hot peppers should take it easy on the spicing since chile overindulgence can cause a form of diarrhea known as *jaloproctitis*. Peruvians generally do not serve *picante* to small children, nursing mothers or the infirm.

Home of a world staple: Those hot peppers are often used to spice up the mainstay plate in Peru – potatoes. Known as *papas*, they come in at least 200 varieties (some small farmers have up to three dozen different varieties in a single field) and they are served

Seafood smorgasbord.

in nearly as many different dishes. Those who think potatoes came from Ireland are mistaken – they were taken to Europe from the Peruvian Andes and even today new varieties of the tuber are being exported from South America. Those varieties include the yellow *Limeña* potato, the purple potatoes whose color describes both the peel and the vegetable beneath it, and the freeze-dried *chuno* potato that is grown in the high plain surrounding Lake Titicaca. Chuno is a generic term for the frost-resistant potatoes that can be stored for up to four years. They are also known as *papa seca* and show up in a dish called *carapulcra* in which the potatoes (which look like hard stones) are boiled until

where French fries are combined with steak strips and tomatoes in a spicy dish.

Potatoes are also served alone. *Papa Ocopa* is sliced, boiled potatoes smothered in a spicy peanut sauce, served over a bed of rice and garnished with hard-boiled eggs and olives. Nearly identical in appearance but very different in flavor is *Papa a la Huancaina* covered in a sauce of cheese and hot peppers. *Causa*, a cold casserole of mashed potatoes mixed with hot peppers and onions (occasionally layered over chicken or fish) is another favorite dish. And *papa rellena* is a fried oblong of mashed potatoes stuffed with a tasty mixture of meat, onions, olives, boiled eggs and raisins.

soft in a stew of meat and spices. Aymara Indians at Titicaca still ritually stuff potatoes with coca leaves and bury them as a tribute to the earth mother, Pacha Mama, in hopes of a bountiful harvest.

Another tuber, *olluco*, ranges in color from red, pink, yellow and orange to white and has a taste much like new potatoes. It is shredded and served with dried llama meat or *charqui* (similar to beef jerky) in another stew dish. In fact, potatoes are an indispensable ingredient in most of the hearty one-pot dishes so common in highland cuisine. They are present in *estofado* – a mild stew of chicken, corn, carrots and tomatoes and in *lomo saltado*,

Ritual food: Found in nearly as many colors and varieties as potatoes is corn, perhaps the most sacred crop of pre-Hispanic times. Corn was used not only as a food but also as a commodity for bartering. Purple corn is converted into a refreshing drink called *chicha morada*, as well as the purple pudding-like dessert known as *mazamorra morada*. These last two dishes are considered so typically products of Lima that when Peruvians speak of someone born in Lima, they say they are "limeño and mazamorrero". Another type of chicha, a thick whitish fermented corn drink, is a sort of poor man's beer and is ceremoniously poured in the earth during harvest and planting ceremonies in the highlands. In ancient times, only the Chosen Women in the Inca court could prepare this drink. *Choclo*, large-grained ears of corn are sold as snacks, boiling hot with slices of cheese and hot sauce. Large, boiled corn kernels are served with pork in a dish called *chicharron con mote*.

As far as grains go, corn best survived the Spanish Conquest. Other grains such as purple-flowered kiwicha and golden-brown quinoa – forms of amaranth – were banned by the Vatican and for many centuries disappeared from the Peruvian diet although they have resurfaced in recent decades. Prior to the ban, kiwicha and quinoa were not only

or guinea pig prepared in a variety of ways ranging from stewed to fried; and *cau cau* – tripe and potatoes. Also commonplace is *rocoto relleno*, a hot red pepper stuffed with meat, potatoes and eggs.

Another novelty of the Sierra is the *pachamanca* – a combination of meats and vegetables cooked together over heated stones in underground pits. Peruvians, quick with a double entendre (often at the expense of the tourist), may use the word as the verb *pachamanquear* which technically means to hold a *pachamanca* picnic but more commonly means to engage in public displays of affection. If asked, tell them you are going to a *pachamanca*, not that you are going to

nourishing food sources high in protein but they were ceremonial foods. Nowadays, they are found prepared like rice, in breads and cookies and as an ingredient in soups.

Corn, potatoes and grains such as kiwicha are most often found in the cuisine of the highlands where they are grown. This is hearty food, often prepared in one pot, where the greatest amount of elaboration goes into the spicing. Highland dishes include *anticuchos*, shish-kebabs of beef heart; protein-rich *cuy*

pachamanquear.

For those who shy away from hot peppers, a *sancochado* is a good option. This is a boiled dinner, usually consisting of beer, onions, potatoes, yams, corn and carrots and finished with a cup of consomme. Typically, the servings are generous and one *sancochado* usually is enough for at least two or three people.

Desert dishes: Like the highland cuisine, food prepared on the desert coast may be hearty, accompanied by potatoes or rice – or both – but rather than beef it employs fish, chicken, duck or even goat. A favorite northern coastal dish is *seco de cabrito* –

Left, street *ceviche* stall. **Above**, *anticuchos*, shish kebabs of beef heart.

roasted goat (actually, kid) cooked with fermented chicha and served with beans and rice. If lamb is substituted, it is called *seco de cordero*. Even better is *aji de gallina*, a rich concoction of creamed chicken with a touch of hot peppers served over boiled potatoes. *Arroz con pato a la chiclayana* is a duck and rice plate originating in the port town of Chiclayo.

Undoubtedly the best coastal dishes are those with seafood bases, led by the ever-popular *ceviche*. This plate of white fish in a spicy marinade of lemon juice, onion and hot peppers is found in other coastal countries but never prepared quite as well as in Peru. Traditional *ceviche* is made with fish and

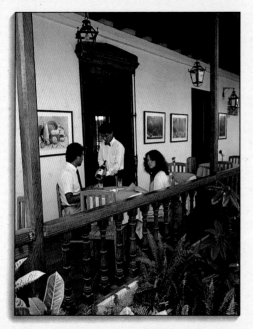

served with corn – both fried and on-the-cob, potatoes, yucca, sweet potatoes and sometimes seaweed, but variations of the dish include *ceviche mixta* in which shellfish are added. Another delicious fish dish is *escabeche de pescado*, cold fried fish covered in a sauce of onions, hot peppers and garlic then adorned with olives and hard boiled eggs. (It is also possible to order *escabeche de gallina*, made with chicken.)

Fish is believed to have rejuvenating powers and *aguadito* – a thick rice and fish soup (although sometimes prepared with chicken) is traditionally what was served to all night revelers after the three-day wedding cel-

ebrations once common along the coast. An *aguadito* may also be served to remaining guests after a party that goes into the wee hours of the morning and, at the multitude of informal vendors' kiosks in working class areas of Lima, a sign promising *Aguadito para recuperar energia* ("Aguadito to recuperate energy") can be found over many of the food booths.

Fruits of the sea: For fish alone, *corvina*, or white sea bass is an excellent choice, as is trout – *trucha* – for freshwater fish (especially Lake Titicaca trout). *Camarones* (shrimp), *calamares* (clams) and *choros* (mussels) are prepared in a number of ways – all delicious. Any dish listed as *a lo macho* means it is steeped in a shellfish sauce.

Fish from the Amazon River and its tributaries are the central ingredient in much of the cuisine from Peru's jungle. These fish range from the small, sharp-fanged *piranhas* to the huge, succulent *paiches*. Broiled or grilled, the fish is accompanied by jungle fruits and vegetables, including *palmito* – ribbons of hearts of palm (that look deceptively like mounds of wide pasta), yucca and fried bananas. The fish may be wrapped in banana leaves and baked in coals in a dish known as *patarashca*.

The best known of the jungle dishes are *juanes* – a sort of tamale stuffed with chicken and rice, turtle soup (*sopa de motelo*), *sajino* (roasted wild boar) and fried bananas. *Masato*, an alcoholic drink made from fermented yucca, is used to wash down the meals.

As evidence of the Peruvian sweet tooth, desserts are in abundance. Favorites include *manjarblanco*, a sweet made from boiled milk and sugar, *cocadas* (coconut macaroons), and *churros* – deep-fried tubes of pastry dough filled with *manjarblanco* or honey. During October, the streets of Lima are filled with a seasonal special, *turron*. This shortbread covered in molasses or honey is prepared in conjunction with the Catholic celebrations honoring the Lord of the Miracles (*El Señor de los Milagros*). *Champus*, (pronounced like the product used to wash one's hair), is a pudding texture sweet made from wheat.

In the summer, cones of crushed ice flavored with fruit syrups (and optionally topped with condensed milk) are sold on nearly every street corner, although it is best to steer clear of those *raspadillas* since the water may upset travelers' stomachs.

Other sweets include *yuquitas*, deep fried yucca dough balls rolled in sugar, *picarones*, deep-fried doughnuts slathered in honey; and *arroz con leche* (rice pudding).

One of the oldest traditional desserts is the crunchy cookies known as *revolución caliente* dating from the independence area. Sellers of these sweets wander through the streets calling out, *"Revolución caliente, música para los dientes. Azúcar, clavo y canela para rechinar las muelas."* ("Hot revolution, music for the teeth. Sugar, cloves and cinnamon to gnash the molars.")

Fruits from the jungle and desert are

A range of thirst-quenchers: Peruvians don't eat without drinking and there is a mixed bag of beverages beginning with the national cocktail, *pisco sours*. This potent drink made from a clear grape-based liquor features fresh lemon juice, bitters, egg whites and sugar mixed and topped with ground sugar. Peru also produces Cartavio rum and wine, although it is generally disappointing except for Tacama and Ocucaje labels. For something less potent, there is mate de coca, a tea brewed from coca leaves, or *manzanilla* (camomile) tea. Peru produces a small amount of fine coffee although it is increasingly exported and is difficult to find. However, you may inquire in restaurants if they serve

wonderful and are served plain or in desserts and juices. *Maracuya* – the seedy passion fruit – is best as a juice or to flavor ice cream, but the *tuna*, the fruit of the desert cactus, is delicious alone. *Chirimoya* or custard apples are tasty and *lucuma*, a small brown fruit with a strong, exotic taste similar to maple syrup is one of the favorite ice cream flavors in Peru. It is recognizable by its dark peach color. Papaya and mango are also grown in Peru.

__Far left__, elegant dining. __Above__, a quick *churro* for the road.

good *cafe Chanchamayo*, named for the region where it is grown. For those who cannot live without carbonated beverages – known here as *gaseosas* – the local soft drink is the bright yellow *Inca Kola*.

As for beer, the main brands are *Cristal, Arequipeña* or *Cusqueña*. It is customary for a group of Peruvian men drinking together to ask for only one or two short glasses to accompany their large bottles of beer. One of the drinkers will raise his glass to a friend, toast him by saying "Salud" and drink the contents of the glass. The glass is then refilled by the toast giver and passed to the friend – who repeats the process with the next person.

TREKKING IN THE ANDES

The great Andes mountain chain stretches the entire length of the South American continent, and is made up of dozens of individual mountain groups known as *cordilleras.* In Peru, these snow-capped peaks have been the source of superstition, frustration and inspiration to mankind for thousands of years.

Pre-Colombian cultures worshipped individual mountains and made ritual offerings to the deities they believed abided within. Mountain worship, in remote areas, is still practiced by Indian groups under the thin veil of Christianity.

The Spanish conquistadors, led by Francisco Pizarro, found the Peruvian Andes daunting. Hernando Pizarro, brother to Francisco, wrote, "…we had to climb another stupendous mountainside. Looking up at it from below, it seemed impossible for birds to scale it by flying through the air, let alone men on horseback climbing by land."

Long after the Spanish Conquest, a new breed of conquistadors came seeking victory over high altitudes rather than indigenous cultures. In the early 1900's, mountaineers "discovered" the Andes of Peru and began the assault, which still continues, on the highest tropical range in the world. More than 30 majestic peaks rise well over 6,000 meters (20,000 feet) in a region that can only be compared to the Himalayas in splendour.

And modern-day outdoor enthusiasts have found that walking around mountains is as much of a thrill as climbing them. For these trekkers, Peru is a paradise.

Mountain cultures: Except for the most remote and rugged areas, the Peruvian Andes offer little in the way of untouched "wilderness". Only 23 percent of Peru's land is arable, and every fertile meter is farmed by local Indians. For most trekkers, then, "getting away" means leaving behind the 20th century and becoming acquainted with an indigenous lifestyle centuries old.

The formidable Peruvian Sierra, or mountainous region, was tamed by the Incas, whose terraced system of agriculture enabled large areas of steep yet fertile land to be cultivated. This unique system is still employed in some areas, and countless remains of ancient terracing give an insight into the productivity achieved by this civilization.

The mountain Indians, or *campesinos*, today cultivate numerous small plots of ancestral land. During growing season the hillsides are plowed in a variety of geometric shapes and, as the crops begin to mature, the mountains are carpeted in colors ranging from deep green to warm gold. It is into these

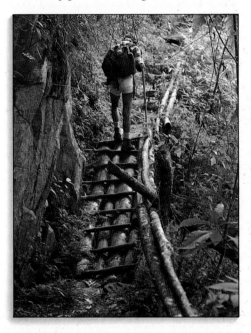

areas that trekkers wander along ancient paths, occasionally pausing to allow a herd of llamas or goats or sheeps to scramble by, crossing high Andean passes at altitudes above 4,000 meters (13,000 feet), and marveling at the glacier-covered peaks which serve as a spectacular backdrop.

It is the very presence of humanity that makes trekking in Peru a unique experience. There is always the opportunity to stop and converse in simple words or hand signals with local inhabitants. Many of the older *campesinos*, especially the women, speak only a little Spanish – Quechua, the language of the Incas, is more often heard. Though the highland people are typically reticent with strangers, curious children or brave adults may initiate a conversation by wanting to know where you're from, what's your name, or do you have any sweets – the last question being the most relevant.

Passing remote, populated areas is like stepping back into the past. One or two-room huts constructed of crude mud bricks and topped with ichu grass have changed little in design since Incan times.

There is no electricity, and fresh running water is taken from nearby streams. Small courtyards house chickens and *cuy*, or guinea pig (considered a delicacy in the sierra), and corn along with other grains

places to start is in Lima at the South American Explorers Club, a non-profit information network for the continent. The clubhouse, at Avenida Republica de Portugal 146 (Breña), has available an invaluable stock of reports about trails, maps and guidebooks. The friendly staff are more than willing to give advice to both beginners and experts. Written inquiries can be sent to the postal address: Casilla 3714, Lima 100, Peru.

The first thing to realize is that, despite the fact that Peru is located in the southern hemisphere, the seasons are not the opposite of those in the northern zone as one would expect. Being so close to the Equator, Peru experiences only two climate changes – a

Inca Trail
4 km / 2,5 miles

To Quillabamba

Puentes Ruinas
Railway Station

Rio Urubamba

Railway Tunnel
Km 88

Rio Pacamayo

Third Pass

Rio Aobamba

O'ente Ruin

Second Pass-
(3998 metres)

Llactapata

To Ollantaytambo

First Pass-
Warmiwañusca
(4198 metres)

Rio Llullucha

Rio Huayruro

CORDILLERA

Lake

VILCABAMBA

Three Stones Camp

Paucarcancha

To Salcantay

Legend:
1 Huayna Picchu
2 Machu Picchu Hotel
3 Machu Picchu Ruins
4 Intipunku Ruins
5 Huiñay Huayna Ruins
6 Phuyupatamarca Ruins
7 Inca Tunnel
8 Sayajmarca Ruins
9 Runturacay Ruins
10 Camp Sites
11 Three Stones Camp
12 Huayllabamba Village
13 Aguas Calientes

can often be seen drying in the midday sun. This typical scene provides an interesting present-day glimpse of an ancient lifestyle, with the trekker as an anachronism in its midst.

Preparing for a trek: Trekking differs from mountain climbing in that it requires little technical skill and the routes are more lateral than vertical. Most treks in the Peruvian Andes are simply extended walks along often steep paths and can be attempted by any reasonably fit and healthy person. Local porters or *arrieros*, burro drivers, can be hired to help with a heavy load.

When planning a trek, one of the best

rainy season and a dry season. Knowing when to trek is as important as knowing where.

Technically called winter, the months from May through October are the finest for trekking when the weather is clear and dry. During the rainy season, from November through April, skies are often cloudy and rain frequent. Travel during this time can often mean long delays due to washed-out roads and trekking takes on the characteristics of long mud slogs.

Most treks wander through the Andean highlands at an altitude of 3,000 to 5,000 meters (10,000 to 16,000 feet). Days are usually sunny with temperatures of 18-24 C (65-75 F). The equatorial sun is strong and frequent applications of sunscreen is a must. Nights can feel bitterly cold, especially at higher altitudes, so lightweight thermal underwear, a few layers of warm clothes, and a pile or down jacket are necessary. A tent and good sleeping bags are also essential, as well as a dependable stove. White gas, called *bencina*, is usually available, but is often of low-grade quality which can clog up a temperamental cooker. Kerosene and leaded petrol are other choices for use in a multi-fuel stove.

Lightweight hiking boots are suitable for the majority of trails. The best equipment is

thin, high-altitude air can quickly exhaust the unaccustomed and cause physical discomfort. Headaches, mild nausea, shortness of breath and sleeplessnes are some of the common symptoms of high altitude sickness, or *soroche*. By avoiding alcohol and fatty foods in the first few days, and drinking plenty of liquds, the affects of altitude will be minimized. Many find that sucking on hard candies and drinking tea made from the cocoa leaf, called *mate de coca*, also help to reduce the symptoms.

Food for treks can be easily found in the larger villages, but the freeze-dried variety, along with many Western luxuries, is nonexistent. Package soups and dried pastas, as

available in your home country, but if the idea of lugging around an assortment of gear does not appeal, most necessities can be hired in the major trekking centers of Huaráz and Cuzco for only a few dollars a day. The quality of hired equipment can vary widely; be sure to check that it is at least adequate. Stoves, especially, have been known to "conk out" after just a few miles into the trek!

Thin mountain air: Before setting off, spend a few days becoming acclimatized to the altitude with short hikes around the area. The

well as dried fruits and grains, are readily available in the markets. Favorite spices brought from home take up little room and add flavor to the evening meals. Take as much as will be needed for the duration of the trek since it is unlikely that anything will be available on the way other than the occasional piece of bread or fruit in the most populated areas.

A multi-fuel cooker is essential since there is no wood for fires at higher altitudes, and using up the scarce reserves at lower levels only adds to the serious problem of soil erosion that plagues the area.

All drinking water should be treated by

Above, ruins on the Inca trail.

using purification tablets, iodine solution or a filtering pump. Iodine works better than chlorine-based purifiers because of its ability to kill more pesky bacteria. The taste of treated water is not especially palatable, but drink-flavored powder can be bought in most shops, and not only hides the chemical taste but adds energy-boosting sugar to the diet.

The Peruvian Andes offer unlimited trekking possibilities. Still, trekkers are drawn to a few special places.

The Inca Trail to Machu Picchu: Of all the popular treks in South America, the three-to-five day Inca trail is legendary. The adventure begins with a four-hour train ride along the Urubamba river, known to the Incas as top of this 4,000 meters (13,000 feet) pass is no small challenge. Laboring up the seemingly endless trail, the hiker soon identifies with its name. In English it translates as "Dead Woman's" pass.

From here, Inca history begins to unfold. The small guard post of **Runkuraqay**, overlooking the valley and often shrouded in early-morning mist, is the first reward of the Inca Trail. Farther along, the more elaborately-constructed site of **Sayajmarka** (Dominant Town) perches atop a narrow cliff. The fine stonework for which the Incas were famous is apparent. An incredible "paved highway" of neatly-fitted stone snakes along the valley below, masterfully con-

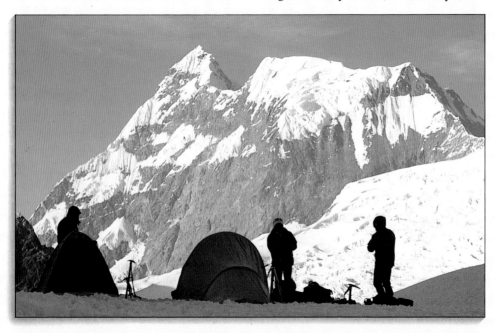

the Sacred Valley. Legions of early-rising *campesinos*, loading and unloading their marketable goods at every station, crowd together in what begins to look more like a cattle car than a passenger train. At **Kilometer 88** the train pauses briefly allowing hikers to disembark. Here at the trailhead, a footbridge temporarily separates the trekker from a rich history dating back more than 400 years.

The first 7 miles (11 km) meander through easy terrain of dusty scrub bushes, low-lying hills, and a few rustic huts. The first barrier is the **Warmiwañusqu pass**. Beyond lies a wealth of Incan ruins, but struggling to the structed by a culture the Spaniards considered uncivilized.

As the trek progresses, the archaeological sites become more complex. **Puyapatamarka** (Cloud-level Town) is fascinating for its circular walls and finely engineered aquaduct system which still provides spring water to the ancient ceremonial baths. Below, the trail offers up yet another delight to the trekker.

Huge steps, a virtual stone stairway almost a half mile in length, lead down into high jungle vegetation where wild orchids and other exotic flowers bloom. Curiously, this section of the trail laid undiscovered until

1984. Until then, a modern footpath served to connect this interrupted section of the Inca highway.

Tenaciously clinging to the side of a steep ravine, is the last set of ruins, and the most stunning. **Wiñay Wayna** presents an unbelieveable picture when first seen in the distance. The ability of the Incas to construct something so complex in an area so vertical defies comprehension, yet the series of ritual baths, long stretches of terracing and intricate stonework certainly prove what would appear to be impossible.

An hour away lies the jewel in the crown – **Machu Picchu**. From the high pass of **Intipunku**, the Sun Gate, the first glimpse of the fabled city is bestowed. This is the culmination of days of walking; the immersion into an ancient culture complete. Arriving as the Incas did centuries ago, the trekker begins the final descent into Machu Picchu, sharing a path with history.

Other treks from Cuzco: The Cuzco area is rich in superb trekking. Routes around the high mountains of Salcantay and Soray originate from the small village of Mollepata and provide some exquisite views of the Cordillera Vilcabamba.

With permission from the government, the more adventurous trekkers can make a stab at getting into an area called Espiritu Pampa, thought to be the "lost city" of Vilcabamba – a place never visited by the Spaniards, a treasure-house of Inca riches. Whether its lost Inca treasures or unparalleled mountain scenery, trekkers will not be at a loss for adventure.

Considered by many seasoned hikers to be one of the finese areas is the **Auzangate Loop** route around Nevado Auzangage (6,270 meters/20,900 feet). A truck from Cuzco is the usual transport, and the village of Tinqui the destination for the start of this five-day trek. The eight hour ride is hot and dusty by day, and bitterly cold at night – apt preparation for the days ahead.

The route meanders up and down, through one valley after another, each divided by passes nearing altitudes of 5,000 meters (16,000 feet). Soothing hot springs welcome the hiker on the first day and give a warm goodbye at the finish. Huge moraines, rock

and silt deposits left behind by the Ice Age, and glacial lakes, each a stunning yet different shade of blue, provide plenty of visual feasts for the days ahead.

The close-up views of Auzangate are spectacular, and frequent. At one point along the trail, the tongue of a glacier extends down within walking distance. A little exploration will reveal a huge ice cave within. It's easy enough to break the few icicles concealing the entrance and roam through the numerous chambers.

Wild vicuña, a cameloid cousin to the llama, are elusive creatures valued for their fine wool. Herds of these skittish beasts are often seen, but only from a distance. Their

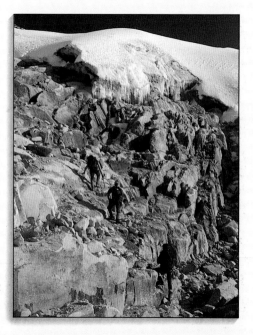

domesticated relatives, llamas and alpacas, also graze along the route, usually tended by traditionally dressed *campesino* children. The Andean condor, the world's largest bird with a wingspan up to 3 meters (10 feet), may be sighted soaring high above on the mountain winds.

Several nights of camping will be near the foot of Auzangate and promised bouts of shivering will last until the early-morning sun drives the cold away. On other nights, campsites are set up near inhabited areas, and the trekker may be rewarded with gifts of boiled potatoes brought around by a generous local. Nothing is asked for in exchange,

Left, camping out in the Cordillera Blanca. **Above right**, scaling the heights.

but a sharing of food is common, and the response greatly enhances the evening meal.

In spite of the strenuous effort this trek requires, the days pass too quickly and in almost no time the final hot spring is reached. The last of the dust is washed away, but not the memories of this marvelous experience.

The Cordillera Blanca: Eight hours by bus north of Lima is one of the most popular trekking areas in Peru. At least for its diversity and large number of mountain peaks clustered so conveniently in one central area, the **Cordillera Blanca** is a trekkers' dream-come-true.

The small city of **Huaráz** is the hub for all hiking activity, and frequent rural buses transport enthusiasts to a variety of trailheads. A **Casa de Guias**, located just off the main street, will provide the latest information about routes and mountain conditions, and can provide trekkers with a list of porters and arrieros, burro drivers, who can help carry gear on the long trek ahead. Along the main street of Luzuriaga, colorful billboard signs lend distinction to an otherwise dull facade of street-front shops. Most of these promote tourism in some form, so finding a comfortable day tour, renting hiking gear, or buying souvenirs is as easy as locating the proper agency by identifying its sign out front. A number of good restaurants (whose status are often elevated to excellent after a long hike) serve up a variety of food and a couple of lively *peñas*, featuring groups playing the traditional music of the Andes, provide a place to loosen up before or after a strenuous four days' trekking.

The Cordillera Blanca is full of striking views and unique adventures. Hikes from one day to ten are possible, combinations producing even more possibilities if desired. Here limitations are only the result of a lack of imagination.

The highest mountain in Peru, **Huascarán** at 6,768 meters (22,200 feet), and what many consider to be the most beautiful in the world, **Alapmayo** at 5,945 meters (19,500 feet) are just the toppings on an already rich cake. Glacial lakes dot the landscape, and fresh running streams serve up tasty trout to even the most amateur of fishermen. The days are warm and scented with eucalyptus. Snow-covered peaks stretch as far as the eye can see.

Trekkers wanting to get the legs and lungs in shape for longer treks can start with a variety of short day hikes in the Huaráz area. Just above the city is **El Mirador**, a scenic lookout marked by a huge white cross. The route heads uphill east along city streets which eventually turn into a footpath beside an irrigation canal lined with eucalyptus trees. Fields of wheat ripening in the sun add a serene, pastoral feel.

At the top, the highest mountain in Peru, Huascarán, dominates the northern horizon, the lower Vallunaraju (5,680 meters/18,600 feet) peeks out over the foothills to the east, and the city of Huaráz sprawls below.

Another choice of many is the **Pitec trail** to **Laguna Churup**. There is no public transport to this small village 10 km (6 mile) from the center of Huaráz, but often a taxi driver can be persuaded to navigate the terribly rough road to Pitec. Walking is also an option, but it's nicer to get a fresh start at the trailhead and then walk back to Huaráz after the hike.

The trail begins at the "parking lot" before the actual village of Pitec is reached. A well-worn footpath heads north up a ridgeline and the Churup massif rises just above 5,495 meters (18,000 feet) in the distance. At the base of this mountain is the destination of the hike, Laguna Churup, fed by the glacial melt-off and surrounded by huge boulders. A picnic lunch and a midday siesta in the warm sun reward the effort of getting here. A leisurely hike back to Huaráz follows a cobbled road through *campesino* homesteads.

The Llanganuco to Santa Cruz Loop: One of the most frequently hiked trails is the five-day loop into the Cordillera Blanca which begins at the Llanganuco lakes. A more perfect mountain hike could not be imagined. The route passes under a dozen peaks over 5,800 meters (19,000 feet) and panoramic views abound.

Buses frequently leave Huaráz, loaded with an assortment of *campesinos*, their chickens, *cuyes* and children, for the small village of **Yungay**. Here *camionetas*, small pick-up trucks, wait in the plaza to transport hikers and sightseers up the valley to the dazzling, glacier-fed lakes of **Llanganuco**.

The trailhead lies a few kilometers above the lakes, near the **Portachuelo** (high pass) of Llanganuco, and the trek begins with a descent towards the village of **Colcabamba**. Immediately the steep face of **Chopicalqui**

(6,350 meters/20,800 feet) towers over the trail like a sentinel and soon a few thatched-roofed houses come into view. A sampling of local cuisine may be possible here.

At this point, the trail begins a steady ascent up the **Huaripampa Quebrada** (narrow valley). The snow-capped peaks of **Chacraraju** (6,110 meters/20,000 feet) and **Pirámide** (5,880 meters/19,285 feet) provide splendid photo opportunities, and a chance to rest, as the trekker labors up the steepening trail towards the high pass of **Punta Unión**. In the last hour before sunset, as camp is set up, the mountains are cast in the silver and pink of "alpenglow".

At over 4,750 meters (15,500 feet), Punta

dramatic mountain vistas to open, marshy pasture land where herds of llamas and goats graze. Farther along, the trail narrows as it begins to wind through forests of stunted trees and follows the easy meandering of a small stream. With luck, trout could be served up for dinner.

Mountaineering: For the more adventurous and technically-minded mountain enthusiast, the Cordillera Blanca is unrivaled for the pursuit of mountaineering. With glacier-covered peaks varying in altitudes from 5,495 meters (18,000 feet) to 6,795 meters (20,000 feet), and technical levels from very easy to extremely difficult, there is something for everyone. However, because all climbing

Union becomes both literally and figuratively the high point of this journey. **Taulliraju**, over 5,830 meters (19,000 feet), glistens in the midday sun, and a number of glacial lakes lie like scattered jewels in the distance. The valley below opens up to reveal a wide stretch of snow-capped peaks, a mere hint of the magnitude of the Cordillera Blanca, and huge Andean Condors can often be seen soaring high above the pass.

As the trail descends toward the village of **Cashapampa**, the scenery changes from

Climbing Alpamayo in the Cordillera Blanca.

here is at high altitude, and any glacier travel requires technical knowledge, climbing in the Cordillera Blanca should be attempted by those with at least some degree of experience. Besides the usual trekking equipment, a rope, ice ax, crampons and ice stakes or screws are necessary.

Trekkers generally don't experience anything more than *soroche*, or mild altitude sickness, but at higher altitudes serious complications can occur. *Pulmonary Edema* occurs when the lungs begin to fill with fluid. Early symptoms include a dry, incessant cough, a rattling sound and tightness in the chest. *Cerebral Edema* occurs when fluid collects in the brain. Symptoms include loss of coordination, incoherent speech, confusion, and loss of energy. Both of these illnesses are extremely serious and possibly fatal. The condition progresses rapidly and the only cure is an immediate descent to a significantly lower altitude. The victim is usually the last one aware of the problem, so it's essential that each person in the group keep an eye out for symptoms in the others.

Another high altitude problem is *hypothermia*, or exposure. This occurs when the body loses more heat than it can replace. The symptoms begin with uncontrolled shivering that will eventually cease, though the body is still cold. Lack of coordination, con-

actually draw off body heat when wet. Layering clothes is an effective way to regulate body temperature during times of exertion and rest. Food also helps stove the internal generators, so eating quickly assimilated food like chocolate will help keep the system functioning.

Many climbers feel that acclimatization comes with activity – getting the legs in shape for the more demanding climbs is as important as having the lungs working at capacity. To this end, several short warm-up climbs are favored. **Nevado Pisco**, just over 5,800 meters (19,000 feet), is popular for its steep, yet quick ascent, and the views from the saddle are some of the finest anywhere in

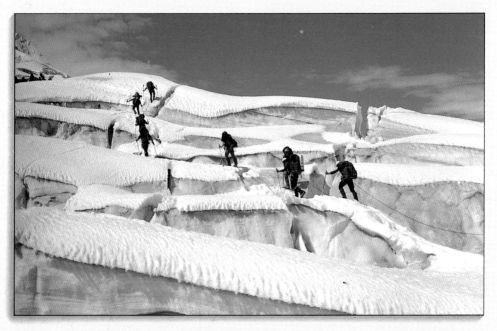

fusion, drowsiness and even a feeling of warmth are other symptoms. A victim suffering from hypothermia will need to be immediately dried-off, placed in a warm sleeping bag, and given warm liquid to drink. In advanced cases, the victim will not be able to generate any body heat and will need the warmth of other bodies to get his temperature back to normal. Hypothermia is prevented by staying warm and dry. Wearing wool or a synthetic insulating material next to the skin will help hold in warmth, even when wet. Cotton has no insulating properties and will

Above, scaling Peru's highest Peak Huascarán.

the Cordillera Blanca.

The approach to base camp begins just above the Llanganuco lakes. The 5-km (3-mile) hike follows a footpath along the crest of a lateral moraine and gains 750 meters (2,460 feet) in altitude.

Camping is in a flat, grassy area below an incredibly steep moraine, which unfortunately must be negotiated the next day. Some groups choose to continue on past the base camp, tackle the difficult moraine the same day, and continue on up to the high camp just below the glacier.

An early morning start from here allows climbers to make the summit and be back in camp for afternoon tea. The next day descent is quick and climbers are usually back in Huaráz by evening.

Scaling Peru's highest peaks: When the acclimatization to altitude is adequate, and climbers are ready for some real work, they'll often head for the highest mountain in Peru, **Huascarán**. There are two huge summits separated by a lower saddle giving a sort of double-humped camel look. The south summit at 6,768 meters (22,205 feet), is 113 meters (370 feet) higher than its north sister, and the most frequently climbed.

The hike into base camp begins at the small village of **Musho**, where *arrieros* can be hired to help carry the heavy load of climbing gear and food provisions to the first camp. The trail wanders through farmland and eucalyptus groves for the first few hours, and then a sharp ascent above treeline finally leads to a flat, grassy area known as Huascarán base camp.

Another two hours up a very steep ridge lies the moraine camp and some climbers opt to make it to this point in one day. The load-relieving burros, however, can't make it up this section of the trail, so it means donning the heavy weight and sallying forth.

It's usually on the second or third day when climbers pack up at moraine camp and head for Camp One on the glacier. The hike starts with a scrambling across rock slabs, the path marked with stone carins. At the glacier's edge it's a question of finding the best access to the snow through sometimes massive icefalls.

Once on the glacier, the route up to the next camp will often be "wanded" by previous climbing parties. Small flags are placed at intervals for an easy descent afterwards and to avoid getting lost on the glacier during a "whiteout" when clouds obscure everything. The climb up to Camp One is unforgettable. Wide crevasses yawning deep, icy cracks and pillars of tumbled ice are constant reminders that glaciers are anything but static piles of snow.

Camp One at about 5,200 meters (17,000 feet) is a welcome relief after five to seven hours of traversing the lower glacier, but the pleasure is short-lived as the sun goes down and temperatures drop to well below freezing. It is in this bone-chilling cold that climbers rise early the next morning and prepare to set off for the final high camp at **La Garganta**

(the throat) at 5,790 meters (19,000 feet).

This section is probably the most interesting of the entire climb. About an hour after leaving camp and crossing a wide crevasse, the first technical part of the route appears. A 30-foot, 70 degree ice wall must be climbed, and quickly because it is a natural avalanche chute. Early morning is the best time as the snow pack is still frozen and likely to stay in place. Above the chute, the route remains steep and prone to avalanche activity. It's important, but extremely strenuous, to move as quickly as possible, leaving little chance to rest the aching lungs and reeling head.

At La Garganta Camp it's difficult to make any more of an effort than set up camp and melt and boil snow for a hot drink. Nightfall brings a dazzling array of stars, but the intense cold quickly drives everyone into tents to nestle in warm sleeping bags. At this altitude sleep can be elusive; it's a long night of tossing and turning and trying to stay warm.

Another early morning finds climbers preparing for the summit attempt. Stiff fingers attempt to sort out gear and groggy minds work out the plan ahead. A small blessing is that the heavy equipment can be left behind in camp. All that's needed are spare warm clothes, food, water and a camera for those magnificent summit photos.

The summit route heads up across the saddle between the two peaks of Huascarán, and the climber is treated to a view of distant mountains set ablaze in the early morning sun. Shifting south the climb ascends several steep snow slopes and the first few hours involve zig-zag traverses up and up until the final approach is reached.

Here the abstract concept of "forever" seems to become tangible. Rather than being just one long, gradual slope to the summit, the climber encounters a series of gentle inclines.

From the highpoint of one, all that is seen is yet another. Each time, the climber summons what strength, both mental and physical, is left and trudges on for what he hopes will be the summit view, and each time he finds only another long slog, and no sign of a summit. At this altitude, about 22,000 feet, the breathing becomes so labored that three or four breaths are needed for each step taken. Finally the tricks play out, "forever" is ended, and the summit of the highest mountain in Peru is conquered.

The Andes of Peru have been heavily populated by wildlife for thousands of years. In Inca times all types of Andean wildlife enjoyed a form of protection, and although periodic hunts occurred, these were few and the privilege of the ruling class. After the Spanish conquest and the breakdown of the Inca infrastructure, wild animals were hunted indiscriminately and consequently suffered a population decline which was further advanced by the cutting of high Andean woodlands, which provide essential cover for many animals. Today the persecution of wild animals continues, in some cases because of damage caused by animals to crops, in most cases because of misconceptions. The careful observer, however, can still find a wide variety of Peruvian fauna while traveling in the Andes.

Endangered species: The most conspicuous animals encountered by a visitor to the Peruvian Andes are the cameloids. There are two wild cameloids in Peru, the vicuña and the guanaco. The vicuña, reputed to have the finest wool of any animal, has been brought back from the verge of extinction by the establishment of reserved areas for the species, such as the Pampas Galeras reserve in south-central Peru. They are now to be found in quite large numbers in many areas but are still considered vulnerable. In Inca times, vicuña wool was obtained by running the animal to the ground, picking its fleece by hand and then releasing it. This not only assured a regular supply of wool each year, it also maintained population levels. The modern day illegal hunter resorts to firearms, the primary cause of the vicuña's demise. Prosecution is difficult, however, since the people who possess guns are often influential or otherwise immune. Fortunately, due to the concerted conservation efforts, the vicuña is making a welcome comeback in the Peruvian highlands.

The other wild cameloid of the Andes is the guanaco. This species reaches its northernmost limit in the highlands of central Peru, and from here extends down the Andean chain to the southern tip of South America – Tierra del Fuego. In Peru the guanaco is most likely to be seen in the departments of Tacna, Moquegua, Arequipa and Puno and is to be found in isolated rocky ravines with bunch grass. Guanacos are wild relatives of the llama and alpaca but are at once distinguishable from their domesticated cousins by their bright tawny coloration, similar to that of the vicuña. The exact relationship between domestic llamas and alpacas and the wild guanacos and vicuñas is not clear. All possible crosses of the four cameloids mentioned have been accomplished and the offspring of all crosses are fertile. Most tax-

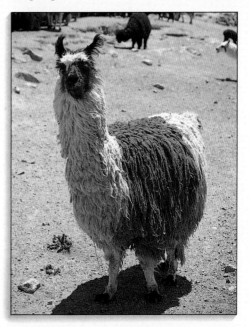

onomists now agree that the domestic llamas and alpacas are a product of the cross breeding of the guanacos and vicuñas. Whatever the relationships, the domesticated cameloids are to be found throughout the Peruvian highlands.

The only natural enemy of the cameloids is the puma or mountain lion. This large tawny, unspotted cat was much revered by the Incas as a symbol of power and elegance. Unfortunately since the conquest, Andean man has lost the conservationist outlook of the Incas, and the puma has suffered dramatically as a result of indiscriminate hunting. The habit of picking off an unwary llama has not endeared the puma to the Quechua peoples, and now it is only possible to catch a fleeting glimpse of this magnificent cat as it crosses remote Andean valleys or stalks mountain viscachas. Two smaller members of the cat family are also to be found in the high Andes. Both species are shy and little is known of their status and habits. The pampas cat (Felis colocolo) is typically an animal of the intermontane Andean valleys although it does occur close to the coast in Northern Peru and in the high cloud forest of the eastern slopes of the Andes. The Andean cat (Felis jacobita) is rarer still and in Peru is limited to the southern highlands. This is a high altitude species, mostly nocturnal, and seems to prey on mountain viscachas. Tracks

Andean woodlands which provides essential cover. The white-tailed deer is still relatively abundant in remoter areas where hunting pressure is low since this species shows a remarkable adaptability to various habitat types. It occurs from the coastal plain (in zones of sufficient vegetation) to 4,000 meters (13,120 feet) above sea level and then into the cloud forest of the eastern slopes of the Andes, down almost to the Amazon basin at 600 meters (1,968 feet). This animal is commonly encountered while hiking in the Andes. Its much rarer relative, the Andean huemal (or taruka as it is known in Peru), is much harder to see. The taruka is a species in danger of extinction and is found at ex-

of this species can be seen at snow line nearly 5,000 meters (16,400 feet) above sea level, but for the short term visitor to the Andes, an encounter with any of the Peruvian wild cats is a rare event indeed.

Woodland creatures: More conspicuous and more commonly seen by backpackers in the highlands are the two species of deer. Both species were once more common than they are now, and the principle cause of their demise is hunting and the cutting of high

tremely high altitudes. Its presence is governed by the availability of cover, mostly small isolated patches of woodland. This type of woodland is disappearing at an alarming rate as it is a primary source of fuel at high altitudes. Consequently the barrel chested, short legged taruka is sadly on the decline. If encountered, it is easily distinguished from the white-tailed deer by its two pronged antlers (the white-tailed deer has one prong only). It is still possible to find this species on the Inca trail to Machu Picchu.

Easier still to see while hiking through the highlands of Peru are the rodents and omnivores. The Andean fox is ubiquitous in all

<u>Left</u>, an ungainly llama. <u>Above</u>, Andean white-tailed deer in mid-flight.

parts of the Andean region, and can be found at all altitudes up to 4,500 meters (14,760 feet). This species of fox is larger and longer legged than its North American and European counterparts and commonly investigates any empty cans or leftover food left outside tents. The Andean fox is everywhere regarded as a dangerous stock killer, especially of sheep. The stomachs of this animal often contain quantities of vicuña wool, but it is not known whether it is a predator of this species or only a carrion eater. Whenever possible, this animal is killed by the local people, yet it remains common.

While walking along stream banks or drystone walls, the observant will notice a black-chested buzzard-eagle, and aplomado falcon. The guinea pig, or *cuy* as it is known in Peru, is domesticated extensively in the Andes, and the wild version is also not uncommon along stony banks and drystone walls, where it lives in colonies. Any Quechua household will have its colony of guinea pigs living in the kitchen area, and the cooked animal is regarded as a delicacy to be eaten on special occasions.

The last two conspicuous animals of the Andes are the hog-nosed skunk and the mountain viscacha. The former which should be familiar to visitors from North America, is mostly nocturnal and can often be picked up in car headlights. The latter is a very

large number of small rodents, ranging from the typical house mouse type familiar to all of us, to mice with a striking combination of chocolate brown and white. It is not that there are a greater number of mice-like creatures in the Andes, but simply that because of very low temperatures at night, most Andean rodents are diurnal. These diurnal rodents are the principle food source of a variety of predators including the Andean weasel (Mustela frenata), a vicious mustelid that will tackle prey twice its size. The abundance of diurnal rodents also accounts for the high density of birds of prey, such as the red-backed and puna hawks, cinereous harrier,

sociable creature commonly found in rock screes and boulder fields. Very well camouflaged, it often betrays its presence with a high pitched whistle. Looking like a cross between a chinchilla and a rabbit, the mountain viscacha can be seen sunning itself on the top of boulders in the eary morning and late afternoon. Mountain viscacha colonies often attract the larger carnivores previously mentioned.

The cloud forest: On the eastern slope of the Andes the environment is dominated by humid temperate forest. Where left undisturbed by man, the forest continues from 3,600 meters (11,800 feet) down to the tropical rainforest of the Amazon basin. The type of forest above 2,500 meters (8,200 feet) is commonly known as "cloud forest", a name derived from the fact that for most of the year the trees are shrouded in mist. Indeed most of the moisture needed by the forest is captured from the enveloping clouds. The cloud forest grades into high grassland at about 3,400 meters (11,200 feet) and harbors some exotic animals that will not be forgotten if glimpsed.

The spectacled bear is perhaps the most impressive animal of the zone. About the size of a North American black bear, this animal is a true omnivore, eating a wide variety of foods such as fruits and berries, large insects, succulent plants and, at high elevations, the lush hearts of terrestrial bromeliads. The spectacled bear will also eat small mammals and rodents when given the opportunity. An important animal in Andean folklore, the bear has a poor reputation among small farmers due to its habit of raiding maize crops at the edge of hill forests. A bear can cause significant economic damage to the smallholder: farmers complain bitterly of the killing of livestock by the spectacled bear. These habits and attributed habits have not boded well for the bear, and it is extensively hunted to the point where population levels are dangerously low.

Other shy inhabitants of the cloud forest include two species of small deer. The larger of the two is the dwarf brocket deer. About half the size of the white-tailed deer, it is found to a height of 3,300 meters (10,800 feet) in the southern Departments of Puno and Cuzco. The other is the pudu, a deer the size of a small dog, difficult to see and mostly nocturnal. It is relentlessly hunted with guns and dogs and must be considered vulnerable at present. Occupying the same habitat as the pudu is the wooly monkey (Logothrix cana), which is found in small family groups where hunting pressure is low. A large primate, the wooly monkey can still be found fairly commonly in the cloud forest beyond the town of Paucartambo on the road to Shintuya in the Department of Cuzco.

The Andes are not just the home of mammals of course, and it is true to say that the south-east Peru has the greatest diversity of

bird life of any place on the planet. The majority of these species occur in the cloud forests and lowland rainforests of the eastern Andean slopes, but a wide variety can be seen right up to the snowline. The bird that first comes to mind when writing of the Andean peaks is of course, the Andean condor. This very large member of the Vulture family is a carrion feeder but is not adverse to starting his meal a little prematurely. The condor is not a hunter and is incapable of grasping or carrying prey, having feet not unlike those of a chicken. (Reports in newspapers of condors carrying off unattended babies must therefore be dismissed.) The sight of a condor sailing

effortlessly against a backdrop of ice-capped Andean peaks will not be forgotten. The condor is still a common sight when hiking through the high country, but much more commonly seen are the smaller songbirds such as sierra-finches, cinclodes, miners and seedsnipes. Once one reaches the limit of the cloud forest, the number of species increase dramatically and birds become more brightly colored. Anyone taking a stroll here in the morning will notice mixed species flocks of brightly colored mountain-tanagers, flycatchers and furnarids moving amongst the moss festooned branches (here birds of a different feather do flock together).

Left, majestic flight. **Above right**, the puma.

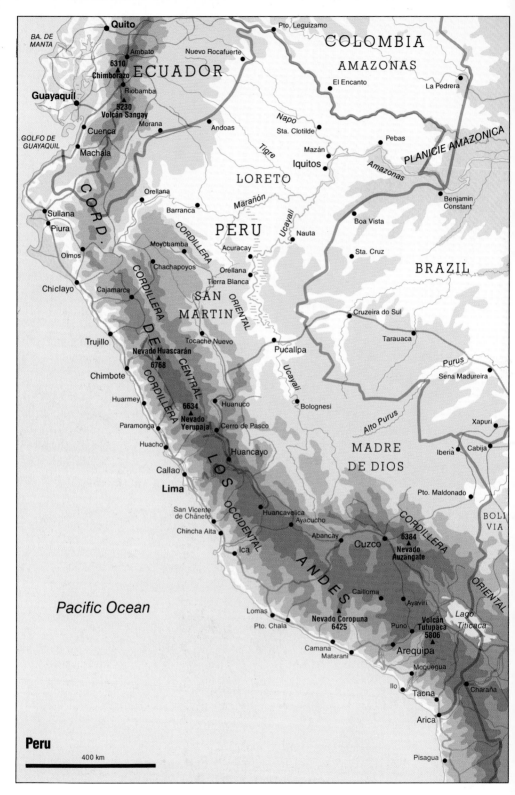

Peru

400 km

EXPLORING PERU

Mapping out an itinerary for Peru might seem a daunting prospect. The country is three times as large as California and many times more varied, with the Andean mountain range and Amazon jungle creating some imposing barriers to travel. Yet journeys that were all but impossible fifty years ago are now everyday events: each of Peru's major cities is linked by safe, modern jet flights; regular coach services run to lesser urban centers; and even tiny mountain villages can be reached on a rattling ancient bus or in the back of one of the ubiquitous Peruvian trucks.

Most travelers to Peru begin their journeys in Lima. As the former center of Spanish South America, it boasts some of the continent's finest colonial architecture as well as Peru's most impressive museums, as well as being the hub for most of the country's domestic flights.

Almost nobody comes to Peru without heading for the ancient Inca capital of Cuzco, and for many people this mountain city is the highlight of their visit. A half-hour flight from Lima – one of the most spectacular on earth – takes travelers straight into the heart of the Andes and this jewel of Inca and colonial architecture. Apart from its own attractions, Cuzco serves as a base to visit the Urubumba valley and what is perhaps the most famous sight in the continent: Machu Picchu. No matter how many times you have seen these ruins in photographs and tourist brochures, nothing will quite prepare you for the reality. Nobody comes away disappointed.

Also in the Andes, Arequipa is one of Peru's most elegant colonial cities set in the shadow of the snow-capped volcano Misti and renowned for its intellectual life. From Cuzco and Arequipa, many travelers fly or take a popular railway journey to Puno, by the shores of Lake Titicaca. The world's highest navigable lake is populated by fascinating Indian communities, who still ply its waters in totora reed canoes.

Increasing numbers of foreign travelers are visiting an area that takes up over half of Peru's land mass: the Amazon basin. In the northern Amazon, the city of Iquitos is the traditional center for beginning tours. And in the south, Puerto Maldonado (reached by flights via Cuzco) has become the gateway to the new Manu National Park, possibly the purest section of rain forest open to visitors in South America.

South of Lima, the Pan-American highway runs along the barren coastal desert to Nazca, whose plains are etched with gigantic drawings made by a mysterious pre-Inca culture, and only visible from the air. Meanwhile, Peru's north has its own distinctive character, with relaxed coastal cities like Trujillo and the beautiful Andean market town of Cajamarca. Then, in the mountains north of Lima is the region of Huaráz, considered by experts to have Peru's most impressive mountain scenery – quite an accolade in a land full of breathtaking views.

Preceding pages: dawn over the Sierra (Sierra); Lacompañia church, Cuzco; putting out to sea near Trujillo.

BATO I IN QUADG
Ad Vesperas Hymnus

AUDI benigne Cón-
ditor, Nostras pre-
ces cum flétibus,
hoc sacro jejúnio
...sas quadragenário.

...erutátor álme córdium,
...firma tu scis vírium:

Ad te revérsis éxhibe
Remissiónis grátiam.

Multum quidem peccávimus
Sed parce confiténtibus:

...i nóminis laudem tui,
...ófer medélam línguidis,
...scede nostrúm córdi...
...púus per abstinénciam...
...per ut reliquum pábuli...
...rébeit a Trínitas...
...les Simplex Trinitas...
...aboósa sint tui...
...uni ménora ténue...

SABBATO

DOMINICAM PASSIONE

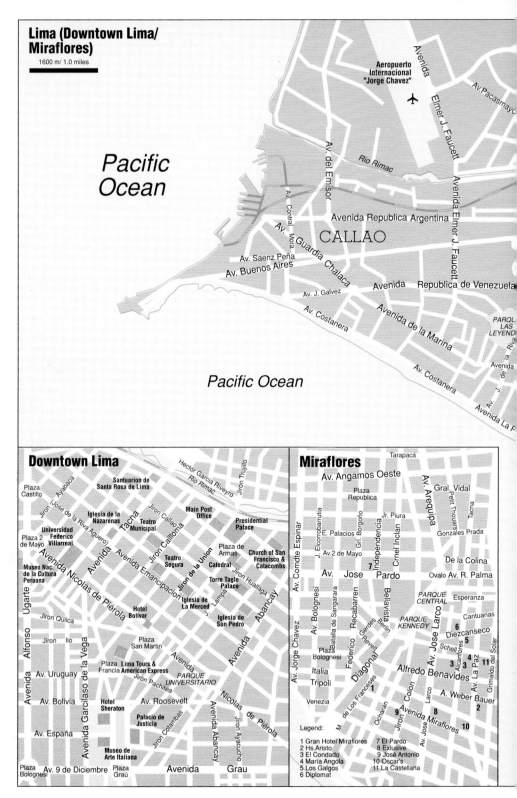

Lima (Downtown Lima/ Miraflores)

1600 m/ 1.0 miles

Pacific Ocean

Aeropuerto Internacional "Jorge Chavez"

Av. del Emisor

Rio Rimac

Av. Pacasmayo

Elmer J. Faucett

Avenida Elmer J. Faucett

Avenida

Avenida Republica Argentina

CALLAO

Av. Contra Mora

Av. Guardia Chalaca

Av. Saenz Peña

Av. Buenos Aires

Av. J. Galvez

Republica de Venezuela

Avenida

Av. Costanera

Avenida de la Marina

PARQU LAS LEYEND

la Riv

Avenida

Av. Costanera

Av. J.

Avenida La P

Pacific Ocean

Downtown Lima

Plaza Castillo

Santuarion de Santa Rosa de Lima

Hector Garcia Riveyro

Rio Rimac

Jiron Trujillo

Ayabaca

Jiron (Jose de la Riva Aguero)

Iglesia de la Nazarenas

Tacna

Jiron Callao

Teatro Municipal

Main Post Office

Presidential Palace

Universidad Federico Villarreal

Avenida Nicolas de Piérola

Avenida

Jiron Callona

Avenida Emancipacion

Jiron Callona

Teatro Segura

Jiron de la Union

Plaza de Armas

Church of San Francisco & Catacombs

Plaza 2 de Mayo

Catedral

Jiron Huallaga

Catedral

Torre Tagle Palace

J. Lampa

Museo Nac. de la Cultura Peruana

Ugarte

Jiron Quilca

Hotel Bolivar

Iglesia de La Merced

Iglesia de San Pedro

Jiron Ilo

Alfonso

Avenida Garcilaso de la Vega

Plaza San Martin

Avenida

Abancay

Av. Uruguay

Plaza Lima Tours & Francia American Express

Avenida

Jiron Pachitea

PARQUE UNIVERSITARIO

Av. Bolivia

Hotel Sheraton

Av. Roosevelt

Nicolas de Piérola

Av. España

Palacio de Justicia

Jiron Cotanbas

Avenida Abancay

Jiron Ayacucho

Museo de Arte Italiana

Plaza Bolognesi

Av. 9 de Diciembre

Plaza Graú

Avenida

Grau

Miraflores

Tarapacá

Av. Angamos Oeste

Plaza Republica

Gral. Vidal

Av. Arequipa

Petit Thouars

Tacna

Jr. Piura

Crnel Inclan

Gonzales Prada

J. Elcorrobarrutia

E. Palacios

Gdl. Borgoño

Independencia

Av. Comdte Espinar

Av.2 de Mayo

7

De la Colina

Av. Jose Pardo

Ovalo Av. R. Palma

Av. Bolognesi

Av. Jorge Chavez

Batalla de Sangarara

Federico Recabarren

Gerdes Berlin

Bellavista

Revell

PARQUE CENTRAL

Esperanza

PARQUE KENNEDY

Cantuarias

6

Diezcanseco

Av. Jose Larco

Schellfors

Alcanfores

3

4

Alfredo Benavides

La Paz

11

Grimaldo del Solar

Plaza Bolognesi

Italia

Diagonal

M. de los Franceses

Colon

A. Weber Bauer

2

Tripoli

Venezia

Ocharan

9

Jiron

Larco

Avenida Miraflores

Av. Jose

8

10

Legend:
1 Gran Hotel Miraflores
2 Hs.Aristo
3 El Condado
4 María Angola
5 Los Galgos
6 Diplomat
7 El Pardo
8 Exlusive
9 José Antonio
10 Oscar's
11 La Castellana

marra de L.Velarde

enida Toma Valle

Panamericana Norte

Cerro la Milla ▲

Avenida Tupac Amaru

SAN MARTIN DE PORRAS

Av. Peru

Av. E. de Habich

A. Pizarro

Av. Zarumilla

Rio Rimac

Av. Mayor Elespuru

Av. S. Alcazar

Cerro Arrastre Bajo ▲

Musea Virreynal

Av. Tacna

H. Garcia Riveyro

Av. Caqueta

RIMAC

Plaza de Toros (Achos)

Cerro Attilo ▲

SAN JUAN DE LURIGANCHO

Cerro Lurigancho ▲

de la Independencia

Av. Malecon M. Checa Eguifuren

Rio Rimac

Avenida Republica Argentina

(Avenida Colonial)

Av. A. Ugarte

Av. G. de la Vega

Catedral (Cathedral)

Av. Abancay

Rio Rimac

Jirón

Ancash

Jirón Ancash

EL AGUSTINO

Cerro El Agustino ▲

Via de Evitamiento

Rio Surco

enida Republica de Venezuela

Av. Tingo Maria

Av. Arica

Inset Downtown Lima

Avenida

Grau

Autopista a Chosica

seo Arqueolog. .. Herrera

Museo Nacional de Historia

Avenida Brasil

PARQUE JAPONES

Paseo de la Reserva

Avenida 28 de Julio

Av. Aviacion

Mercado Mayorista

Av. Chosica

Av. Chosica

Rio Surco

Via de

Museo ológico y ueologico

la Marina

Av. Sucre

Avenida

Av. Sucre

Hospital Central No.2

Av. Mariategui

Bolivar

Salaverry

Avenida Arequipa

PARQUE DE LA RESERVA

de

la

Avenida Mexico

Av. San Nicolas Arriola

Av.

Av. San Luis

Rio Surco

Avenida Brasil

Av. F.S. Carrion

Museo de Historia Natural J. Prado

Av. Canada

PARQUE UNION PANAMERICANA

Av. Canada

Avenida

Republica

Av. Nicolas Arriola

Av. Canada

SAN LUIS

GOLF CLUB

.Perez Aranibar

Avenida Javier Prado

Avenida Javier Prado

CAMPO DE GOLF

Jac. Lara

Av. los Conquistadores

Avenida Arequipa

Paseo de la

Av. del Aire

Avenida San Luis

Avenida Aviacion

Avenida Panamericana Sur

Hippodromo de Monterrico

POTA CLUB

Av. Perez Aranibar

PARQUE TAHUANTINSUYO

Avenida

Paseo de la

Panama

Avenida Tomas Marzano

Av. Principal

Angamos

Avenida Angamos

Ministn. de Guerra

Av. Velasco Astete

Av. Wilca Umo

Av. Jose Pardo

Av. Larco

Av. M. Benavides

Avenida

Republica

Benavides

Avenida Panama

Av. Benavides

Av. Caminos del Inca

Av. Reynaldo Vivanco

Av. Panamericana Sur

Cerro San Francisco ▲

Inset Miraflores

Pacific Ocean

Avenida Panama

Av. Balta

Rio Surco

Avenida Tomas Marzano

SURCO

Av. Panamericana

Sur

Avenida Pachacutec

LIMA

Herman Melville called **Lima** "the saddest city on earth". Many visitors agree with him, while residents have been even less complimentary – "Lima the horrible", was how writer Sebastian Salazar Bondy described his native city in the early 1960s. But the tourist who is tempted to take such descriptions – and his or her own first impressions – at face value risks missing out on a city of rare fascination and unexpected pleasures. And while locals may gripe, most have an enduring love-hate relationship with their paradoxical city. Lima has both decaying colonial splendour and the teeming vitality of an oriental bazaar; melancholy cloudy winters and warm breezy summers; impoverished urban sprawl and quiet, elegant corners among ancient buildings where the night air is scented with jasmin.

The City of Kings: Lima was founded by the Spanish *conquistador* Francisco Pizarro on January 5 1535, the eve of the Epiphany of the Magi – from which it derived its evocative original name of La Cuidad de los Reyes or "The City of Kings". Pizarro traced a grid of thirteen streets by nine to form 117 city blocks on the site of an existing indigenous settlement beside the southern bank of the River Rimac (from which the name Lima seems subsequently to have been derived). But the city's first inhabitants numbered fewer than a hundred *conquistadores*.

Pizarro had originally made his capital at Jauja, in the Andes. The rapid switch was determined by his strategic need to be close to his ships – his only lifeline in a rebellious country that was still largely unconquered. The Rimac valley provides the best line of communication through the Andean peaks to the interior of central Peru while the rivers Chillon and Lurin also reach the sea within the present-day boundaries of the city, making the site one of the best-watered in the coastal desert. Several *huacas*, or funeral mounds, along with other pre-Colombian ruins, survive in greater Lima as testimony that the area was populated before the conquest. Indeed, the most important pre-Inca religous site in coastal Peru was nearby at Pachacamac.

The only drawback was the future city's micro-climate. Because of a meteorological phenomenon known as thermal inversion, Lima is draped in a damp blanket of low cloud from May to October, though the summers are agreeable. And though the visitor may often forget the fact, seeing exuberant gardens of yellow amancaes or purple bougainvillea (the product of careful irrigation), rainfall rarely amounts to more than a few nights of winter drizzle, insufficient to wash the desert dust from the facades of buildings that require frequent repainting.

Spain's capital in the New world: For two centuries after its foundation, Lima was the political, commercial and ecclesiastical capital of Spanish South America, the seat of the Inquisition as well as the Viceroys. But its beginnings were modest, and gave little clue to its later splendour. The *mestizo* chronicler Garcilaso de la Vega described it as having "very broad and very straight streets, so that from any of its crossroads the countryside can be seen in all four directions", adding that the houses were roofed with reeds rather than tiles. But by the early-17th century, Lima's population had risen to about 25,000, the majority of them Indian servants and artisans or African slaves. In the 1680s a protective wall with 12 gateways was built around the city, because of fears of raids by English privateers. (The wall was demolished in the 1870s, although fragments can still be seen beside the railway line in Barrios Altos.) Despite being frequently damaged by earthquakes, the city was rich as well as powerful. Palaces and churches, mansions and monasteries were rebuilt and expanded while across the river pleasure gardens for the aristocracy were carefully laid out.

Lima's gradual decline from pre-eminence began in the late 18th century, as new Vice Royalties were created in Bogotá and Buenos Aires and the city's monopoly on trade between Europe and South America was broken. As befitted a royalist city, independence from Spain came from outside, as expeditionary forces, first from Argentina under José de San Martín and subsequently from Colombia under Simón Bolívar, occupied the city. Installed as Republican Peru's dictator in the suburb of Magdalena, even the stern Bolívar was affected by Lima's sybaritic elegance. It was at a ball in Lima that Bolívar met and fell in love with Manuela Saenz, the Ecuadorean wife of a British doctor who was to become "the Liberator's" lifelong companion.

Bursting urban boundaries: After a period of stagnation immediately after independence, the city's development resumed in the mid-19th century. The first railway in South America opened between Lima and its port of Callao in 1854, followed swiftly by further lines to connect the city with the growing coastal villages of Miraflores and Chorillos. But setbacks followed, as Lima was occupied and partially sacked by Chilean troops in 1881 during the disastrous War of the Pacific. It was only early in the 20th century that the city burst its 17th century Spanish limits and embarked on a process of change and growth that has lasted to the present day, the product both of massive migration from the Andean hinterland and the decline of the aristocracy as Peru moved falteringly towards democracy. The outline of the modern city dates from the beginning of this period. Industry began to spread westwards along the Callao railway, and up the central highway to Vitarte in the east. The building of Paseo Colón and Avenida Nicolas de Piérola or La Colmena (beginning in 1898) and of the Plaza San Martín (1921) created new arteries and a new central focus to the south of Pizarro's Plaza de Armas. The rising urban upper middle class moved away from the crowded center to the spacious south, towards Miraflores and the new district of San Isidro, laid out as a leafy garden suburb. Working class suburbs sprung up over the river in Rimac, in El

Mall in the Correo Central.

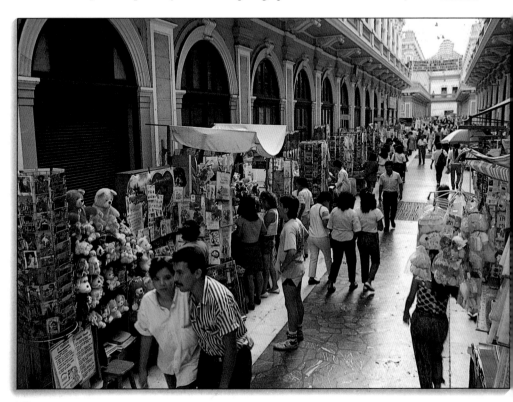

Agustino to the east and La Victoria to the south-east. By 1931, Lima's population had reached 280,000, having doubled in little more than two decades.

In the sixty years since then, two trends have given Lima its present urban structure. Infill development of middle-class suburbs has completed a triangle enclosing the area between the city centre, Callao and Chorillos. Outside this triangle, Andean migrants made their homes in sprawling self-built shanty towns stretching north, south and north-east, occupying the vacant desert sands in the shadow of the Andean foothills. The shanty towns now contain perhaps half the city's estimated population of 6 million. Starting as squatter land invasions of rush matting huts, decades of hard work have turned some into pleasant districts. Many others remain desperately poor, lacking electricity, piped water or paved streets. But the migrants and their children have changed the character of the city irrevocably. They may be poor, but they are not idle. In the face of massive

The Plaza de Armas.

unemployment, many have created their own jobs as street vendors, thronging the streets of the city centre. In turn, the business elite has moved its offices out from the centre to San Isidro, and the wealthy have created new residential districts in the Andean foothills in Monterrico and La Molina.

The colonial heart: The usual starting point to exploring Lima is the **Plaza de Armas**. Stand in the middle of this spacious and handsome square, by the 17th-century bronze fountain, and you are at the historic heart of the city. Though most of the buildings are later reconstructions, the spirit of Pizarro permeates the square. On the north side is the **Government Palace**, on the site of Pizarro's own house. The present building (which is not open to the public) was completed in 1938, and suffers from the taste of Peru's dictators of the time for grandiose French baroque. But much of the groundplan at the rear remains the same as in Pizarro's day. On weekdays at 12.45 p.m., you can catch the changing of the guard, performed in the front

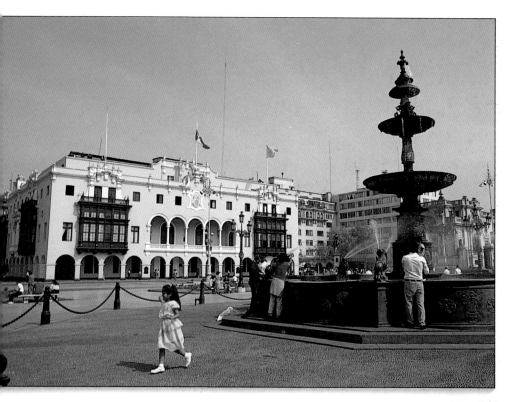

courtyard by goose-stepping troops from the Hussares de Junin regiment, dressed in the red and blue ceremonial uniforms and ornamental helmets of the independence period.

The eastern side of the square is dominated by the **Cathedral**, again on the site chosen by Pizarro, but reconstructed several times after earthquakes. The present building was begun in the 18th century. Much of the exterior was painted in yellow-ochre in the mid-1980s, as part of a successful policy to brighten up dusty facades with colours used in the colonial period. Inside, the Cathedral is large and unusually austere. Notable are the 17th-century wooden choir stalls. To the right of the entrance is a small side chapel dedicated to Pizarro. His skeleton is here in a sealed wooden coffin. It was found in 1977 during excavations in the Cathedral crypt and put on display in 1985, to mark Lima's 450th anniversary. (It replaced the remains of an anonymous *conquistador*, long mistakenly thought to have been Pizarro). Next door to the Cathe-

dral is the **Archbishop's Palace**, rebuilt in the 1920s with an impressive wooden balcony.

Opposite the Cathedral is the **Municipalidad de Lima,** or town hall, built in the 1940s after fire destroyed its predecessor. The pleasant interior includes a fine library. Next to it on the square is the headquarters of the **Club de la Union**, a lunchtime haunt of politicians and professionals. Between them at the mouth of Pasaje Santa Rosa is a monument, in the form of a large chunk of rough-hewn stone, to Taulichusco El Viejo, the last *cacique* (chief) of pre-conquest Lima, unveiled in 1985 as a belated antidote to the ghost of Pizarro. The fourth, southern side of the Plaza de Armas contains shops and offices.

To the left of the palace, in a small side square, stands an equestrian statue of the ubiquitous Pizarro. Behind him, the building topped with antennae houses an office of Peru's National Intelligence Service; to the left is the Café Haiti, with tables on the pavement – a good place for a coffee and a rest while sightseeing.

Bones in the San Fransico catacombs.

Nearby is the **Cental Post Office**, its offices grouped around a handsome neoclassical arcade, whose roof is sadly missing most of its glass. Further up towards the river are a couple of splendid old hat shops, where you can acquire a felt stetson for US$11 or a Panama for US$6. Round the corner lies a taste of Lima's contemporary social reality – the booming contraband market of **Polvos Azules**, selling Chilean wine, Scotch whisky, watches and cigarettes much cheaper than in the shops (it also sells handcrafts). It is usually packed with shoppers. Thieves abound, and tourists should take great care of their valuables. (This warning goes for the whole of the city centre. Until you become accustomed to Lima, you would also be best advised not to wander alone in the center by night.)

Doubling back into the Plaza de Armas again, to the right of the Presidential Palace is a charming street corner (the intersection of Jiron Carabaya and Jr. Junin) that contains the oldest buildings in the square (dating from the early 18th century), with the wooden balconies in the form of enclosed galleries projecting on the first floor that were colonial Lima's most graceful feature. Further up Carabaya, past several shoe shops (hand-stitched cowboy boots made to measure for about US$100) is the **Desamparados Station**, the terminal for the Central Railway to Huancayo, a neo-classical building painted in green and white and dating from 1908. Opposite the station, on the corner of Jr. Ancash, is the **Cordano restaurant** – tasty Peruvian food served in an old-fashioned dining room. There are several cheap hotels popular with back-packers in this area.

Ancient books and bones: Walk along Jr. Ancash and you come to the **San Francisco Monastery**, the jewel of colonial Lima. Even if you are not a fan of colonial churches, don't miss this one. The monastery faces a small paved square, full of pigeons and portrait photographers. The outside is currently painted in a pink wash. But it is the interior that is fascinating, much of it is

Visiting the new Museo de la Nación.

decorated in the geometrical Mudejar (Andalusian Moorish) style. Founded in 1546, it was heavily damaged by an earthquake in 1646, reconstruction being completed in 1672. Outstanding features include the 17th-century library, with 25,000 leather bound volumes and 6,000 parchments dating from the 15th to the 18th centuries. The cupola has a superb Mudejar carved wooden ceiling of Panamanian cedar, dating from 1625. In a gallery above the nave of the church are 130 choir stalls and 71 panels with carvings of Franciscan saints, of the same wood. Recent work has exposed (under eight layers of paint) 17th-century murals in the cloister and adjacent chambers. The monastery's collection of religious art includes paintings by the Rubens and Zurbaran workshops and a *Last Supper* attributed to Van Dyck. San Francisco has survived more recent earthquakes because of its catacombs, used as Lima's cementary until 1810. A network of underground chambers open to the public contain hundreds of skulls and bones, stored in racks according to

type. A secret passage (now bricked up) led from here to the government palace.

There are half a dozen other colonial churches in the centre, but most will be mainly of interest to the specialist. **Santo Domingo monastery** (on the corner of Jiron Camana and Conde de Superunda, just past the Post Office) has a pleasant cloister with Sevillian tiling. Its church contains an urn with the ashes of Santa Rosa of Lima, the patron saint of the New World and the Philippines. **San Pedro Church** (Jiron Azangaro) is for lovers of baroque and gold leaf altars. The **Sanctuary of Santa Rosa** (Av. Tacna) contains relics of Santa Rosa. **Las Nazarenas** (also Av. Tacna) houses the image of El Señor de los Milagros (The Lord of Miracles), the black Christ painted by a freed Negro slave which has become the most important focus of popular religiosity in Lima. On three occasions in October, the image is borne around the streets of the city centre on a one-ton litter by teams of men wearing the purple robes of the brotherhood of El Señor de los Milagros. Hundreds of thousands of people turn out to accompany the image in what is one of the largest public gatherings in South America.

Colonial mansions: The city centre also contains several fine examples of secular colonial architecture. Outstanding is the **Torre Tagle Palace**, completed in 1735. It houses the Foreign Ministry, but tourists are allowed into the courtyard and can see the finely carved wooden balconies. It gives a good idea of the opulence of Lima in its colonial prime. Opposite, in another colonial mansion, is the **L'Eau Vive Restaurant**, run by French-speaking nuns. They serve excellent and reasonably-priced French cooking; customers are encouraged to join them in singing the Ave Maria at 10 p.m. each evening. Also worth visiting is the **Casa de Osambela**, in Jr Conde Superunda, a late 18th-century mansion with an ornamental cupola, beautifully restored between 1982 and 1984. It houses a small art gallery and the offices of various cultural institutions and is open to the public. Conde de Superunda is one of several streets in the center

Colonial altar.

with good colonial balconies. Many others are in a sad state of decay. Other colonial buildings include the **Casona de San Marcos**, in Parque Universitario, the original site of San Marcos University, founded in 1551 and the oldest university in the Western Hemisphere. The Casona contains a library and is used for meetings and seminars. (Most of the University's activities moved in the 1940s to a large campus on Av. Venezuela.) Visits to other colonial houses in the centre can be arranged through the Lima Tours travel agency.

The **Puente de Piedra** or stone bridge behind the Presidential Palace, built in Roman style in 1610 (its mortar reputedly bound with thousands of egg whites for strength), leads over the river to **Rimac**, once the playground of the aristocracy and now a lively working class district. The Hatuchay peña (nightclub with Peruvian music and dancing), popular with both tourists and locals, is in Jr. Trujillo. At the **Plaza de Acho** is the **Bullring**, the oldest in the Americas and with a small museum including some Goya prints. The bullfight season is in October and November. Behind the large Backus and Johnston brewery (founded 1879) and at the foot of the **San Cristóbal hill** is the **Alameda de los Descalzos**, laid out in 1610 as a pleasure garden with statues and wrought iron railings, but now tatty. It leads to the **Monastery of the Descalzos** (barefoot friars), recently restored. To the right is the **Paseo de Aguas**, another pleasure garden created in the 18th century by Viceroy Amat for his famous mistress La Pericholi, but also in need of repair. Nearby is the **Quinta de Presa**, a mansion in 18th-century French roccoco style, now the Museum of the Viceroyalty.

Republican Lima: Six blocks south of the Plaza de Armas is the **Plaza San Martín**, the hub of the contemporary city center. The two squares are linked by the pedestrianised **Jirón de la Union**, once Lima's most elegant shopping street. As recently as the 1940s it was considered scandalous for women to stroll along Jirón de la Union without wearing a hat. Now it is a teeming mass of street vendors, shoppers, and fast-food joints. All human life is here, including an Andean version of *tombola* in which prizes are decided by a guinea pig scuttling at random into one of a number of small cardboard arches set up on the pavement. From time to time the police clear the street of vendors, but these attempts to repress reality never last long.

The colonnaded Plaza San Martín, its buildings painted red several years ago, is an important gathering place used for political meetings. In the center is an equestrian statue of José de San Martín, Peru's Argentine independence hero. The square is shabby but lively, thronged with clowns, storytellers and, at weekends, by courting couples or domestic servants or soldiers on their day-off. On its west side is the **Hotel Bolívar**, built in the 1920s. Though now it often seems to have more elderly waiters and bellboys than guests, the hotel retains much of its former atmosphere. A Palm Court trio serenades afternoon tea in the domed lobby, while its giant Pisco Sours (called

Skyscraper in Miraflores.

"Cathedrals") remain justly famous. Even if you are not staying here, the Bolívar is the perfect place to stop and rest during a city tour.

Next to the Bolívar is **Jiron Ocoña**, the center of Lima's street foreign exchange market, where money changers buy or sell dollars round the clock. The market is sophisticated – in times of high inflation, rates change hourly and are communicated by walkie-talkie throughout the city. Across La Colmena from the Bolívar is the **Club Nacional**. The watering hole of Peru's once all-powerful oligarchy, it has become an anachronism since business and the elite abandoned the city center. On the opposite side of the square, above a fast-food bakery, is the **Phoenix Club**, a British businessman's club, while a third club, the **Circulo Militar** is on the north side. Next door is a small shop of the **Instituto Geográfico Militar**, selling good maps of Peru.

A city full of museums: Lima has more than a score of museums and visitors will want to make their own selection.

But don't miss the **Museum of Anthropology and Archaeology** in the Plaza Bolívar in the suburb of Pueblo Libre. It is one of the most interesting museums in South America, with a superb collection of pottery and textiles from all the main cultures of ancient Peru, as well as stone idols from Chavín. It is well laid out, in chronological order and the curators have resisted the temptation to swamp the visitor with too many exhibits. (Next door is the **Museum of the Republic** or National History Museum, in a mansion Bolívar lived in during his stay in Lima, with exhibits from the colonial and independence periods.)

Second on the list is the **National Museum**, opened in 1990 in a neo-brutalist mausoleum on Av. Javier Prado Oeste in San Borja. It was built in the 1970s as the Fisheries Ministry and subsequently used as the National Bank. The Museum is not yet complete, and should improve each year. So far it has relied on loans from private collections and other museums. It contains im-

The Bridge of Sighs in Barranco.

pressive mock-ups of pre-Colombian archaeological sites, and an ingenious replica of the Chavín *stela*, a massive carved stone idol. The museum's large models of Machu Picchu and other Inca sites are a good preparation for Cuzco. See also the exhibition of Peruvian costume on the ground floor.

The **Gold Museum** (Av. Alonso de Molina in Monterrico) contains a private collection with some fine items but suffers from overcrowding of exhibits and poor labelling. There is also a collection of armaments. The **Rafael Larco Herrera Museum** (Av. Bolívar, Pueblo Libre) has good pre-Colombian pottery and textiles, but also suffers from overcrowded layout. A small annexe holds a fascinating and amusing collection of erotic pottery.

The **Museum of the Inquisition** (Plaza Bolívar, next to Congress in the city center) is in the building where generations of supposed heretics were tortured and tried. See the main hall (a fine 18th-century wooden ceiling) and the underground dungeons and torture chambers. The stocks are original, while there are mock-ups of other torture techniques. It's a grim and macabre reminder that the torments inflicted by recent Latin American military dictatorships have a long history.

The modern capital: Two main arteries, the Avenida Arequipa and the Paseo de la Republica expressway, connect the city center with the business district of **San Isidro** (pause at the **Bosque del Olivar**, an attractive olive grove reputedly planted in Pizarro's day and now a park) and **Miraflores**, the main area for shopping, restaurants, cafés and theatres. Av. Larco is the main shopping street. Good, though expensive handicrafts are sold in Av. La Paz (cheaper are the handicraft markets on Avenida La Marina, on the way to the airport). At the top end of Av. Larco is the **Parque Kennedy**, where artists sell paintings at the weekend. Here next to the Pacifico cinema is the **Café Haiti**, a prime spot for people-watching. Round the corner in Ricardo Palma, is the more upmarket **Vivaldi café**, while down the Diagonal

Looking out at La Rosa Nautica restaurant at Costa Verde, Miraflores.

is a pedestrianised side street crammed with pizzerias with open-air tables, a haunt of upper middle-class teenagers. Continue down the Diagonal and you reach the cliffs overlooking the Pacific, laid out with gardens – a lovely place to watch the sunset. A cobbled road leads down a gulley to the **Costa Verde**, as the sweep of beaches is called. Though Limeños flock here in thousands to bathe on summer Sundays, the sea is polluted – the resorts to the south are better for swimming. But the Costa Verde is an attractive place for a stroll or a drive – the coast road sweeps on round (with fine views of the city) to the isolated beach of **La Herradura**, a popular spot to eat *ceviche* (the delicious Peruvian dish of fish marinaded in lemon juice with onion and hot pepper) while watching the Pacific breakers. Closer to Miraflores are two superb fish restaurants (international prices) – the Costa Verde on the beach, and the Rosa Nautica, built on a pier surrounded by the ocean.

From La Herradura, the road doubles back through a tunnel to **Chorillos**, an interesting area of mixed social composition high on the sandy cliffs. Down on the beach is a fishing wharf, where small boats can be hired by the hour. Moving back towards Miraflores we come to **Barranco**, a beautiful district of colonial and 19th-century housing, much of it recently restored and in excellent condition.

This romantic neighborhood is the home of many bohemians, writers and artists (including Mario Vargas Llosa, the novelist) and is celebrated in Peruvian waltzes. It has recently become the centre of the city's nightlife, with a score or more of peñas and bars where music of all kinds is played. Opposite the attractive main square is the wooden **Puente de Los Suspiros** or Bridge of Sighs, a traditional meeting place for lovers set among gardens overlooking the Pacific.

The Pacific port: Now joined to Lima, the port of **Callao** was originally a settlement apart, 6 miles west of the city on a low-lying bay. Though Callao is now poor and tatty, it has several points of interest. Permission is required to enter the docks, but at the wharf next door launches take passengers for trips round the bay. Along the shore is the **Yacht Club**, with a good restaurant open to visitors for lunches. Behind the docks, there is an area of colonial housing with balconies, though in poor repair. Nearby is the 18th-century **Real Felipe Fort**, the last Royalist redoubt in Peru. It was captured by Bolívar's forces in 1826 after a year-long seige. It now contains an interesting **Military Museum**.

Finally, on the outskirts of Lima, 20 miles south of the centre, are the ruins of **Pachacamac**, once the largest pre-Colombian settlement on the Peruvian coast. The cult surrounding its idol was so important that Pizarro sent his brother Hernando on a lengthy detour to destroy it in 1533. The ruins of the original pre-Inca temple occupy a large site crowning a low sandhill overlooking the ocean. The temple complex was expanded under the Incas and there is an interesting reconstruction of the Inca Temple of the Virgins.

Left, Pedro Osma Museum. **Right**, summer swimming on the Costa Verde.

PERU'S HIGH-PROFILE NOVELIST

Mario Vargas Llosa is Peru's best known intellectual and novelist, the author of works such as *The War of the End of the World* and *Aunt Julia and the Scriptwriter*. Possessed of a precocious literary talent, he first emerged as a hot property in international publishing in the 1960s, a youthful prodigy of the "boom" in Latin American fiction.

He has not been content to remain simply his country's chronicler. Though the continent's intellectuals have rarely shunned politics, few have sought such an active political role as Vargas. But the novelist's bid to become President of his country in 1990 ended in a failure as resounding as his literary success.

Prodigious output: Vargas Llosa, the author of ten novels, three plays and a prolific essayist, was born in Arequipa into a middle-class family in 1936. His parents were estranged, and he scarcely knew his family until he was ten. He went to school in the northern city of Piura and the Military College in Lima. Both were to provide material for books. His first novel, translated as *The Time of the Hero* and set in the Military College, is a taut exploration of adolescence lived in a closed, authoritarian world. The military authorities responded by burning copies of the book on a public bonfire.

Vargas Llosa is a meticulous and sophisticated stylist, a conscious craftsman of words. For many Peruvians, his greatest novel remains *Conversation in the Cathedral* – a complex, multi-layered tableau of power and its perversions, set mainly in Lima in the 1950s during the dictatorship of General Odria. But Vargas Llosa himself prefers *The War of the End of the World*, his 1981 historical novel about a fanatical backwoods rebellion in turn-of-the-century Brazil.

"Peru is for me a kind of incurable disease," he has written, "and my feeling for her is intense, bitter, and full of the violence that characterizes passion." But to express that passion in writing, he chose to live in Europe for 16 years, returning to Peru mainly for summer vacations to his impressive house,

Mario Vargas Llosa, a man as intense as his works.

on a cliff overlooking the Pacific in Barranco, Lima.

As a student at Lima's San Marcos University, he briefly joined the Communist Party. He remained a man of the left for almost two decades before gradually mutating into a supporter of the radical Right, an admirer of British Prime Minister Margaret Thatcher and a bitter detractor of the Cuban revolution he once defended. Vargas himself identifies a common thread in his political positions: an ongoing concern for freedom of expression.

Push for the presidency: Vargas's plunge into active politics began when he led a public campaign in opposition to President Garcia's bid to nationalise the country's private banks. Out of this came, first, a political movement called "Libertad" (Freedom), and then a presidential candidacy for the right-of-center Democratic Front which Vargas used to expound a radical free market economic program, promising to sell-off all of Peru's state companies.

It was a strange role for someone who once said that "when politics invades…the writer dies." But this was not the only paradox. "I left my books because I think there is a real, immediate possibility of changing the history of Peru," he told his final campaign rally. Uttered by a character in one of his novels this might be intended to reveal the kind of dangerous, messianic obsession that is a favourite Vargas Llosa theme. The underlying contradiction was between the writer who frequently claims to be an enemy of absolute truths and the politician who preached a doctrinaire liberalism as the only way to "modernize" Peru.

Though Vargas Llosa has written so penetratingly about his country, the campaign suggested that he lacked an understanding of the aspirations and perceptions of ordinary Peruvians. They turned their backs on him. Vargas slipped 20 points in the opinion polls in a month, before finally losing decisively to Alberto Fujimori. Within days, the novelist was on a plane to London, where he owns a flat in Knightsbridge, saying that some time in the future he would write a novel about his experiences.

LIMA'S OASIS OF HOPE

Villa El Salvador is a microcosm of Peru's past, present and future. Tucked behind the sand dunes not far from the Inca shrine of Pachacamac, about 30 km (19 miles) south of Lima, it is more than just another shanty town bundled together by homeless Andean migrants in search of the Big City. It is a fiery prototype of self-determination by Peru's marginalized Indian majority. Villa El Salvador has prospered in an era of national decline.

Founded in May 1971 by an initial wave of 10,000 migrants who had fled from the mountains around Huaráz in the wake of an earthquake, its first martyr was Edilberto Ramos. He was shot dead resisting police efforts to expel the settlers. His death forced the government to hand over the desert. Reed huts blossomed, numbers swelled, schools were built and a parish installed. The newly-born shanty town or *pueblo jovén* was named after the image of Christ the Savior.

Today, about 300,000 people live here. Most of the houses are of adobe bricks or concrete. Most have drainage and are connected to water and electricity. The community is crisscrossed by roads and dotted generously with poplar, eucalyptus, pomegranate and banana trees.

Reclaiming the desert: Little by little, clever irrigation, its ingenuity worthy of the inhabitants' Inca forebears, has converted hundreds of hectares of sandy desert into arable land: fruit and cotton are grown, as are corn and fodder crops for the thousands of privately and communally-owned cattle whose milk and cheese are sold locally. The secret is that the agricultural zone is watered with processed sewage.

"We are the only district of Lima which does not throw its sewage into the sea," says the former mayor, Michel Azcueta, a leading member of the United Left, a broad socialist coalition which enjoys the historic support of most residents. "We are now trying to collect the sewage from the surrounding districts in order to irrigate the rest of the desert." Sewage ponds, which have been built with foreign grants, are perfumed off by a curtain of eucalyptus trees.

Villa El Salvador's success has enjoyed international recognition. It has been nominated for the Nobel Peace Prize, won Spain's prestigious Prince of Asturias award for social achievement and has been designated by the United Nations as a Messenger of Peace. Its key is the Andean tradition of community organization centered on the family unit.

Each block of houses or *manzana* comprises 24 families; 16 blocks make up a residential group and 22 of these form a sector. Health centers, communal kitchens and sports grounds bond each group to-

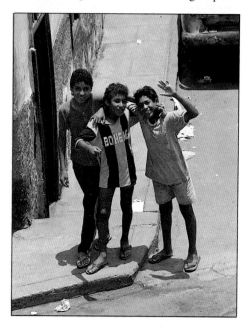

gether. The powerful sense of local identity, forged by collective action in combating poverty with no expectations of help from a poor and neglectful central government, has also kept terrorism at bay. Shining Path militants have been unable to penetrate the community without being quickly exposed. Common crime is at unusually low levels in the area, too.

Hope for the future: "We have proved that Peru has a way forward despite the absence of state investment," said Mr Azcueta. "The municipality gives land titles to the communtiy – *perestroika* came here years ago! Villa reactivates itself because bad leaders are voted out. We are learning all the time. The community is an example of new Peru, a mixture of the Andes and the coast."

Carnival (February), which is profoundly perceived as a rite of the renovation of life, features the *Yunsa* fiesta in which presents hanging from a tree fall to the ground while it is struck in turn by the participants' axes. He whose axe finally fells the tree must provide the tree the following year.

Fifteen libraries, a community radio station and all kinds of written bulletins demonstrate the determination to communicate and the striking belief, by no means visible in the urban slums of many richer countries, that education genuinely harvests self-advance-

ary war, reads the Mass in Quechua as well as Spanish. "Many don't understand Quechua," he says, "but they are so dumbfounded a foreigner speaks it that they reconsider their parents' language. There is a perpetual process of re-evaluation." Masses for the dead are especially popular. "Everything was against these people," he stresses. "Villa represents the struggle of life over death and negativeness. It is like a plant which was trampled in the desert but has grown."

The old and new are still meeting, each growing with the other. Hundreds of ancient Indian pots are being gathered from around Pachacamac to furnish a municipal museum

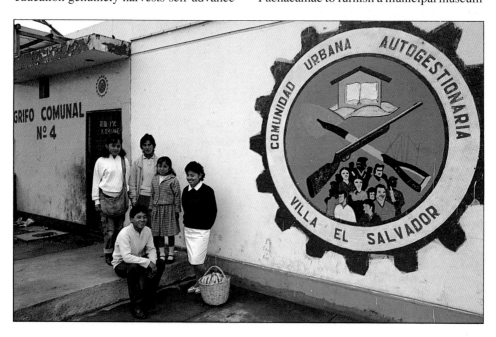

ment and change. Illiteracy is minimal. Audio-visual techniques are harnessed in free classes at cultural centers; individual loudspeaker systems run by residential blocks carry local, national and international news as well as music. Villa is the only *pueblo joven* whose own theater groups have performed overseas.

Catholicism plays its traditionally influential role. An Irish priest, Eugene Kirk, whose wooden home faces a rare wall of graffiti vaunting Shining Path's revolution-

Left, back from the soccer. **Above**, in Villa El Salvador.

which will tell both the history of pre-Colombian times and the history of Villa El Salvador. Meanwhile, its industrial park is springing to life. Already, 45 small factories producing everything from textiles to handbags are yielding 1,000 jobs. The businesses, which because of bureaucratic red tape and extortionate costs exist like most in Peru outside the formal sector, pay only municipal taxes. They export as far afield as Canada, the United States and the Soviet Union.

Villa flourishes despite underemployment and malnutrition. It is an oasis which has tapped a spring of hope from deep beneath the desert floor.

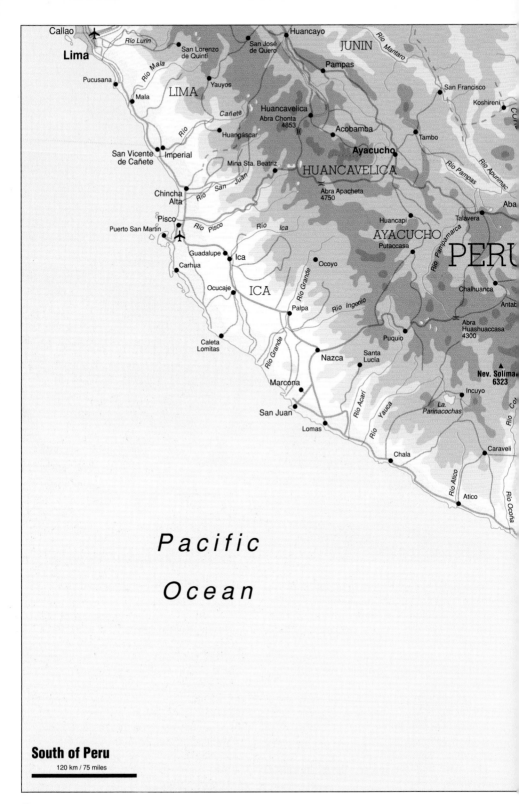

Callao ✈
Lima
Río Lurín
Pucusana
Mala
LIMA
Yauyos
Cañete
San José
de Quero
Huancayo
JUNIN
Río Mantaro
Pampas
San Francisco
Koshireni
San Lorenzo
de Quinti
Huancavelica
Abra Chonta
4853
Acobamba
Tambo
Ayacucho
Río Apurímac
Aba
Huangáscar
San Vicente
de Cañete
Imperial
Mina Sta. Beatriz
HUANCAVELICA
Río Pampas
Chincha
Alta
Río San Juan
Abra Apacheta
4750
Huancapi
Talavera
AYACUCHO
Río Pampamarca
PERU
Pisco
Río Pisco
Río Ica
Putaccasa
Puerto San Martín ✈
Guadalupe
Ica
Ocoyo
Chalhuanca
Antab
Carhua
Río Grande
Ocucaje
ICA
Río Ingenio
Abra
Huashuaccasa
4300
Palpa
Puquio
Río Col
Caleta
Lomitas
Río Grande
Nazca
Santa
Lucía
Nev. Solima
6323
Marcona
Incuyo
La.
Parinacochas
San Juan
Río Acarí
Río Yauca
Lomas
Caraveli
Chala
Río Atico
Río Ocoña
Atico

Pacific

Ocean

South of Peru
120 km / 75 miles

RAILWAY TO HUANCAYO

Two and a half centuries ago, European monks boarded ships bound for Peru, embarking on a mission to carry Christianity to the depths of the Amazon rainforest. Surviving the ocean voyage, they crossed the Andes on mules, their saddle bags packed with theology, astronomy and science books. Those books, many of them copied by hand, are just where the monks left them – in a tiny mountain monastery reached by a trip on the world's highest train.

Although the monks' mountain trek was decidedly more hazardous, the journey on this 600-mile single gauge rail line is not for those weak of heart or those bereft of humor. Passing over one of the world's most forbidding mountain ranges, passengers face the likelihood of mountain sickness, a journey that will last at least 10 hours but feel like forever, with the prospect of arriv-

ing at an unknown mountain city late at night. But this zigzagging journey over the rail line built by eccentric North American Henry Meiggs is a joy for the adventurous.

This journey scales oxygen-robbing heights, twists by 1,115 curves, through 68 tunnels and over 54 trestles. At nine spots along the route, the train must stop and backup to negotiate hairpin turns. But the reward is a haunting voyage over the Andes – soft and green at the journey's start and bleak and forbidding hours later at 4,900 meters (16,000 feet) above sea level. One can almost imagine the awe and fear the monks on muleback faced making the same sojourn.

Breathless heights: Most likely, somewhere along the trip the monks began to experience headache, queasiness, a quickened pulse and breathlessness. That was altitude sickness or, in Spanish, *soroche*. Unfortunately for them, they did not have the easiest remedy for that malaise: oxygen tanks. But modern train passengers do, thanks

The construction of the railway.

to conductors who rush up and down the aisle administering oxygen to passengers feeling a little under the weather. Not everyone gets *soroche*, of course, and those who do will survive the experience. Indians claim altitude sickness can be easily relieved with a cup of *mate de coca*, a tea brewed from coca leaves and far less of a stimulant than coffee. More curious cures include padding one's chest and back with newspapers then sucking a lemon drop, chewing fresh ginger or breathing into a paper bag. For most, going lightly on food, drink and reading on the trip, as well as a good rest at the destination, should be all that's needed.

From the capital into wilderness: This curious voyage begins at the Desamparados train station beside the presidential palace in **Lima** and ends at the market city of **Huancayo**. In between, it passes the country's mining region, one of the country's fiercest rivers, Peru's first capital and the burg that hides the monastery and its priceless books.

Leaving Lima, the train sets out for **Chosica**, now a suburb of the rapidly expanding capital but once a summer resort for the rich. A glimpse of those villas can be grabbed en route, although more obvious along the track are the shantytowns or *pueblos jovenes* populated nowadays by the poor, many of whom ride the train or spend hours in buses traveling from their sunny town to jobs in Lima. Outside of Chosica is **Villarte** – home to one of Peru's finest statesmen, Victor Raul Haya de la Torre, founder of the political party APRA (Alianza Popular Revolucionaria Americana). Haya de la Torre's home, **Villa Mercedes** is open to visitors; best are its library and photos of its former occupant's friends, including Albert Einstein.

Back on the train after Chosica, the upward grade of the route becomes steeper and the scenery turns from arid to lush green then to grayer, starker mountains – a transformation appropriate for one's now *soroche*-bound constitution. *Soroche* usually peaks just as

An unscheduled stop en route.

the train does at *Ticlio*, a spot nearly 4,900 meters (16,000 feet) above sea level. The site is marked only by a Peruvian flag atop a barren mountain. At this altitude the vegetation has disappeared and the rugged Andes are their most powerful and forbidding. The tourists speak in hushed tones and only the clicking of cameras and the sound of the struggling train engine break the silence.

The harsh landscape begins to soften and llamas reappear on the hillsides as the train begins its descent past the dreary mountain town of **Oroyo** and the raging **Rio Mantaro** – the River of Destiny. This tributary is so named because on its banks the fierce Huanco Indians stood up to the conquering Incas and, later, here as well that the Spanish wrestled control from the Inca troops. Bloody battles were waged beside this river during the Peruvian struggle for independence in the 1800s, then Chilean soldiers invaded as far as the Mantaro during the Pacific War a century ago.

Missionaries' outpost: The highland's bloody past contrasts strongly with the tranquility at **Ocopa**, the sleepy village where the monks settled and where one of the continent's oldest libraries houses their precious books.

Tucked away in the nearly 270-year-old **Rosa de Ocopa monastery**, a marvelous gallery began as the private book collection for this complex, the jumping-off point for missionaries headed into the Amazon jungle to convert the Indians to Catholicism. The missions met with resistance; a monastery wall bears the portraits of 54 priests martyred by indigenous people. But the Franciscans who managed to enter the rain forest and escape unscathed kept detailed journals documenting paths through mountain and rainforest regions previously unseen by white men. Some say Henry Meiggs consulted those journals before he defied critics and began planning the Lima-Huancayo rail line.

The overpowering scent of eucalyptus and a calming silence accompany visitors as they walk up the long driveway to the well-kept Ocopa monas-

tery. At its entrance Indian women sell cornmeal sweets while children shyly peek out from behind their mothers' layered skirts. Inside the austere religious complex, visitors speak softly and their footsteps echo on the tiled floors as guides lead them past 17th-century paintings, religious icons and the simple architecture characteristic of the Franciscans.

The prize of this tour is the library, with volumes dating back 500 years. The oldest books were hand-copied in Venice and accompanied their owners over two continents before reaching this home. Guides claim the cool dry mountain air acts as a natural preservative for the 25,000 books. Anyone is free to enter and use the library with help from the monks. A strict no-smoking rule covers the library, the monastery and its grounds.

The library is a single room two stories high with walls cut horizontally by long wooden balconies allowing access to upper rows of books. Its oldest and most valuable volumes are housed in a glass display case in the center of the room and include ancient science and astronomy texts, theology books written by hand and some of the first journals chronicling the Spanish conquistadors' arrival in the New World. A card catalogue adds an anachronistic touch.

Down the hall, butterflies, stuffed animals, textiles and Indian artifacts collected by the missionaries over the past two and a half centuries fill a rainforest museum. For a modest fee, the monks open their doors to overnight guests, offering them spotless communal sleeping quarters, shared bathrooms and a generous supply of hot water.

Peru's sunniest village: The closest train stop to Ocopa is **Jauja**, a delightful place in its own right. This was Peru's first capital but Francisco Pizarro transferred that title to Lima when his soldiers protested they were too far from a sea escape route. The town's cathedral with 15 side altars, the silver altar columns in the Chapel of Carmen and a handful of colonial buildings are evidence of the short-lived Spanish presence.

In more modern times, Jauja was home

to Peru's tuberculosis sanitarium, now a general hospital, and the Indian women wandering in the main plaza selling fresh-baked bread and herbal drinks called *emolientes* claim that the village never has a day without sunshine. It was this sun and the dry mountain air that lured TB sufferers, including author Ciro Alegria who wrote the haunting novel *Los Perros Hambrientos* (The Hungry Dogs) while seeking treatment for his own respiratory ailments.

Close enough to Jauja for day trips are **San Jerónimo** where fine silver filigree is tooled, the trout farms of **Ingenio** and the tranquil **Laguna de Paca** (Paca Lagoon) where legend has it that 11,000 gold-laden llamas drowned while carrying ransom for the release of the last Inca, Atahualpa. The drivers learned that their ruler had been executed by the Spanish and sent the treasures to the bottom of the lagoon.

On the shores of Laguna de Paca is a small state-run tourist hotel where those seeking solitude can watch black garza birds, fish for trout or borrow one of the hotel's launches for a trip over icy waters. Otherwise, the closest comfortable lodgings are in **Huancayo** at the end of the rail line. Huancayo has lost its Andean charm as it has grown but its Sunday market, stretching over ten blocks of Huancavelica streets, is still one of Peru's best. Historically, too, this city is important. On November 20, 1820 Huancayo declared Peru's independence – eight months before Lima. Some three decades later, the decree that abolished slavery in Peru was signed in this city.

A wealth of handicrafts: Nowadays it is the outdoor market that draws visitors. Increasingly overrun with modern goods, it runs the gamut from pots and pans and sewing machines to tennis shoes and spare tires. But mixed among that merchandise are delicately etched gourds, tooled leather and a quality selection of woven belts and tapestries. With diligence, it is possible to find weavings with train engine designs in homage to the metal machine that linked Huancayo to the outside world.

Small farm in the Sierra.

CUZCO AND VALLEY OF INCAS

The Indians selling goods in the open markets speak Spanish with tourists and Quechua with one another. Roman Catholic nuns live in buildings once inhabited by vestal virgins of the Inca rulers. Paintings of the last supper show Christ and the apostles eating Andean cheese and roast guinea pig. **Cuzco** is a city that lives simultaneously in the past and present and the mix is not always an easy one. Nearly half a millenium after the Spanish reached Cuzco, the city remains a crossroads of two cultures.

Of course, the Cuzco of today is dramatically different from the awesome city that Francisco Pizarro and his soldiers found when they entered the capital of the Inca empire. Five hundred years ago, an estimated 15,000 people – noblemen, priests and their servants – lived in Cuzco. Where now daily rail, plane and bus services connect this city to the rest of the country, once *chasquis* – swift long-distance Indian runners – carried news and messages from Cuzco to the four corners of Tawantinsuyo, as the empire was called. Although today this is a fairly modern Andean community with a population of about 225,000, many traces of the past remain.

Cradle of an empire: The Incas called their most important city Cuzco, or "belly button of the world", because they believed the navel was the source or center of life. Legend has it Cuzco was founded by Manco Capac and his sister-consort Mama Ocllo sent by the sun god Inti and, gold staff in hand, began the divine task of finding a spot where the staff would sink easily into the ground. That place was Cuzco and there Mano Capac taught the men to farm and Mama Ocllo taught the women to weave. The Inca dynasty started regionally here with the empire coming into being during the reign of Inca Pachacutec Yupanqui, who began a great expansion, imposing Quechua as the common language, conquering other Indian nations, creating a state religion and turning Cuzco into a glittering capital as large as any European city (see "The Incas").

Pachacutec's reign stemmed not from his desire to conquer but from his valiant effort to save the city. His father, Viracocha Inca, was in power when the fierce Chancas Indians began an assault on the Inca kingdom and Viracocha and his eldest son gave up the fight as futile. However, the younger son – who later took the name Pachacutec – led his troops to victory over the invading forces and declared himself the new Inca leader.

(An eight-story stone statue of Pachacutec, with a stairway and lookout area inside, was under construction on the south side of Cuzco to pay tribute to the Inca ruler who ruled for 40 years and was one of the empire's greatest warriors, innovators and unifiers of Andean civilizations. Perhaps thankfully, the plan has been put on hold.)

Pachacutec's son Topa Inca continued his father's work, expanding even further the empire's boundaries. But Cuzco's advances do not mean it was

Preceding pages: Inca terraces at Pisac; the Plaza de Armas, Cuzco. **Left,** Cuzco's narrow streets. **Right,** woman with a glass of home-brewed *chicha*.

always ruled by wise and competent leaders. One Inca chief, Urco, was behind such atrocities that his name later was banned from being mentioned. Another ruler hung his enemies along the roadsides in the empire's cities – a gruesome message for the disloyal. Yet another had the entire population of a nearby city excuted for the rape of a chosen woman who had dedicated her life to the sun cult. However, these excesses fail to overshadow the magnificance of a civilization that left an indelible culture.

Some of the best-loved Inca legends have been transferred to the Peruvian theater, among them *Ollantay* – the story of Pachacutec's most famous general. Under Ollantay's military leadership, the empire was extended into what is now Ecuador, Bolivia, Colombia, Chile and portions of Argentina. A grateful Pachacutec asked his general what he would like in compensation, agreeing to grant any wish. Ollantay boldly asked for the hand of Kusi Kuyur, the monarch's daughter.

But the Inca, the son of the sun, could not allow a member of the monarchy to marry a common person even though the daughter professed her love for the military leader. Ollantay rebelled against Pachacutec and was eventually ordered imprisoned for the rest of his life. Kusi Kuyur refused to marry anyone else and was sent to be a chosen woman, dedicating her life to serving the sun god.

The story does not end here, however, because years later an unforeseen occurrence brought the couple together again. The play is staged frequently in Cuzco and Lima and is worth seeing by those who understand some Spanish.

A brief moment of glory: At its peak, Cuzco was a city with sophisticated water systems, paved streets and no poverty. But it had only been an imposing urban center for about 70 years before the Spanish arrived. It was Pachacutec who turned Cuzco from a city of clay and straw into a thriving metropolis with grand stone buildings in the second half of the 15th century. Even so, Cuzco was very different from

The Inca masonry of Calle Loreto.

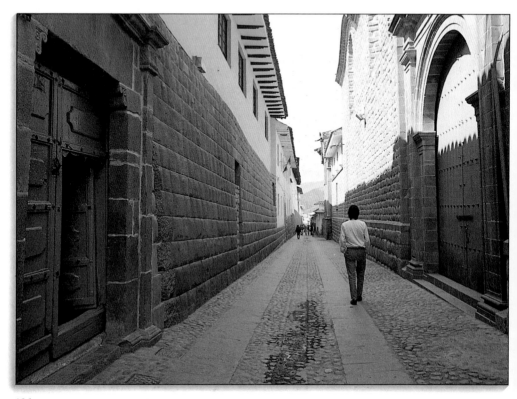

the city shown by early European cartographers, including the German Sebastien Munster. He drew Cuzco as a walled city, laid out in a grid, surrounded by featherly trees. In actuality, there was no wall and its blocks were irregular. That was in part owing to the design of the city – which reputedly followed the shape of a puma, a religious power symbol, with the fortress of Sacsayhuaman outside Cuzco as the head and the Tullumayo River as its spine.

Of course, since the Incas left no written records and the Spanish explanations of what they found are contradictory, theories about Cuzco's design are numerous. One specialist in archaeology and astronomy even speculates that one city boundary was warped to make it coincide with the midpoint in the Milky Way, reflecting the Indian sensitivity to astronomy and movement of the heavenly bodies.

Many other details of how the Inca capital looked must be drawn from the often unreliable memoirs of the conquistadors. Pizarro and his men did not set off for Cuzco, the city of wonders, until they executed Atahualpa in Cajamarca. Entering for the first time the fertile valley where Cuzco is located, the Europeans found rain-washed countryside of green, patchworked with barley, alfalfa, corn and gold and purple fields of kiwicha and quinua – varieties of amaranth grain.

The Spaniards were certainly impressed by the order and magnificence of Cuzco, and wrote back to Spain that it was the most marvelous city of the New World. But the Incas' cultural achievements were merely a minor distraction in comparison with the lure of their treasures: conquistadors greedily pushed their way into ancient temples, seized their gold and silver artworks to promptly melt into portable bars.

In addition to palaces and gold-filled temples, indestructible buildings, and advanced medical techniques, the Spanish soldiers found the Inca society full of skilled artisans. In Cuzco a storehouse full of delicate, bright-colored feathers from tropical birds was

Typical dress of the Urubamba valley.

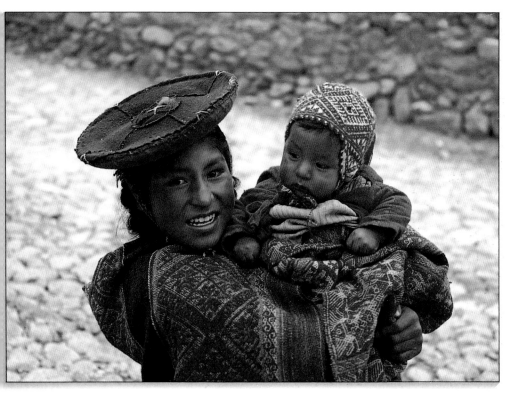

used solely for the weaving of fine capes for the Inca and his priests. Rescued examples of the capes or *mantas*, which may reflect the most extreme test of patience and handiwork, are found in museums in Lima. These survived because the Spanish wanted precious metals and their thirst for gold was so great they overlooked many of the empire's other treasures.

Although the Inca reign is certainly what most intrigues visitors to this city, Cuzco retained a level of importance for the first few decades after the Spanish conquest. It was here that Diego de Almagro's faction of Spanish soldiers attempted to wrest control from Pizarro; in fact, de Almagro was executed on Cuzco's main plaza. Also in this city, the Spanish struggled against Inca Manco as the Indian made a fated attempt to stop the European conquest. But by 1535 the capital of this new Spanish colony had been set up in Lima, Cuzco's wealth had been stripped and silver from Bolivia turned attention away from this valley.

But finally, after centuries of provincial oblivion, Hiram Bingham's discovery of Machu Picchu and the subsequent construction of a roadway in 1948 up to the lost city transformed Cuzco into the jumping off point for visits to one of South America's most famous tourist attractions.

Walking into the past: The most startling and curious characteristic of Cuzco at first glance is its architecture. Huge walls of intricately fit stone pay testimony to the civilization that 500 years ago controlled much of the South American continent. The Spaniard's attempts to eradicate every trace of the "pagan" Inca civilization proved too ambitious a task; the Europeans ended up putting their own buildings on the mammoth foundations of the Inca ones, often using the same stones that had been finely cut and rounded by the Indian masons. When earthquakes shook the city, the colonial walls crashed down but the Inca foundations remained intact.

To explore this intriguing city, the **Plaza de Armas** is a perfect place to start. In Inca times it was not only the

View of Cuzco from Sacsayhuaman fortress.

exact center of the empire known as Tawantinsuyo – or The Four Quarters of the Earth – but was twice as large as it is now. A sample of soil from each of the conquered areas of the empire were joined at this spot and the plaza itself, flanked by Inca palaces, was surfaced with white sand mixed with tiny shells, bits of gold, silver and coral.

This was the spot where the most important Inca religious and military ceremonies were held. The section that remains today was a portion that some say was known as Aucaypata, the Square of War, featuring a stone covered in sheets of gold where offerings were made before military actions. However, other experts claim the real name of this portion of the main plaza was Huacaypata – or Weeping Square – because it was here that deceased Incas were mourned.

During the days of Spanish control, the plaza was the scene of much bloodletting such as the execution of Indian rebel leader Tupac Amaru II in a successful effort by the Spanish to stop an uprising. Captured while trying to flee with his pregnant wife, Tupac Amaru – a *mestizo* whose real name was Jose Gabriel Condorcanqui – was ordered drawn and quartered in the square. Spanish chronicles say the young leader was so strong that the horses tied to his arms and legs were unable to dismember him on the first try, so the conquistadors beheaded him – after forcing him to watch the decapitations of his four children and strangulation of his wife.

Festival focus: Nowadays, the people assembled in Cuzco's Plaza de Armas are most often there for festivities, both modern and ancient, solemn and colorful. Annually on International Workers' Day, the parade of workers through the square continues for hours with each group lined up behind their respective banners – from the organization of transportation workers to the union of informal street vendors (*ambulantes*) made up mostly of women with their babies strapped to their backs. This, like many ceremonies in Cuzco opens with the raising of the red and

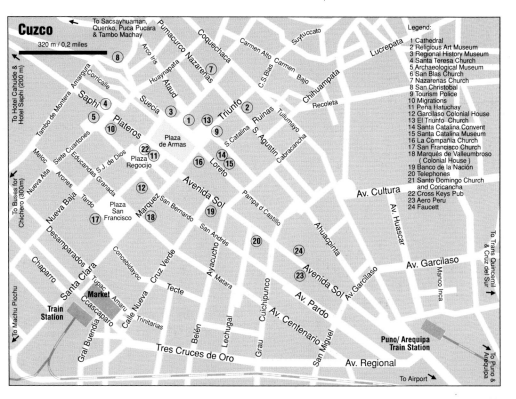

white Peruvian flag and the rainbow-colored standard of the Inca empire. Solemnity marks the beginning of celebrations for Corpus Christi Day, a movable feast usually held in June at which statues and silver are paraded through the streets. But that ceremony usually ends on a more festive note as increasingly generous quantities of alcoholic beverages are imbibed and masked devil dancers frolic among the shrubberies.

The most spectacular view of the plaza comes after nightfall when dramatic lighting transforms the square. Although the night is best for outside photos, the interior of Cuzco's magnificent **Cathedral** can only be seen during the day – and it shouldn't be missed. Built on what once was the palace of Inca Viracocha and made in part from stones hauled from the fortress of Sacsayhuaman outside the city, the Cathedral mixes Spanish renaissance architecture with the stoneworking skills of the Indians; it took a century to build and an equally awesome investment of money.

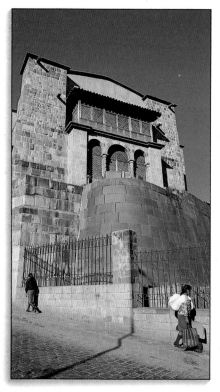

The altar is solid silver. In the corner next to the sacristy is a painting of the last supper with Christ and his apostles dining on roast guinea pig and Andean cheese. Another painting of Christ's crucifixion in the church is believed to be the work of Flemish painter Sir Anthony Van Dyck. The third side altar from the left contains a curious painting of a pregnant Virgin Mary.

Locally, the Cathedral's best known statue is the crucified Christ known as *El Señor de los Temblores* – or Lord of the Earthquakes. Depicted in a painting in another Cuzco church, El Triunfo, this is the statue that was paraded around the city during the 1650 earthquake. After the tremors eventually stopped, the statue was credited with the end of seismic activity. Borne on a silver litter, this statue – a gift to the New World from Spanish King Charles V – is still regularly taken from the church and paraded around Cuzco on feast days. Inside the Cathedral, candles are perpetually lit to this icon and it is their smoke that has blackened the statue.

The Cathedral's María Angola bell in the north tower can be heard up to 25 miles (40 km) away. Made of a ton of gold, silver and bronze, the more than 300-year-old bell is reportedly the continent's largest. But when it was cast, it had a partner – the Magdalena, which was dropped by workers during a storm at the edge of Lake Titicaca, where the bells were made. Indians in Cuzco now say that the echoes from the first peals of the María Angola each morning are actually the tolling of the Magdalena on the bottom of the Lake.

Cuzco's first Christian Church: El Triunfo – literally "the triumph" – is the church to the right of the Cathedral, up Triunfo street off the plaza. It was built in honor of the Spanish victory over the Indians in the great rebellion of 1536, when Cuzco was under siege for many months. The uprising was led by Manco Inca, a descendent of an Inca leader whom the Spaniards assumed would be their political puppet. They were surprised, then, to find Manco surrounding the city with some 200,000 followers – against the Spaniards' 200

Left, the Inca temple Koricancha, at the base of Santo Domingo Church.

RIDING THE RAPIDS

High in the Peruvian Sierra, where icy waters churn and boil over huge boulders and rush through narrow canyons, river travel has never been practical. Not, at least, until the sport of white-water rafting was introduced. With the staggering number of rivers in Peru – the Andes having been at work for thousands of years forcing new waterways to carry their glacial melt-off – choices for river adventures are unlimited.

The Cuzco area is well-suited for river rafting. The **Urubamba River** winds through the Sacred Valley of the Incas, and floating along its waters gives a unique perspective to one of the most culturally-rich areas in all of Peru. Remains of ancient terracing are evident on the hillsides and simple mud huts with thatched roofs dot the riverbank. Women can be seen washing clothes in the shallows, children herding cattle and sheep, and men working the fields – all of whom will pause briefly to watch with surprise as the floating rubber dinghy makes it way down river. The tranquility lulls you into a peaceful daydream until the next set of rapids brings you to life and starts you paddling for all you're worth.

White water challenges: Trips on the **Apurimac River**, just a few hours from Cuzco, are for those looking for a longer and rougher ride. Superb white water is found in a spectacular, mile-deep tropical canyon on this source river of the Amazon. When not occupied with immediate survival in the challenging rapids, rafters have time to enjoy steep waterfalls cascading down the canyon walls, and search for wildlife including otters, deer, puma, and, of course, the ever-present Andean condor. Afternoons are spent relaxing in camp on a sandy beach, trying a hand at fishing, or hiking along goat trails. The last remaining Inca bridge, stretches across the Apurimac just above the common take-out point.

Several hours from the city of Arequipa is the

Tackling the Urubamba River.

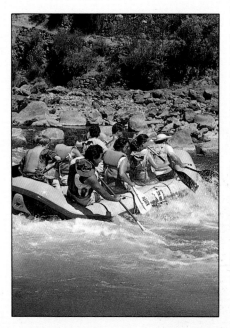

spectacular **Colca Canyon**, thought to be the deepest in the world, with the crystalline waters of the **Colca River** snaking along its bottom. It wasn't until 1981 that a complete exploration of the river was undertaken by the CanoAndes Polish Expedition. Many sections of the river are technically difficult – enough to test the limits of experts. This, along with a setting devoid of vegetation, a lunar landscape of rocks and volcanic lava, makes a trip along the Colca one of the most impressive. Excursions to this zone must be arranged in advance.

Huck Finn on the Urubamba: For the Huckleberry Finn-type, a completely different sort of rafting trip is possible. This one requires a spirit of adventure, the ability to swim, and an itinerary flexible enough to go with the flow (literally!) of things. The first step is to take the train from Cuzco to the end of the line and start of the jungle at **Quillabamba**. From here, it's an eleven hour truck ride to the village of **Kitini** on the upper Urubamba River, where a boatman is hired for a six-hour trip to an even smaller village called **San Iriate**. Here the fun begins. In San Iriate you can hire someone to build a balsa raft in about 4 hours, or sit by the riverbank and wait for an abandoned one to float by. These average about one a day. Also, be sure to buy a good quality paddle from one of the villagers since balsa paddles are not strong enough. When the raft is ready, and before the journey can begin, another boatman must be located to ferry the passenger and drag the raft down through a stretch of the river known as the **Pongo de Mainique**. Below the Pongo, the raft is loaded with passenger and possessions for a four-day (or longer) float down the Urubamba. Gear should be tied securely to the raft, and a plastic sheet helps for waterproofing. The river is not dangerous, but unexpected rapids have been known to dump the unsuspecting. It's easy enough, however, to swim after the raft and climb back on. Little food is necessary because of the communities situated all along the way – someone will always offer a meal and a place to sleep. The larger village of **Sepahua** has a mission and landing strip with sporadic flights available. Farther along is the town of **Atalaya** with real hotels, ice cold beer and a lift back to civilization.

men and loyal Indians.

The turning point of the siege was a great attack on the city, with Manco's men slinging red hot stones to set the thatched roofs alight. Almost all the Spaniards were gathered in the old Inca armory of Suntur Huasi as much of Cuzco began to burn. But when the fiery stones hit the armory roof, they "miraculously" went out. Priests later declared that the Virgin of the Assumption had appeared to put out the flames and inspire the Spaniards on to defend the city. El Triunfo – the city's first Christian church – was built on the site.

Entering El Triunfo church today, the painting to the right of the entrance shows the 1650 earthquake which shook down the Spanish-built structures but left nary a stone out of place in the Inca buildings. Also in this church is the grave of Spanish chronicler Garcilaso de la Vega, who died in Spain in 1616 but whose remains were returned to Cuzco a few years ago. On the other side of the Cathedral is the Church of the Holy Family, or Jesus María. At nearly 260 years old, it is one of Cuzco's "newer" structures.

In a city with so many churches, it is an honor to be dubbed the "most beautiful". That distinction belongs to **La Compañía**, sitting in the main plaza where once stood Inca Huayna Capac's palace. Construction of the church, with its intricate interior, finely carved balconies and altars covered in gold leaf, started in 1571 and took nearly 100 years to complete, in part because of damage in the 1650 earthquake. During its construction, this splendid building drew so much attention that the Bishop of Cuzco complained it outshone the Cathedral. By the time the Pope was called into the spat and ruled in favor of the Cathedral, La Compañía's construction was too advanced to turn back.

The Sun God Temple: The street to the side of El Triunfo led to what was the most important place of worship in the Inca empire. Now the **Santo Domingo Church**, this was known as Koricancha – Temple of the Sun – and was the most magnificent complex in Cuzco. Walls

Below left, example of the Cuzco school of colonial art. Right, ancient street.

there were covered in 700 sheets of gold studded with emeralds and turquoise, and windows were constructed so the sun would enter and cast a near blinding reflection of golden light off the precious metals inside.

The mummified bodies of deceased Inca leaders, dressed in fine clothing and adornments, were kept on thrones of gold here, tended by women selected for that honor. In that same room, a huge gold disk representing the sun covered one full wall while a sister disk of silver, supposedly to reflect the moonlight, was positioned on another wall.

Spanish chronicles tell of how the Europeans were stunned when they saw Koricancha's patio filled with life-sized gold and silver statues of llamas, trees, fruits, flowers and even delicately handcrafted butterflies. Legend has it Atahualpa's ransom included 20 of Koricancha's life-sized golden statues of beautiful women.

Spanish historian Pedro de Cieza de Leon described the patio "in which the earth was lumps of fine gold...with stalks of corn that were of gold-stalks, leaves and ears...so well planted that no matter how hard the wind blew it could not uproot them. Aside from this there were more than 20 sheep of gold with their lambs and the shepherds who guarded them, with their slings and staffs, all of this metal," wrote the Spaniard after his visit to Cuzco.

The conquistadors forced the Indians to destroy this art, melting down the finely crafted gold and silver into easily transportable bars. Although the temple's wealth can only be imagined, its Inca architecture is still left standing to appreciate. Visible from inside Koricancha is the perfectly fitted curved stone wall that has surved at least two major earthquakes.

Another chronicle writer confirmed the extravagence of Koricancha. Some of the most detailed accounts of what the conquistadors found in Cuzco came from Garcilaso de la Vega, himself born in Cuzco in 1539 to a Spanish captain and the niece of the 11th Inca, Huayna Capac. When he was 21, Garcilaso de la

Inca wall inside the Hostal Loreto.

Vega went to Spain and wrote "royal Commentaries" based on things he heard and saw while in Peru. According to this multi-volume work, a fabulous Hall of the Sun – of which there is no longer a trace – was located in Koricancha. Meanwhile, around a patio there were four chapels dedicated to lesser gods – including the moon, stars, thunder and the rainbow.

The rainbow had special significance for the Incas and it remains a good omen for the Indians today. Any Peruvian child asked to draw a picture of the *sierra* or highlands almost always will sketch a house with mountains in the background and a rainbow arching the sky. It was in honor of the rainbow that the Inca flag displayed all the colors of the *arco iris*.

Chosen women: In modern Cuzco, yet another Christian enclave was formerly used as an Inca holy place. This is the **Santa Catalina Convent** that centuries ago housed a different group of cloistered females, the Chosen Women who dedicated their lives to the sun god.

Foremost among these were the *mamacunas*, consecrated women who taught religion to selected virgins called *acllas*. The *acllas* were taught to prepare the alcoholic beverage *chicha* for use in religious ceremonies, to weave and to pray. They made the fine robes that the Inca wore – only once – out of vicuña, alpaca and, according to one Spanish chronicle, a silky soft black fabric that was made from bat skins.

Turned into a colonial style building occupied by Roman Catholic nuns, this complex off the plaza on the street later known as Arequipa, was once home to 3,000 women and girls trained to serve their heavenly husband, the sun, or attend to the pleasure of his son on earth, the Inca.

An important contribution to the art world grew out of this mixing of the Indian and Spanish cultures and the latter's failure to erase all brushings of gold, is known as the School of Cuzco. In these often violent and bloody paintings are archangels dressed as Spaniards and carrying European guns, but

Below left, picking out a tapestry. Right, handicrafts for sale on the Plaza de Armas.

surrounded by cherubs with Indian faces; or Christ appearing with Indian-looking apostles. The Virgin Mary wears Indian clothes and, in scenes of the crucifixion, Christ is hung on a cross decorated with Indian symbols.

A fine collection of this art, which flourished from the 16th through 18th centuries is found at the **Museum of Religious Art** on Calle Palacio at the corner of Hatunrumiyoc (heading downhill from the Plaza de Armas). Once the palace of Inca Roca, under whose rule Cuzco's schools were started, this now Moorish building has complicated carvings on its doors and balconies. Just outside is the famous **Twelve Angled Stone**. Called Hatunrumiyoc by the Indians, this masonry masterpiece was left by Inca architects who proved no piece of granite was too irregular to be fitted without mortar.

Heading straight up Hatunrumiyoc street is the church of **San Blas** with its carved pulpit, said to be one of the world's finest pieces of woodwork. Made of a solid piece of wood, there is some dispute about the craftsman who produced the ornate masterpiece: some say it was an Indian leper who initiated the work after he was miraculously cured of his illness.

The streets around San Blas form Cuzco's artists neighborhood, with galleries, studios and small shops. Heading straight back down the same street and past the Plaza de Armas takes you to **La Merced**, another important church tucked behind the Trattoria Adriano Italian restaurant and a bookstore. Destroyed by the massive earthquake in 1650, this church was erected a second time four years later. Today, it contains the remains of Francisco Pizarro's brother Gonzalo and conquistador Diego de Almagro, who returned to Peru after an unsuccessful search for riches in Chile. Its connected **Museum of Religious Art** contains several paintings, including a Rubens, and gold and silver altarpieces. The most ostentatious of these is a jewel-studded, solid gold monstrance.

Garden Square: Continuing down the

Below left, girl with Andean pipes. Right, blind musician on Calle Loreto.

same street away from the Plaza de Armas lies another public square, the **Plaza San Francisco**. This square has been planted entirely with Andean flora, including the once-outlawed amaranth grain. Here, too, is Cuzco's coat of arms featuring a castle surrounded by eight condors. The castle represents Sacsayhuaman and the emblem refers to the bitter and bloody battle fought there in 1536 as the Indians tried futilely to cast off the Spanish conquerors. The condors circling over the coat-of-arms castle are a vivid reproduction of the scores of flesh-eating birds that circled over the Inca fort as the bodies of the dead piled up there.

Plaza San Francisco is named for the 16th century church and monastery banking one side. Simple in comparison to other houses of worship in the city, it has an extensive collection of colonial art – including a painting showing St. Francis de Assisi's family tree and reportedly one of the largest canvases in South America.

Continuing down Marquéz street past the plaza, you will find **Santa Clara Church**. Although this is part of a convent closed to the public, it is possible to enter the church at the time of the 6 a.m. mass. The cloistered nuns at this 16th century religious chapel sit at the back of the church, behind a floor to ceiling metal grill, and form the church's choir. The most impressive part of this building, however, is the infinite number of tiny mirrors covering its interior.

Returning to the Plaza de Armas and over to the corner of Tucumán and Ataud is the **Admiral's Palace**, once the home of Admiral Francisco Aldrete Maldonado and now the Regional Historical Museum. A coat of arms over its doorway belongs to a subsequent owner, the arrogant and self-important Count of Laguna who died under mysterious circumstances. His body was found hanging in the mansion's courtyards shortly after he mistreated a priest who had complained about the count's behaviour. In that same courtyard are visible miniature profiles of Pizarro and Spain's Queen Isabel. An optical illusion at this **The Urubamba Valley.**

196

house is found in a corner window column which looks like a bearded man from inside and like a nude woman from outside.

Before heading for landmarks outside the city, stop by the **Cross Keys Pub**, two blocks from the Plaza de Armas. In this city of contrasts, what could be more natural than a British-owned watering hole for offbeat travelers, cartographers, self-styled pioneers, eccentric scientists and some of the world's most famous bird-watchers. Cozy up to the bar to hear an exchange of their latest adventures, consult them on out-of-the-way tourist stops and help Barry Walker, an expatriate-ornithologist-jungle guide supplement his income as co-owner of the pub with wife Margot.

Monolithic fortress: The best known of the ruins outside Cuzco is the overwhelming fortress of **Sacsayhuaman**, a bold showing of ancient construction skills. Made of massive stones weighing up to 17,000 kg (125 tons) apiece, this military complex overlooking Cuzco

has a double wall in a zigzag shape – some say to imitate the teeth of the puma figure, whose head the fort may have formed. Sacsayhuaman also once had at least three fabulous huge towers and a labyrinth of rooms large enough to garrison 5,000 Inca soldiers. It marks the birthplace of the river that runs under Cuzco, channeled through stone conduits cut by ancient Indians to invisibly supply the city with water.

This fortress served as the focus of the Great Rebellion led by Manco Inca against the Spanish in 1536. From here, the Incas beseiged Cuzco for 10 months. Historians say if Manco Inca had been able to defeat the Spanish here, he may effectively have saved the empire. But, no matter how valiantly his troops fought and died, the Spanish responded in a desperate manner and eventually wrestled back control of the fort, Cuzco, and ultimately all Peru (see "The Conquest").

Archaelogists estimate tens of thousands of workers labored on this massive structure for up to seven decades, hauling the immense stone blocks that

Market day in Pisac.

make up its double outside walls and erecting the near indestructible buildings that transformed the complex into one of the most wondrous in all the empire. Although the outer walls are basically intact, the buildings in the complex have been destroyed – in part to provide building stones for many of the structures in Cuzco. Still, visitors can see the so-called **Inca's Throne** from which parading troops were allegedly reviewed.

Hearty travelers reach Sacsayhuaman after a half hour hike from Cuzco; there are also cabs available and they will wait at the summit. This is one of the area's most spectacular spots to take photos at dawn and, like much of Cuzco, provides a startling contrast of the Indian and Christian cultures. Beside this complex built during the reign of Inca Pachacutec is a giant white statue of a Christ, his arms outstretched over Cuzco in the valley below.

Those seeking a quiet place for a picnic lunch or for reading will also find it at Sacsayhuaman. Visitors perched on

almost any stone there have an amazing view of the red tile roofs of Cuzco and the lush fields of the surrounding valley. The ribbon and yarn decorated llamas wandering through the ruins are smelly but harmless, and giggling children tending them will almost certainly ask you to take a photo – make sure to give them a tip.

Peruvian archaeologists and Inca scholars say Sacsayhuaman is not out of danger, although it lies in ruins. They claim that the 100,000 tourists and Peruvians that annually attend the colorful Inti Raymi festival to celebrate winter solstice – a recreation of one of the Inca's most important festivities – damage the fort, not only with their litter but by moving and defacing stones. There has been in recent years an effort to move the festival from Sacsayhuaman although there has been resistance from those who insist Cuzco's largest celebration each year must be held in the Inca stronghold. Since 1944, when the outlawed June 24 celebration was publicly revived, this festival has become

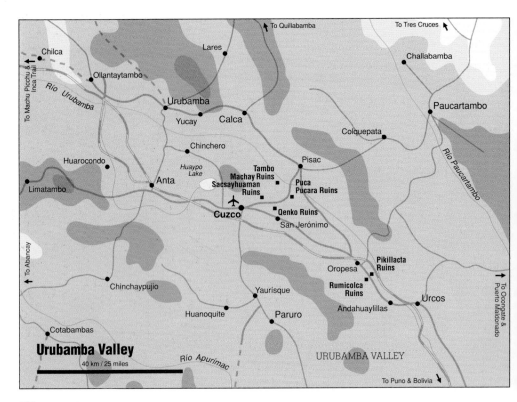

the area's main producer of tourism revenues.

The sacred valley of the Incas: Fewer than 7 km (4.5 miles) from Sacsayhuaman is **Quenko**, an Inca shrine with a circular amphitheater and an 5-meter (18-foot) high stone block that locals claim looks like a puma. Its name means labyrinth and this ceremonial center – dedicated to the worship of the mother earth – includes water canals cut into solid rock and a subterranean room. Unlike Sacsayhuaman, which is a complex made up of huge stone blocks transported to the spot and assembled, Quenko was honed from a huge limestone formation found at the site. Into its walls were carved the typically Inca-style niches and alcoves used to display gold and holy items in pre-Hispanic times. Local residents also say the shrine contains a number of drawings etched into its stone, among them a puma, condor and llama.

Farther along the road to Pisac is a smaller fortress, **Puka Pukara**, believed to have guarded the road and the Sacred Valley of the Incas. Like Machu Picchu, this pink stone complex has hillside terraces, stairways, tunnels and towers. And to the north is **Tambomachay**, the sacred bathing place for the Inca rulers and their royal women. A hydraulic engineering marval, its aqueduct system still feeds crystalline water into a series of showers where once water rituals were held by worshippers of the sun. The ruins now consist of three massive walls of Inca stonework tucked into a hillside. There are Peruvian historians who say this was used by Inca Yupanqui as a hunting lodge in addition to being a shrine. Some claim it was the place where the Inca leader Pachacutec received a prophetic vision of the Incas as conquerors. Others say the water running through the aqueduct came from a holy spring and his may have been one of the rare spots where sacrifices of children were made.

From there, the journey plunges down some 400 meters (1,500 feet) into a valley on the curvy road leading to **Pisac**, a friendly village known for its good

Young boys at Chincheros.

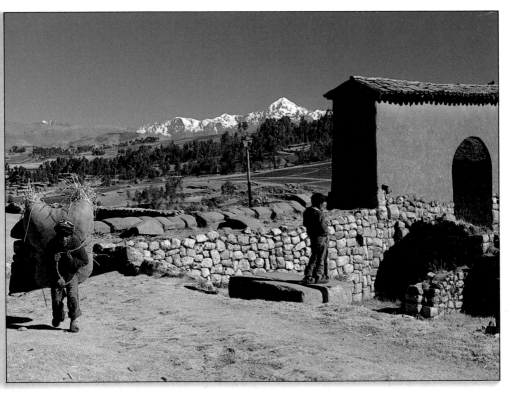

fishing, Sunday market and the ruins above the town. The ruins can be reached by climbing past the mountainside terraces (Indian children will serve as guides for a small fee) and, at this high altitude, even the most fit travelers find themselves winded and their hearts pounding, increasing the likelihood they will be grateful when they round the bend on an isolated trail only to find themselves face to face with one of the many *Inca Kola* vendors scattered throughout the site.

The steep farming terraces and dramatic architecture are the elements of an impressive scene at this one-time fortress city whose many features include ritual baths fed by aqueducts and one of the largest known Inca cemeteries. The stones making up Pisac's buildings are smaller than those at Sacsayhuaman but the precision with which they are cut and fit is amazing, as is the lovely view here. In fact, in some respects, this is a more awesome example of stonemasonry than the more famous ruins at Machu Picchu. There are residential buildings and towers that some scientists say may have been astronomical observation spots. Higher up, there is a second set of ruins. Owing to the style – smaller stones more haphazardly arranged – a number of theories have arisen as to the origin of this section. Some say it was used by servants or other community members with low social standing; another theory says it predates the main part of the complex.

Sunday festivities: Pisac's Sunday market is a riotous occasion in a town where the people work hard and – apparently – play hard. The beer tent is the favorite haunt of the motley brass band that adds an increasingly out-of-tune touch to the festivities. Sometimes it seems that the beer tent is the favorite stop for most of the other villagers, too. For that reason, the later in the day visitors arrive, the better their chances for some congenial bargaining for the fine alpaca blankets and sweaters available. (Although, of course, the biggest selection is found earlier in the morning.) For a bite to eat, stop by Frank's Cafe on **Market at Pisac.**

Avenida Pardo; all the profits from this small restaurant go to a local fund for emergency care for children.

Those unable to make it to Pisac should consider a trip to **Chincheros**, another spot to catch the action at a weekend market. Once again, the Indians use it as a place to buy and barter over goods as much as a place to socialize. This "town of the rainbow", as it was known in pre-Hispanic days, has kept many of its ancient traditions and its inhabitants live in centuries-old houses, wear traditional clothing and locate their outdoor market in a plaza banked by a massive wall built by the Incas. It is said that Chincheros was one of the favorite spots of Tupac Inca Yupanqui, who built a palace and had farming terraces cultivated here at the mouth of the Vilcanota River. Other historians say it was actually quite an important population center in Inca times and Topa Inca, the son of Pachacutec, had an estate here. If the Inca royalty was lured to Chincheros, it might have been by the view: there is a commanding vista of snowcapped mountains and the river.

To do a full circuit of the valley, it is necessary to continue on to **Urubamba** and the great fortress of **Ollantaytambo** 72 kilometers (45 miles) from Cuzco. Urubamba lies at the center of the valley and has a number of simple lodging houses – including a government-run Hotel Turistas – for travelers who want to spend more than a day in this area. This is a peaceful village of flowering trees and a strong Indian favor. The coat-of arms on the city hall bear witness to this; no Spanish symbols are found in the emblem bearing pumas, snakes and trees. It was the beauty and calm of this village that prompted the 18th century naturalist, Antonio de Leon Pinelo, to expound on his theory that Urubamba was actually the biblical Eden.

Fortress village: Continuing onto Ollantaytambo, travelers find themselves facing an elegant and intricate walled complex containing seven rose-colored granite monoliths which puzzle scientists, who say the stone is not mined

Below left, jewelry at a roadside stall near Urubamba. Right, the Pisac ruins.

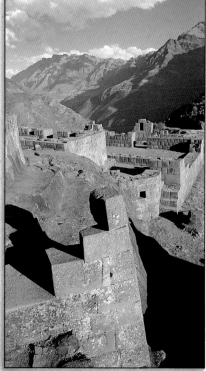

in the valley. A steep stairway enters the grouping of buildings, among which the best known is the **Temple of the Sun** – an unfinished construction in front of a wall of enormous boulders. Some of the original carvings on these huge worn stones can still be seen although it is unclear if they really were pumas, as some authorities claim.

Some specialists say the unfinished condition of the temple lies less in Spanish destruction of Ollantaytambo than in the fact that it simply was not completed. They point to huge boulders found at the stone quarry 6 km (3.6 miles) away, at the same time they marvel that the Indians were able to transport those massive boulders such a distance when the trip involved crossing the Urubamba River and hauling the building material up steep grades. Ollantaytambo, strategically placed at the northern end of the Sacred Valley, also has plazas with sacred niches, shrines, an area of stone stocks where prisoners were tied by their hands and ritual shower areas, including the **Princess' Bath**, or Bano de la Nusta.

The village's military fortification was so well planned that it took the Spanish by surprise when they arrived there in search of Manco Inca during the 1536 Indian uprising. Hernando Pizarro led a contingent of about 100 men and a number of Indian assistants to the fort with the intention of capturing and executing the rebel Indian. Chronicles say that as the Spaniards sneaked up to the side of the fort just before dawn, they looked up to see the silhouettes of multitudes of Indian warriors ready and willing to take them on. It is even said they saw Manco Inca himself, directing troops from inside the Ollantaytambo complex while mounted on a captured horse. Manco Inca's men had also diverted the Patacaucha River through some water canals and they opened barriers that allowed the water to rush out and flood the plain the Europeans were crossing. However, the Spaniards managed to escape to Cuzco, where they recruited a force of 300 soldiers to return to confront Manco Inca. The In-

Below left, young girl in the Sacred Valley. Right, bargaining a price.

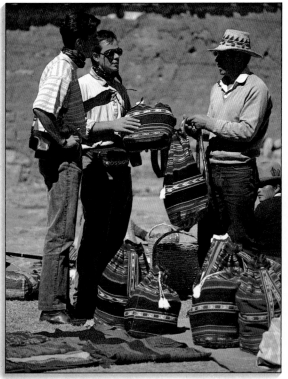

dian noble, outnumbered, abandoned the walled city and fled to Vilcabamba, where he was eventually killed by Spanish treachery.

Woolen weavings and wild music: Back in Cuzco, stroll around and look at the artisan work for sale. The best quality goods are found in the stores, including those around the Plaza de Armas, although some bargains can be obtained from the insistent Indian women selling items on blankets under the archways along the square. Don't believe it when you're assured the rugs or weavings you're eying are antiques; as one traveler said, "They smell like they've been around a hundred campfires – but I think the fires were lit in my lifetime." Besides, the centuries-old textiles found in museums in Peru were rescued from the arid coast where the absence of moisure protected them from decay. In the damp highlands, wool does not endure indefinitely.

The most commonly heard phrase when tourists pass by the arches in the Plaza de Armas is a chorus of *Cómprame*, or "Buy from me." Cuzco depends on tourism and some visitors feel literally assaulted by the men, women and children who pester them to buy goods. Be patient. It appears that the Spanish conquest was successful in imposing one condition that did not exist with the Incas: poverty.

Bear in mind that petty theft has gone in tandem with the growth in tourism and valuables should be kept in money belts or where they are not easily accessible. It is not unheard of for tourists' purses, bags and backpacks to be expertly slit and their contents stolen where there are distractions. Police, meanwhile, say they receive reports of at least one camera theft each day. The Plaza de Armas is perfectly safe day and night but the market area near the train station where tickets are sold for Machu Picchu has become a favorite haunt of thieves in recent times (and some tourists claim they found their stolen items on sale there later in their vacations).

However, that is not to say that the market area should be avoided. Leave your valuables in the hotel safe deposit box or put your passport in a money belt and head off to this outdoor collection of a little bit of everything. Here you'll find woolen items, shoes, potatoes in every size, shape and color and even bags of coca leaves.

In the evenings, highland music can be heard wafting out of restaurants all over the city. One of the finest floor shows is at **El Truco**, where the pisco sours pack a punch and the musicians and dancers are first rate. Eating a plate of *anticuchos* – a shish kebab of beef heart – and watching the performers in their traditional clothing, singing in Quechua and playing reed flutes makes visitors temporarily forget that the Incas lost their showdown with the Spanish. But after the foot-stomping dance songs, the quieter mountain music will seem haunting – even sad. Some Indians will tell you their music was always *alegre* or happy until the Spanish came and the last Inca was killed. From that day on, the world went dark; the sun god turned his back on his children and the music has had a melancholy strain ever since.

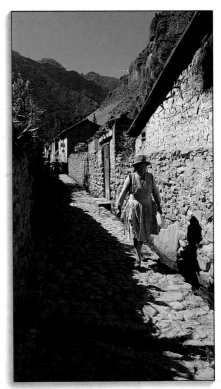

The ancient streets of Ollantaytambo.

FIESTAS IN CUZCO

Fiestas! Who can pass one up? The dry season (May through September) is the main fiesta season in southern Peru, although there are some wonderful celebrations throughout the year. The good news for weary travelers is that there are several fiestas you can attend right in Cuzco.

Cuzco was the political and ceremonial center of the Inca Empire with a major festival celebrated in the city every month. On the theory that if you can't beat them, co-opt with them, the Spanish attempted to transform Andean feast days and sacred sites into Catholic events and shrines. Building the church of Santo Domingo on top of the Temple of the Sun, Coricancha, is a perfect example of this tactic.

The Wrath of God: On March 31, 1650, Cuzco was devastated by a violent earthquake, which the clergy attributed to sin and idolatry. To commemorate the disaster they hauled out an image of Christ on the cross dating from about 1560 and called it *Nuestro Señor de los Temblores* (Our Lord of the Earthquakes). The *indigenas* dubbed him Taitacha (Little Father) Temblores and credited him with saving the city from complete destruction. Every year on March 31st Taitacha was paraded through the streets of Cuzco followed by penitents begging for protection from earthquakes. Eventually Tatiacha's feast day was moved to Monday afternoon during Holy Week, the week before Easter – when it is still celebrated today. Taitacha, on a silver litter, is carried on a three hour circuit of the city, while red flower petals are thrown in his patch symbolizing the blood of Christ. He always stops at the church of Santa Teresa, which customarily provides his litter bearers. Thousands of Cuzqueños turn out along with the civic, religious and military hierarchies of the city.

When a severe earthquake battered Cuzco in 1950, Taitacha was set up in the Plaza de Armas for three days while the populace implored him to make the earth stop trembling. Shortly after Easter in 1986 another

Preceding pages: festival of the sun at Sacsay-huaman, Cuzco. **Right**, dancing in Cuzco's Plaza de Armas.

206

earthquake hit the city, killing several dozen residents and damaging many buildings. The word around Cuzco was that Taitacha was angry because, unlike former times, many people did not prostrate themselves during his procession. If you're in Cuzco on the Monday of Holy Week, you might put in a good word with Taitacha for all of us.

Parading mummies and saints: In June the major Inca festivals included the celebration of the rise of the Pleiades, called Collca (storehouse), about June 8th and the winter solstice festival, Inti Raymi, on June 21st. At important Inca celebrations, the mummies of the dead Inca rulers and their queens were carried on litters to visit one another (pre-

devotees and led by a brass band and the faithful of the parish carrying banners and candles. San Sebastián and San Gerónimo and eight or nine other statues pay an overnight visit to the Virgen of Belen in San Clara Church in Cuzco, where presumably they all catch up on the news of the year just like the Inca mummies.

On Corpus Cristi the Plaza de Armas comes alive. Large altars decorated with flowers, tin, mirrors, crosses and images of the sun are erected on three sides of the Plaza and vendors set up booths with food prepared especially for Corpus. These treats, well worth sampling, include *chiriuchu*, made with guinea pig, chicken, corn, cheese, eggs and

sumably to gossip and consult on matters of import) and then to the Cusipata (now the Plaza de Armas) where they sat in state. If you're in Cuzco during the Corpus Cristi fiesta, you will see vestiges of this tradition.

Corpus Cristi (in honor of the Eucharist) is a moveable feast, held on the Thursday after Trinity Sunday. It usually falls in early to mid June. On Wednesday, the vespers of the fiesta, thirteen statues of saints and of the virgin are brought into Cuzco from their churches in Cuzco's *barrios* and suburbs. Effigies of San Sebastián and San Gerónimo race into Cuzco from the little towns of those names, borne on enormous litters by their

peppers; and baked *achira*, a rhizome that resembles the sweet potato.

Precious Metals: After high mass, the statues are paraded around the plaza, stopping to bow at each altar – no mean feat when some of the gilded and silver-covered palequins weigh up to a ton. It's a honor to be a litter bearer and some of the men wear traditional carrying cloths on their backs, a symbol of humility since Inca times. Each parish has its own brass band, costumed dance groups and devotees and the plaza is a melange of color and sound. At the end of the procession comes the priest bearing the Eucharist, almost forgotten in the crush. Slip inside the cathedral if you can because some of the old women remain there to sing Quechua hymns before their patron saint in the high, bird-like voices typical of traditional Quechua music.

A week later, the statues are again paraded around the Plaza de Armas and then taken home. If you're in Cuzco in June, the sound of music or fireworks coming from the center of town should bring you to the Plaza de Armas on the run.

Most travelers come to Cuzco for Inti Raymi (the Festival of the Sun) on June 24th and miss Corpus Cristi, which is a shame, since Corpus is an authentic local celebration. Still, Inti Raymi isn't just for tourists. If you want to see Inti Raymi be sure to make

They're lit to bring back the sun during the longest nights and shortest days of the year.

In the 1940s residents of Cuzco revived Inti Raymi, basing their fiesta on colonial accounts of the Inca festival. On June 24th, *campesinos*, townspeople and travelers all head to the fortress of Sacsayhuaman for a pageant that combines the hokey and the authentic in a slightly surreal manner. In comes the Inca-for-a-day on a litter, dressed in tin foil and cheap cloth, with a palace guard consisting of costumed Peruvian army troops. Off go the dancers from the mountains beyond Ollantaytambo, dressed in hand-woven traditional dress that would have made the Inca Pachacuti proud.

hotel reservations and arrive by June 20th because the city is mobbed.

Bringing back the sun: Inti Raymi was the Inca winter solstice celebration, held on June 21st or 22nd. Conveniently for the Spanish, the Catholic feast of Saint John the Baptist (San Juan Bautista) falls on June 24th, so the solstice events could be transferred to an ostensibly Christian fiesta. The fires that burn throughout the night of June 23rd don't have much to do with John the Baptist.

<u>Left</u>, the Inca returns in the Festival of the Sun. <u>Above</u>, watching the dancers at Sacsayhuaman, Festival of the Sun.

The pageant, in which the fires of the empire are ceremonially relit, a llama is "sacrificed" to the sun, and music and dance groups perform, lasts about three hours, but the city becomes a giant fair for the entire week. It's irresistible, but do watch for pickpockets in the crowd.

On Christmas Eve there is a beautiful festival in Cuzco's Plaza de Armas and side streets called Santo Rantikuy (Saint Buying). People come into Cuzco to buy and sell *nacimientos* (nativity sets). You will see crafts for sale that are available only that day, including locally made statues of the holy family and the three kings.

THE QUEST FOR LOST CITIES

The "Golden Beast": When the Admiral Christopher Columbus first approached the coast of South America, he believed that he had come to the place where the sun rose on the day of the creation. The earth, he wrote, was like a "round ball, and on one part of it something like a woman's breast" rose up toward heaven. The Earthly Paradise was located on the nipple of this breast, and the breast itself was to be found on the equator of the South American continent. Columbus was also convinced that the tribe of Amazon warrior women of classical antiquity lived somewhere in this same region.

Although the Admiral's mind had certainly come somewhat unhinged at the time that he wrote about these matters, his ideas did not seem all that fantastic to most Europeans. So many true wonders were soon reported by the explorers and conquerors of the Americas that the line between reality and fantasy was completely blurred. Large land iguanas were confused with medieval dragons, and underwater manatees with breasts merged into mythical mermaids. The innocent natives, "as naked as the day they were born", were certain proof that the Garden of Eden was to be found in the vicinity. And the fierce women warriors of the Carib tribes were obviously related to the Amazons.

However, although such marvels were cause for speculation, they held no intrinsic interest for the more materially minded *conquistadores*. None of the ancient texts mentioned gold mines in Paradise, and the Spanish crown cared little for mermaids. But once the royal coffers began to bulge with the riches of the conquered Aztec and Inca nations, the belief in the existence of the Earthly Paradise took on another dimension.

If such empires existed, why should there not be another golden city hidden somewhere in the vast rainforests of South America? If the Terrestial Paradise consisted of something more than lost innocence and spiritual serenity – if it happened to also contain untold riches – it became something worth discov-

Watching the dawn on a recent expedition.

ering. And, of course, conquering.

Thus the Garden of Eden – located, according to Columbus, on the nipple of the breast of the world – was the teat at which a strange, semi-mythical golden beast was suckled. Once weaned, this beast would undergo many incarnations and be responsible for the deaths of thousands of men and women. In the 16th century it would be transformed into a chimera known as El Dorado, "The Golden One". By the 17th century it would become Paititi, the last refuge of the Incas who had taken with them all of the gold they had hidden from the Spaniards. And in the late 1900's it would merge with Vilcabamba, the city which the

present-day Colombia made sure that the quests would continue when they told Spaniards about a tribal chieftan who, in an annual ritual, anointed himself in gold dust and then plunged into a lake. It is likely that this ceremony had actually taken place in a lake near modern Bogotá, but the destruction of the Muisca culture assured that it would not occur again. However, the plunge into the lake was the baptism which gave the beast its first name – El Dorado, the Golden Man.

As this legend spread throughout Spanish America, El Dorado became "The Golden City". There was no lack of men and women willing to risk their lives and endure enormous hardships on the hunt. A typical expe-

rebellious Incas had actually occupied and which had been "lost" since its conquest by the Spaniards in 1571.

Today the golden beast, in its manifestation as Paititi, still haunts the fevered imaginations of the explorers of South America – particularly in Peru. In the course of the search for it, hundreds of minor "lost cities" have been found, but the beast itself continues to elude its seekers. And it continues to devour the lives of those who would hunt it.

Death in the jungle: No sooner had the Inca empire been destroyed than *conquistadores* began setting off into the Amazon, searching for the Lost City. The Muisca Indians of

dition was led in 1540 by Gonzalo Pizarro, half-brother of the conqueror of the Incas. He left Quito with no less than 220 horses and 5,000 live pigs for food. A year and a half later, he returned with less than 100 diseased Spaniards. However, 50 of his men under the command of Fransisco de Orellana had built a ship and made the first descent of the river that would be called the Amazon – because an Indian captive had told them that a tribe of Amazon women lived near the river.

The beast itself would survive in other forms, and over the centuries hundreds of expeditions set off after it – most of them disastrous. Its fascination has lasted into the

20th century, making world-famous two modern explorers in South America, Colonel Percy Fawcett and Hiram Bingham.

A modern obsession: Percy Fawcett was a British army officer who came to South America in 1906, contracted by the Bolivian and Brazilian government to help define their jungle borders. But his real interest was in tracking down a golden city that, according to an 18th-century Portuguese document, had been found in Brazil by a group of adventurers. Fawcett also possessed a stone idol of supposed Brazilian origin which, according to the psychics whom he consulted, had actually come from the lost continent of Atlantis. The idol contained mysterious in-

fear of any failure." Then he and his party "disappeared", mysteriously swallowed up by the beast.

However, that was not the end of the story. Over the years various explorers reported that they had either met Fawcett or had heard rumors of his whereabouts. According to some of the tales, he was living with a group of Indians, while Jack had married one of the tribal women who had given birth to a white, blue-eyed son. A number of expeditions set out in search of him, but all were unsuccessful.

And this was perhaps the strangest metamorphosis of the golden beast: for Colonel Percy Fawcett had himself become the beast he had stalked!

scriptions which he claimed were identical to some strange scribbling at the end of the Portuguese document.

Armed with this conclusive proof of the existence of the Atlantean city, Fawcett plunged into the "green hell" of the Amazon in search of it. On his second expedition in 1925, in which he was accompanied by his son Jack and a man named Raleigh Rimell, he sent a message back to his wife which ended with the words: "You need have no

Left, early explorers became obsessed with tales of El Dorado. **Above**, a 19th-century expedition near Cuzco.

Success in Peru: The golden beast, however, is only semi-mythical, and not all of its mutations have been chimerical. In 1536 the Incas rebelled against the Spaniards and then withdrew to Vilcabamba in the jungles to the northeast of Cuzco. There they remained for 35 years before they were finally defeated. Vilcabamba itself was rapidly consumed by the forest, but as such it became one of the beast's real manifestations – known as "The Lost City of the Incas".

There was little interest in discovering the whereabouts of Vilcabamba until the latter half of the 19th century when there was a revival of enthusiasm for American archaeology; and it was this beast that Hiram Bingham was tracking when he "discovered" Machu Picchu. Bingham and his party left the Inca village of Ollantaytambo on mule-back one morning in 1911 and, following a recently dynamited road down the Urubamba canyon, they arrived in the evening at a small hut. Bingham was told by the owner, Melchor Arteaga, that there were some fairly good ruins on the ridge above. The next morning Arteaga took him up a path where he met two farmers who had been cultivating the Inca terraces. A photo taken at the time even shows the famous Intihuatana Stone in the midst of a cornfield! The entire demanding journey had lasted just one and a

Still, Espíritu Pampa is only one of many Inca ruins in the region, and in 1976 the Peruvian archaeologist Edmundo Guillén claimed another site as the true Vilcabamba. Other explorers think that neither identification is correct and the real city is yet to be found. The controversy thus promises to continue for a long while – especially as more explorations turn up more ruins.

In 1985 Savoy uncovered another pre-Inca site in the jungles of northern Peru which he claims covers 120 square miles and consists of over 20,000 structures. Called Gran Vilaya, it may turn out to be the largest single complex of ruins to have been found in South America. In the same year, the

half days.

To give Bingham credit, he did continue on to find many other Inca sites under far more arduous circumstances. He even came across some ruins in a place called Espíritu Pampa, but he did not bother to investigate. In the 1960's, however, another American explorer, Gene Savoy, did explore the area and declared this site to be the true Vilcabamba. The most convincing evidence to support his claim is the existence of piles of roof tiles – since a 16th-century chronicle affirms that the Incas roofed one of the Vilcabamba palaces with tiles in imitation of Spanish architecture.

University of Colorado announced the discovery of another "lost" city – Gran Pajatén. But this time the beast had outdone itself in chicanery – for the UC scholars had failed to mention that these ruins had been described by Savoy in 1965 and that they had been excavated in 1966 by the Peruvian archaeologist Duccio Bonavía!

However, all of these are just appendages of the beast. The truly romantic explorer is still after its heart – Paititi.

The Legend of Paititi: With the destruction of the Inca Empire, the chameleon-like chimera underwent yet another metamorphosis, this time into Paititi – and as such the golden beast clings tenaciously to life to this day. According to the legend, a group of disaffected Incas fled into the jungle, taking with them thousands of llamas loaded with gold. Anyone who enters the rainforests to the east of Cuzco will come across countless tales of Paititi. The most common is that of a peasant who follows the trail of a lost animal for several days into the cloudforest. Disoriented, he stumbles through the fog, falls asleep and awakens to find himself in Paititi. Inevitably, one of the Incas gives him a golden ear of corn to take home with him. But he is never again able to find the site.

Is this manifestation of the beast mythical or real? According to documents from the late 16th and early 17th centuries, a son of the Inca Huayna Capac discovered a small range of mountains in the jungle, conquered its peoples and populated it. He cultivated its rich soil, mined its vast gold veins and built temples. He then sent a delegation to Cuzco to inform the Inca of the land, but because he was jealous of his holdings, he warned them to say nothing of the gold. They were to tell the Inca, "*Paytiti*" ("That place is just lead"). However, when they arrived in Cuzco they found the Spaniards already there. They thus returned to Paititi, taking with them many Inca nobles, gold and hundreds of llamas.

All of this could be simple legend, of course, but according to one early testimony, the Incas of Paititi had communication with Cuzco. And in 1602, when Melchor Carlos Inca (a grandson of Huayna Capac) was sent back to Spain, it was said that many Incas never before seen in Cuzco arrived from Paititi to wish him well. But if the beast is real, where is its lair? The documents indicate a wide range of habitat – as far as the forests of northern Bolívia and western Brazil – but the beast has taken most of its victims in the high jungles to the east of Cuzco.

In the cat's lair: There are two other possible explanations for the name "Paititi". "Titi" is also the Agmara word for a wild mountain cat, and many legends state that the lost city is guarded by pumas or jaguars. However, most of the those who have hunted the cat in the forested slopes east of Cuzco would probably agree with the Guarani approximation – for in this jungle language, "Piatitti" means "sadness, affliction, anguish".

In 1970 an American journalist named Bob Nichols set off with two Frenchmen – Serge Debru, a photographer, and Geraud Puel, a sociologist – up the Shinkikibeni River into the Pantiacolla mountains. Coming across a massive rockface covered with ancient petroglyphs, they followed a stone road until it was lost and then proceeded up the canyon. They were never heard from again, but a Japanese adventurer, Yoshiharo Sekino, later met a group of Machiguenga Indians who claimed to have killed them. The Machiguengas are also said to be guardians of Paititi.

Petroglyphs are common in the forests of the region; and Father Juan Carlos Polentini, an Argentinian priest who has searched for the golden beast for 13 years, has found some which he claims to be a map to the lost city. In his book, *Por las rutas de Paititi*, he recounts a tale told him by an old man of three young men who found Paititi near a lake on top of a mountain called Apu Katinti (or Qatini). Starving and weak, they were only able to cut off a finger of a golden idol; and one of them died and was buried up there. According to the old man, who was 92 at the time, he himself had gone up the mountain and found the gravestone carved with a cross and the man's initials.

I would not put much credence in this tale, but in 1989, I and a group of Paititi-seeking friends found a stone etched with a cross and letters on Apu Katinti. We also arrived at the lake, but we were unable to climb to the top and found no sign of ruins (later we were to find out that another explorer, Gregory Deyermenjian, had actually made it to the peak – but he also discovered no ruins).

Over the years we have stumbled upon many small ruins and followed many Inca roads which lose themselves in the impenetrable forests, but we have yet to find any golden idols (with or without fingers). Still we continue to search. Those roads must lead to somewhere.

Does Paititi exist? Those of us who have stalked the golden beast can answer with an unqualified yes. It prowls somewhere in the jungles of the soul of the seeker, animating one's dreams with its growls and stirring one's heart with its musky scent. And if the actual Paititi were ever to be discovered, we seekers would soon have to invent another.

Left, Machu Picchu at dawn.

to Huayna Picchu

1 Terrace Caretakers' House (main entrance)
2 Agricultural Sector
3 Dry Moat
4 Ritual Baths
5 Principal Bath
6 Temple of the Sun
7 "Palace of the Princess"
8 "Fountain Caretakers' House"
9 Royal Sector
10 Watchman's Hut
11 Funerary Rock
12 Quarry
13 Temple of the Three Windows
14 Principal Temple
15 "Sacristy"
16 Intihuatana (gnomon)
17 Sacred Rock
18 Common District
19 Mortar Building
20 "Prison Group" or "Condor Temple"
21 Intimachay

to Train Station

to Inca Drawbridge

to Intipunku

MACHU PICCHU

When Hiram Bingham discovered **Machu Picchu** in July 1911, he was actually searching for the ruins of Vilcabamba, the remote stronghold of the last Incas. Today we know that he almost certainly found Vilcabamba without realizing it, when he visited the jungle-covered ruins of Espiritu Pampa, some 100 km (620 miles) west of Machu Picchu, two months before his spectacular find on the Urubamba gorge. But Bingham only saw a small part of Espiritu Pampa, and dismissed it as insignificant. Considering what he found later, who can blame him?

Bingham was a Yale graduate, later a US Senator, who became fascinated with Inca archaeology in 1909, while in Peru studying the terrain of Bolívar's independence struggle. He returned with the Yale Peruvian expedition in 1911, and took the narrow mule trail down the Urubamba gorge in July of that year. Melchor Arteaga, a local *campesino* whom he met by chance while camping on the river banks, led him to the jungle-covered ruins.

The locals called the mountain above the saddle-ridge where the ruins were located Machu Picchu – Ancient Peak; and its sister mountain was Huayna Picchu – Young Peak. But Bingham felt that the real name of these ruins should be Vilcabamba. He believed he had discovered the last refuge of the Incas. More than that, he also speculated this was Tampu Tocco, the mythical birthplace of the Ayar brothers, founding ancestors of the Incas.

Bingham's mistake in thinking he had found the location of Vilcabamba is understandable. Who would imagine there were not one, but two lost cities in the jungle north of Cuzco? But today there is overwhelming evidence against the Machu Picchu-as-Vilcabamba hypothesis. So Bingham presented us with an enigma even deeper than he imagined. If Machu Picchu was not Vilcabamba, then what was it?

Outpost in a "lost" province: Bingham had carried out further explorations between 1911 and 1915, discovering a string of other ruins and a major Inca highway (now known as the Inca Trail) to the south of Machu Picchu. Later still, in 1941, the Viking Fund expedition led by Paul Fejos discovered the important ruins of Huiñay Huayna above the Urubamba gorge, about 4½ km (3 miles) due south of Machu Picchu. Thus, Machu Picchu was not merely a lost city, but part of an entire lost region – a fact generally ignored by popular histories. The usual account portrays Machu Picchu as some secret refuge known only to a select few, and concealed from the Spaniards. But this would have been impossible; the location of an entire active and populated region could not have been concealed from the Spaniards, who had many Indian allies.

And yet the Spaniards did *not* know of Machu Picchu's existence. How? The only possible conclusion is that the Incas did not know of it either. Somehow the city and its region was abandoned and depopulated before the Conquest, and the memory lost even to the Incas themselves. Perhaps the area was devastated by plague, or overrun by the Antis, the fierce jungle tribesmen. But then, why the total amnesia concerning its location? This cannot have been accidental. The Incas had a caste of *quipucamayocs* – oral history recorders – who kept detailed accounts of the Inca past. But this was *official* history, and the Incas are notorious among modern historians for wiping inconvenient details off the record. Perhaps this was Machu Picchu's fate: a province that rebelled and was dealt with so ruthlessly that its existence was erased from official memory.

Well, the foregoing is simply one theory that fits the known facts. Here is another: according to new evidence unearthed from Spanish colonial archives, and recently presented by the archaeologist J.H. Rowe, there was a "royal estate" (sort of a western concept, but how else to put it?) of the emperor Pachacuti at a place called "Picchu", north of Cuzco. This leads to an interpretation that Machu Picchu was built and populated by the *panaca* (royal house) of Pachacuti, and that the eventual disappearance of the panaca, a generation or so after Pachacuti's death, led to the depopulation and abandonment of the region.

Signs of a pre-Inca occupation at Machu Picchu, going back 2,000 years, have recently been discovered, but there was certainly no pre-Inca city of any consequence here. If we accept that Machu Picchu was built for Pachacuti, we can speak of the construction dates of Machu Picchu with reasonable confidence. According to a widely accepted chronology, the Inca expansion began in the year 1438, after Pachacuti's defeat of the Chanca invasion from the north. Various chronicles tell us that for strategic reasons (to keep the retreating Chancas out) this mountainous area was the first to be settled in the headlong rush toward empire. The building style of Machu Picchu is "late imperial Inca", which supports this thesis, and there are no signs of post-Conquest occupation. So Machu Picchu was built, occupied and abandoned in the space of less than one hundred years. The rest is speculation. And who can resist speculating when faced with something as affecting and impenetrable as the mystery of these silent stones?

Piecing together the past: What kind of settlement was Machu Picchu? John Hemming states that the site has only 200 habitation structures, leading him to estimate a permanent population of about 1,000 people. It is interesting that the agricultural output of the area would have greatly exceeded the needs of the population; for, besides the large extension of agricultural terracing at Machu Picchu itself, there were also much larger terraced areas at Inti Pata (just behind Machu Picchu peak to the southwest), and Huiñay Huayna along the Inca Trail. More than one archaeologist has lately proposed that the principal material function of the Machu Picchu region was to create a reliable supply of coca leaves for the priests and royals of Cuzco.

Hiram Bingham called the ruin a "cita-

A guide explains the ruins.

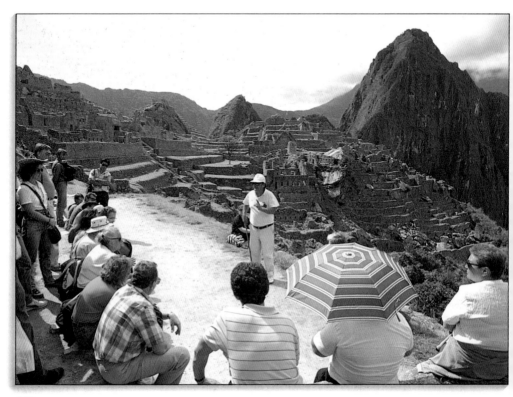

del", existing for strategic and defensive purposes. But besides its outer walls and moat, Machu Picchu contains an unusually high proportion and quality of religious architecture. Modern opinion leans more to the view that Machu Picchu was essentially a site of spiritual and ceremonial significance, with important agricultural functions. Its strategic purposes, if any, were secondary.

Bingham's fortress idea did not prevent him from speculating that the city was a refuge of Cuzco's Virgins of the Sun, an idea inspired by the revelation that more than 75 percent of the skeletal remains found there were from females. This exciting piece of news has been on the lips of tour guides ever since. Yet there is a difficulty with the argument. The Yale expedition found only skulls, the other bones having disintegrated in the humid climate. It is extremely hard to pronounce on the gender of a skull, particularly if, like the expedition's medical authority Dr. Eaton, you are not very familiar with bones of the racial sub-group it comes from. Dr. Eaton

Inca terraces.

pronounced most of the skulls "gracile", and therefore, he assumed, female. But they could as easily have been young or small men. The skulls still exist, and could be studied again by modern experts, but so far no-one has done it.

Allegedly, the terms of Bingham's permission to excavate at Machu Picchu were unclear. This led to vague accusations of smuggling after he shipped all his relics back to Yale University, where most of them remain to this day. There were no precious metals, however, and it is not a visually spectacular collection, so the dispute is mainly for scholars.

Breakthroughs in archaeology: Starting in about 1985 an astonishing number of new discoveries have been made around Machu Picchu. Taken as a whole they support and expand the emerging view of Machu Picchu as the ceremonial and possibly administrative center of a huge and quite populous region. The alluring myth of Machu Picchu as some kind of Andean Shangri-la perched alone on its remote crag must now be laid to rest.

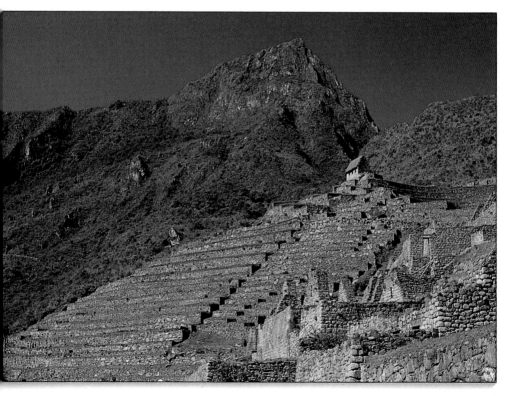

The most extensive finds have been made across the river to the northeast, on a sloping plateau known as Mandorpampa about 100 meters (328 feet) above the railroad. Its outstanding feature is an enormous wall about 3.5 meters high by 2.5 meters wide (11.5 by 8.2 feet), and more than a kilometer long, which runs straight up the mountainside, toward a pointy peak known as Yanantin. It was apparently built to protect the adjacent agricultural terraces from erosion, and may also have served to demarcate two areas with separate functions. A road running along its top heads off northeast into densely forested mountains towards Amaybamba, or perhaps some other Inca settlement yet undiscovered. Other finds on the pampa include quarries, circular buildings, a large number of stone mortars, and a large observation platform.

Closer to Machu Picchu itself, the sector on the north slope of Huayna Picchu known as the "Temple of the Moon" has been cleared to reveal a subterranean temple, a fine wall with an imposing gateway, and an observatory directed toward the aforementioned Yanantin peak.

Farther upriver two important burial sites known as Killipata and Ch'askapata have been discovered, and the ruins of Choquesuysuy, just upstream from the hydroelectric project, now appear to be much larger than had been previously believed. Of all these sites only the Temple of the Moon has been opened to the public so far, and at this writing it is closed again.

In the years following Bingham's discovery the ruins were cleared of vegetation, excavations were made, and later a railroad was blasted out of the sheer granite cliffs of the imposing canyon. Visitors began to arrive. Pablo Neruda came in 1942, and was inspired to write his most famous poem. In 1948 a sinuous 12-km (7 mile). road from the river banks to the ruins was inaugurated by Hiram Bingham himself.

A walking tour of the ruins: Bingham classified the ruins into sectors, naming some of the buildings, and so on. But some of his conclusions appear wide off the mark to modern archaeologists; others seem too arbitrary, resting on minimal evidence. However, for the sake of clear directions we need to name different sectors, and since nobody has come up with a better system than Bingham's, here we go:

You enter the ruins through the **"House of the Terrace Caretakers"** (1), (see map) which flank the **Agricultural Sector** (2). This great area of terracing was undoubtedly for agricultural purposes, and made the city self-sufficient in crops. The terraces end in a **Dry Moat** (3), beyond which lies the city itself. If you continue straight ahead you come to the **Fountains** (4), which are actually small waterfalls, in a chain of sixteen little "baths", varying in the quality of their construction. These were probably for ritual, religious purposes relating to the worship of water. Bingham speculated that Machu Picchu might have been abandoned because this water supply dried up, or became inadequate to irrigate the terraces. The hotel consumes most of this spring water today. The **Main Fountain** (5) is so called because it has the finest stonework and the most important location; it is just above you to the left as you arrive from the terraces.

Here, too, is the **Temple of the Sun** (6). This round tapering tower features the most perfect stonework of Machu Picchu. It contains sacred niches for holding idols or offerings, and the centerpiece is a great rock, part of the actual outcrop onto which the temple is built. The base of this rock forms a grotto which is casually referred to as the Royal Tomb, although no bones were found there.

Recent archaeo-astronomical studies have shown how this temple served as an astronomical observatory. The rock in the center of the tower has a straight edge cut into it. This is precisely aligned through the adjacent window to the rising point of the sun on the morning of the June solstice. The pegs on the outside of the window may have been used to support a shadow-casting device, which would have made observation simpler.

View through a trapezoid window.

The temple's entranceway has holes drilled about the jamb, less complex than a similar doorway at the Coricancha in Cuzco. The adjacent building (7) has two stories and was obviously the house of someone important. Bingham named it the **Palace of the Princess.**

Next to the Sun Temple, just above the main fountain, is a three-walled house (8), which has been restored and its roof thatched as an example of how these structures looked in Inca times. It is usually called the **Fountain Caretaker's House** – but it's unlikely to have been a house at all, since it is open to the elements on one side. The thick stone pegs high up in the wall are thought to have served as hangers for heavy objects.

Students of the more esoteric aspects of the Inca culture have suggested that this complex of adjacent structures forms a temple to the four elements: the Temple of the Sun (Fire); the "Royal Tomb" (Earth); the open-fronted "Fountain Caretaker's House" (Air); the Principal Fountain (Water).

The structures directly opposite the Sun Temple, across the staircase, have been classified as the **Royal Sector** (9), because of the roominess of the buildings, and also for the huge rock lintels (weighing up to 3 tons) which generally characterized the homes of the mighty in Inca architecture.

At the top of the agricultural terraces, high above the city, stands a lone hut (10) that backs onto a gently-sloping area known as the cemetery. Bingham found many bones and mummies at this spot. This is a great place for an overall view of the ruins. A few meters from the hut lies a curiously-shaped carved rock (11), called the **Funeral Rock**. Bingham speculated that this rock was used as a place of lying-in-state for the dead, or as a kind of mortician's slab, on which bodies were eviscerated and dried by the sun for mummification.

Mysterious stone: At the top of the staircase leading up from the fountains you come to a great jumble of rocks (12) that served as a quarry for the Inca masons. There is a fascinating discovery in this sector – a partially-split rock

that seems to show precisely how the builders cut stone from the quarry. The rock bears a line of wedge-shaped cuts where tools were hammered in to form a crack. The problem with this rock, though, is that it was reportedly cut by a 20th-century archaeologist, Dr. Manuel Chavez Ballon!

Follow the ridge away from the quarry with your back to the staircase, and you come to one of the most interesting areas of the city. Here is the **Temple of the Three Windows** (13). Its east wall is built on a single huge rock; the trapezoidal windows are partly cut into it. On the empty side of this three-walled building stands a stone pillar which once supported the roof. On the ground by this pillar is a rock bearing the sacred step-motif common to many other Inca and pre-Inca temples.

Next to this site stands the **Principal Temple** (14), another three-walled building with immense foundation rocks and artfully-cut masonry. It is named for its size and quality, and also because it is the only temple with a kind of sub-

The trail to Huayna Picchu.

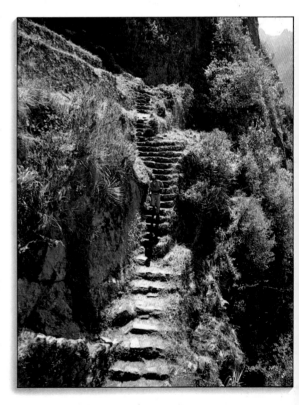

temple attached to it. This is generally called the **Sacristy** (15), because it seems a suitable place for the priests to have prepared themselves before sacred rites. The stone which forms part of the left-hand door-jamb has no fewer than 32 corners in its separate faces.

Ascending the mound beyond this temple leads you to what was probably the most important of all the many shrines at Machu Picchu, the **Intihua-tana** (16), the so-called "Hitching Post of the Sun". This term was popularized by the American traveler Squier in the 19th century. But nobody has ever unraveled the mystery of how this stone and others like it were used. Every major Inca center had one. It seems likely that the stones somehow served for making astronomical observations and calculating the passing seasons. There was at least one other "Intihuatana" in the vicinity, located near the hydro-electric power station in the valley below, to the west. The second stone was probably situated to make a specific astronomical alignment with the main one. The main

Intihuatana is a sculpture of surpassing beauty. It is the only one in all Peru to have escaped the diligent attention of the Spanish "extirpators of idolatry" and survive in its original condition.

The group of buildings across the large grassy plaza below comprises another, more utilitarian sector of the city. At the north end, farthest from the entrance to the ruins, you find two three-sided buildings opening onto a small plaza, which is backed by a huge rock (17) generally called the **Sacred Rock**. An intriguing aspect of this plaza is that the outline of the great flat rock erected at the northeast edge is shaped to form a visual tracing of the mountain skyline behind it. Then, if you step behind the masma (three-sided hut) on the southeast edge and look northwest, you find another rock that echoes the skyline of the small outcrop named **Uña Huayna Picchu** in the same way.

Walking back towards the main entrance along the east flank of the ridge you pass through a large district of cruder constructions that has been labeled the **Common District** (18). At the end of this sector you come to a building with two curious disc-shapes cut into the stone of the floor (19). Each is about two feet in diameter, flat, with a low rim carved around the edge. Bingham called these mortars for grinding corn, but this is doubtful. True, he did find some pestle stones in the same building, but the normal mortar used by the Quechua Indians today is much deeper and more rounded within; also it is portable, not fixed in one spot. These "mortars" would not have served well for that function. However, to date nobody has suggested a more plausible explanation than Bingham's for these enigmatic carvings.

Just across the next staircase you come to a deep hollow surrounded by walls and niches, which is known as the **Temple of the Condor** (20). Bingham called this the Prison Group, because there are vaults below ground, and man-sized niches with holes that might have been used for binding wrists. But the concept of "prison" probably did not exist in Inca society; punishments tended to involve loss of privileges, or physical

The view from Huayna Picchu.

suffering, or death. Some early Spaniards reported pits full of snakes or pumas into which offenders were dropped to see if they would survive, but this is hardly a prison. The complex was probably a temple. A rock at the bottom of this hollow bears a stylized carving, apparently a condor, with the shape of the head and the ruff at the neck clearly discernible.

There is a small cave known as Intimachay (21) above and to the east of the Condor Temple. It has been identified as a solar observatory for marking the December solstice. The cave is faced with coursed masonry and features a window carved out of a boulder that forms part of the front wall. This window is precisely aligned with the winter solstice sunrise, so that morning light falls on the back wall of the cave for ten days before and after that date.

Further explorations: Having seen the Machu Picchu ruins proper, these are three short walks worth attempting.

Firstly, above the ruins to the southeast you can see a pass scooped out of the ridge, with a small ruin at the center. This is **Intipunku**, the Sun Gate. You can actually see the sun rise in this gateway from the western heights of the ruins at certain times of year. The trail that you can see traversing the mountainside from this point was the main Inca highway from Huiñay Huayna and other sites farther south. It is well preserved, and makes for a fairly easy climb, taking about an hour and a half there and back. The view of Machu Picchu from Intipunku is magnificent.

The second walk is to the **Inca Drawbridge.** A trail winds back from the heights of the ruins, by the cemetery, leading along the west flank of the mountain behind Machu Picchu. This trail grows narrower, until it is cut into the side of a sheer precipice, and you find yourself taking each step with care. Follow it until you come to a spot so abrupt that the ancients had to build a huge stone buttress to create a ledge for the path to cross. They left a strategic gap in the middle of the buttress, bridged by logs which could be withdrawn. Beyond this point the trail quickly peters out, becoming unstable and extremely dangerous. The path has been fenced off shortly before the bridge, ever since a man tried to hike beyond it and fell to his death. To the bridge and back is an exciting one-hour walk demanding a cool head for heights.

Hardy visitors also like to climb **Huayna Picchu**, the towering granite peak that overlooks Machu Picchu from the north. The path is very steep; it's the original Inca path, stepped in places. Approach it with caution – but don't be put off by the peak's fearsome appearance. You don't have to be a mountaineer. If you are reasonably active and healthy you will get to the top – and back.

Everyone planning to climb Huayna Picchu must sign in at the control point along the trail leaving the principal ruins. Start before 1 p.m., as visitors are barred from starting the climb after that time.

As you near the top of Huayna Picchu you pass through ancient terraces so inaccessible and so narrow that their value for agricultural purposes would have been negligible. Hence, it's thought that these were probably ornamental gardens, to be admired from the city below. About 1 to 1½ hours gets the average person to the peak for a stupendous view.

The **Temple of the Moon** stands inside a cavern halfway down the north face of Huayna Picchu. It was discovered as recently as 1936, and contains some of the finest stonework of the entire Machu Picchu complex. The Inca pathway which leads to the temple forks off the main trail to the left about one third of the way up to the peak of Huayna Picchu. The trail and ruins are closed to the public at this writing, but may be open when you read this.

Physically active people staying overnight at Machu Picchu can also consider taking the **Inca Trail** to **Huiñay Huayna.** The round-trip takes about four hours, including some time to look at the ruins. (Note: they charge the Inca Trail fee, minus entrance fee to Machu Picchu, for this hike.) The journey itself is rewarding, since the trail passes through exotic tropical forest, and is worth the effort.

Dawn on the winter solstice at the Temple of the Sun.

LAKE TITICACA

Lake Titicaca is the world's highest navigable lake and the center of a region where thousands of subsistence farmers eke out a living fishing in its icy waters, growing potatoes in the rocky land at its edge or herding llama and alpaca at altitudes that leave Europeans and North Americans gasping for air. It is also where traces of the rich Indian past still stubbornly cling, resisting in past centuries the Spanish conquistadors' aggressive campaign to erase Inca and pre-Inca cultures and, in modern times, the lure of modernization.

When Peruvians talk of turquoise blue Titacaca, they proudly note that it is so large it has waves. This, the most sacred body of water in the Inca empire and now the natural separation between Peru and Bolivia, has a surface area exceeding 8,000 square kilometers, not counting its more than 30 islands. At 3,856 meters (12,725 feet) above sea level it has two climates: chilly and rainy or chilly and dry. In the evenings it becomes quite cold, dropping below freezing from June through August. In the day, the sun is intense and sunburn is common.

According to legend, this lake gave birth to the Inca civilization. Before the Incas, the lake and its islands were holy for the Aymará Indians, whose civilization was centered at the Tiahuanaco, now a complex of ruins on the Bolivian side of Titicaca but once a revered temple site with advanced irrigation techniques. Geologically, Titicaca's origins are disputed, although it likely was a glacial lake. Maverick scientists claim it had a volcanic start; a century ago, Titicaca was popularly believed to be an immense mountain top crater. A few diehards today stick to the notion that the lake was part of a massive river system from the Pacific Ocean.

Indian legend says the sun god had his children, Manco Capac and his sister-consort Mama Ocllo, spring from the frigid waters of the lake to found Cuzco and the beginning of the Inca dynasty.

Preceding pages, totora reed raft on Lake Titicaca. Left, tapestries for sale on the Uros islands. Right, a llama by the lakeside.

Later, during the Spanish conquest, the lake allegedly became a secret depository for the empire's gold. Among the items supposedly buried on the lake's bottom is Inca Huascar's gold chain weighing 2,000 kilos and stored in Koricancha – the Temple of the Sun in Cuzco – until loyal Indians threw it into the lake to prevent it from falling into Spanish hands.

Oceanographer Jacques Yves Cousteau spent eight weeks using mini submarines to explore the depths of the lake but found no gold. (What he did discover, to the amazement of the scientific world, was a 60-centimeter long, tri-colored frog that apparently never surfaces!)

Urban base: On the Peruvian side of the lake is **Puno**, an unattractive commercial center settled as a Spanish community in 1668 by the Count of Lemos. Although much of Puno may seem unappealing, during the Spanish period it was one of the continent's richest cities because of its proximity to the Laykakota silver mines discovered by brothers Gaspar and José Salcedo in 1657. The mining boom drew 10,000 people to an area not far from what is now Puno. It also brought a bloody rivalry that ended only when the iron-handed Count traveled to Puno, ordered José Salcedo executed and transferred Laykakota's residents to Puno.

At an altitude of 3,827 meters (12, 628 feet), Puno is still the capital Peru's *altiplano* – the harsh highland region better suited to roaming vicuñas and alpacas than to people. It is also Peru's folklore center with a rich array of handicrafts, costumes, holidays, legends and, most importantly, more than 300 ethnic dances.

Among the latter, the most famous is Devil dance performed during the feast of the Virgin of Candelaria during the first two weeks in February. Dancers fiercely compete to outdo one another in this *Diablada*, famous for its profusion of costly and grotesque masks. The origins of the dance have become confused with the centuries but it is believed to have started with pre-Inca Indian cultures, surviving through the Inca conquest and the Spanish takeover of the country, modifying costumes each time.

Dance and wild costumes: As numerous as the dances themselves are the lavish and colorful outfits the dancers wear. They range from multicolored *polleras* (layered skirts) used by barefoot female dancers to the short skirts, fringed shawls and bowler hats used in the highland version of the Marinera dance. For centuries the Indians in the *altiplano* were accustomed to working hard then celebrating their special days with gusto. In fact, many of the dances incorporate features of the most repressive times for the Indians with dancers dressed as the mine overseers or cruel landowners – the characters that are mocked during the festivities. It is difficult to find a month in Puno without at least one elaborate festival, always accompanied by music and dance.

Within Puno, there remain a handful of buildings worth seeing. The **Cathe-**

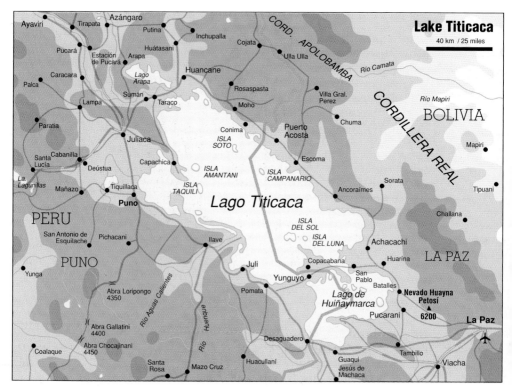

dral is a magnificent stone structure dating back to 1757 with a weather-beaten baroque style exterior and a surprisingly spartan interior – except for its center altar of carved marble plated in silver. Over a side altar to the right side of the church is the icon of The Lord of Agony, commonly known as El Señor de la Bala. Beside the Cathedral is the famous **Balcony of the Count of Lemos** found on an old house on the corners of Deustua and Conde de Lemos streets. It is said that Peru's Viceroy Don Pedro Antonio Fernandez de Castro Andrade y Portugal – the Count – stayed here when he first arrived in the city he later named "San Carlos de Puno".

On the **Plaza de Armas** is the **library** and the municipal *pinacoteca*, or **art gallery** and half a block off the plaza is the **Museo Carlos Dreyer** – a private collection of Nazca, Tiahuanaco, Paracas, Chimu and Inca artifacts bequeathed to the city upon the death of their owner, for whom the museum is named.

One of the most valuable pieces in the museum is an Aymara *arybalo*, the delicate pointed-bottomed pottery whose wide belly curves up to a narrow neck. Throughout the continent, the *arybalo* stands as a symbol of the Andean culture. (The museum is open daily except Sunday from 9 a.m. to 7 p.m.)

Views of the Sierra: Three blocks uphill from the plaza is **Huajsapata Park**, actually a hill that figures in the lyrics to local songs and an excellent spot for a panoramic view of Puno. Huajsapata is topped by a huge white statue of Manco Capac gazing at the lake from which he sprang.

Another lookout point is found beside **Parque Pino** at the city's north side in the plaza four blocks up Calle Lima from the Plaza de Armas. Also called Parque San Juan, it boats the Arco Deustua, a monument honoring the patriots killed in the battles of Junín and Ayacucho, the decisive battles in the Independence War with Spain.

The "San Juan" moniker for the park comes from the San Juan Bautista church within its limits; at its main altar is a

Procession during the Feast of the Virgin of Candelaria, Puno.

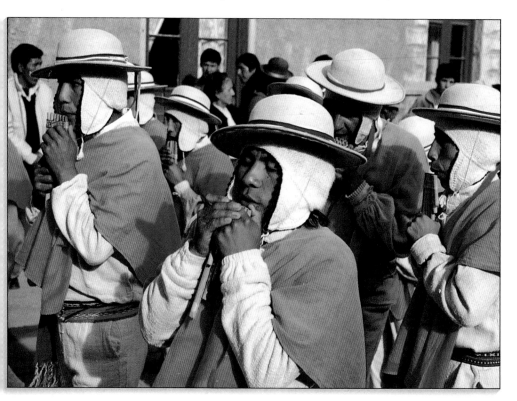

statue of the patron saint of Puno, the Virgin of Candelaria. Also in the park is the Colegio Nacional de San Carlos, a grade school founded by a decree signed by Venezuelan liberation leader Simon Bolivar in 1825. It was later converted into a university, then subsequently used as a military barracks.

Two blocks down F. Arbulu street from Parque Pino is the city **market**, a colorful collection of people, goods and food. Tourists should keep their eyes on their money and cameras while here, but it is worth a stop to see the wide range of products – especially the amazing variety of potatoes, starting with the hard freeze-dried *papa seca* that looks like gravel to the purple potatoes and yellow and orange speckled *olluco* tubers. Woolen goods, colorful blankets and ponchos are on sale here, along with miniature reed boats like those that ply Titicaca. Among the more intriguing trinkets are the Ekekos, the ceramic statues of stout jolly men laden with a indefinite number of good luck charms, ranging from fake money to

little bags of coca leaves. Believers say the Ekekos smoke and they are often found with lit cigarettes hanging from their mouths. Those who really believe in the power of these statues say they only bring luck if they are received as gifts – not purchased.

Exploring the Lake: Puno is the stepping off point for exploring Titicaca with its amazing array of islands, Indian inhabitants and colorful traditions. Small motorboats can be hired for lake trips or for catching the 30 pound-plus lake trout that make it one of Peru's best-known fishing destinations.

Launches leave from the dock at the end of Avenida del Puerto. It is also possible to take a lake tour on a British steamship that was carried piece by piece by train to Lake Titicaca more than a half century ago and recently was reactivated as a tourist ship.

Run by the National Train Company, the steam-powered *Ollanta* originally was used to take cargo and passengers from Punto to the Bolivian port of Guaqui but was taken out of service in

Navigating in totora reed boats.

1986 after flooding damaged the Bolivian lake town. Although its schedule depends more on passenger demand than an actual timetable, the *Ollanta* offers an overnight voyage from Peru to Bolivia as well as a half-day trip to the lake's islands. Tickets are sold at the Puno train station and officials said they are refurbishing a second vessel, the *Inca*, which was taken to the lake on muleback decades ago. Both are among only a handful of steamships remaining in Peru.

A British businessman, Meriel Larken, is also attempting to put back into service a 19th-century steamship built in his great uncle's shipyard in England. The *Vavari* (which temporarily had its name changed to *BAP Chucuito* when used by the Peruvian Navy in the 1970s) was built in 1861 and is one of the world's last riveted iron-hulled ships still afloat. Its original trip from the ocean port at Tacna to Titicaca involved packing pieces of the vessel onto the backs of mules and porters for an uphill journey that was expected to take six months. A number of interruptions, including a local revolution, poor weather and slow paychecks, stretched the project out to six years and it wasn't until Christmas Day in 1870 that the passenger and cargo vessel was launched, its boilers burning llama dung for fuel.

Steamships are understandably the novelty on Lake Titicaca, where most of the transportation is done in motorized launches or the Totora reed boats that Norwegian Thor Heyerdahl studied in preparing for his 4,300-nautical mile journey from Peru to Polynesia in the reed boat Kon-Tiki in the 1940s.

Floating Islands of Reed: The best known of the islands dotting Titicaca's surface are the **Uros**, floating islands of reed named after the Indians who inhabited them. Legend has it the Uro Indians had black blood that helped them survive the frigid nights on the water and safeguarded them from drowning.

The last full-blooded Uro was a woman who died in 1959. Other Uros had left the group of islands in earlier years – owing

The Uros Islands, made of reeds.

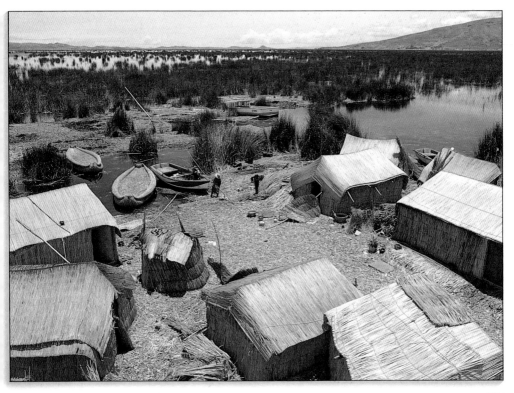

to a drought that worsened their poverty – and intermarried with Aymará and Quechua-speaking Indians. But the Indians who now inhabit this island – a mix of Uro, Aymará and Inca descendants – follow the Uro ways.

The Uros' poverty has prompted more and more of them to move to Puno. That same poverty has caused those who remain to take a hard-sell approach to tourists and, besides pressing visitors to buy their handicrafts, they frequently demand "tips" for having their photos taken.

Some tourists suggest that bartering with fresh fruit is better than money exchanges. However, there continues criticism that tourism has not only opened the Uros islands to the stares of insensitive tourists but has destroyed much of the culture as the Indians modified their handicrafts to appeal to outsiders or abandoned traditional practices to dedicate more time to the influx of outsiders.

The Uros islanders fish, hunt birds and live off lake plants, with the most important element in their life being the lake reeds they use for their houses, boats and even as the base of their five islands – the largest of which are **Toranipata, Huaca Huacani** and **Santa Maria**. The bottoms of the reed islands decay in the water and are replaced from the top with new layers, making a spongy surface that is a bit difficult to walk on. Even the walls of the schools on the bigger islands are made of totora. The soft roots of the reed are eaten.

Another island that lures tourists is **Taquile**, the home of skilled weavers and a spot where travelers can buy well-made woolen and alpaca goods as well as colorful garments whose patterns and designs bear hidden messages about the wearer's social standing or marital status. The residents of this island run their own tourism operations in the hope that the visits of outsiders will not destroy their delicate culture. There are no hotels on Taquile but the islanders generously open their homes to tourists interested in an overnight stay. (See "The Weav-

Women on Taquile island.

ing Co-ops of Taquile".)

Handicrafts also play an important role in life on **Amantaní,** a lovely and peaceful island even further away from Puno than Taquile. Amantaní has archaeological remains, including a stone "throne" and well-known trout farms. The Amantaní residents sell woven items. (See "Amantaní Opens its Doors".)

Esteves, though an island, is connected to Puno by a bridge and contains one of the finest hotels in the state-run Turistas chain. This luxury hotel, Turistas Isla Esteves, is a far cry from what used to be the main structure on the island – a prison that housed the patriots captured by the Spanish during Peru's war for independence.

James Orton, a naturalist and explorer who died crossing Titicaca on a steamship in 1877, is buried on Isla Esteves; his memorial sits beside one honoring the liberation fighters who perished in the war with Spain. Orton, a natural history professor from Vassar University, was on his third expedition to explore the Beni River in the Amazon area. The Beni's link to the Mamore River – both crucial conduits during the jungle's rubber boom – was named the Orton River in his honor.

Mysterious burial chambers: Some 35 kilometers (21 miles) from Puno is **Sillustani**, with its circular burial towers or *chullpas* overlooking **Lake Umayo**. The age of the funeral towers, which are up to 12 meters (40 feet) high, remains a puzzle. A Spanish chronicle keeper described them as "recently finished" in 1549, although some still appear as if they were never completed and the Indians that built them were conquered by the Incas about a century earlier.

The *chullpas* apparently were used as burial chambers for nobles of the Colla civilization, Indians who spoke Aymará, had architecture considered more complicated than that of the Incas and who buried their nobility with their entire family.

Not far away is **Chucuito**, a village that sits upon what was once an Inca

A procession on Taquile.

settlement and which boasts an Inca sundial. Stop by the **Santo Domingo Church** with its small museum in this altiplano village; also worth visiting is **La Asunción Church**.

Juli, once the capital of the lake area, has four beautiful colonial churches under reconstruction. Although it now appears odd to see so many large churches so close together, at the time the Spanish ordered them built they hoped to covert huge masses of Indians to Catholicism.

In addition, the Spanish were accustomed to having one church for the Europeans, one for the mixed-raced Christians and yet another for the Indians. The largest of Juli's churches is **San Juan Bautista** with its colonial paintings tracing the life of its patron, Saint John the Baptist. From the courtyard of **La Asunción church** visitors have a captivating view of the lake. The other churches are **San Pedro**, once the city's principal place of worship and the church in which a choir of 400 Indians sang each Sunday, and **Santa Cruz** beside the city's old cemetery. Santa Cruz was a Jesuit church upon the front of which Indian stonemasons carved a huge sun – the Inca god – along with Christian symbols.

It is from Juli that the Transturin hydrofoils leave for Bolivia. (Information is available at the Transturin office in Puno, Av. Giron Tacna 201, Tel: 737). There is catamaran service from Juli and Puno to Copacabana, Bolivia.

Pilgrimage Site: Copacabana can also be reached by taking a mini-bus ride around the side of the lake, passing the reeds waving in the wind, shy but curious children at the bends in the road and always the brilliant blue of Titicaca on the roadway that ends the lake. This pleasant trip involves a short ferry trip at the **Strait of Tiquina** and the destination is a pleasant one – Copacabana. This friendly little town accustomed to tourists has a number of modest but clean restaurants and hotels. It is most famous for its cathedral containing a 16th-century carved wood figure of the Virgin of Copacabana, the Christian guardian of the lake. The statue, finished in 1853, was the work of Indian sculptor Francisco Tito Yupanqui, nephew of Inca Huayna Capac.

One of the loveliest outings in Copacabana is a dawn or dusk walk along the waterfront, watching the sky explode into color with sunrise or slip into the blue black of night at sunset.

It is also possible to reach Bolivia by crossing around the other side of the lake via the Desaguadero border crossing, but this border town is one of the continent's filthiest and there is no acceptable lodging there in the event buses on the Bolivian side are not running (owing to holidays, strikes or lack of demand). From Copacabana, launches can be hired to visit the Bolivian islands on Lake Titicaca – the **Island of the Sun** and the **Island of the Moon**. The Island of the Sun (also accessible via a public ferry) has a sacred Inca rock at one end and the ruins of Pilko Caima with a portal dedicated to the sun god at the other. The Island of the Moon, also called Coati, has ruins of an Inca temple and a cloister for Chosen Women.

Left, steering on the lake. **Right**, burial *chullpa* at Sillustani.

THE WEAVING CO-OPS OF TAQUILE

Taquile, the island of weavers has a long history. In the 16th century it was awarded by the King of Spain to a man named Pedro Gonzales and became a colonial *hacienda*. After Peru won its independence, Taquile was used as a prison island. Little by little, the Taquile Indians regained ownership of their ancestral lands and, since 1970, they have run their own tourism operations in an attempt to ensure that the old ways are not lost in the effort to bring in visitors.

The tourism operations began after enterprising Puno residents began transporting visitors to the island; the Taquile residents wrestled control from the entrepreneurs and began operating their own passenger boats, regulating the number of outsiders that arrive and their activities. Once on the island, visitors are free to wander to the small Inca ruins dotting the hilltops or take photos of the farming terraces. The liveliest photos, however, are taken on July 25, St. James Day, when the island explodes into celebration with dancing, music and merrymaking.

A world of color: Taquile is devoted to weaving, and even men can be seen walking around knitting finely spun sheep's wool into the stocking hats they wear.

The colors and designs also reveal information about the wearer. Certain colors tell marital status or social standing, certain garments are worn only on holidays. Single men wear knit hats with white tufts on top; married men have red points on their hats. Belts are seasonal and some contain coded calendars, signaling that marriages will take place one month, houses will be roofed in another and crops will be planted in another. Blue and red are the predominant colors.

Samples of these ethnic garments, ranging from delicately embroidered blouses to the belts, hats and jackets that the men used, can be purchased at the island's weaving cooperative store. There is also a small museum of antique garments made by the ancestors of the current island residents.

Family accommodation: Although there are no hotels on the island, visitors can spend the night in the home of an island family, and the Taquile residents have a reputation for hospitality. Arrangements can be made with the Indians waiting at the top of the steep stone staircase at whose base the boats dock. Keep in mind that the accommodations are rustic and the blankets offered visitors unaccustomed to the cold nights may be insufficient. Many overnight guests bring their own sleeping bags, flashlights and food for eating and sharing with their host family; the charge

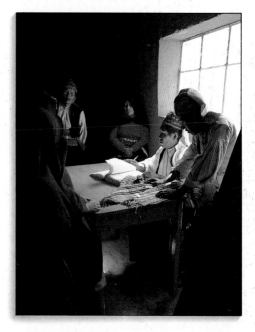

for the lodging is usually under a US$2.

There are some small eating establishments on the island, with fried trout offered as one of the delicacies. Bottled soft drinks are also usually available, although tourists are advised to carry water with them in the event refreshments run out.

It is possible to take the morning boat trip – a four hour journey – to Taquile, spend a couple of hours there and return on the early afternoon boat. However, travelers who have roughed it on an overnight at Taquile say watching the moon rising over frigid Lake Titicaca from the island is well worth any minor discomforts.

Left, a weaver with her loom. **Right**, signing in guests on the island.

AMANTANÍ OPENS ITS DOORS

For centuries lying all but forgotten at the eastern end of Lake Titicaca, the island of **Amantaní** is fast becoming one of South America's more exotic traveler's meccas.

It is not exactly Club Med Peru. The island's beds are made of long, hard reeds. Potatoes are served up for breakfast, lunch and dinner. There is no running water or electricity and the temperatures are freezing even at the height of summer. But Amantaní is catching on, and travelers now come from far and wide to stay on the latest Titicaca island to

of Taquile Island and control the flow of visitors. The Taquile Indians have kept out foreign middlemen and sell their weavings directly to tourists. But it is a balancing act that few other Indian groups in South America have been able to manage: Lake Titicaca's own Uros Islands can be a depressing reminder of the dangers of unbridled tourism.

Visiting Amantaní is a fascinating experience, but it also leaves travelers with an uncomfortable sensation: They may be unwitting actors in the cultural clash between

open its doors. For the equivalent of US$2 a night for bed and board in a family house, you can gain a unique glimpse of an Andean agricultural society that has maintained its traditions for centuries.

To the bitterly poor islanders, the tourist money is a small fortune. Yet the sudden influx of outsiders is a double-edged sword: the abrupt end to isolation, islanders fear, may put at risk the culture that makes Amantaní unique. Many of the island's inhabitants speak only Aymará and have never made the crossing to the mainland.

Wary of losing their ancient traditions, the island elders are trying to follow the model

the Andean and Western cultures that has been going on in Peru ever since Spaniards first arrived here over 450 years ago.

Family accommodation: The journey to Amantaní begins at the Puno docks with a wooden launch that the islanders run themselves. They make no pretense at an efficient commuter service; supposedly leaving at 5 a.m., the launch doesn't get moving until 8.

Four long hours later, you will finally arrive at Amantaní. A dry wind brushes past the few green trees poking up from the orange soil, while clusters of thin sheep munch sulkily in stone pens. Every passenger is taken to register on the island and be formally rostered to a "host" family, represented by one of the shy elderly men who gather at the docks.

Many of the mud-brick houses are set around open courtyards, where white pebbles spell the owners' names. The whole family gathers to heartily pump new arrivals' hands and show them their room, usually a simple affair with a bed, chair and whitewashed walls plastered with religious pictures. Communication can be a little awkward at first as the older family members rarely speak Spanish, but everyone quickly relaxes.

The mother of the family soon disappears through a smoky doorway to prepare lunch. Many travelers are relieved to discover that the islanders are almost exclusively vegetarian. The meal is usually a soup of potatoes and the Andean grain quinoa, followed by boiled potatoes and potato fritters. Any pieces of fruit brought from the coast as gifts are accepted by the families as if they were precious gems.

Exploring the island: Usually one of the younger family members speaks Spanish and will guide you around the island, pointing out the different herbs used in medicinal teas and explaining a few of the islanders' customs. There are several ruins that can be visited and the views over the island are often spectacular. Meanwhile, Indian women wander by in their traditional black and white lace dresses, always carrying slingshots to kill scavenging birds.

Folk memory holds that Amantaní was taken over by Incas, but the invading Spanish conquistadors slaughtered the inhabitants. A Spanish landlord later brought other Indians here to work the land as virtual slaves – with his white descendents still ruling the island after Peruvian independence. Then, within living memory, after a particularly riotous fiesta, the Indians went to the landlord's house and cut him down with their hoes. Land was then spilt up.

But the island's cold and unpredictable weather still makes farming difficult. Crops are offered up to Pachamama, the Earth Mother, every year at a fiesta. Most agree that tourism is a more reliable source of income.

Ancient world on the brink of change: But there is not always agreement as to how tourism should be managed. Many of the younger islanders are more enthusiastic about welcoming the outside world than the elders. "We want as many gringos as we can get," says Daniel, a 20-year-old who speaks Spanish and prefers Western clothes to traditional island garb. "Not dozens – hundreds."

Some visitors, impressed by the serenity of the island, have suggested that they should beware of gringos bearing gifts – that the Western presence might not be the unmitigated boon some expect. The young backpackers that now dribble onto the island might be the shock troops of mass tourism,

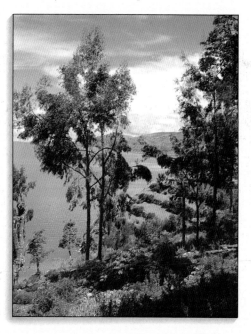

leading Amantaní down the same path as the forlorn and empty Uros islands.

But pro-tourism islanders regard these suggestions cynically, seeing no idyllic pleasure in the dull round of tending pastures, or the death rate left by using only traditional herbal medicines. With no outside aid, they argue, the Amantaní Indians will sell their only asset: their culture.

A couple of nights on the stiff reed bed and eating potatoes for three meals a day soon detracts from the romance for many visitors as well. The spluttering launch is always ready to head back to the coast, one step closer to the encroaching world outside.

<u>Left</u>, a wedding on Amantaní. <u>Above right</u>, the tranquil shores of Lake Titicaca.

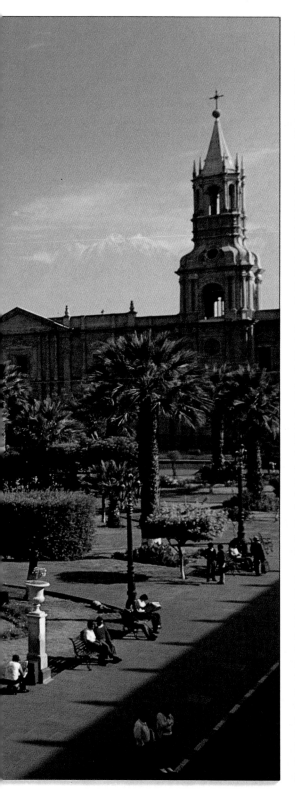

AREQUIPA

Far from Lima, isolated in a fertile valley tucked between desert and mountains and crowned by turquoise skies, **Arequipa** was a key stop on the cargo route linking the abundant silver mines of Bolivia to the coast. Built from the white sillar rock that spewed from **Misti**, one of a trio of imposing volcanoes looming behind it, this appropriately named "City of White" is Peru's second largest urban area and one of the country's most prosperous. In colonial days it boasted the largest Spanish population and strongest European traditions; the cattle and farming industries that started then remain principal sources of income for the region.

In 1541 the King of Spain granted this oasis at the foot of the snow-capped volcano the title "Most Noble, Most Loyal and Faithful City of the Ascension of Our Lady of the Beautiful Valley of Arequipa". Aymara Indians living here beside the **Chili river** more concisely called it Ariquepa (sic), "the place behind the pointed mountain". Another legend has it that one of the Incas, Mayta Capac, was moved by the beauty of the valley during one of his journeys and here he ordered his entourage to stop. His exact words were said to be "Ari quipay" – or "Yes, stay" in Quechua. Whatever the truth, Arequipa has grown into a magnificent city and the intellectual capital of modern Peru.

The heart of the city: Arequipa's **Plaza de Armas** is one of Peru's most beautiful. One full side is occupied by the massive twin-towered **Cathedral**, rebuilt twice in the 1800s after it was destroyed by fire and earthquake. The Cathedral's ominous and ornate exterior misleads because the church's interior is unusually bare and simple, except for its elaborate chandelier. The Cathedral clock is the city's unofficial timepiece and the place where disputes over punctuality (rare as they are among ever-tardy Peruvians) are settled. The church's organ, recently restored, is from Belgium and its elaborately carved wooden pulpit, the work of French artist Rigot in 1879, was brought to the city a century ago by a local aristocrat's daughter.

Two-story arcades grace the other three sides of the plaza, where palm trees, old gas lamps and a white stone fountain nestled in an English garden attract strollers and those looking for a bench. It is here that outspoken Arequipeños congregate for political rallies, protests or fiestas. The plaza's thick stone buildings with busily carved portals, their Moorish touches evident, breathe 450 years of history.

This city is full of dignified patricians' homes built in the 18th century and which have, for the most part, withstood the tremors that regularly shake this city. The one-story colonial structures are replete with massive carved wooden doors, grilled French windows and high-ceilinged rooms clustered around spacious central patrios. The best for visiting are **Casa Ricketts**, built as a seminary in 1738 and now used as a bank, the 200-year-old **Casa de la Moneda** or former mint and the **Casa Moral**, named after

the venerable mulberry tree on its patio and now operating as a bank with a small museum.

Upon close scrutiny, the carvings above the door of Casa Moral show pumas from whose mouths snakes are slithering – the same designs found on the ceramics and fabrics of the Nazca Indians. Meanwhile, an inscription inside the Casa de la Moneda gives visitors an idea of the social status enjoyed by Arequipa's wealthiest families at one time. When the mint was acquired as a home for the Quiróz famoly, those patricians, had inscribed – in 1738 – their family slogan: *Despues de Diós, Quiróz* (After God, Quiroz).

Also worth a stop on **Calle La Merced** is the **Goyeneche palace** with its huge patios, bedroom alcoves and colonial doors and windows. As with most colonial houses from the period, this mansion had a series of patios – one for formal occasions, one for the family, one for the servants and animals. The main patio breaks with the traditional white stone decor; at its center is a

Preceding pages: gazing over the Colca Canyon; Arequipa's Plaza de Armas. **Below**, the Santa Catalina convent.

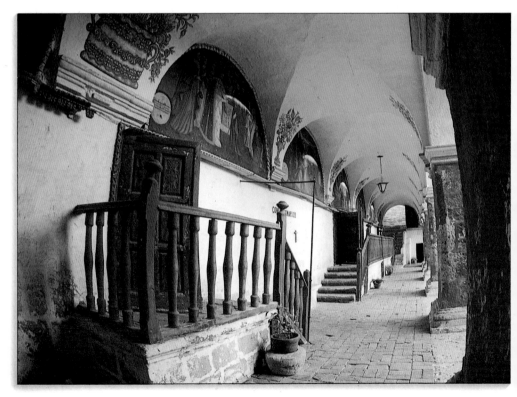

248

fountain of black rock.

Indian angels: On the non-secular side of this city, no visit is complete without a stop at the Church of **La Compañía**. The frontispiece of this two-story church is a complicated compilation of columns, zigzags, spirals, laurel crowns, flowers, birds and grapevines into which is embroidered in rock the abbreviations of the masses on Holy Fridays, the city's coat of arms (with the Misti volcano at its center) and the date the massive work was completed: 1698. But a careful look shows that even the European influence had its limits. The angels have Indian faces; one Indian face is even crowned with feathers.

What lies inside La Compañía is equally impressive. The sacristy's ceiling is covered with miniature paintings and carvings of crimson and gold. The view from La Compañía's steeple is fabulous, especially at sunset when the late afternoon light casts a pink, then mauve, glow on the city's gracious white buildings.

On the Morán street side of the church

is its cloister, where stark architectural lines are broken by detailed columns, demonstrating the high level stone carving reached in this city during the 17th century.

Nearby is **San Francisco Church**, the focus of attention every December 8 during the Feast of the Immaculate Conception. From the small chapel of the Sorrowful Virgin found in the church, the devout remove a fairytale-like coach topped with the image of the Virgin Mary surrounded by angels and saints. This is paraded through the streets in a colorful procession of pilgrims carrying flowers and candles.

Secret world of the past: The most astonishing stop in Arequipa is the **Santa Catalina convent**, opened in 1970 after 400 years as a cloister for nuns. Despite the closed doors, there was little heed paid to the nuns' vows of poverty and silence, at least in the early days. During its heyday this convent's sleeping cells were actually more akin to luxurious European chambers, with English carpets, silk curtains, cambric and lace

Below left, newspaper and a shoeshine. Right, an Arequipeña.

sheets and tapestry-covered stools. As for silence, French feminist Flora Tristan, visiting the convent in 1832 said the nuns – daughters of aristocrats – were nearly as good at talking as they were about spending huge quantities of money. Each had her own servants and dined with porcelain plates, damask tablecloths and silver cutlery.

Three blocks from the Plaza de Armas, Santa Catalina takes visitors back into the 16th century. Those who enter the cloister can see the spacious patios, the kitchen and slave quarters and stone wash tubs of this convent where entrance requirements were among the strictest in Peru. Novices had to prove Spanish origin and come up with a dowry of at least 1,000 gold pesos to join the order. The narrow streets, arches and gardens of the convent bear their original names: Córdova street, its whitewashed walls stark against the pots of bright red geraniums, Zocodovar square with a granite fountain and Sevilla street with archways and steps. About four dozen nuns still live in a section of the tile-roofed convent, which once housed up to 500 women.

When the convent was opened up twenty years ago, its anecdotes and scandals were resurrected. Among them is the story of Sister Dominga, the 16-year-old who entered the convent when her betrothed left her for a rich widow. The religious life did not agree with this beautiful young woman and she staged her own mock death to escape. Dominga really did place the body of a deceased Indian woman into her bed one night and set the room on fire, but it didn't happen here as some people claim. That scandal belongs to the **Santa Rosa convent** seven blocks from Arequipa's main square. Santa Rosa's mother superior refused to believe the rumors that the young nun was really alive and living outside the cloister – until Dominga wrote her demanding return of the dowry she paid the convent!

Although Santa Rosa remains cloistered, there are plans underway to renovate one earthquake-damaged section and make it accessible to the public.

Below left, restful colonial courtyard. **Right**, Virgin in Santa Catalina convent.

The Santa Rose convent was founded in 1747 by four nuns from the much larger Santa Catalina; nearly two dozen cloistered nuns still reside there.

Even older than Santa Catalina is the ancient colonial church of **San Lázaro**, the oldest neighborhood in Arequipa and possibly the spot where the city's founding took place. This small hermitage sits in front of a square bearing the same name; the fountain at the plaza's center is fed from Inca aqueducts there when the Spanish arrived.

Seceding from the north: Arequipeños are a proud, even haughty lot and their perennial attempts to secede from the rest of the country are a source of entertainment for Limeños, who jokingly ask Peruvian travelers if they have their passport before heading to Arequipa. In fact, the Arequipeños designed their own passports and flag in one of their futile attempts to separate from the rest of the union. From Arequipa's well-educated and politically passionate ranks have come two of the country's best-known figures, former President Fernando Belaunde Terry and novelist and failed Presidential hopeful Mario Vargas Llosa.

This regionalist passion peaks at annual celebrations marking the anniversary of the city's founding. Every August 15 Arequipeños cut loose with parades, bullfights and nighttime revelry highlighted by fireworks. The birthday celebration is accompanied by a weeklong handicrafts and folk festival.

To unwind in Arequipa in the evening, do what the locals do and head to a *picantería* for a cold Arequipena beer and some spicy food – stuffed peppers, pressed rabbit or marinated pork. If you opt for the peppers (*rocoto relleno*), take care. These red peppers scorch tongue, gullet and bowel of the inexperienced, and tourist reactions to the screamingly spicy pepper are a source of amusement for other diners and concern for restaurant owners. The beer will be accompanied by a dish of *cancha* or salty fried corn for munching.

Restored ruin: Outside Arequipa is **Sabandía** with its flour mill made of

Monastic library.

volcanic rock that was restored, stone by stone, in 1973. Architect Luis Felipe Calle had, in 1966, restored an old mansion in Arequipa (now functioning as the main branch of the Central Reserve Bank there), when he was given a task he long sought: restoring this old mill in ruins outside the city. He set up a tent beside the mill and lived there for the two and a half years it took him to finish the project, which he did using old documents and interviews with residents who remembered when the mill last operated nearly a half century ago. After the restoration the bank put the mill up for sale – and Calle himself purchased it.

"(The Arequipa area) is unique for its mixed architecture," said Calle, who not only lives at the mill but grinds wheat there to be transformed into mouth-watering bread. "It's not the case of superimposition, like one sees in Cuzco where the conquistadors constructed their buildings upon Inca foundations, nor is it like the purely Spanish architecture of Trujillo".

"Architecture of Arequipa is a fusion. The big *sillar* (stone) houses are humble but at the same time vigorous, a faithful reflection of the spirit of their people," added Calle, whose 18th-century property – open to visitors – is set in some of the area's most beautiful countryside.

A little farther out from the city are the thermal springs of **Yura** in the foothills of the extinct **Chachani volcano**. Crude cement pools fed by the sulfurous waters are open for bathing and lunch is available at the government-run Turistas Hotel at the springs. Two hours from the city on the road to Lima are the **Toro Muerto Petroglyphs**, hundreds of volcanic rocks believed engraved and painted more than 1,000 years ago by Wari Indians living in the region. The petroglyphs show depictions of llamas, condors, pumas, guanacos, dancers and warriors. A 145 km (90-mile) drive to the coast takes birdwatchers to **Mejía**, where rare and exotic species of the feathered creatures congregate at a series of lagoons.

Deeper than the grand canyon: Four

Colonial church near Arequipa.

hours away from Arequipa and drawing almost as much tourist attention these days as the city is the **Colca Canyon**, one of the world's deepest gorges cut 3,182 meter (10,607 feet) into the earth's crust. Twice the depth of the Grand Canyon, the Colca is shadowed by snow-topped peaks – many of them volcanoes – and sliced by the silvery Colca River. The base of this profound canyon is cold and windy and draws only daredevil kayak enthusiasts and researchers. Above, at the brink of the chasm, Indian farmers irrigate narrow terraces of rich volcanic earth much the same way their ancestors did centuries ago.

Though isolated, the Colca was a productive farming area before the Incas claimed it and, even when the Spanish reached the 64 km (40-mile) long valley where this canyon lies, they found terraced fields and thriving herds of lamas and alpacas. When the canyon became part of the route between the silver mines of Bolivia and the coast, the Colca farmers were snatched from their homes and forced to work in the mines. Later, when the railroad reached Arequipa, the Colca valley was forgotten – along with the small villages along its canyon.

When a multinational consortium began investigating the possibility of diverting the Colca River for a desert irrigation project, eyes once again turned to this valley and its gorge. From a lost chasm in a valley trapped in a time warp, the Colca – upon whose basalt sides cactus and brush cling desperately and whose visitors come in jeeps and on mules – has become one of the hottest tourist attractions in southwestern Peru. A flurry of tourism activity has surfaced with the Colca as its focus and there has been an accompanying modification in the valley's crops as it has more and more contact with the outside world. Barley is now grown on some terraces for use in the brewery in Arequipa.

The canyon is an average of 900 meters (3,000 feet) deep through most of its journey through the valley. A popular section is the "*Cruz del Condor*" – literally, the "Condor Crossing" – where visitors scan the skies for a glimpse of the majestic birds soaring

above in pairs.

A series of canyon trips, usually starting with a bus ride from Arequipa then a transfer to burros or trekking allow travelers to explore this rift full of small towns seldom visited by outsiders. Visitors may be puzzled in passing sections of the gorge named "the Polish Canyon" or "John Paul II Canyon". The first in-depth expedition of the chasm's bottom in 1978 was done by Canoandes, a group of white water experts from Poland who spent 17 years on the swift Colca River patriotically naming the areas they passed.

Although train travel in Peru has become increasingly difficult, some travelers still use Arequipa as the starting point for rail travel to Lake Titicaca then onto Cuzco. Rising transportation prices combined with heavy government subsidies on rail travel have made trains the Peruvians' most popular way to journey. That means tickets are in short supply.

From here, thrice weekly trains leave Arequipa at 7.45 p.m. for the more than 10-hour journey to Puno.

Lush terraces of the Colca Canyon.

THE PERUVIAN AMAZON

Those who have seen Werner Herzog's 1972 film *Aguirre, Wrath of God* which opens up with an expedition of armored conquistadors, horses, llamas and manacled Indian slaves making their way over the eastern edge of the Andes and down into the cloud forest, already have a vision of just how dramatic Peru's upper Amazon can be. The film, based on a true account of a mad conquistador's brutal search for El Dorado, ends appropriately enough with Aguirre and a few survivors drifting on a raft dwarfed by the enormity of the surrounding jungle, the raft circling slowly and infested with marooned monkeys.

Aguirre actually traced the same route of the Amazon and many of its tributaries. The river itself begins at 5,160 meters (17,200 feet) in Peru's snow-capped Andes, then gradually plunges in waterfalls through the cloud forest before broadening and swelling through the immense lowland jungles that stretch over 3,500 km (2,200 miles) to the sea. Although it often surprises the first-time visitor, 60 percent of Peru is actually jungle, even though less than 6 percent of its population lives there. Because the physical barrier of the Andes has prevented Peru from rapidly integrating the jungle portion of its country and because the upper Amazon is so distant from the Amazon's mouth and the sea, much of Peru's jungle is still intact. In a nutshell, Peru has some of the best untouched rainforest in the world.

Jungle from a prehistoric sea: Two hundred million years ago, South America, Africa and the rest of the world's continents were all part of one enormous continent called Gondwanaland. The Amazon basin at that time formed a giant inland sea while much of Gondwandaland was covered in a tropical forest that had no flowering plants but rather tree ferns, cyclads and roaming dinosaurs. Around 100 million years ago South America broke off from Af-

rica and the continent became an island where evolution continued in isolation. A menage of bizarre animals began to evolve, among them the sloths, the capybara (the world's largest rodent), armadillos and anteaters. As the eastern edge of the continent began to fold, the inland ocean became a gigantic inland lake where other unusual animals such as freshwater dolphins, piranhas and electric eels began to evolve. Gradually an ancient mountain formation in eastern Brazil was breached and the lake suddenly emptied, exposing an enormous, almost uniformly flat basin below. Even today the difference in elevation between Iquitos and the mouth of the Amazon – a distance of 3,200 km (2,000 miles) – is only 200 meters (660 feet)! About 4 million years ago the Andes mountains thrust up and the present contours of the basin were formed. Rivers flowing out of the Andes soon converged on the path of least resistance through a basin as large as the continental United States. After nearly 100 million years of isolation, it wasn't

Preceding pages: aerial view of the Amazon basin in the Madre de Dios region; a jaguar surprised in the wild. **Left**, waterfall in the lush jungle. **Right**, a macaw.

until only a few million years ago that Central America arose forming a landbridge to the north and allowing such modern animals as jaguars, deer and peccaries to move south.

Because of the characteristics of abundant water, light and heat (straddling as it does the equator) and a continuous growing season (there is little difference between winter and summer), plants flourished in incredible profusion, forming enormous 60-meter (200-foot) canopies. Unlike other biomes which were wiped out by the massive ice blocks rolling over the southern and northern hemispheres during the ice age, the jungle persisted – it is thus the oldest continuous terrestrial habitat on earth. The plants and animals have had millions of extra years to interact with one another and to evolve into increasingly more specialized forms. It is no wonder, then, that although the tropical rainforests presently cover less than 4 percent of the earth's surface, they house over 50 percent of all of its species. An estimated 50 percent of those have yet to even be discovered.

It was only within the last 50,000 years that mankind – who had evolved only a few million years before in Africa – was afforded an opportunity to pass into North and hence South America in his modern form. As the polar ice caps grew during the different phases of the ice age, the sea level sank, thus exposing the Bering Straight as a land bridge. Mongol tribes from Asia presumably followed herds of animals over the bridge and roughly 20,000 years ago arrived in the enormous hot-house now called the Amazon. Adapting to the rainforest over a period of thousands of years, the Indians learned to live in harmony with the jungle, using slash and burn methods of agriculture and learning to harvest the jungle's resources well within the limits of what this complex yet surprisingly fragile environment allowed.

Dreams of the conquistadors: That balance was immediately disrupted, however, with the arrival of the first Europeans. Far from home and wishing only to

Elegant jabiru birds in the Manu National Park.

stay long enough to gain instant wealth and fame, Europeans viewed the Amazon more as a storehouse of raw materials than as a place to be permanently inhabited. Having found immense Indian empires and plentiful gold in Mexico and the Andes, it was perhaps only natural for the Spaniards to suspect that there might be more golden empires to the east. In 1542 Fransisco de Orellana and his men became the first Europeans to raft down the Amazon. Attacked at one point by bow and arrow-bearing warriors wearing grass skirts and with long hair, the surprised Spaniards confused them with women, later christening the river the *Río de las Amazones*, after the Greek myth of a nation of warrior women.

In southern Peru, close to the Inca's capital of Cuzco, the story of glistening cities of gold gave rise to the legend of *Paititi*, a supposedly lost jungle city where the last Incas had hidden their gold. Various adventurers have sought Paititi – thought to exist somewhere in Peru's southern jungle department of Madre de Dios. (See feature "Search for Lost Cities".) Thus far only scattered petroglyphs, remote tribes and small Inca ruins have been found.

The search for gold, however, was eventually replaced by other valuable commodities native to the Amazon and found nowhere else in the world: quinine (which allowed British troops to conquer malarial India), cocoa (the basis of the world's chocolate industry), mahogany, vanilla, and others. No product made a bigger impact on the world, however, than that which naturally exudes from three species of Amazonian tree: the sticky-white latex called rubber.

The Rubber Boom: Almost 500 years ago Columbus reported seeing Indians who used strange elastic (rubber) balls for games. In 1743 the French scientist La Condamine used rubber latex to waterproof his instruments and was the first European to introduce the substance to the Old World. Although an English chemist soon began putting "rubbers" on the end of pencils, wider commercial

A caiman by the riverbank.

use was limited due to the fact that natural rubber grew soft and sticky in hot weather and brittle and hard in cold. In 1844, however, the process of vulcanization was discovered by Charles Goodyear, thus allowing rubber to stay tough and firm at all temperatures. With Dunlop's later invention of the pneumatic tire, suddenly an enormous demand was created which only the Amazon could satisfy. The ensuing rubber boom, which lasted roughly from 1880 to 1912, completely transformed the Amazon's economy. Rubber trees in the remotest regions were soon being tapped, the latex gathered in cups, then coagulated into large balls that were cured over a fire. The tappers themselves were bankrolled by entrepreneurs who amassed enormous wealth and lived in luxury in newly-burgeoning jungle cities such as Manaus in Brazil and Iquitos in Peru. In southeastern Peru the rubber baron Carlos Fitzcarrald extended his empire by dragging an entire steamship over a jungle pass that now bears his name (located between the Urubamba and Manu rivers) and thereby linking the remote Madre de Dios region with the rest of Peru (the fictionalized story was made into the 1982 film *Fitzcarraldo* by Werner Herzog).

In the midst of the boom, however, an English adventurer named Henry Wickham quietly collected 70,000 rubber seeds and smuggled them out of the Amazon. First planted in Kew gardens in England and then transplanted to tropical Asia where they were safe from indigenous disease, the seeds flourished. By 1912 the Amazon rubber boom was at an end.

Delicate ecology: Viewed from the air, Peru's Amazon looks like an endless sea of lumpy green sponges, stretching in all directions to the horizon. It is this thick umbrella of trees – the jungle's equivalent to an enormous housing project – that creates the millions of homes for animals and specialized plants to live in below. If you were to enter the upper canopy slowly from the top you would soon discover that the first layer **Dense** is virtually a desert of sorts. The crowns **rainforest.**

of the trees are exposed both to the fierce tropical sun and to winds that frequently snap and topple the tallest of trees. To reduce evaporation, the leaves at this level are quite small. many of the epiphytes here – plants that live on top of other plants – actually take the form of cacti, to reduce their loss of water. As you descend through the upper canopy, however, you immediately begin to enter a different world of reduced light. Protected from direct sun and wind, the leaves are thus larger in size than those above and the struggle for light has begun. Traveling further down towards the jungle floor, leafy plants are much less abundant. Although explorers traveling by river often reported thick and impenetrable jungle, under the canopy away from the rivers one can move quite easily as most branches and leaves are well off the floor. Like living beneath the sea, even in strong storms the air here is calm and at other times, completely still. The overpowering sound of insects above is enormous as millions call to one another unseen. At the bottom most level the leaves are very large; less than 5 percent of the sun's light reaches the jungle's floor.

It is this enormous variation of light, wind, temperature and thousands of different species of plants that affords a million different homes for animal and plant species. Whole communities of insects, birds and other animals are specialized and adapted to different levels of the rainforest which not surprisingly contains the highest species diversity in the world. Manu National park in southeastern Peru, for example covering an area roughly half the size of Switzerland, houses over 800 bird species (the same number as found in all of North America), 20 percent of all plant species found in South America, and more than 1,200 species of butterflies (Europe has 400). A recent study of the insects in Manu's upper canopy by the Smithsonian Institution has increased the number of the world's estimated animal species by 30 million.

Push towards conservation: Although jungles have existed for hundreds of

A cautious young puma.

millions of years, it is only within the last 100 years that they have been on the decline. The trend is in direct relation to the population of human beings. A million years ago man had an estimated population of 50,000. That population has now grown to over 4 billion. In the last century humans have destroyed half of the world's rainforests. At the present rate of destruction, most experts agree, the majority of the remaining rainforests will be gone within the next 25 years.

In Peru, the largest destructive force on the Amazon has been the unmanaged influx of peasants from the Andes and the coast. Since the 1960's, both military and civilian governments have viewed the eastern Andean slopes and the Amazon basin as an El Dorado of unexploited natural resources, believing that development of the region would provide a politically painless "solution" to land hunger in the Andes, migration of rural poor to coastal cities, and the need to populate remote border regions to defend national sovereignty. As a result the government financed the construction of a "marginal highway", a road paralleling the Andes to the east which the government hoped would help open up the area to colonization and industry.

The idea of settling the Amazon, however, ignored reality: less than 5 percent of the Peruvian Amazon's soil is suitable for agriculture, and much of the region supports populations of indigenous people and settlers that are already large in relation to exploitable resources. As a consequence, agriculture that began on a few relatively fertile terraces in the eastern Andes has spread to land ill-suited to continuous exploitation. With little knowledge of better practices, many farmers work the land too long, allowing no time for it to renew. Once the soil has been drained of nutrients, poor farmers unable to buy fertilizer move on, carving yet another plot from the forest. The result has been extensive deforestation of Peru's cloud forest where incredibly an estimated 50 percent of all neotropical plant species

Poison-dart frog in the Manu National Park.

are found. Thus far over 70,000 square kilometers of the Peruvian Amazon has been deforested; 300,000 hectares are deforested every year.

An additional impact on Peru's rainforest has been the illegal, 1.6 billion dollar/year cocaine industry, mostly concentrated in the north-central jungle's Huallaga valley. Hundreds of thousands of hectares of virgin rainforest have been destroyed in order to grow illegal plantations of coca shrubs – all to support the surprising need of North Americans and Europeans to snort the potent white powder. In the last few years the U.S. government has pressured Peru to use a major defoliant – Spike – on coca plantations. Protests among local and international conservationists about the effect such a chemical could have on the surrounding jungle, however, has prevented its use. In the meantime, the entry of Shining Path guerrillas into Huallaga area and the U.S.'s offer of military equipment and increasing numbers of advisors, has further complicated the situation.

System of protection: In spite of increasing rainforest destruction, however, a number of encouraging developments have taken place. Peru currently has roughly 5 percent of its territory protected by a system of 24 national parks, reserves, sanctuaries and other designated areas, a process which began only in the 1960's. In the last 20 years considerable ecological awareness has developed and, as a consequence, a proliferation of conservation organisations has begun. Five of the largest are: The Nature Conservancy Foundation (FPCN, Lima); Ecologia y Conservacion (ECCO, Lima); The Conservation Association for the Southern Jungle (ACSS, Cuzco); The Peruvian Association for the Conservation of Nature (APECO, Lima); and the Environmental Development Group (IDMA, Lima). In 1983, with the help of the Canadian government, the U.S. Fish and Wildlife Service and the World Wildlife fund, Lima's La Molina Agrarian University began the only graduate school in the tropical Andean countries to offer advanced

River transport near Iquitos.

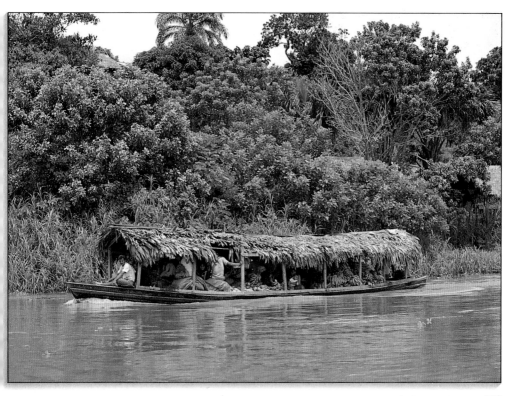

degrees in Wildlife conservation and management. Also begun at La Molina is the Conservation Data Center (CDC) which is computerizing an inventory of Peru's biological diversity, one of the highest in the world.

In February, 1990 a giant new 1.5 million hectare "reserved zone" was declared in the Madre de Dios region – Peru's southernmost department which houses some of the richest rainforest found anywhere in the world. This new area – including almost the entire watershed of the Tambopata river – is currently at the forefront of tropical rainforest conservation. The idea is to convert the zone not into a park but rather an "extractive reserve". The latter is an area of rainforest where renewable yearly harvests of Brazil nuts, rubber and other rainforest products will create more revenue over the long run than the permanent destruction caused by unmanaged farming, logging and cattle-ranching. Pioneered by the Brazilian rubber tapper Chico Mendez (who was murdered in 1988 by Brazilian cattle ranchers and whose story has recently been made into a film by David Puttnam), the pressure is currently on to see how such extractive reserve ideas fare.

Also developing in Peru's rainforest within the last 10 years is the practice of "eco-tourism", based on the belief that rich natural rainforest can not only be preserved by use as an extractive reserve, but also as a lure to attract tourist dollars. Pumped into local economies and national park infrastructures, tourist dollars may well prove to be one of the few counter-destructive economic forces currently available for preserving the jungle. The more people that travel to virgin rainforest areas, the more people who will become involved in the international fight to save them. And, just as importantly, tourism can prove the monetary value of intact rainforests to the many hard-pressed, third world countries that can't afford the luxury of the industrialized west's "untouchable" parks and reserves.

The northern jungle: Three thousand two hundred kilometers up-river from **Calm jungle morning.**

the Amazon's mouth lies the jungle-locked city of Iquitos. It has a population of 350,000, with only rivers linking it to the exterior world. At one time the clearing house for the millions of tons of rubber shipped to Europe, Iquitos still displays the vestiges of its former status as one of the most important rubber capitals in the world. Houses near the main plaza and near the river are still faced with *azuelos* (glazed tiles) which at the height of the rubber boom (1880-1912) were shipped from Italy and Portugal along with other luxury goods such as turn-of-the-century ironwork from England, glass chandeliers, caviar and fine wines. On the **main plaza** is an iron house which was designed by Gustav Eiffel for the Paris exhibition in 1898. The house is said to have been transported from Paris by a local rubber baron and is entirely constructed of iron trusses and bolted iron sheets. Also on the plaza is the house of Carlos Fitzcarrald, the Peruvian rubber baron who dragged a steamship over the pass that bears his name thus opening up the

department of Madre de Dios. The German film maker Werner Herzog shot part of his 1982 film *Fitzcarraldo* here (he also filmed on the Urubamba river near Camisea) and several of the refurbished steamships that he used are still in port. Hundreds of Iquiteños were used as extras.

Iquitos today is a quiet, colorful, friendly city which seems to have a monopoly not on rubber but on three-wheel taxis (roughly $0.50 a ride), motor scooters, Amazon views and atmosphere. Located some 80 km (50 miles) downriver from where the **Marañon** and **Ucayali** rivers join to create the Amazon river, the local dish here is *Paiche a la Loretana*, a fillet of a huge primitive fish, together with fried manioc and vegetables. Exotic fruit juices are sold on the street corners as are ice-creams flavored with mango, papaya, guanabana, granadilla, zapote, pochote, spondia and others.

You can take a taxi or simply walk from the main plaza to the picturesque waterfront district of **Belén**, many of the

Lunch by an Amazon tributary, Manu National Park.

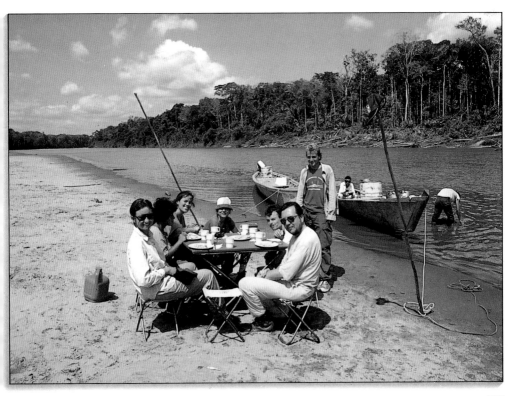

houses of which float on rafts in the water. A Venetian-like labyrinth of canals, canoes and stores, Belén is the nerve center for an incredible variety of Amazon products: exotic fruits, fish, turtles, herbal medicines and water fowl. Plowing the waterways are a plethora of small canoe-taxis paddled by Iquiteños as young as 5 years old. You can take a canoe tour of this floating metropolis for roughly $3.00 – it's one of the most unusual waterfronts in the world.

A short excursion just south of the city is the beautiful **Lake Quistocoche** set in lush tropical jungle. The lake-reserve has a zoo (Parque Zoológico de Quistococha) where animals such as jaguars, ocelots, paiche, parrots and anacondas can be seen (entrance US$1, closed Mondays).

Jungle lodges: Due to its character as a stop-over for those going by river to Brazil and for international flights, Iquitos has long been a center for excursions into the surrounding jungle. It should be remembered, however, that because there are a lot of people in this area and that this is a main waterway, you must travel well beyond a 60 kilometer radius of the city if you want to see wildlife such as caimen, monkeys, macaws or pink dolphins (the latter are found only on remote tributaries of the upper Amazon and Orinoco rivers). One way to become quickly acquainted with the jungle is to visit one of a number of lodges set up on nearby rivers. Although many of the two or three day lodge tours can be booked through a travel agent in Lima, the tours are much cheaper if booked in Iquitos and are roughly $40 a day. One should avoid the numerous individuals in the airport and city trying to set up a "jungle lodge tour". Since these men are paid a commission, you can get the same package deal much cheaper by simply walking into a lodge's downtown office, most of which are clustered around Jiron Putumayo near the Plaza de Armas.

Explorama Tours (Putumayo 150) is one of the largest companies with three different lodges all well-run and efficient; **Explorama Inn**, 40 km (25

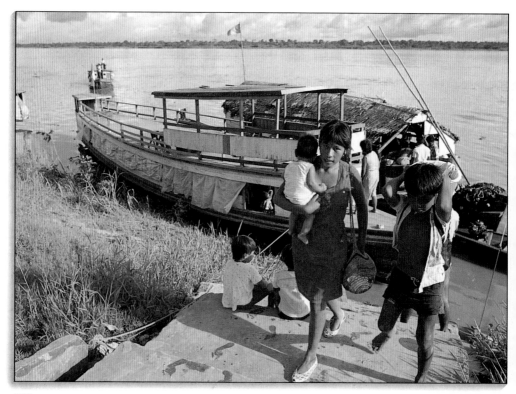

Riverboat near Iquitos.

miles; 1½ hrs) from Iquitos and which has not water, comfortable bungalows, good food and attractive jungle walks, is recommended for those who want to see the jungle (though few large animals) in comfort; **Explorama Lodge** (60 km/ 37 miles from Iquitos), is at Yanamono; **Explornapo** (140 km/88 miles from Iquitos) is located on the Napo river and is one of the best lodges for seeing wildlife in the Iquitos area. Other lodges are **Amazon Lodge Safaris** (Putumayo 165), which also owns the **Amazon Lodge** and another, smaller lodge for more adventurous visitors; (**Amazon River Tamshiyacu Lodge** (Putumayo 184) which runs the **Tamshiyacu lodge** ($30/day) and includes a tour of the beautiful Yarapa river (where there are often numerous river dolphins); and **Amazon Camp Tourist Service** (Putumayo 196) which runs a lodge on the rio Momon ($20/day). All lodge routes and prices are controlled by the Ministry of Tourism (Calle Arica) and can be double-checked there.

Slow boats through the jungle: Another way of seeing the Amazon is to take a commercial riverboat traveling either upriver towards Pucallpa or downriver towards Brazil. Although not much will be seen in the way of wildlife along the way (boats traveling upstream hug the banks, those in the opposite direction travel down the center of the river), the traveler will still see how people live along the Amazon as well as enjoy beautiful sunsets and magnificent scenery. One should be warned that life along the Amazon is slow and leisurely – you should never travel by riverboat if you are in a hurry or have an inflexible schedule. Boats break down, linger sometimes for days in port, and are generally unpredictable. Even so, riverboat travel is an unforgettable experience and well recommended. The best place to look for boats in Iquitos is by actually going down to the docks and asking around or by visiting the following offices: **Menesses** (Jirón Prospero); **Hurtado** (Av. Grau 1223); **Bellavista** (Malecon Tarapaca 596), and **Casa Pinto** (Sargento Lores 164). A seven-

Paddling near the Belén markets, Iquitos.

day trip to Pucallpa can cost anywhere from $20-30, and includes food (generally rice, meat and beans cooked in river water – which might prompt you to bring tins and fruits of your own), deckspace for your hammock (you can buy one in Iquitos for $10) and a cabin ticket if you want a berth. Traveling to Manaus in Brazil takes around 15 days and requires a boat change at the border. Both the *Clivie* and *Almirante Monteiro* frequently make this journey, are clean and have reasonable food. If you want to make the trip in style, try the *Juliana*, the refurbished riverboat used in Herzog's film, *Fitzcarraldo*. Travel to the border of Brazil costs around $15.

A third way to see the Amazon, and one highly recommend for those who have a little more time and want to get off the beaten path, is to hire a small boat and guide of your own. In every Amazon port there are boat owners who are willing to rent you their services at only a fraction of the cost paid to a typical jungle lodge. Once with a boat, the entire Amazon suddenly opens up for your exploration. By sharing expenses, for example, a party of four can travel the Amazon daily for as little as $7-10 per person. The best way to locate a guide and boat in Iquitos is to go to the tourist office (Foptur, Jr. Prospero 163 on the Plaza de Armas) or simply ask about on the wharves. Only 100 km (62 miles) from Iquitos, for example is the 2.1 million hectare **Pacaya-Samiria National Reserve**, a wildlife-packed lowland jungle area that can only be reached by hiring a private boat and staging your own expedition. The reserve is managed by COREPASA in Iquitos.

Yet another interesting introduction to the jungle open to the visitor who wants a more "hands-on experience" is a number of "jungle survival" courses offered in the Iquitos area. The nature, length and location of the course depends a lot on the participant – they can be anything from jungle camping trips to rigorous, live-off-the-land expeditions. You should be very fit; the experience is unique. Freddie Valles of

Camping in the jungle.

Amazon Adventure Tours (Sgto Lores 220, Tel: 235151) and Moises Torres Viena of **Expediciones Jungle Amazonica** (Soledad 718), (the latter a former Peruvian army jungle survival instructor), both offer excursions for a negotiable $80/day.

The central jungle: Seven days travel upriver from Iquitos on the Ucayali river is **Pucallpa**, a rapidly growing city of 90,000 which can be reached from Lima by air. The city was joined to Lima by a highway in the 1960s which has fueled lumbering, oil exploration and also drug trafficking. Most people arriving in Pucallpa, however, prefer to stay on the nearby **Lake Yarinacocha** a 20-minute bus ride from the city and the main tourist attraction of the area. Both the **Hospital Albert Schweitzer**, which serves the local Indians, and the **Summer Institute of Linquistics**, a non-denominational missionary organization studying many of Peru's jungle Indian languages (visited by appointment only), are based here. In the small town of Yarinacocha at the edge of the lake is the fascinating artesanal cooperative, **Moroti Shobo**, where extremely high quality ceramics and weavings of the Shipibo Indians are displayed and are sent to museums all over the world. Although several lodges are on the lake, as there is little wildlife to see due to the nearby population, they are more for scenery and relaxation: **Hotel La Cabana**, run by a German and **La Perla** run by a Frenchman. The lodges also arrange jungle excursions. Private excursions by motor canoe into the surrounding jungle and canals are easy to arrange from the port at Yarinacocha for about $17/day. On the canals are numerous piranhas, caimen and occasional monkeys. Trips can also be arranged to the numerous Shipibo villages whose culture has been in the area for at least the last 1,000 years.

The southern jungle: The traditional hopping off point into Peru's little-explored southern jungle is the city of **Cuzco**, where a variety of trip options are available. A recommended agency in Cuzco to visit is the Peruvian Conser-

Giant water lillies.

vation Association for the Southern Rainforests (ACSS), a non-profit group dedicated to preserving the rainforests in southern Peru and an excellent source of information on some of the southern jungle's parks.

The adventurous traveler can go from Cuzco by rail and truck to **Quillabamba** and **Kiteni** and from there to hire a boat through the **Pongo de Manigue**, a narrow gorge surrounded by lush jungle and waterfalls on the upper **Urubamba river**, a journey described in Peter Matthiesson's 1962 classic novel *The Cloud Forest*. After visiting the Pongo you can either return to Cuzco or else continue on down the Urubamba past small missions and Machiguenga Indians settlements. It should be emphasized that travel is infrequent through this area and should therefore be extremely flexible. There is a twice monthly government plane lower down on the Urubamba at the mission town of **Sepahua** which goes to Pucallpa and then Lima, or you can continue all of the way to Pucallpa and points beyond by boat.

The Manu National Park: Also accessible from Cuzco is the largest rainforest park in the world, located in Peru's southernmost jungle department of **Madre de Dios**. At 4.5 million acres, **Manu** is without a doubt one of the best areas for seeing wildlife anywhere in the Amazon rainforest. In many other jungle areas, because of the proximity to humans, you will be lucky to see anything more than birds, insects and the occasional large animal, but in Manu you are guaranteed to see so many monkeys (there are 13 different species) that you run the risk of getting tired of them. Besides abundant macaws, turtles, and other wildlife, you'll have the best opportunity you'll ever have of seeing giant otters, peccaries, capybaras, tapir and even the occasional jaguar.

The easiest way to visit Manu is with a local tour operator such as **Manu Nature Tours** or **Expediciones Manu**, since all preparations for the trip must be made in advance and permits are required for entry into the reserve. The **A tropical downpour.**

tour operator arranges all permits, transport, equipment, gasoline, and food supplies for the trip. It can take two days to reach this isolated area by traveling overland from Cuzco, down through the cloud forest and later transferring to a boat – an unforgettable experience. There is also the option of chartering a small plane which can fly to the junction of the Madre de Dios and Manu rivers. Most tour operators offer rustic camping trips from about $30 per person per day. In 1987 Manu Nature Tours built the first tourist lodge in Manu, **Manu Lodge**, which is presently one of the finest Amazon wildlife viewing facilities in the world. Because of the extreme isolation of the area and the fact that it houses only a maximum of 25 visitors at a time, the lodge isn't cheap, averaging around $60/night. Dedicated to conservation, however, in terms of seeing wildlife it's probably the best money per animal seen that you'll spend anywhere in the Amazon.

Boom town of the south: Linked by road or by air from Cuzco, **Puerto Maldonado** is the capital of the Peruvian department of Madre de Dios. Long cut off from the rest of the world by rapids on the **Madeira river** and by the Andes, only with the discovery of gold in the 1970's and the building of an airport in the early 1980's has the city developed into a gold rush "boom" town. Still, however, Madre de Dios has some of the greatest expanses of pristine jungle that exist anywhere on earth. Not only are there four protected wildlife reserves (including Manu National Park) that rank among the best in the world, but it is also here that three of Peru's last uncontacted Indian tribes are hidden.

Set on a bluff overlooking the Madre de Dios and Tambopata rivers, Puerto Maldonado has a pleasant **town square**, a large government bank (to buy the gold sifted from the river), and numerous hotels for miners on brief trips to town. In 1897 the rubber baron Carlos Fitzcarrald traveled through here after having dragged his steamship, with the help of hundreds of Indians, over the Fitzcarrald pass and down the Manu

The notorious piranha.

and Madre de Dios rivers on his way to Iquitos via Brazil. If you go down to where supposedly Fitzcarrald's steamship is located, a half an hour from the city and stranded a short ways inland in the jungle. Despite their claims, however, this isn't his boat; it is that of a German hospital ship which plowed the Madre de Dios in mid-century. Buy a bag or two of Brazil nuts while you're here. Buying the rich, abundant and inexpensive nuts will help encourage the preservation of Madre de Dios' rainforest where 70 percent of the population is involved in Brazil nut extraction.

Only an hour south of Puerto Maldonado is **Lake Sandoval**, a beautiful jungle lake which can be reached by boat from Puerto Maldonado's port. Three hours further downriver, and well worth an overnight fishing expedition, is **Lake Valencia** which is quite remote and relatively free of tourists. A several day expedition can be mounted to the 100,000 hectare **Pampas de Rio Heath National Reserve**, a wild area of plains and swamps located on the Heath River bordering Bolivia. Guides and their boats can be rented for roughly $30/day. Travelers wishing to go to Bolivia (about five hours to the border) can easily buy a passage with the weekly cargo boats traveling the Madre de Dios river. Many of the boats stop in small river communities for rubber and Brazil nuts thus allowing the traveler a privileged view of a way of life that has little changed in the last 100 years.

The new Tambopata-Candamo Reserve: Created by the Peruvian government in 1989, this 1.5 million hectare "reserved zone" has been set up both as an extractive reserve (for rubber, Brazil nuts and other products) and for eco-tourism. The reserve encompasses the entire watershed of the **Tambopata River**, one of the most beautiful and least disturbed areas in Peru. The river begins high in the Andean department of Puno; several tour companies lead kayak expeditions down the Tambopapa which offers a spectacular transition from the Andes to the low jungle. Recommended is **Mayuc Tours**; a week and a half expedition runs around $800. Tambopata Nature

Tours also visits the area.

Within the same reserve, about a four-hour river journey from Puerto Maldonado on the Tambopata, is the **Explorer's Inn Lodge** owned by Peruvian Safaris. With world record numbers of birds and butterflies, a two day/three night package runs about $150. Tours are led by biology graduate students; yet because there are settlers in the area, large mammals are only occasionally to be seen. The area is beautiful, however, and side trips are available from the lodge to one of the world's largest macaw coplas (salt-licks), located some four hours further up-river where hundreds of spectacularly colored macaws can be seen everyday.

Closer to the Puerto Maldonado area (and hence in a more disturbed, yet accessible area) are two other jungle lodges: **Cuzco Amazonico** located 45 minutes downriver from Puerto Maldonado on the Madre de Dios River, and **Tambo Lodge**, on the opposite side of the Madre de Dios only 8 km (5 miles) from town.

Below, ecologist marks a baby caiman. Right, watching from above.

The forests along the western edge of the Amazon Basin, nudging the Andean foothills, contain the highest diversity of bird species of any region on Earth.

The richest, least disturbed part of this unique belt is found in the unlogged, unhunted rainforests of southeast Peru. Here a typical square-mile of forest boasts over 500 species of bird – 40 percent more than a similar area in the central Amazon of Brazil. This species-rich area ranges from the cloud forests of the Andean foothills to the rainforests of

creepers, gnateaters, and foliage-gleaners all search for insects amongst the leaves and epiphytes in a flurry of activity. Identifying the many constantly moving individuals in these large mixed-species flocks poses one of the real challenges for tropical birders. Other insect-eaters, like the black-spotted bare-eye, specialize in following army ants so as to catch the insects fleeing from the invading ant swarm.

Fruit-eating birds on the other hand are often attracted to the fig tree with its small,

the Amazonian lowlands, and offers unrivalled opportunities to see rare and fascinating birds. There are many species of birds which only occur at higher elevations. These can be seen in the mountain cloud forests, and include golden-headed quetzals, large green military macaws, and orange-red male cock-of-the-rocks that use elaborate wing displays to attract females.

In the lowland rainforests every level, from darkened forest floor to sun-dappled canopy, supports a variety of insect – and fruit-eating birds. Many of the insect-eating birds gather together in mixed flocks containing dozens of different species. Small antbirds, wood-

soft fruits. Paradise tanagers, colorful euphonias, brilliant blue cotingas, fruitcrows, squawking parrots, and large-billed toucans may all visit the tree creating a day-long birding spectacle.

Entry to the jungle: However, to see these birds it is necessary to have a network of trails giving birders access to many types of forest. Such trail systems are provided by lodges located in the protected forests of two huge preserves in southeast Peru.

The largest of these, the **Manu Biosphere Reserve** is one of the few truly pristine regions of the tropics. Its 4.5 million acres harbour over 1,000 species of bird – 300 more species than are found in the U.S. and Canada together. In fact, the world record for the number of species seen and heard in one day was set in Manu in 1982 when 331 species were recorded in just a few square-miles of forest.

The only lodge located in the Manu preserve is **Manu Lodge** ($60/night), operated by Manu Nature Tours. The lodge overlooks a tranquil rainforest lagoon, and accommodates just 25 visitors. Its expanding trail system provides access to seasonally flooded forest, high ground forest, and patches of bamboo. There are also experienced guides to help visitors find shy bird species, like the Amazonian Antpitta.

Lodge. The list of birds seen at the lodge is still growing, and may soon exceed 550 species. All of this makes Manu Lodge one of the most attractive lodges to birders in the Western Amazon.

There are more chances to see birds in the second large reserve: the **Tambopata-Candamo Reserve**. This 3.7 million acre preserve protects the largest macaw lick in South America. Here birders can view one of the world's phenomenal avian spectacles.

Forest for macaws: Hundreds of red, blue, and green parrots and macaws gather at the lick daily. Squawking raucously, they wheel through the air before landing together on the river bank to eat clay. This breathtaking

Large, rare game-birds such as razor-billed curassows and piping-guans have been hunted out of most areas, but are easy to see at Manu Lodge. Also seen are macaws, pale-winged trumpeters, 5-foot-tall jabiru storks, roseate spoonbills, and five species of large eagle including the majestic harpy eagle.

New species are continually being discovered along the lodge trails. The extremely rare rufous-fronted ant-thrush, for example, was previously known from only one location but has now also been found at Manu

display can only be seen where there is undisturbed rainforest with healthy populations of wild macaws, as in southeast Peru.

Rustic accommodation is provided at the macaw lick by Tambopata Nature Tours, with six days including transportation costing about $500. Trails around the macaw lick offer birding in both floodplain and high ground forest. Orinoco geese and large horned screamers can also be seen along clear-water streams near the Andean foothills.

Also in the Tambopata reserve is the **Explorer's Inn** lodge, owned by Peruvian Safaris, with 2 days/3 nights at $150. Up to 500

Left, birdwatchers spot their prey. **Above,** the Peruvian cock-of-the-rock (Rupicola Peruviana).

bird species can be seen around the lodge. These include quetzals, manakins, and many antbirds as well as a recently discovered species new to science. The lodge trails also provide good access to patches of bamboo with bird specialities like the Peruvian recurve-bill, white-cheeked tody-flycatcher, and goeldi's antbird.

With all this, the forests of southeast Peru offer the finest birdwatching experience. However, identifying all the different species, and finding elusive birds in the forest undergrowth can prove overwhelming for an ornithologist inexperienced in tropical forests. An expert guide familiar with the rainforest and its bird-life is invaluable for a rewarding bird-watching trip to southeast Peru. **Manu Nature Tours** at Avenida Sol 627-B, officina 401, in Cuzco provide bilingual guides on their birding tours. High quality tours with expert guides are also provided to many parts of southeast Peru by **Victor Emmanuel Nature Tours** at P.O. Box 33008, Austin, TX 78764.

Bird-watching tours like these help support many local families who will conserve rainforest birds if their livelihoods depend on it. Local people will not hunt macaws for trade or feathers if they can make more money by taking visitors to see wild macaws at clay licks, as in the Tambopata Reserve. By choosing such tours, visitors can make a positive conservation impact while enjoying the spectacular bird-life. However, the birds cannot survive without the pristine rainforests in which they live. A non-profit group dedicated to preserving these virgin forests is the **Peruvian Conservation Association for the Southern Rainforests** (ACSS), based at Avenida Sol 627-B, oficina 305, in Cuzco. ACSS works to protect the forests upon which this incredible bird-life depends.

Some preparations: The most appropriate clothing for a jungle trip is long-sleeved shirts and trousers of a close-woven material. These protect against biting insects. Cotton is more comfortable in tropical climates than synthetic material. Bring a hat as protection.

Visits to the rainforest are generally more comfortable during the dry season (May-October) when it may not rain for weeks at a time. Most of the rainfall occurs during the rainy season (November-April).

Colorful macaws at a salt lick.

THE VALLEY OF COCA

The eastward-flowing Andean rivers have carved out over millenia a distinct ecological region where the mountain flanks meet Peru's Amazon basin. Here in what Peruvians call *la ceja de la selva* (the eyebrow of the jungle) are broad tropical valleys. The largest is the valley of the 935-km (581-mile) long **Huallaga river** in the northeast of the country.

Opened up for colonisation with the extension of the Central Highway from Lima as far as Pucallpa in the 1940s, successive governments have nurtured great hopes for the Huallaga valley as a potential larder for the country. In the 1960s a highway (the Carretera Marginal) was built through the valley to connect it with Lima and the north coast (now in very poor condition in many places). But though maize and rice are grown on a large-scale, in the past decade the valley has become known for another product – coca.

Everyday use: To the outside world, the small green coca leaf is best known as the raw material for the drug cocaine. But in the Andean highlands of Peru – as in Bolivia and Ecuador – it has been a part of the traditional Indian culture for over 4,000 years and is still an integral part of daily life.

Coca leaves are for sale in any mountain town market. Ask at a café for mate de coca, and you will receive a tea-bag of the leaf for a hot and refreshing drink – normally taken by travelers as the best cure for *soroche* or altitude sickness.

Some 3 million South Americans still chew coca, adding a little bicarbonate of soda to get the saliva going, and keeping a wad of the leaf in their cheeks. It gives energy, and dulls the senses against cold and exhaustion. The biggest consumers have always been miners, who use up to half a kilo a day.

Coca is also used at every stage of the Indians' lives. Before giving birth, a woman chews the leaves to hasten labor and ease the pain. When the child is born, relatives celebrate by chewing the leaf together. When a young man wants to marry a girl, he offers coca to her father. And when somebody dies, mate de coca is drunk at the wake and a small pile of leaves is placed in the coffin before burial.

Ancient tradition: Archaeologists say that coca was first cultivated in the Andes around the year 2,000 B.C. – or 3 millenia before the rise of the Inca dynasty. But it was the Incas who turned its production into a monopoly, as one more means of controlling subject populations. Its use was restricted to royalty, priests, doctors and the empire's messenger runners, known to travel up to 250 kilometers a day by chewing the leaves.

By the arrival of the first European explorers, the Incas had relaxed their monopoly on coca and its use had spread beyond their empire. The Catholic Church first tried to ban chewing of the leaf, denouncing it as "the delusion of the devil".

But they quickly changed their tune when it was found that Indians needed it to survive the brutal conditions in the colonial mines and plantations. Realizing that coca was essential to keep the captive labor force under control, the Church then went into the coca business itself, establishing its own monopoly.

Back in Europe and the United States, coca was almost unheard of until the mid-1800s, when a chemist in Paris by the name of Angelo Mariani marketed a wine made from the leaf. Immensely popular at all levels of society, this Vin Mariani inspired American soft drink companies to produce other drinks based on coca, such as Coca-Cola. At the same time, cocaine was first being developed. The white substance was quickly taken up by such modern luminaries as Sigmund Freud, who called it a "magical substance".

But by the early 1900s, moves were afoot to ban the drug. In the 1970s, cocaine became more popular, especially in the United States. Much of the coca grown in the Andes is now crushed by foot in chemicals, turned into a gummy paste and flown to Colombia. After being refined into powder, the cocaine is then smuggled into North American and European cities.

Cautious exploring: Cocaine has brought violence to the Huallaga valley, in the shape of a complex conflict involving the drug police, backed by United States Drug Enforcement Administration agents, Colombian cocaine traffickers, left-wing guerrillas and the coca farmers themselves. Only the foolhardy tourist will venture into the heart of the valley. But the Huallaga is an area of great natural beauty, and around the fringes there are points that can be visited safely.

Tingo Maria, surrounded by jungle-clad mountains, is the main center for the Upper Huallaga. Founded in 1936, its population is now about 30,000. Police action has driven the cocaine industry further north, and the town is now generally quiet.

It has little to recommend it architecturally, but it has a pleasant State Tourist Hotel, set in beautiful gardens, on the edge of town. A stiff walk up a nearby mountain, with fine

nated by left-wing guerrillas, as far as Juanjui, a maize growing center. Further on, up the side valley of the River Mayo, is **Tarapoto**, the main commercial center for the Middle Huallaga with a population of about 60,000. It is a pleasant, bustling pioneer town, surrounded by exuberant vegetation. A short walk away from the main square, the streets are of dirt and the back gardens are full of mango trees. There is a good State Tourist Hotel on the edge of town, with a swimming pool and tropical gardens. An excursion can be made to the **Laguna Azul**, a lake (with hotel) deep in the countryside. Tarapoto has a busy airport, with daily commercial flights from Lima and air-taxis from Tingo Maria.

views, will take the visitor to the Cueva de las Lechuzas, a natural cave full of owls and bats.

North of Tingo Maria, the valley opens out and the river broadens, with huge meanders. Here are the towns of **Uchiza** and **Tocache**, the main centers of the cocaine trade. Full of *cantinas* and brothels, they have a wild west atmosphere and are dangerous for *gringos* to visit, since they may well be taken for DEA agents. Between the two towns there are two large palm oil plantations. Continuing north, there is a thinly-populated stretch, domi-

Coca leaves for sale in an Andean market.

From Tarapoto the Marginal Highway goes on up the Mayo Valley, a great rice-growing area. A side road leads to **Lamas**, a small town peopled by jungle Indians who have preserved their traditions. The main road goes on to **Moyobamba** and **Rioja**, both pleasant and peaceful towns that were badly damaged by an earthquake in 1990, before crossing the Andean Cordillera and eventually reaching the coast.

Another road, in poor condition, leads from Tarapoto to the riverport of **Yuri-maguas** on the lower Huallaga. From here river boats run to Iquitos, a 2-day journey when going downstream (6 days upstream).

CALLEJÓN DE HUAYLAS

Stretching for 160 km (256 miles) and ranging in altitude from a mere 1,800 meters (5,900 feet) to 4,080 meters (13,380 feet), the valley known as the **Callejón de Huaylas** rates as one of the finest areas in all of South America for its superb mountain vistas and a wealth of opportunities for outdoor pursuits. Many dedicated enthusiasts arrive prepared for trekking and climbing to snowboarding, parapeting and skiing, while others are content to spend their days relaxing in a spectacular mountain setting and exploring the traditional villages which sprawl along the hillsides.

The Callejón de Huaylas is bordered on the east by the Cordillera Blanca (white mountains) – a mountain range with the greatest number of 6,000-meter peaks outside of the Himalaya – and on the west by the more diminutive range known as the Cordillera Negra (black mountains) for their sparseness of vegetation and complete lack of snow. To the north, the valley terminates with the Cañon del Pato, a narrow gorge of a canyon with sheer rock walls, steep precipices and a dirt road winding its way through numerous crudely constructed tunnels down toward the coast. In the past few years, access through this northernmost area has been limited due to the security measures surrounding the State hydroelectric plant in operation there. The 40-km (25-mile) wide Callejón de Huaylas is renowned not only for its breathtaking scenery, but for Inca and pre-Inca history, unusual flora and fauna, lively markets and traditional villages.

Regional pride: If one trait was left as a legacy by the early inhabitants of this region, it would be that of independence. Dating from 1000 B.C., the Chavín culture emerged with a highly developed art style and cult whose influence lasted longer than the Roman Empire and was so widespread that archaeologists have termed this formation period "the Chavín Horizon".

The Huaylas culture, occupying the valley during the Inca expansion, was briefly dominated, though not entirely conquered, by this more sophisticated civilization who set up Andean crossroads between the important centers of Cajamarca and Cuzco. When the Spaniards arrived, they were considered liberators of sorts, for the daughter of Kuntar Guacho, the lord of Huaylas, was given as mistress to the *conquistador* Francisco Pizarro himself. In later history, the early 1800s, an Indian uprising against heavy taxation and labor abuses took the Spanish by surprise, requiring several months to crush. Today, the tradition of independence can be sensed in the people who carry themselves with pride, and is evident in the policies of the regional government which maintains a certain distance from the central authorities in Lima only 8 hours away by road.

The Callejón de Huaylas is also well known for a history of natural disasters. Earthquakes and alluvions, floods of water combined with avalanches and landslides have caused considerable damage over the past 300 recorded years. The capital city of Huaráz was severely damaged by an alluvion in 1941 when an avalanche broke loose from a nearby mountain and caused Laguna Palcacocha to overflow. The resulting mixture of water, rock and snow tumbled down the narrow Cojup valley and inundated the city. Much of the central district was destroyed and nearly 5,000 lives were lost. The most tragic disaster occurred in 1970, when an earthquake measuring 7.7 on the Richter scale devastated the entire region and was responsible for more than 80,000 deaths. Huaráz again suffered with the loss of more than 30,000 lives and over 80 percent of the city flattened, but hardest hit was the village of Yungay. The entire town and most of its inhabitants completely disappeared under a massive avalanche of rock and snow when part of the Huascarán massif broke loose and plunged down the valley.

In the aftermath of these catastrophes many of the towns and villages have been almost completely rebuilt, but with a dubious eye for design. Progress has been introduced in the form of uninspiring concrete structures with little thought given to preserving an architectural heritage. The colonial charm encountered in other highland areas has been all but lost in the Callejón de Huaylas. Sadly, these natural disasters also took a heavy toll on the archaeology of the region. Notably lacking are many ancient remains, primarily Inca, which did not survive the calamities.

Mountain retreat: The center of most commercial activity and the common destination for visitors to the Callejón de Huaylas is the city of **Huaráz**. As the capital of the Department of Ancash and with a population of more than 60,000 inhabitants, this highland mecca is well suited to support the demands of tourism. At first glance, Huaráz appears to be little more than a "one-horse" town, but a closer look proves that all necessities are readily available. Scores of low-cost hostels offer accommodation ranging from very basic to quite comfortable. Edward's Inn is a popular place to stay for its location away from the city center and its warm, family atmosphere. A few higher-priced hotels are available for those who require a bit of luxury during their mountain retreat. Hostel Colomba offers individual bungalows in a lovely garden setting, and the Swiss-run Hostal Andino has great views of the Cordillers Blanca.

Before departing for remote regions or after a long trek in the mountains, you'll find plenty of activity in the bustling town of Huaráz. Along the main street of Luzuriaga, *campesino* street vendors sell a wide selection of woolen goods, pan flutes and ceramic replicas of the Chavín temple. Other traditionally-dressed highlanders sell regional food specialities from wooden carts. Andean cheeses, rich honey and *manjar blanco* (a sweet, milk-based paste used as a topping or filling), are a few tasty edibles that are worth trying. Storefront tour companies set out brightly-colored billboards promoting day trips to popular tourist sites and advertise an assortment of climbing and trekking gear for hire. A wide range of restaurants cater to international tastes. Pizzerias, Chinese food and hamburgers are found along with the more typical dishes of *lomo saltado, pollos a la brasa*, and *cuy*, roasted guinea pig.

Worth a visit is the **Archaeological Museum,** off Ancash on the **Plaza de Armas**. It is a humble affair, yet considered noteworthy for its collection of stone monoliths from the Recuay culture which date from 400 B.C. to 600 A.D. Also on display are mummies, ceramics and household utensils dating from the same period. The museum is open most days from 9 a.m. to 5 p.m. A modest entrance fee is charged.

Huaráz nightlife also has plenty to offer. Several cinemas show recent American films in English with Spanish subtitles, though the sound system frequently leaves something to be desired. Often the amusement comes more from observing the reaction of the highlanders to the "first-world" dramas and watching the silliness of American films from another perspective. Peñas, or folklore nightclubs, entertain with tra-

ditional Andean musical groups in the early evening, and switch to disco later on for serious high-altitude dancing. El Tambo Peña is one of the most popular and is packed to capacity on weekends during the high season. Offering a more laid-back atmosphere and a good meeting place is the Tasco Bar, which also serves up some fairly decent Mexican food for being so far south of the border.

The outlying area of Huaráz is replete with many opportunities for day excursions. Footpaths lead to a number of small villages and agricultural areas within walking distance of the city center. Rataquenua, Unchus, Marían and Pitec are just a few of the *pueblos* which can be visited in a few hours.

Ancient remains: Lying about 8 km (5 miles) north of Huaráz and easily reached by foot is the small pre-Inca ruin of **Wilcahuaín**. Little is known about this three-storied structure which stands in the middle of an agricultural valley, but it is thought to date from 1000 A.D. and is a replica in miniature of the temple of Chavín. The masonry style is typical of the Huari-Tiahuanacu culture which expanded from the coastal region between the 7th and 11th century. The windowless inner chambers can be explored with a flashlight, or with candles proffered by any one of the hordes of schoolboys who haunt the site and offer their services as guides. Most of the rooms within the construction are inaccessible from the debris of centuries, but a few have been opened up to reveal a sophisticated ventilation system and skilful stone craftmanship.

Longer excursions to the surrounding countryside area are as simple to arrange as locating the proper rural bus to take you there. A major road stretches the length of the Callejón de Huaylas running alongside the Santa river and local transportation is readily available to a variety of villages situated along the route. Quite often the ride can be as fascinating as the destination, when local *campesinos* overcome their shyness and initiate a conversation. A bus ride can turn into a rollicking affair of giggles, stares and laughter as the *gringo*, or foreigner, attempts to answer questions about himself in broken Spanish.

The village of **Monterrey**, just 5 km (3 miles) outside of Huaráz, is worth a visit for its *baños termales* (hot springs). Two swimming pools of warm water, and private baths of the steaming variety are extremely inviting, especially after a rigorous trek in the mountains. A few kilometers farther up the valley is the village of **Chancos** which claims to have its own Fountain of Youth – more thermal baths with natural saunas and pools of flowing hot water.

Yungay lies north down the valley and is the turn-off point for the 2-hour ride up to the popular **Llanganuco lakes**, an excellent day excursion from Huaráz. It is this village which was completely destroyed by the 1970 earthquake. This disaster was a near repeat of an earlier catastrophe when, in 1872, the town was almost wiped out by an avalanche. In 1962, Yungay was graced with a "near miss" when an avalanche decimated the neighboring village of Ranrahirca. During the most recent re-

Mountain flowers.

building of Yungay, the village site was shifted a few kilometers north of its original location in the hope that it would now be out of the way of any future disasters. All that remains of the abandoned Yungay is a solitary monument dedicated to those whose lives were lost, and a few battered palm trees that once lined the charming Plaza de Armas.

About an hour by local bus south of Huaráz awaits the small town of **Catac** often visited by those keen to see the giant *Puya Raimondi*. This unusual plant is often referred to as a cactus, but is actually the largest member of the Bromeliad family. It is a rare species, considered to be one of the oldest in the world, and is found in only a few isolated areas of the Andes. At its base, the Puya Raimondi forms a huge rosette of long, spiked, waxy leaves – often reaching a diameter of 2 meters. As it begins to flower, a process which takes its entire lifespan estimated to approach 100 years, it sends up a phallic-like spike which can reach a height of 12 meters. As the final flowering begins,

Girls in the Cordillera Blanca.

usually in the month of May for mature plants, the spike is covered in flowers – as many as 20,000 blooms on a single plant. During this season groups of Puya Raimondi will bloom together, creating an unbelievable picture set against the backdrop of the snowy peaks of the Cordillera Blanca.

Reserve in the Sierra: Much of the Cordillera Blanca above 4,000 meters (13,000 feet) and the area around Huascarán mountain fall within the confines of **Huascarán National Park**, first conceived in 1958 and finally established in 1972. This, along with other national parks set up at the same time, marked Peru as a frontrunner in Latin America in the area of conservation. Huascarán National Park was formed to protect the indigenous wildlife, archaeological sites, geology and natural beauty of an area threatened by mining and other commercial interests. A small entrance fee is charged to help offset the cost of providing park guardians. Of the more interesting wildlife that you can possibly see, with a little patience and a bit of luck, is the *viscacha*, a small, elusive squirrel-like animal with characteristics similar to the North American marmot, the vicuña, a cameloid cousin to the llama, and the stealthy puma. On rare occasions, burros brought along by travelers for help with heavy loads do not finished the trek circuit, having become instead a tasty meal for a hungry puma.

Throughout the Callejón de Huaylas, a lifestyle dating back centuries continues to thrive in the Andean foothills. The traditional dress of the villagers has not changed radically in many years. The women, especially, hold on to their heritage, wearing layers of colorful woolen skirts and embroidered blouses which developed during colonial times. In addition, each wears a hat style which may vary significantly from village to village. The custom of hat-wearing can also be used to indicate marital status, as in the village of Carhuaz. There, a woman with a black band around her fedora is a widow, while a rose color would be worn by a single woman and a white band would show that the woman was married.

Agriculture, the mainstay of the valley, has also seen little change in either means or crop variety. Double-yoked oxen still drag crude wooden plows through the black, fertile soil. Honey-colored wheat can be seen ripening throughout the valley and maturing quinoa plants, a high-altitude grain rich in protein, are easily recognized for the rich colors of burnt orange, firey red and deep purple they produce along the hillsides.

Corn – the sacred crop of the Incas and one of the earliest foods which took man from hunter-gatherer to farmer – is grown in abundance and is the staple of life along with the ever-present potato. From it, a slightly-fermented maize beer, called *chicha*, is made which is drunk in great quantities, especially during festivals. It was originally the royal drink, suitable only to be consumed by the Inca king and his court.

Festivals play a large part in the lifestyle of the indigenous people who inhabit the Callejón de Huaylas. It is a way to break out of the monotony of the day-to-day existence and reaffirm the traditions which give a continuity to life in the Andes. Since the Spanish conquest, festivals have assumed a religious veneer and coincided with Catholic feast days, but underneath still lies a thread of meaning left behind by ancient cultures. Every month of the year sees a celebration, or several, in full swing. Some are particular to one village, while others are observed throughout the region. The festivals of San Juan and San Pedro, celebrated during the last week of June, are particularly lively, especially since they coincide with the national day set aside to honor the *campesino*.

On the eve of San Juan, fires are lit throughout the valley, burning the chaff from the harvest and wild ichu grass on the hillsides. From a high mountain camp, the fires look like starlight brought to earth and the next day the valley is thick with smoke. Semana Santa, or Easter Week, is another widely celebrated festival. Many villages have their

Ice precipice.

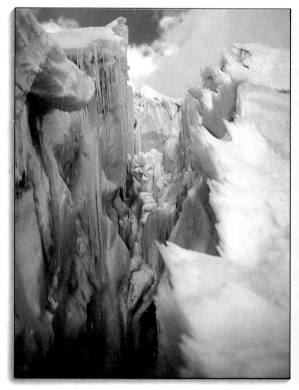

own special traditions, but the celebrations are always colorful and abundant. Processions of finely-adorned religious figures carried on litters, scenes of the resurrection sculpted in flower petals on the ground, and folkoric bands playing music throughout the village are common themes during the festivities of Holy Week.

Jaguar-worshippers' temples: Of the visitors to the Callejón de Huaylas, many not only come for the majestic mountains and typical highland life, but to see one of the oldest archaeological sites designed by one of the most influential cultures in the Americas. The temple complex of **Chavín de Huantar** is actually located across the mountains in the next valley to the east near the village of Chavín, yet transport is most accessible from the city of Huaráz. Here lies the remains of one of the most important cultures that flourished from about 1300 to 400 B.C.

Archaeologists have been able to learn very little about the cult whose architecture and sculpture had a strong impact on the artistic and cultural development of a large part of the coast and central *sierra* of Peru. Because the culture left no written records, much of what is suggested is based on pure supposition. One thing that has been established is that at the time of the Chavín emergence, man was moving from a hunter/gatherer society to one of agriculture, and subsequently was in a position to devote newly-found leisure time to artful development. The theories that have been put forth about this mysterious culture are based on the study of this 17-acre site containing a temple, plazas, and a multitude of stone carvings and drawings. Based on physical evidence, the temple of Chavín de Huantar is thought to have been a major ceremonial center and the feline, or jaguar, the principal deity of the cult.

What first strikes most visitors upon arrival to Chavín de Huantar is the quality of the stonework found in the temple walls and plaza stairways. The dry stonemasonry construction reflects a sophistication not expected from a cul-

Approach to Huascarán in the Cordillera Blanca.

ture that produced it more than 3,000 years ago. Added to this are huge stone slabs with highly stylized carvings of jaguars, eagles and anacondas; the designs are intricate and fluid.

The temple sits above a large, sunken plaza where it is believed pilgrims came to worship during certain seasons. On one side sits a large granite slab with seven hewn-out indentations which must have served as an altarstone for group rituals. Two 3-meter (10-feet) high stone portals overlook the plaza and represent the entry way into the interior of the temple. Both feature a finely-etched bird-like figure, one male, one female, which face each other across a stairway, symbolically divided into two halves – one painted black and the other, white. Its significance is a mystery, but the effect is striking. Niches set around the outside of the temple walls originally held protruding sculpted stone heads, human in shape but with the snarling grin of a jaguar. Some suggest that the eyes were originally inset with crystals which would reflect the light of the moon and ward off evil-doers. Only one of these "keystones" remains in its original place. A few have been stolen and the rest safely stored within the temple.

The interior of the temple is a subterranean labyrinth of passages and galleries set on at least three levels which are connected by a series of ramps and stairs. Though there are no windows, a highly-engineered ventilation system allows the continuous flow of fresh air throughout – another marvel produced by an ancient civilization. Some of the rooms contain what remains of the sculpted heads and intricately-carved slabs which portray a variety of Amazonian and highland animals. These appear to have been originally positioned outside the temple.

At the heart of the underground complex, two narrow passageways cross and at their junction stands the crowning glory of the Chavín religion – the Lanzón de Chavín. This 4-meter (13-feet) high granite monolith is thought to be the principle god-image worshipped

Below left, carving at Chavín de Huantar. Right, keystone.

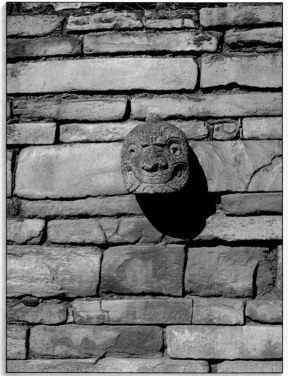

by this cult. Its Spanish name comes from the lance, or dagger-like shape of the monolith which appears to be stuck in the ground. A mythological image emerges from the elaborate stone carving and its demeanor is in keeping with most of the terrifying god images created by the Chavín people. The large head is square, human-like, yet definite feline characteristics are noted in the grinning mouth, out of which protrudes a long fang from each corner. The nose has two big holes for nostrils and an arm and leg are visible on each side. Round earrings dangle from the creature's ears and long flowing hair is made up of intricately-carved serpents. Carved into the top of the head are thin, grooved canals and some speculate that animals, or even humans, may have been sacrificed to this god.

Above the god image, there was once an opening in the ceiling, now closed to preserve the figure from exposure to the elements. Here it is believed that a sacrificial rock may have positioned and, as animals or people were slaughtered,

Carvings at Chavín de Huantar.

the blood would flow through the opening in the ceiling and would run down through the canals in the figure. Other archaeologists disclaim the sacrificial theory and suggest that the Lanzon was merely the dominant figure for worship.

Two other monoliths are considered important in the Chavín cult, but both are now housed in the Museum of Anthropology and Archaeology in Lima. The 6-foot-high stone "Estela Raimondi" was originally discovered by a *campesino* in 1840, who took the piece home to use as a table. Archaeolologist Antonio Raimondi eventually had it transferred to Lima at the end of the last century. It depicts a monstrous feline anthropomorphic god with its arms wide open and holding a large cane. The feet are bird-like claws and serpents represent the hair. The "Tellow Obelisk" was discovered by the anthropologist Julio C. Tellow and brought to Lima just after the turn of the century. Again the feline, or jaguar, image is represented in a mixture of jagged teeth and crawling serpents.

THE NORTH

The essence of **Trujillo**, Peru's most important northern city, is summed up every year during the flower-strewn Spring Festival. Barefoot women in white lace skirts and bouses, with ornate gold filigree ornaments dangling from their earlobes, whirl and curtsy through the streets in the traditional Marinera dance. Charming, simple, formal and delicate – all are characteristics of this coastal city, making it the perfect spot to explore Peru's gentle but fiercely patriotic north.

Founded in 1535 and named after Francisco Pizarro's birthplace in Spain, Trujillo was the resting spot along the Spaniards' route between Lima and Quito. It soon merited the title "Lordliest City" and its well-preserved colonial homes with intricate wooden balconies and complicated window grills pay testimony to an elegant past.

Fiery past: Although Spanish ways were firmly planted here, Trujillanos eschewed blind loyalty to the Spanish crown. In 1820, this became the first Peruvian city to proclaim its independence from Spain and liberator Simón Bolívar, moving down the coast from Ecuador, set the seat of his revolutionary government here. From Trujillo the Venezuelan leader prepared his campaigns for the decisive battles of Junín, Pichincha and Ayacucho. At the latter battle in the plain bearing the same name, soldiers from Venezuela, Colombia, Peru and Boliva – under Bolívar's command – turned back the royalist troops once and for all.

A century later, political fervor coursed through Trujillo when the city gave birth to the progressive and repressive political party APRA, the Alianza Popular Revolucionária Americana. But the ideas of party founder Victor Raúl Haya de la Torre were too radical for the government; the party was outlawed and its militants forced to operate in secret. Government repression and torture of *Apristas* culminated in 1932 in the "Trujillo Massacre" in which a re-bellious crowd of party followers attacked an army post and killed the officers in charge. *Apristas* claim close to 6,000 persons were executed by military firing squads in retaliation.

In one of the more bizarre twists of Peru's political history, Haya de la Torre – by then one of the continent's most revered statesmen – was elected president of Peru in 1962 at age 67. The military alleged fraud and voided the election. Three decades earlier the military had stepped in to block Haya de la Torre from his first presidential bid, forcing him to seek refuge in the Colombian embassy in Lima – where he remained for nearly a dozen years. Haya de la Torre died six years before a 1985 landslide victory finally put the left-of-center party in power under the presidency of Alán García. Even today, on the anniversaries of Haya de la Torre's birth and death, the stateman's Trujillo grave with its eternal torch and inscription "Here Lies the Light" is piled high with flowers. And the mention of his name sparks more out outpourings of

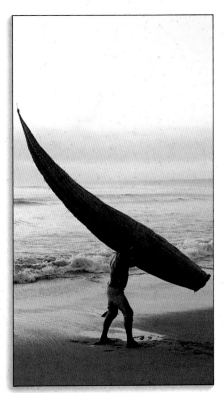

love – and hatred – than any other Peruvian.

Another of Trujillo's militant *Apristas*, Ciro Alegría, was exiled to Chile for his political activity – and there he published the first of the trio of novels that converted him into one of the continent's most acclaimed authors. Although only 22 when he was banned from Peru, repeated jailing and beatings had left Alegria with permanent health problems, compounded later by tuberculosis. He won literary attention with *La Serpiente de Oro* (The Serpent of Gold), but he is best known for *El Mundo Es Ancho y Ajeno* (The World is Wide and Far) – both based on his childhood and rich with material on *campesino* life. When he died in 1967, Alegria was representing Lima in Peru's Congress.

A peaceful present: These tumultuous days of exile, political subterfuge and bloodshed seem distant now in Trujillo, where formality and turn-of-the-century charm hang in the air. The best way to see this city is on foot and the best place to start is the huge and impeccable **Plaza de Armas** at the center of which is a disarming statue of a running winged figure – Liberty – holding a torch. Part of this landmark's oddness is its disproportionately short legs, allegedly to appease officials who feared it would end up taller than the cathedral facing it.

The plaza is bounded by that newly-renovated **cathedral**, **city hall**, the **archbishop's palace** and the colonial-style **Hotel Turistas**, one of the finest hotels in the state-run chain. Travelers who don't spend the night there should consider a breakfast or lunch in its small windowed dining room looking out on to the plaza. From this vantage point one can see the slow-paced comings and goings of the city's elderly men who, morning newspapers in hand, find a shady bench in the plaza, the young mothers carrying their market baskets, toddlers in tow, or the uniformed school girls, huddled together sharing secrets.

Off the main square, dozens of churches, monasteries and convents from the era of viceroys spatter the city. Many are in stages of disrepair or reno-

The Central Club, Trujillo.

vation following earthquakes that shake the northern coast at intervals. But the most intriguing colonial architecture is found in the mansions adorned with the detailed window grills and intricately carved wooden balconies synonymous with this city. The window grills are purely decorative; over the centuries their simple designs became increasingly elaborate as the colonial Trujillanos tried to outdo one another. The cathedral, too, once had elaborate metal grills and railings but they were melted down for armaments during the wars of Independence. The balconies, on the other hand, had a practical purpose: they allowed upper class women to look on to the street but prevented their jealous husbands' rivals from looking in.

Historial houses: La Casa de la Emancipación is typical of the houses built in the 16th and 17th centuries and is one of the few still containing its original furniture. This mansion is open daily to the public and its staff eagerly shows visitors where earthquakes and

remodeling over the centuries have changed the home's original lines. Also worth seeing are **Casa de Mayorazgo, Casa Urquiaga** and **Casa Bracamonte**. Or stop by the **Casa Ganoza**, now an art gallery, and the **Palacio Iturregui** housing the **Central Club**. Here the Marqués of Torre Tagle proclaimed Trujillo's independence from Spain.

Further vestiges of the days of wealth are found on the sugar *haciendas* ouside the city. Owing to its warm climate and gentle nighttime temperatures, the Trujillo countryside produces most of Peru's sugar – an important crop in a country where three spoons of the white granules go in every cup of coffee and where every child seems to be born with a sweet tooth. Land reform beginning in 1969 turned most of the sugar *haciendas* into cooperatives but the opulence of the past is still evident. The most impressive *haciendas* are **Casa Grande**, originally owned by a wealthy German immigrant family, and **Hacienda Cartavio**, where the sugar is used to make Cartavio rum.

Preparing for a cockfight near Trujillo.

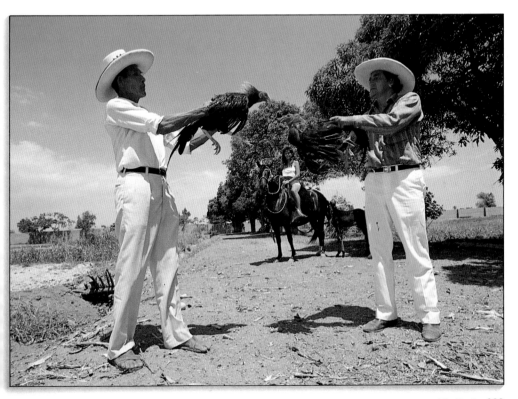

To step back even further in time, Trujillo's pre-hispanic past is on display at the University of Trujillo **Archaeological Museum** a block from the Plaza de Armas. Among the artifacts here are fine pieces of Moche and Chimu pottery found during excavations near the city. An impressive private archaeological collection is at the **Cassinelli Museum**, anachronistically located in the basement of a service station north of Avenida España, the elliptical street where once stood a 12-foot high wall to protect the city from pirate attacks.

Clay and cactus juice: On the fringe of Trujillo are the ruins of **Chan Chan** possibly the world's largest adobe city at the time it was discovered by the Spanish nearly five centuries ago. Perched on 20 square kilometers at the edge of the sea, its seven citadels are enclosed by a massive adobe wall. Chan Chan was home to the Chimú Indians, who fished and farmed, worshipped the moon and had no written records – leaving it to archaeologists to unravel the secrets of their culture. Under the unrelenting sun of Peru's arid north, it is a hollow silence that surrounds visitors to this ancient city where walls bear carvings of fish, sea birds, fishnets and moons and where cash-strapped scientists try to prevent the crumbling of the adobe structures by coating them with a cactus juice varnish.

Aided by sophisticated aqueduct and irrigation systems, the Chimús turned the arid wasteland around them into fertile fields of grains, fruits and vegetables supporting a population that may have reached 700,000. When conquered by the Incas, the Chimús were not forced to change their ways – except for the addition of the sun to their collection of gods; rather, Inca teachers were sent to study the Chimú farming and irrigation systems. It wasn't until the Spanish sabotaged the aqueducts after repeated attempts to invade Chan Chan that the fearless Chimús left the protection of the city – and were conquered.

An entrance ticket to Chan Chan also allows visitors to see the restored **Huaca** **The ruins of Chan Chan.**

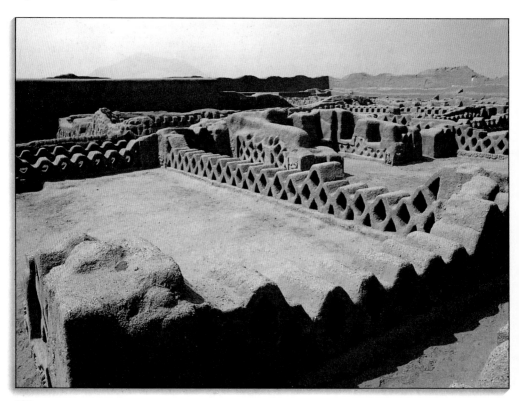

El Dragón temple nearby and the **Huaca La Esmeralda** ruins. Licensed guides can be hired at the ticket office at the ruins. Tourists are advised to begin their visit in the morning and avoid going alone; the tourism police at Chan Chan frequently go home mid-afternoon and there have been reports of robberies at the isolated site. Visitors also are cautioned to steer clear of vendors hawking what they claim is antique pottery. Most of these ceramics are fake. Since Peru is more strictly enforcing laws to halt the trafficking of archaeological pieces, tourists lucky enough to stumble on authentic pottery could find the items confiscated and themselves fined or jailed if they try to take the artifacts out of the country.

Horse hooves and bare feet: Trujillanos are proud of their *Caballos de Paso*, a fine breed of horses with a tripping gait that has made them known worldwide. Another legacy of the Spanish, since there were no horses on the continent at the time of the Inca empire, these horses have been immortalized in Peruvian

Examining rainbow carving at Chan Chan.

waltzes. In particular composer Chabuca Granda, for whom a monument is erected in the bohemian neighborhood of Barranco in Lima, wrote of the *chalanes* or riders in their *jipijapa sombreros* upon their honey-colored mounts. These riders still compete in their own form of the Marinera dance – smoothly guiding their horses through the steps. Granda's most famous waltz to the Caballos de Paso is "Jose Antonio". The best of these trotters are bred in and around Trujillo and buyers from around the world congregate to see them shown at the annual spring Festival – *Festival de la Primavera*.

The festival spotlight, however, is on the Marinera dancers who pirouette and twirl as they rigorously vie for the male and female dance titles. The Marinera is a graceful dance rooted in African and Spanish rhythms and movements; some say its steps mimic the strutting of a cock courting a hen. Shoeless women in ruffled lace skirts seductively flit toward white-garbed men in ponchos before quickly pulling away from the

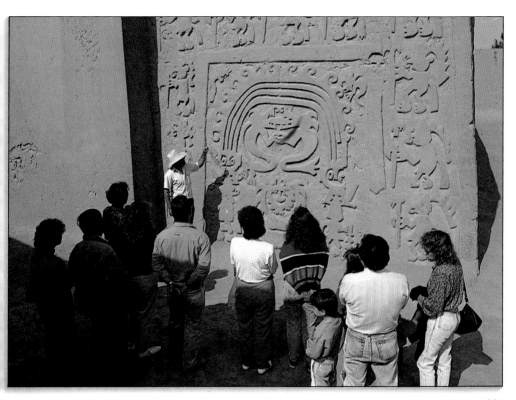

frustrated courter. The men attempt to win back the women's attention, deftly tossing up hats or handkerchiefs then twirling and snatching them in mid-fall.

The dancers are barefoot and the men's trousers stop just above their ankles – a costume in keeping with this region's proximity to the sea, an area where feet and ankles are routinely dampened by the Pacific ocean. Just 7 km (4 miles) from Trujillo it is possible to watch that unbreakable tie with the ocean in the seaside village of **Huanchaco**. Two centuries ago when the Huanchaco residents paid taxes to the Spanish crown and it was used as the storage city for Trujillo, two leagues away, it was a quiet village of men who fished and women who wove baskets in the sunshine. Little has changed.

Today sun-bronzed fishermen head out each morning with their nets tucked into *caballitos de totora,* literally "little horses" woven of totora reed. The design of these curved, peapod shaped boats has changed little from the craft used by pre-Inca fishing tribes and the *cabalitos de totora* contrast startlingly to the brightly colored surfboards sharing the Pacific waves that lap this village.

Excavation and black magic: Three hours to the north of Trujillo is the busy port of **Chiclayo**, the starting point for visits to two of the continent's most exciting archaeological digs. The greatest attention has been lavished on the Moche Indian burial area at **Sipán** where, thanks to funding from the National Geographic Society, the Americas' richest documented tomb was uncovered. (See "Treasures from a Forgotten World".) Nearby is the excavation at the **Túcume pyramids** – a project directed by Norwegina Thor Heyerdahl, who can be seen wandering around the dig. Heyerdahl has rolled out the red carpet to tourists, building a stairway to a look out point over the pyramids and piping water to a picnic area at the entrance to this dig. He planned to construct a catwalk at the excavation so tourists can get close to the delicate work without disturbing the archaeologists. (See "Thor Heyerdahl Returns".)

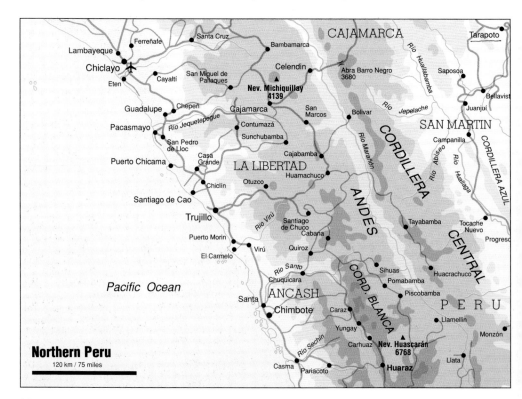

Northern Peru

120 km / 75 miles

Farther north is **Piura**, a hot commercial city best known for its folk dance, the *tondero*, and the black magic practiced surrounding towns inhabited by the descendents of black slaves. The *tondero* is a lively, barefoot Afro-Peruvian dance accompanied by strong rhythmic music and sashaying dancers in multicolored outfits. But Peruvian visitors to this part of the country usually come to see more than the dancers. There are Lima business executives who travel to this region every year to consult with *brujos* – the witches, folk healers and fortune tellers behind the occult practices that permeate the Piuranos lives.

Nearly as famous as its esoteric pursuits is Piura's cuisine, with its sharp flavors and elaborate preparation. The best dishes include *seco de chavelo* (mashed plantains with fried pork), *majado de yucca con chicharrón* (mashed maniocs with fried pork), fried plantain bits known as *chifles*, and the goat milk and sugar cane molasses sweet called *natilla*. It is washed down with *chicha de jora*, a fermented corn drink.

Piura has a proud history, beginning with its founding as a city by the Spanish in 1532 – three years before Lima – and continuing through the War of the Pacific with Chile. That war's most famous hero was Admiral Miguel Grau, born in this oasis in the desert, and his home on Jirón Tacna across from the Centro Cívico has been converted into a museum. Of interest there is the scale model of the British-built Huascar, the largest Peruvian warship in that war. Grau was commander of the vessel and used it to keep invading Chilean forces at bay until his death in a battle at sea. During the war he was called "Gentleman Grau" because of his unceasing string of letters to the Peruvian President, seeking more supplies for his men, and his rescuing of Chilean sailors left in the water after each battle.

Atahualpa's last home: Southeast across the dusty desert into the Andean highlands, far from ocean and magic, is **Cajamarca.** Now dotted by cattle herds and dairy farms where Peru's best cheese

Fishing boats on the coast near Trujillo.

is made, this was one of the biggest cities in the Inca empire and marks where the Indians and Spaniards had their first showdown. According to Spanish chronicles, it was in Cajamarca that the Inca Atahualpa was kidnapped and later executed.

The heavily-armed Spaniards caught the Inca and his royal soldiers off guard and thousands of unarmed Indians were slain futilely trying to protect their leader in a bloodbath on the Plaza de Armas. Despite the Spaniards' numerical disadvantage, their audacity in kidnapping an Inca threw an already split Indian kingdom into confusion. What followed immediately was a cry across the Inca empire to assemble the outrageous ransom the Spanish requested for Atahualpa's release.

Leading llamas weighted down by riches, Indians from as far away as Cuzco began the journey to Cajamarca, filling the **Rescue Room** a block from the Plaza de Armas with some of the Incas most valuable treasures – which the Spanish promptly melted down into bullion. The Rescue Room is still there; a red line on one wall shows where the tall and powerful Atahualpa allegedly drew a mark, agreeing to have his subjects fill the room to that line twice with silver and once with gold. Of course, once most of the treasure had been collected, the conquistadors had the Inca garrotted.

The spot for Atahualpa's execution was the **Plaza de Armas**, still the hub of this slow-paced city of 120,000. Some Peruvians believe the pink grain on a stone slab alleged to be where the Incas was killed is the indelible mark of his blood. What is certain is that in exchange for a promise he would not be burned alive, Atahualpa was baptized "Juan" just before his execution against the backdrop of massive Inca palaces. The palaces are gone and the plaza is now ringed by colonial buildings and two churches – the **cathedral** and lovely **San Francisco Church**. The plaza's center is graced by a stone fountain surrounded by *campesinos* and birds.

Catching a wave.

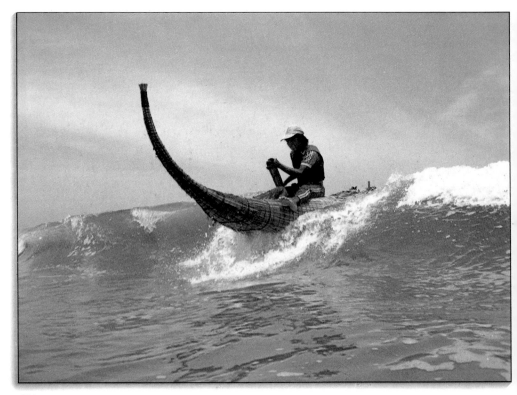

304

No bells toll: The Cathedral, opened in 1776, is the most attention-getting building on the plaza. Its carved wood altars are covered in gold leaf and its facade of intricately carved volcanic rock is impressive. But something is conspicuously absent – its bell towers. They were left unfinished to protest Spain's tax on churches. Next door is the **Hotel Turistas**, a better than average lodging with rooms furnished in heavy wooden antiques.

On the opposite side of the plaza is the San Francisco Church, older and more ornate than the Cathedral, and home to the **Religious Art Museum** filled with its often violent and bloody colonial era paintings and statues. The guided tour of this storeroom of silver candelabras, gold altar vessels, jeweled vestments and portraits of saints and priests includes entrance to the church's eerie catacombs – precursor to the present city cemetery.

Also on the square is the family-run **Salas Restaurant**, described by one Cajamarquino as the "city's nerve center". Here locals catch up on the latest news and gossip while downing the city's best – and most economical – home cooking. Diners can find anything from crisp salads and thick *chupe verde* (potato and vegetable soup) to hearty beef ribs and spicy guinea pig stew. No meal is complete without *panqueque con manjar blanco*, a sweet, rich dessert consisting of a thick crepe bathed in a condensed milk sauce.

Hung on the restaurant's walls are paintings by local artist Andres Zavallos, one of the founding fathers of Cajamarca's longstanding community of poets, writers, painters and musicians. Most notable of these was Mario Urteaga, the only Peruvian artist to have his work in the permanent collection at New York's Metropolitan Museum of Art and a person so loved in his hometown that the procession at his funeral in 1957 lasted into the night. Urteaga's oils depicted *campesinos*, simple yet human, and the Cajamarca countryside was his studio. In much the same way today, local poet Manuel Ibañez Rosazza

Building reed boats near Trujillo.

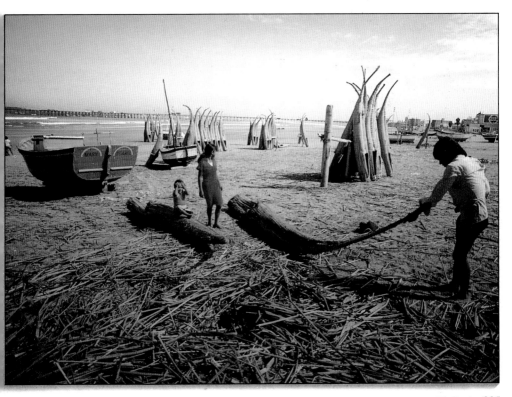

In Search Of Hemingway's Marlin

Ernest Hemingway's name is heard frequently on the lips of Peruvians – not simply because he was enamored with their country for a time and visited it repeatedly, but because they say it was Peru that inspired him to write his novella *The Old Man and the Sea*. Although the book's protagonist, Santiago, was an aging Cuban fisherman battling for the biggest catch of his life, Peruvians insist that Hemingway's sea hunts for marlin off their Pacific coast half a century ago gave him the idea for the plot.

A repeated visitor to the fishing club at **Cabo Blanco** in northern Peru, Hemingway made the village synonymous internationally with deepsea fishing challenges. His love affair with the Pacific coast – and its waters abundant with fish – drew other anglers to the port and, some decades back, the town's modest fishermen who depended on the sea for their livelihood did not even blink an eye when the wealthy *gringos* showed up for their sports fishing vacations.

It's easy to see what brought the author to Cabo Blanco; Peru's northern coast is a veritable fishing goldmine. It is here the cold marlin-bearing Humboldt Current meets El Niño, which carries the smaller fish upon which they feed. This is a hot spot for prime catches of black marlin (*marlin negra*), striped marlin (*per aguja*), yellowfin tuna, broadbill swordfish (*albacora* or *pez espada*), mackerel, big-eye tuna (*atun*), ocean bonito (*cachorreta*) and several varieties of grouper. Not only do anglers claim it is unusual to find all in the same waters but they say enthusiasts can fish here 12 months a year. This is also one of the few places in the world where two-in-one-day takes of swordfish or marlin have been registered by a single fisherman or fisherwoman.

The world's most exclusive fishing club: If Hemingway immortalized Peru's marlin hunt in fiction, another angler put it in the record books. In 1953, Alfred Glassell Jr. set a record with his rod and reel catch of a 710 kilo (1,562 pound) black marlin off the northern coast, breaking his own 1,090-pound record of the year before (Black marlins weighing more than 2,200 pounds have been harpooned in the same waters). Glassell was one of the founding members of the elite group that made up the Cabo Blanco Fishing Club.

A Canadian businessman living in Lima first bragged of the fabulous catches off Cabo Blanco in the mid-1930s, drawing attention to the coastal areas. But the war interrupted and it was not until the 1950s that fishing in this area resumed, encouraged by wealthy Peruvian Enrique Pardo, son of a Peruvian president and the person who built the group's first clubhouse in Cabo Blanco in 1952. The Cabo Blanco fishing club became so prestigious that it was not uncommon for its membership to be offered $50,000 to help get other fishermen on the membership rolls; the club, however, turned down the offers on grounds that the members would include only the finest sports fishing fans and, initially, only 16 people were admitted to the group. Later a second, larger, clubhouse was built on the rise above the beach at Cabo Blanco, boasting not only one of the coast's finest views but undoubtedly the world's finest tackle room. By this time, the club had acquired boats and its members dropped by the area at regular intervals.

The club and Cabo Blanco were abandoned by sports fishermen after a time, but, the refurbished club/resort recently reopened and its 60 rooms are sporadically filled with foreign fishing enthusiasts looking for the catch of their lives. (It is no longer a membership-only operation.) There is camping by the club and the newly renovated Punta Sal resort at Talara offers luxury lodging for well-heeled anglers who want to end their day with more than a sunburn.

Until recently, the big obstacle to retracing Hemingway's steps was the dearth of yachts to take fishermen out to sea. When the fishing club abandoned the area, with them went the yachts they had used to troll the waters. In

newest addition to the Cabo Blanco scenery – a 11-meter (38-foot) yacht purchased in San Diego, California, and sailed to Peru in mid-1990. Yacht owner Joe Rada, who says his goal is to take out to sea an angler who will break Glassell's record catch marlin, can be hired for solo or group trips off the northern coast. A typical day fishing for marlin off his yacht consists of heading out from the shore about 7 a.m. and returning about 5 in the afternoon, just in time to order a *pisco sour* or cold beer and watch the sun set on the coast. Rada provides refreshments, food and fishing gear.

Increasingly, big scores on marlin are now being made where the fish have migrated to

the 1980s, those who visited the northern coast had to content themselves with outings in small boats rented from local fishermen. Some male and female fishing fans still find those low-tech outings a treat and, fortunately, only a few Peruvian old-timers hold to the belief that women in a fishing boat mean bad luck. For those who prefer *terra firma*, there is light tackle surf casting for flounder, sea bass, snook, corvina and mackerel.

New opportunity: Serious marlin-seekers now can make arrangements to fish from the

<u>Left</u>, the day's catch. <u>Above</u>, bringing in the nets.

feed, a few miles from Cabo Blanco at Mancora. Marlin hunters set out from Mancora in the morning and head south toward Cabo Blanco with the wind in their favor and a good catch nearly inevitable. This is a particularly popular weekend outing for foreign oil executives whose companies are drilling in the northern desert.

Rada is also willing to arrange trips from Gabo Blanco to Ecuador's Galapagos Islands, a trip that takes about six days each way. Rada can be contacted through the Peru Tourism Board office in Miami, Florida (Tel: USA [305] 374-0023) or through the tourism offices scattered throughout Peru.

writes verse about these gentle fields swept by brisk mountain winds and photographer Victor Campos Rio captures the beauty of the countryside and its people in photos and documentary films.

A few blocks from the plaza is the newly restored **Municipal Theater**, rescued by this culture-loving city after being used first as a movie theater then as a storehouse for industrial cleaner. Built by a wealthy German merchant using the architectural plans of a small opera house in his homeland, the theater has an impressive stamped metal ceiling and its seating nearly exactly duplicates the original plans of the theater, although the colors have been changed to add more glitter. The ticket office has listings of cultural events, which range from classical music to folklore dances; ticket prices are intentionally kept low to entice students and less affluent Cajamarquinos, along with city patricians.

Scaling the heights: For the physically fit, the best way to delight in Cajamarca's charms is from above. That means climbing steep **Cerro Apolonia**. Stone steps take climbers as far as a little chapel – a miniature version of Notre Dame Cathedral about halfway up the hillside – and the rest of the journey is on a curvy road bordered by cactus, flowers and benches for the fatigued. Near the top is the **silla del Inca** a rock cut into the shape of a throne where, Cajamarquinos say, the Inca sat and looked out over his kingdom. A bronze statue of Atahualpa, and parking for those who arrive by cab or car, top the hill.

The view here is reminiscent of Cuzco with green, rain-fed fields, red tile roofs and whitewashed houses. At night, the Cajamarca skies – which in daytime may switch in minutes from brilliant blue to stormy gray – are clear and star studded. Early risers are in for a special treat; sunrises in these highlands are joyously beautiful and the show is a long one. It can take the sun up to 45 minutes to switch from a silhouetting blue black to brilliant red-orange before lightening to a hazy yellow.

The main square of Chiclayo.

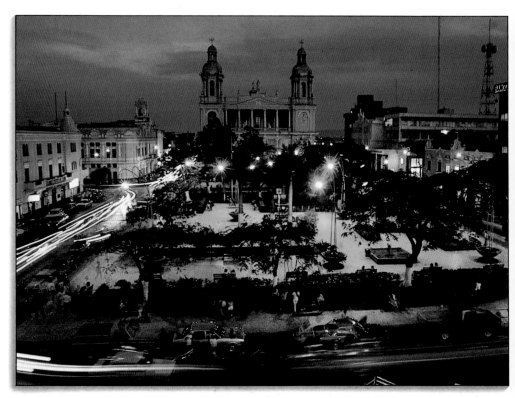

308

Inca's bathing place: Looking from the Cerro by day, a white mist can be seen hovering over the edge of the city. This is the steam rising from the **Baños del Inca** – the Inca's bathing spot. These bubbling mineral springs made Cajamarca the Incas' favorite vacation spot; a sign over a huge stone tub at the springs claims that it was here Atahualpa bathed with his family. The springs are so hot at their source that local Indians use them to boil eggs. Whether they are curative as the locals believe or not, they merit a visit. The city has channeled the water from the springs into a lukewarm Olympic-sized outdoor pool, rustic cabanas where families or groups of friends can splash privately and modern "tourist baths" where up to two persons can soak in tiled hot tubs. There is a minimal entrance fee to the facilities.

At the springs, several tourist hostels have sprung up, all of them with bathtubs or swimming pools fed by the springs. The best known and most impressive, despite it rustic appearance, is the **Laguna Seca**. It is periodically rumored that an international hotel chain is looking at the converted *hacienda*, which has a pool, a pungent sauna where eucalyptus is steamed on hot coals, a weight-lifting room, a small bullfight ring, a cockfight arena and "Baños del Inca" water running into the deep bathtubs of every room.

Back in the city, at the base of Cerro Santa Apolonia, is the **Complejo Belén** housing the Institute of Culture, Cajamarca's most picturesque chapel, a museum and an art gallery. The Belén Church is undoubtedly the city's loveliest with elaborately carved stone and woodwork and brightly-colored statues and side altars. The small white carved dove suspended over the pulpit represents the Holy Spirit and allegedly gives those who stand under it the power of eloquence. The chapel's cupola altar depicts the three levels of life – ground level with the common people, an intermediary area with saints and priests and the top level – heaven – with God and the Virgin Mary, represented by the sky blue dome of the cupola. Many visitors

Below left, northern twins. <u>Right</u>, shopping in Cajamarca.

are fooled by the detail of the brilliantly painted details on the upper walls and ceiling of the church; these saints and cherubs are not made from painted wood or plaster, they are intricately carved stone. More carving is found on the massive wooden doors in the church, most of them from solid pieces of Nicaraguan cedar.

Connected to the church is the **Pinacoteca**, a gallery of local artists' work in what was once the kitchen of a Medieval hospital for men. Off the Pinacoteca is the former hospital ward, a room with alcoves along its side walls. The alcoves were the patients' "bedrooms" and the images of saints originally painted above them corresponded to the illnesses of the infirm. The sickest were bedded closest to the altar, conveniently located near the door to the cemetery. A sample alcove with blankets and its saint painting preserved can be seen across the street at the **Ethnographic and Archaeological Museum**, once the maternity hospital of the same era. The only difference was that from the tops of the women's alcoves dangled long scarves, which the patients pulled to help them during births.

The Ethnographic and Archaeological Museum has a collection of ceramics from Indian cultures that dominated this region of Peru, samples of local handicrafts and costumes used during the annual carnival celebrations – the most raucous in the country. Across the street at the **Cultural Institute**, Spanish-language books and the area's best postcards are on sale. The Institute has details on ongoing archaeological digs that can be visited from October to May, before the highland's rainy season begins. Those excavations include the Huacaloma and Kuntur Wasi digs sponsored by the University of Tokyo.

Recapturing ceramic traditions: The Complejo Belén artisan shop and those near the Plaza de Armas are filled with well-made knit sweaters, pottery, baskets, leather goods and the gilt framed mirrors popular in this northern region. But the most fascinating – and least expensive – spot to buy pottery and

The witchcraft market in Chiclayo.

ceramics is outside the city at **Aylambo**. The brainchild of ecologist Pablo Sanchez of the University of Cajamarca, Aylambo is a series of ecologically balanced workshops. Sewage at the workshops is processed into natural gas used to generate the heat and light in the work rooms. Rather than buy expensive fuel and imported heat-resistent bricks from the kilns that fire the pottery, Aylambo students collect kindling from the hillside and make their own heat-tolerating kiln tiles – much the same way their Indian ancestors did.

Products here range from plates bearing traditional Indian designs to teapots with modern glazes – concocted by the students – and money from pottery sales pays those working in the studios. Sanchez said the Aylambo artisans, who range in age from 9 to 90, are not charged to learn the crafts but economic necessity would force them to leave the workshop to find paying jobs if study stipends were not available. Sanchez's dream is to have the hillside covered with environmentally sound workshops providing jobs, reclaiming ancient pottery designs, keeping *Cajamarquinos* living in the countryside and preventing further deforestation of the hills.

Beyond the city: There are many possible excursions outside of Cajamarca, although these outings are best accomplished through a travel agency with transportation to the isolated areas. Puzzling and awesome are the **Ventanillas de Otuzco**, the cliffside "windows" that served as ancient Indian burial grounds. Anthropologists and archaeologists still have not unraveled the mystery of how the Indians were able to open the burial holes on the sides of sheer cliffs but they counted the openings to get an idea of the population – and importance – of the area before the conquistadors' arrival.

Equally astonishing is **Cumbemayo**, a valley cut by an Inca irrigation ditch of carved rock. The sophistication and precision of the ditch's angles – hewn by Indians using stone tools – leave modern-day hydraulic engineers marveling. Sharp turns in the ditch prevents the water from rushing too fast, as

View of Cajamarca.

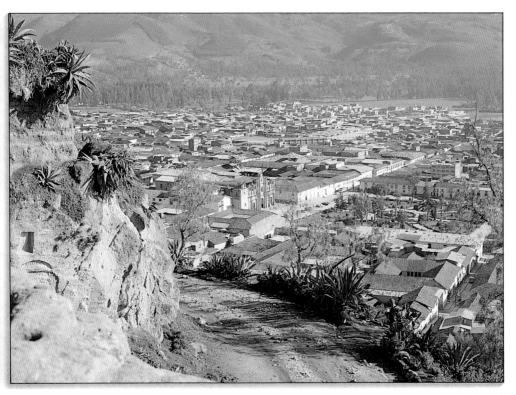

do imperceptible inclines. In the same valley are Los Frailones, huge rocks that have eroded into the shape of hooded monks, sparking a number of local legends, as well as some primitive Indian worship caves and petroglyphs.

Those who start their countryside ramblings early in the day may have time to reach the **Colpa dairy farm** before cow-calling time. Every day, just before 2 p.m., the cows at this cooperative are called by name – to the delight of the crowd that gathers to watch their antics. The bovine respond by sauntering up to the milking areas bearing their names. Once a *hacienda*, Colpa is an example of the many cooperative dairies outside Cajamarca, famous for its butter, cheese and manjar blanco milk sweet. A new city-built hostal at Colpa has opened its doors to travelers seeking a pastoral spot to spend the night.

In the evenings Cajamarca rolls up its sidewalks early as fitting a farm community where work begins at sunrise. But nocturnal souls can listen – and dance – to boisterous local music at the Emperador. Or they can join the camaraderie, and even pick up a guitar if they play, at the more intimate **El Sítio bar** connected to the **Hostal Cajamarca** behind the Belén Complex. Here fans of tunes, ranging from boleros to the footstomping huaynos of the Andean highlands, meet to sing, drink and share their music with tourists.

Hemingway's marlin: Rather than heading inland from Chiclayo, it is also possible to continue along the coast north to Ecuador. Some 135 km (81 miles) north of Chiclayo, **Talara** is a desert oasis and a petroleum producing center with transportation to the warm water beaches of **Mancora**, another beach area where Ernest Hemingway allegedly was inspired to write *The Old Man and the Sea*, **Playa Sol** and **La Pena** beach. **Cabo Blanco** is a popular spot for marlin fishing (see feature "In Search of Hemingway's Marlin"), frequented by Hemingway in his time, but experts say the marlin have actually now been carried south by the current to Mancora. Seaside seafood restaurants in Mancora

Window in Belén church, Cajamarca.

are, for obvious reasons, recommended. This is also a popular spot for Brazilian surfers, as Peru's coast has some of the world's most spectacular waves and is frequently the sight of international surfing competitions.

The hotel offerings in Talara are slim and many fill up with visiting oil engineers. Camping is permitted at Cabo Blanco and some of the other nearby beaches. It is possible also to spend just a short time here, taking an AeroPeru or Faucett flight from the city airport.

South of Talara are the **Brea tarpits** where the Spanish boiled tar to caulk their ships.

Frontier town: Another 141 kilometers (84 miles) north of Talara is **Tumbes**, a somewhat lawless frontier town with a military post and immigration offices for crossing into Ecuador. Although there has been an ongoing effort to give this city of about 40,000 a facelift, there continues to be a problem with theft – particularly affecting tourists who find their suitcases, passports or money snatched most often near the bus offices or at the sprawling and colorful outdoor market. A few miles outside the city at the actual border, known as **Aguas Verdes** on the Peruvian side, travelers are also usually barraged by unscrupulous money changers, porters and over-friendly individuals who often have theft on their minds.

To exacerbate the situation, police corruption is notorious here, although that usually affects Peruvians more than outsiders and focuses upon the widespread cross-border trafficking in contraband items.

Tumbes is also within spitting distance from the few Peruvian beaches that offer white sand beaches and warm water for swimming all year round. **Caleta La Cruz** can be reached by cab or in collectivos, as can **Zorritos** and **Puerto Pizarro**. The latter has intriguing mangroves and an attractive beach; boat rentals can be arranged with fishermen. Offshore here has become increasingly popular among deep sea fishing enthusiasts drawn by the big fish that follow the Humboldt Current.

Cutting sugar cane.

SOUTH COAST

Peru's southern desert coast, although inhospitable at first glance, is a historical land mine. It is the geographical encyclopedia of a handful of highly developed pre-Inca cultures known for their masterful pottery, fine weaving, medical advances and, in the case of one Indian culture, the mysterious mammoth drawings they left on the desert plain at Nazca.

The south coast is also where ancient Indians proved once again they could, if not tame, then accommodate the harsh physical reality of their environment. This time it was not the imposing Andes mountains that separated the Indian tribes, made agriculture difficult and left the humans subject to the subtle changes in climate. Rather it was the parched and desolate desert, often compared to the deserts of North Africa, that proved the obstacle.

Women who captivated the Incas: Although the more recent Inca culture has overshadowed much of the pre-Columbian development of this area, the artisan work left by the earlier civilizations prove they were more sophisticated than the Incas in both ceramics and textiles. They were also renowned, according to Indian legend, for the beauty of their women. It is said that Pachacutec, the Inca responsible for expanding the empire, once sent a mission to the valleys of Chincha to begin work in conquering the Indians there. But Pachacutec's envoys – his brother and son – did not realize they were headed into an area where strong resistance against them was planned.

By chance, after meeting the desert leader Aranvilca in the valley, both men were taken by the beauty of his daughter. The Inca envoys befriended the young woman and she served as a go-between in the peaceful takeover of that Indian group. In appreciation, Pachacutec's men promised to help Aranvilca by ordering 30,000 members of the Inca nation to open a water canal from the Andean highlands into the valley, pro-

viding water. The tradition explaining the source of the waterway now known as Achirana, claims the work was completed in only ten days.

Years later, when Huascar was declared the legitimate heir of Huayna Capac and before he was killed by his half-brother Atahualpa, this heir received as a present from the Indians near Ica, a young consort. Huascar was so awed by the woman's beauty that he called her Kory Koyllur – gold star – and fathered her child. His adoration of her so infuriated his other concubines that they murdered the young woman.

Into the devil's mouth: Heading south from Lima, the first community of note is **Pucusana**. This seaside resort town is actually a charming fishing village with panoramic views from its cliffs and good seafood. During the Peruvian summer, from January to April, beaches can get crowded here on weekends. In the mornings, it is possible to hitch a ride on a fishing launch and spend the day fishing or swimming offshore. The arrangements usually involve bargaining with

Preceding
pages: the
barren
coastal
desert. Left,
sealions on
the Ballestas
Islands.
Right, Nazca
lines seen
from the air.

local fishermen anxious to take a day off. Or, those tired of the crowds at the Las Ninfas or Pucusana beach can ask for a ride to one of the more isolated stretches of sand (arranging for a pickup later in the day), such as Naplo. Take the trip via the **Boquerón del Diablo**, literally the Devil's Big Mouth, a tunnel carved in the rock. It would be fatal to enter the tunnel, either by foot or in a boat, as the astonishing din coming from the Boquerón suggests. The groaning noise inside the tunnel sounds like, as one Peruvian put it, "a thousand devils".

Further to the south lies sunny **Chincha**, the city that for Peruvians is synonymous with wine, fine quality cotton, excellent athletes and ferocious fighting cocks. Its name is believed to be derived from *chinchay* – the Yauyo Indians word for feline – although when the Spanish named it in 1571 it was more pompously called *Pueblo Alto de Santo Domingo*. Grape and cotton crops flourish here thanks to an elaborate system of irrigation and the rerouting of the Cochas River.

The city's fairly modern coliseum pays tribute to the long sports tradition here. Chincha has turned out a number of Peruvian sports stars, principally in soccer and boxing. Great Peruvian boxer Mauro Mina – from Chincha – defeated a number of North Americans including Floyd Patterson but a detached retina prevented him from going for the middleweight world title. Another Chincha athlete, Fernando Acevedo was a Pan American running champion in 100- and 200-meter events. His nickname was "The Harpoon of Chincha".

This is home to much of Peru's black population, descendants of slaves brought to work on coastal plantations, and it is the center for Afro-Peruvian dances, including the energetic and comical *alcatraz* – in which a gyrating male dancing with a lit candle in hand attempts to ignite the cloth tail hanging from his teasing partner's bright-hued skirt. Many of these dances are accompanied by rhythms supplied by *cajones*, or hollow boxes pounded by open-palmed drummers.

Church in Piso.

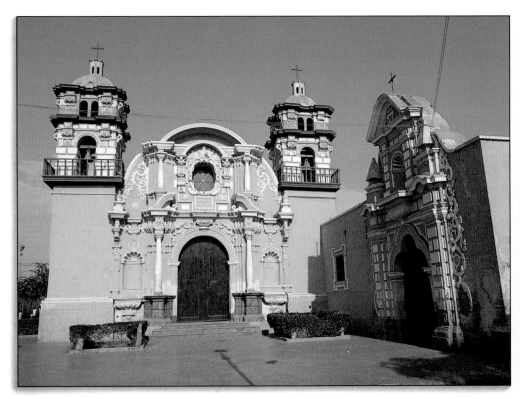

Continuing south on the Panamerican Highway is **Pisco**, a port city that gave its name to the clear white grape alcohol used in Peru's national drink, the *pisco sour*. The invention of pisco was actually a mistake by Spaniards trying to introduce grapes and wine production into the dry coastal area of the New World. However, once they tried this potent, yet smooth, beverage they decided it had merit of its own. Needless to say, this city is a good spot to try a *pisco sour*, the cocktail made from pisco, lemon juice, egg white and bitters, whipped and garnished with cinnamon.

The city, now with 80,000 inhabitants, joined the bandwagon when revolutionary fever overtook the continent in the early 1800s. Half a block from the town's **Plaza de Armas** is the **Club Social Pisco** used as the headquarters for liberation leader General José de San Martín while he was fighting the Spaniards. A statue to this Argentine hero of the independence war is found on the main plaza – the same square where boat trips to the Ballestas Islands can be arranged.

Originally, Pisco stood in another spot not far away. But an earthquake in 1687 and subsequent pirate attacks badly damaged the structures in the city, prompting the viceroy, Count de la Monclova, to order it moved. Construction of the opulent baroque **cathedral** started shortly thereafter only ending in 1723.

Pisco's small airport serves as the emergency landing strip when heavy fog prevents planes from descending in Lima; passengers are then bussed to the Peruvian capital or wait until the weather clears before flying north again. From 1960 to 1970, small propeller planes of the foreign-owned Consorcio Ballenero buzzed the waters offshore in a now defunct project to localize and count groups of whales that regularly close in on Peru's coast.

Then, in late 1988, Peruvian scientists in conjunction with experts from the Natural History Museum at the Smithsonian Institute in the United States announced what appeared to be

Llamas gather on the southern coast.

the discovery of a new whale species. Named the Mesoplodon Peruvianus, one of these mammals was inadvertently picked up by fishermen working the waters between Pucusana and Pisco. The 13-foot long whale is considered one of the smallest members of the whale family.

The poor man's Galápagos: Some 5 km (9 miles) down the coast from Pisco is the **Bay of Paracas**, named after the Paracas winds – blustery sand storms that sweep the coast. Transformed into an ecologically-delicate national park, and a popular spot for New Year's Day camping, this "Poor Man's Galápagos" is a wildlife reserve boasting a wide variety of sea mammals and exotic birds – including red and white flamingos that allegedly inspired General San Martín to design a red and white independence flag for Peru.

The beach is lovely, although craggy for swimming and the waters contain jellyfish. Here a monument marks where San Martín set foot in Peru on September 8, 1820 after liberating Argentina. (A law passed by the National Congress makes Sept. 8 a provincial holiday.) Not long after the Argentina's arrival, a shipload of British troops led by Lord Thomas Cochrane, dropped anchor in the same bay and headed to shore to help San Martín plan his strategy against the Spanish. The British goal was to break Spain's monopoly on trade in the region.

The famous **Candelabro**, a candelabra-shaped drawing scratched on to the highest point of a cliffside overlooking the bay, can be seen from the beach although it is best viewed from a boat. And it would be a terrible omission to leave the bay without first visiting some of the islands. Some scientists link the drawing to the Southern Cross constellation; others say it is actually a stylized drawing of a cactus – a symbol of power from the Chavín culture, which flourished farther north but whose influence has been found great distances from its seat of power. The magic associated with the cactus is related to its hallucinogenic powers and use by high priests in ancient Indian cultures.

Recommended from the Bay of Paracas is a visit to the **Ballestas Islands**, part of a national reserve where sea lions, seals, penguins, guano birds and turtles rarely found at this latitude converge before photo-taking tourists. Dozens of bird species alone thrive here, among them albatross, alcatraz, pelicans and a handful of seagull species. Also worth a visit in a fishing boat or launch is **Punta Pejerrey**, nearly the northernmost point of the isthmus and the best spot for seeing the Candelabro.

On the exact opposite side of the isthmus is **Punta Arquillo** and the *mirador de los lobos*, or sea lion lookout point. This rough and rocky spot, reachable only after an hour trek on foot, takes visitors to a spot above a sea lion refuge. Looking down, the adventuresome find themselves nearly face to face with a congregation of noisy sea mammals. On lucky days, a look skyward is rewarded by the sight of a pair of condors soaring above. These majestic birds sweep down on sea lion carcasses then use the intense coastal winds to

Candelabra engraved into the Paracas desert.

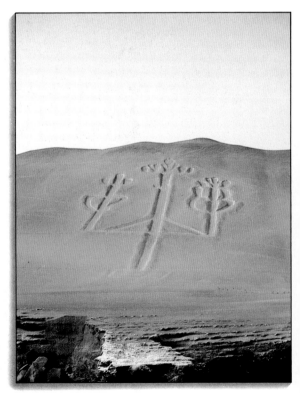

wing themselves up to the high altitudes they normally frequent. So well-known was the Andean birds' presence at Paracas that, when the nature reserve was being named, one scientist pushed for the moniker "Parque Nacional de los Condores" (Condor National Park).

During the last century, this region was important for its guano – the mineral rich bird droppings used as fertilizers in Europe. Extensive exploration of the peninsula is best done with the help of a guide as paths are not always clearly marked and it is easy to become lost. In June and August, Paracas is quite foggy – a reaction to the heat and sparse precipitation combined with the water-laden ocean winds that caress the coast. A meteorological office here recorded only 36.7 mm (1.5 inches) of precipitation during a 20 year period.

Desert burial grounds: Paracas not only refers to the area but also to the ancient Indian civilization living here up to 3,000 years ago, a pre-Columbian culture that was literally uncovered in 1925 when Peruvian archaeologist Julio C. Tello

Mummy at the Julio C. Tello site museum.

found burial sites under the sand dunes. The sand and the dryness of the desert protected the finely woven textiles around and inside those funeral bundles, buried when the Paracas culture thrived from 1300 B.C. until A.D. 200. The best examples of the textiles, as well as examples of the funeral bundles and information about how the burial pits were arranged, can be found in musuems in Lima. Recommended are visits to the Museo de la Nación, Museo Archaeological in Pueblo Libre and the private Amano collection of textiles in Miraflores.

The **Julio C. Tello site museum**, on the isthmus joining the Paracas Peninsula to the mainland, has exhibits about the archaeological find, although part of the collection was lost in a robbery some years ago. The discovery of hundreds of so-called "funeral fards" – or burying cocoons – gave anthropologists and archaeologists yet another tiny clue into this civilization. The fine weaving in cotton and wool still astound modern day textile experts, particularly those who have studied how the Indians were able to develop permanent dyes with such brilliant tones.

Meanwhile, the elaborately wrapped mummies in the funeral bundles show that the Paracas Indians performed trepanation, or a type of brain surgery in which metal plates were inserted to replace broken skull sections – a common injury among these Indians who fought by slinging rocks at one another. The Paracas culture also practiced the intentional deformation or molding of infants' skulls for aesthetic reasons. The results, akin to a conehead shape, not only were considered attractive but they clearly identified an individual's clan, since the molding was slightly different from tribe to tribe.

Heading some 48 km (29 miles) inland from Pisco is **Tambo Colorado**, among the best pre-Inca ruins on Peru's southern coast. There are wall paintings and buildings still standing at this complex, believed to have been a temple.

Grape stomping and fine wine: Farther south along the coast is **Ica**, a bustling oasis amid one of the continents' driest deserts and Peru's richest wine-growing region. Every March, the city goes all out with its annual wine festival, featuring everything from grape-stomping beauty queens to home-made wine that the locals swear is better than anything available on sale. The week-long party, called the *Festival Internactional de la Vendimia* is punctuated by sports events, cock fights, music, drinking, religious ceremonies and general merrymaking.

The wine festival is accompanied by an abundance of dancing, including the energetic dance known as the *yunza*. Hatchet-carrying men and skirt-flouncing women dance around a tree, drinking the alcoholic beverage derived from newly fermented grapes and stopping at intervals to take swings at the unlucky plant. The dance continues until the tree falls; the couple responsible for the felling cuts is promised a year of good luck. In addition, if the woman is unmarried, it is assured she will have a mate soon.

Although the festival is the most riotous time of year to investigate the area's wine reputation, visitors can explore the vineyards and wineries year round. The **Bodega El Carmel** pisco distillery is open to the public; it has an ancient grape press made from a tree trunk. Tours in Spanish only can be taken of the **Vista Alegre** wine and pisco distillery in Ica and its shop is recommended. Peruvian wines tend to be overly sweet although Ocucaje and Tacama are finer. (It is difficult to make arrangements to visit their vineyards but the wines can be purchased all over the country.)

Located on the Ica River, this community's second important festival falls in March when religious devotees to Our Lord of Luren show up for all night processions in which a wood and plaster image of the crucified Christ is taken from a church and paraded around the city. A second procession in honor of the city's patron saint is held every December.

Christ on a wave: The statue arrived in Ica more than four centuries ago, carried to shore on a wave then transported to the town. Records from the San Francisco monastery in Lima show that the Christ image was purchased by a friar in 1570. A storm at sea and the fear the ship in which the statue was being transported would sink apparently prompted the ship's captain to toss much of the cargo – including the wooden box containing the statue – overboard. Religious Ica residents took the icon's intact arrival as a miracle.

Churches worth visiting are **La Merced**, with its delicately carved wooden altars, and **San Francisco** with admirable stained glass windows. Balancing out the Christian importance of Ica is the witchcraft side of the city, known across the country as a center for black magic and folk healing.

A flood seriously damaged much of Ica in 1963, explaining why its colonial buildings have been replaced by more modern structures. Still, the city center retains its square block layout – based on a chessboard design. Although Ica was founded by the Spanish in 1536, European attempts to control the city were fraught with problems. Strong tremors caused damage to the town in 1568 and 1571 before a devastating earthquake in 1664 leveled it and left 500 persons dead – a phenomenal toll in those days. Later, the city residents resisted the Spanish presence. Ica was never granted a coat of arms, owing to its repudiation of attempts to make it a colonial center, and local residents remain proud of that rebellious image.

One of the city's most famous sons is José de la Torre Ugarte, author of Peru's national hymn. He was born in Ica in 1786 serving as a local judge until he joined the revolutionary troops under General San Martín. After Peru's independence, he turned to politics but found that an even more dangerous line of work than freedom fighter; in a power struggle between factions of the Congress, he was condemned to death. When spared by the colonel commissioned to execute him, Torre Ugarte returned to a career in law.

At the same time, the first civilian to be named president of Peru was also from Ica. Domingo Elias' tenure in office was short-lived owing to political upheaval in the newly independent Peru. His attempt in 1854 to start a revolution of his own failed, although he was able to take control of Arequipa before fleeing to exile in Chile.

Knotted strings: Today, just a 20-minute walk from Ica's center, this region's role in the revolution is traced in a room at the **Museo Regional**. Even more interesting are the exhibits of mummies, ceramics and skulls from the Paracas, Nazca and Inca cultures. On display are *quipus* (also spelled *kipus*), the mysterious knotted strings believed to have been used to keep calculations, records and historical notes for the Incas, who had no system of writing. Since only selected members of the Inca civilization were permitted to "read" the *quipus*, their meaning has been lost, although some experts say they were a sophisticated accounting system in which colored strings represented commodities and knots showed quantities. It is theorized the *quipus* were crucial in keeping food inventories throughout the Inca empire.

The regional museum also boasts an excellent collection of Paracas textiles and feather weavings. And it is a rare visitor who does not find his or her curiosity piqued by the rehydrated mummy hand on exhibit – a "must" for those who think they have seen everything. Placed in a saline solution after being buried centuries on the dry desert coast, this hand was part of an experiment by scientists who hoped rehydrating would provide medical information about the deceased individual.

An unmarked private museum on the **Plaza de Armas** (at Bolívar 170) is intriguing for the number and variety of stones it contains, but the scientific community has pooh-poohed its owner's theories that the rocks come from a technologically-advanced Stone Age civilization. Javier Cabrera, the eccentric descendant of city patricians, however, is happy to have an audience for his offbeat theories and visitors are welcome to see the more than 10,000 rocks in this collection. The only drawback here is the hefty entrance fee, roughly

Bodega near Ica.

US$5.

Consuls and curers: Outside Ica is **Las Dunas**, a full-scale resort and one of the most luxurious hotel complexes on the continent. With a restaurant, swimming pool, horses for riding, sand surfing and its own airstrip for flights over Nazca, this hotel regularly attracts diplomats and was featured in the US television series "Lifestyles of the Rich and Famous". It is said that several foreign diplomats make an annual pilgrimage to Ica, staying at Las Dunas and consulting with *curanderos* or curers and occult practitioners in the city.

Las Dunas has led the sand surfing frenzy that recently overtook this dune-covered coastal area. Principally attracting European sports fans, especially from Italy and France, the hotel has sponsored competitive sand surfing events on Cerro Blanco – a massive dune some (14 km/8 miles) north of Nazca.

Also on the outskirts of Ica is **Laguna de Huacachina**, a green lagoon of sulfur waters that Peruvians claim have me-dicinal value. Since Angela Perotti, an Italian living in Ica, began espousing the curative properties of the waters in the 1930s, this spot has become a favorite pilgrimage center for persons suffering from rheumatism and skin problems. Local residents claim up to 1,000 persons daily come to the waters to swim and soak. This peaceful setting just 5 km (3 miles) outside Ica also draws those looking for sun and solitude beside the palm trees and sand dunes that ring the lagoon.

Thanks to irrigation, cotton fields and ribbons of orange trees mark the landscape on the voyage farther south along the coast to **Nazca**, the home of the mysterious lined drawings that have prompted theories ranging from the fanciful to the scientific.

Desert drawings: Sixty years ago Nazca was like any other small Peruvian town with no special claim to fame, except that it was necessary to cross one of the world's driest deserts to reach it from Lima. But it is that desert – a sketching pad for ancient Indians – that has since

Laguna de Huacachina, an Oasis resort near Ica.

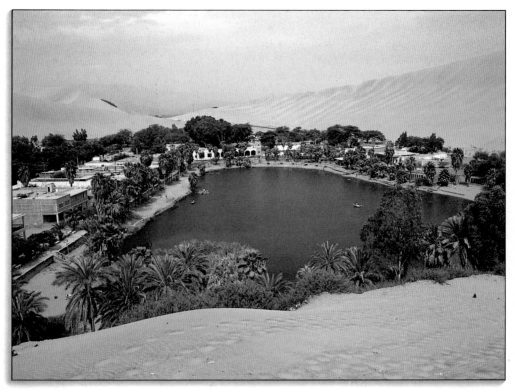

drawn thousands to this sun-bleached colonial town of 25,000 and made the pampa, or plain, north of the city one of the greatest scientific mysteries in the New World.

The Nazca lines are a series of drawings of animals, geometric figures and birds ranging up to 300 meters (1,000 feet) in size, scratched onto the arid crust of the desert and preserved for about 2,000 years owing to a complete lack of rain and special winds that cleaned – but did not erase – the pampa.

It wasn't until 1939 that Paul Kosok, a North American scientist flying over the dry coast in a small plane, noticed the lines, then believed to be part of a pre-Inca irrigation system. A specialist in irrigation, he quickly concluded this had nothing to do with water systems. By chance, the day of the flight coincided with the summer solstice and, making a second pass over the area, Kosok discovered that the lines of the sunset ran tandem to the direction of one of the bird drawings. He immediately dubbed the Nazca pampa "the biggest

Relaxing on the beach near Ica.

astronomy book in the world".

But instead of Kosok, it was a young German mathematician who became the expert on the lines and put the backwater on the map. Maria Reiche was 35 when she met Kosok, serving as his translator at a seminar on the lines. She had arrived in Peru eight years earlier to teach the German consul's children in Cuzco. Following Kosok's speech, she spoke with the scientist and he encouraged her to study the pampa. She dedicated the next half century to the task (see "Guardian of the Nazca Lines").

Pampa guardian: Now nearly 90, blinded by glaucoma and her movements restricted by Parkinson's disease, Reiche can no longer see the lines that she studied, measured, cleaned and charted daily from both the air and a 15-meter (49-foot) high metal platform she built. But hers are the most widely accepted theories on the hundreds of delicate drawings that cover a 50-km (31-mile) belt between Nazca and Palpa.

"This work was done so that the gods could see it and, from above, help the ancient Peruvians with their farming, fishing and all their other activities," says Reiche, who calls the pampa an "astronomical calendar". For example, she speculates that the drawing of the monkey – her favorite – is the Indian symbol for the Big Dipper, their constellation representing rain. When rain was overdue – a common occurrence in this plain where it only rains the equivalent of about half an hour every two years – the Indians sketched the monkey so the gods, looking down, would be reminded that the earth was parched.

Reiche also broke the key to the puzzle on how the Nazca Indians and their hawkish nation of fishermen and traders could have drawn the huge sketchings with such symmetry. She has determined that they used a basic unit of measurement, probably the distance from their elbows to their forefingers, and based all calculations upon this. As for symmetry, Reiche believes they used ropes tied to stakes to form circles and arcs that they cut with straight lines.

There are, of course, those who do not accept Reiche's theories, denying that the ancient Indians would have drawn something that they themselves could not see. Because the drawings can only be seen from the air, the International Explorers Club set out in 1975 to prove a theory that the Nazca Indians had aircraft. The Explorers Club made a cloth and reed hot air balloon, the *Condor I* and flew it for 60 seconds, reaching an altitude of 100 meters (300 feet). But the flight, 14 minutes shorter than planned, has hardly resolved the issue.

Writing from the planets?: The most damaging theory about the Nazca lines came seven years earlier when Erich Von Daniken published his volume *Chariots of the Gods*, in which he argued that the pampa was part of an extraterrestrial landing strip – an idea that Reiche discards impatiently.

Von Daniken's book drew thousands of visitors to the lines, but the newcomers set out across the pampa in search of the drawings on motorcycles, four-wheel drive vehicles and even horses – leaving the unerasable marks of their visits. Now it is illegal to walk or drive on the pampa and Reiche uses the profits from sales of her book, *Mystery on the Desert* to pay four guards to patrol the plain.

Other theorists say the lines marked tracks for running competitions, that they were enlarged designs used in weavings and textiles or that they are actually a huge map of the Tiahuanaco civilization which flourished near Lake Titicaca.

Reiche's last trip to the pampa was in 1987 with Phyllis Pitluga, the US astronomer Reiche has chosen to be her successor. Although she does not live in Peru year round and still retains a post at the Max Adler Planetarium in Chicago, when in Nazca, Pitluga gives a daily lecture about the pampa. When she is not in Peru, Reiche's sister Renate gives the free hour-long chat each evening at the Hotel Turistas. Pitluga's initial computer-based research on the Nazca lines appeared to support their link to the constellations. Other researchers have pointed to the elaborate vividly-painted Nazca pottery, with its clock-shaped pieces and elaborate solar calendars as further evidence this civilization was closely linked to the movement of the heavenly bodies.

There is a metal ladder at the side of the Pan America highway for those who want to view the pampa from ground level, although not much can be seen from so low. The best way to capture the impact of the lines is to fly over them in small propeller planes. AeroCondor offers flights from Lima, Ica and the small airport in Nazca. A lunch and a stop in the archaeological museum in downtown Nazca is included in the day-long Lima package. Other flights can be taken on Aeroica from Ica or Nazca. The Nazca flight is about 45 minutes and is best taken in mid-morning. Earlier there is sometimes a haze over the pampa, later the winds that buffet the plane leave observers more concerned about their stomachs than about the spectacle over the Nazca airstrip and wait around for pilots who are willing to bargain on the price for carrying tourists over the lines.

From the ground, the Nazca pampa is hot, dry and dusty, but from the air it is an amazing puzzle that thrills those trying to decipher the lines and figures they represent. Unfortuntely, unless visitors take the AeroCondor flight from Lima, the only way to reach Nazca is by bus – a trip that can take up to eight hours from the Peruvian capital. For several years there has been discussion of building an international airport at Nazca but the project has never gone farther than the drawing board.

Red dot in the desert sky: Occasionally, Nazca is deluged with astronomers who find the desert plain to be an optimal spot for viewing some rare cosmic happenings. On September 23, 1989, the autumn equinox, scientists went to Nazca to view Mars – which appeared as a red light in the desert sky for a 12-hour period. Laden down by telescopes, the astronomers said the phenomena would not present itself again until the year 2005.

Although the perplexing Nazca lines are what draw tourists to this area, they are by no means the only thing to see here. Some 30 km (18 miles) from the city is the fascinating **Cemetery of Chauchilla**, where sun-whitened bones and skulls, as well as pottery shards and mummies, litter a plain. The cemetery remains as it is in part to avoid further desecration of the area (most of the mummies were unearthed during tomb looting) and in part because there is no funding to arrange proper storage or exhibition of the mummies and their grave artifacts.

Local tours to the cemetery usually also stop at the **Paredones ruins** beside the Cantalloc aqueducts, an immense and complicated system built by the Incas and still supplying water to irrigated fields nearby.

Inland from Nazca on a well-paved road, **Camaná** is a popular summer resort for Arequipa residents and, coincidentally, the hometown of Peru's chess grand master, Julio Granda Zuñiga. Buses from the city center head to La Punta and the fine, but undeveloped, beach area. Camaná was, in colonial times, the unloading point for cargo headed to Arequipa then on to the silver

Hummingbird etched into the desert.

mines in Potosí, Bolivia.

Mollendo to the south is another summer beach resort, busy with Arequipeños from January to March but sleepy the rest of the year. Mollendo was a principal port before being replaced by **Matarani**, about 14 km (8 miles) to the northwest. Now its attractions are its three sandy beaches and its closeness to the **Lagunas de Mejía** nature reserve that attracts a number of coastal and migratory birds.

At the spot where the Peruvian coastal desert reaches its driest point lies **Moquegua**, a parched and dusty town on the banks of the Moquegua River. Buildings here – even the cathedral – are roofed with sugar-cane stalks daubed with mud. Its streets are cobblestones and its residents' topiary skills are evident on the **Plaza de Armas** where most of the bushes are trimmed into the form of llamas. Wine and avocados are shipped out of this city and both are worth sampling.

Repatriated city: Peru's southernmost coastal city is **Tacna**, repatriated from Chile in 1929 and separated from that country only by a mined stretch of desert that marks the border between the two nations. The Atacama Desert region from Tacna as far as Antofagasta once belonged to Peru and Bolivia but the nitrate-rich territory was lost to Chile in 1880 at the beginning of the War of the Pacific. A vote more than six decades ago returned it to Peru and, in the 1980s, it was one of the main spots for contraband activity in Peru. Government-subsidized milk and medicines were smuggled into Chile while less expensive clothing and imported cosmetics were brought back into Peru.

Unlike other border cities on the continent, Tacna is fairly well developed and boasts some of Peru's best schools and medical facilities – perhaps owing to its importance as a military base. The downtown area has been refurbished and its main boulevard is cut by an attractive flower and tree studded promenade. A pedestrian mall passes by the shops and here ice cream or cold drinks such as the popular icy cinnamon-laced soy milk beverage helps off-

set the intense heat during the Tacna summer. The tree-shaded **Plaza de Armas** is a welcome relief from the unrelenting sun that beats down on this town, although biting ants have invaded many of the plaza's benches.

The centerpiece of the plaza is the monument to the heroes of the War of the Pacific. The bronze fountain nearby is the work of Gustave Eiffel, of tower fame. He also designed the Cathedral, with its onyx high altar and interesting stained glass windows.

The **Museo Ferroviario** at the railway station has turn of the century train engines from the days when the British began constructing the complicated and, in some cases, daredevilish railway system in Peru. The museum also has a collection of railway-theme stamps from around the world.

Visitors should be on the alert in the train and bus station areas, avoiding entirely the street with the bus companies in the evening. Pickpockets and thieves work these areas and tourists are an easy mark.

Below, spider etched into desert near Nazca. **Right**, Maria Reiche, now nearly 90. **Following pages**: fiesta mask in Cuzco.

GUARDIAN OF THE NAZCA LINES

It was 1946 when German mathematician Maria Reiche began to haunt the Nazca pampa, measuring the lines there, sweeping them with a broom and walking alongside them day after day. The townspeople in the tiny town closest to the lines watched her hitch rides on cotton trucks before dawn every morning, a woman alone traveling to that isolated desert plain – sometimes even camping out all night on the pampa. The rumors began.

Some said she was a fortune hunter, looking for gold treasure buried in the desert. Others said she was a German spy. Still others accused her of being a witch. "Children used to run from me," Reiche says now in a barely audible voice. "The women in the market told their children that if they didn't behave I'd take them with me."

But the self-confessed loner didn't care. She was obsessed with the Nazca lines and saw their study as a mission from which she could not turn back.

"It was the happiest time of her life. She would never say that she has sacrificed," said Dr. Renate Reiche-Grosse, Reiche's sister, companion and physician since 1985 when Parkinson's Disease left the official "Guardian of the Pampa" unable to walk unassisted. Glaucoma, meanwhile, robbed her of her vision.

Battling illness: The walls of Reiche's room at the Turistas Hotel in Nazca, where she has lived free of charge for more than a decade is covered with charts and maps of the lines. She can no longer see them and she hasn't walked on the pampa since 1987 but the nearly 90-year-old woman claims every line, every drawing is imprinted in her mind.

Ironically, it was poor eyesight when she was very young that left a much younger Reiche pegged as stupid at school and relegated to the back seat of the class – making it even harder for her to see the teacher and the blackboard. Once they discovered that she simply needed eyeglasses, she had already withdrawn into herself.

In her youth, the pampa was all Reiche had. Her parents and only brother were dead. Her sister was married and living in Germany. When

Reiche was 26 she began teaching math in Germany; three years later she left her homeland to take a job teaching the German consul's children in Cuzco. Since 1946, when she began studying the lines, she has only taken one break – several months in 1959 in which she returned to teaching to help in a Peruvian literacy program. For more than 50 years, every speech she has given, every trip she made, every paper she wrote was somehow linked to the Nazca lines.

Reiche concedes her spartan lifestyle as the unpaid pampa guardian may be linked to her current health problems. When she first began studying the lines, supporting herself through translations and assistance at scientific conferences, she sometimes lived on only a mango or avocado a day – whatever she could stuff into her pocket on her way to the pampa. There were also the years when a *hacienda* owner let her stay in a small windowless, abandoned building with neither electricity nor running water. But she says it was preferable to living in cheap and dirty hotels in Nazca.

Appointing a Successor: Speaking frankly about how her death is not far off and how she feared to leave the lines without a caretaker, Reiche says she waited for a sign to indicate who could take over her work. Then one night she dreamt about a US astronomer who had visited her. The astronomer was Phyllis Pitluga and she came to Nazca with her husband while on vacation from her job at the Max Adler Planetarium in Chicago.

Since then, Pitluga has spent her vacations at Nazca and her free time doing the first computer analysis of the Nazca lines. Scientists have not yet responded to her initial findings but Pitluga says much of it supports Reiche's theory that the drawings are linked to the constellations.

Reiche, a national hero in Peru and one of the few living people who has appeared on a Peruvian postage stamp, says Pitluga's job will be heard. Like Reiche, this outsider will have to win the confidence of Nazca's residents as well as the Air Force – the group that so frequently gave Reiche airplane rides over the lines so she could take notes or photograph the pampa. "But Phyllis is fanatical about it," says Reiche. "She sees it as her mission, as I did."

Getting There

332 By Air
332 By Sea
332 By Land

Travel Essentials

332 Visas & Passports
332 Money Matters
333 Health
333 What to Wear
334 What to Bring

Getting Acquainted

334 Climate
334 Time Zones
334 Weights & Measures
335 Electricity
335 Business Hours
335 Festivals & Holidays

Communications

336 Newspapers
337 Postal Services
337 Telephone/Telegram/Telex

Emergencies

337 Security & Crime
338 Medical Services

Getting Around

338 Orientation
338 Maps
338 From the Airport
339 Domestic Travel
340 Private Transport
340 Public Transport
341 On Foot

Where To Stay

341 Hotels

Food Digest

346 What To Eat
346 Where To Eat

Things To Do

349 General
349 Lima
350 Pisco
350 Ica
350 Nazca
350 Arequipa
351 Puno (Lake Titicaca)
351 Cuzco
352 Huaráz
352 Trujillo
352 Chiclayo
352 Cajamarca
352 Iquitos

Culture Plus

352 Museums
354 Antique & Art Galleries
355 Concerts
355 Theater & Music

Nightlife

356 Live Music
356 Nightclubs
357 Bars
357 Discos

Shopping

357 What To Buy
358 Shopping Areas

Sports

359 Participant
359 Spectator

Further Reading

359 General
360 Archaeology & Pre-Inca Cultures
360 Inca Society
361 Colonial History
361 Machu Picchu
361 Other "Lost Cities"
361 Andean Wildlife
361 Amazon Jungle

Useful Addresses

362 Embassies & Consulates
363 Airline Offices
364 Tourist Information Offices (FOPTUR)

GETTING THERE

BY AIR

From Europe, direct flights to Lima are available with Lufthansa, Air France, KLM, Iberia, Viasa and Avianca.

American Airlines and Aeroperu make daily flights from Canada and USA via the South American gateway – Miami. Flying direct is also possible from several major cities including New York and Los Angeles aboard CP Air, Avianca, Aerolineas Argentinas, Air Panama, Varig, Lan Chile and Equatoriana.

There is no shortage of flights to other South American countries. Lloyd Aero Boliviano now flies between Cuzco and La Paz, Bolivia, twice a week. To and from Mexico use either Aerolineas Argentinas or Aeroperu.

The best route from Australia or New Zealand is probably with the Aerolineas Argentinas direct flight to BA, connecting with Lima. There are also weekly flights from Sydney and Auckland to Santiago in Chile (via Tahiti with Qantas or UTA, connecting with Lan-Chile to Santiago, stopping over at Easter Island). In Santiago, change for Lima. Other travelers go to LA and make a connection there.

BY SEA

Few people arrive at Lima's port of Callao by either ocean liner or freight ship. The limited services available are expensive and inconvenient by comparison to flying.

BY LAND

Peru has borders with four other countries: Chile, Bolivia, Brazil and Ecuador. The border crossing with Chile is at Tacna on the Peruvian side, Arica on the Chilean; taxis regularly make the crossing and some long distance buses operate Lima-Santiago. From Bolivia, efficient minibus services will take you from La Paz to Puno; alternatively, Crillon Tours in Bolivia offers a hydrofoil across Lake Titicaca via Copacabana and the Island of the Sun – an extremely pleasant way to arrive (*pisco sours* are served en route). The journey from Ecuador is also straight forward: take a bus to the border at Huaquillas and walk through to Tumbes. Other buses operate from there (note that the "international service" advertised in Quito still requires you to change buses at the border, so is actually more expensive and occasionally much less convenient than doing the trip with seperate legs).

TRAVEL ESSENTIALS

VISAS & PASSPORTS

Visas are not required by citizens of South American countries, (other than Chile and Venezuela), western European countries, the United States, Canada or Japan. Australians and citizens of New Zealand do require visas. These can be obtained overnight from Peruvian consulates for a US$10 fee. Note that for a visa, their consulates insist on your showing a ticket out of the country, which can be inconvenient if you plan to travel overland.

All visitors, however, must have a passport and are issued with an entry stamp and tourist card on arrival in Peru. These are valid for 90 days and the card must be surrendered to immigration on departure. These tourist cards can be extended for 60 days at the Ministerio del Interior, Paseo de la Republica at Av. 28 de Julio, Lima.

MONEY MATTERS

In 1986, the unit of currency was changed from the *sol* to the *inti*. One *inti* was worth 1,000 *sol*. It is impossible to state the current value of the *inti*, given its extreme fluctuation and the possibility that it will again be replaced. However, as an indication, at time of press, US$1 was worth 2,000,000 *intis*.

Denominations of this currency are notes ranging from 1,000 to 1,000,000 *intis* and soon to be 5,000,000 *intis*.

There is certainly no shortage of money changing facilities in Lima, formal and otherwise (i.e if you don't mind haggling on street corners). On the Plaza San Martín, in downtown Lima, hundreds of outdoor bankers run alongside the traffic – the rate is usually a little better than in the banks. It is legal to change with these "cambistas" and usually quite safe – although if you don't feel comfortable with it, there are plenty of alternatives. Banks will change your currency at the slightly inflated "official" rate and good hotels have exchange services or will send a hotel courier to one of the Casas de Cambio for a better rate (give him a tip, though). Travel agents accept payment in some foreign currencies and exchange small amounts.

The Banco de Credito and the Banco de la Nacion are recommended for any international banking business such as receiving US$ or DM from overseas. Ask for a *liquidacion por canje de moneda extranjera*.

Upon arrival in Lima, and especially when traveling in the provinces of Peru, it is convenient to carry some US cash as well as your travelers' checks, credit cards or cash advance card (although the cities of Cuzco, Arequipa and Iquitos, which have large numbers of visiting tourists, boast every money changing facility). It is not always possible to change checks, and cash dollars get a better rate, although you run the risk of theft. American Express will replace lost travelers' checks only in Lima.

The Visa "cash advance" card is quite useful in major cities (the Banco de la Nacion handles these transactions), while credit cards such as Diners Club and Mastercharge are accepted by good hotels and restaurants.

HEALTH

The most serious illnesses to guard against are yellow fever and malaria, both apparent only in some jungle areas of the north and south Amazon. There have been outbreaks of yellow fever in Puerto Maldonado, so visitors should ensure they are vaccinated.

There are drugs which can be used against malaria and visitors are advised to consult their physician before leaving home. Malarial mosquitoes only bite at night so always use a mosquito net when sleeping in jungle towns.

Hepatitis A is caused by ingesting contaminated food or water. Stick to bottled drinks, peeled fruit and good quality restaurants, thereby ensuring your standard of hygiene. A gamma globulin injection, taken shortly before your trip, is considered by many doctors to protect against hepatitis.

A less serious and much more common condition for travelers in Peru (or any third world country, for that matter) is upset stomach and diarrhoea – often caused by a change in culture and diet, unclean water or utensils, or simply the change of place. Traveling itself places extra pressure on the immune system, so take it easy until you feel stronger. In most cases, the symptoms will improve after a day or so of fasting and drinking plenty of fluids (hot tea without milk is ideal). If the more serious condition of dysentery develops (i.e. any blood or pus in the stool), you should be treated by a doctor.

Don't be surprised if your exaltation at flying into Andean mountain cities is followed by a less pleasant sensation called "soroche" or altitude sickness. In most cases the symptoms are very mild – fatigue, shortness of breath, slight nausea and headache. The best prevention and cure is to lie down for a few hours upon arrival at your hotel and then slowly introduce yourself to physical activity. If the symptoms are severe – i.e. vomiting, rapid irregular pulse, insomnia – the immediate treatment is to descend to a lower altitude (although this usually happens only to mountain climbers).

A last word about sunburn. The tropical sun can feel very gentle but might burn you to a crisp. Effective sunscreen such as 35+ strength is not available in Peru, so take it with you.

WHAT TO WEAR

Good traveling clothes are comfortable and durable and often made of natural fiber, although one or two synthetics in the form of evening wear won't crush in your suitcase and come in handy for those formal Latin nightspots. Take some good walking shoes that won't look too out of place in a casual restaurant.

One rarely regrets traveling light, especially in a land where clothes shopping is a dream. Remember all those alpaca sweaters and leather goods – you can buy as many warm clothes as you like when you arrive.

The most appropriate clothing for a jungle trip is long-sleeved shirts and trousers of close-woven material. These protect the wearer from most biting insects. A hat gives valuable protection while traveling on the river or birdwatching on the lakes.

It is advisable to leave your valuable jewelry at home and not to carry cameras or walkmans in public areas.

WHAT TO BRING

What you bring depends on your itinerary, Peru being a country of such diversity. For example, those planning adventure travel will need specific items like tents that other travelers can do without. Bring warm clothes for the Sierra, light clothes for the jungle and a combination for the coastal deserts (which are warm by day and cool at night). See the section on "Climate" for more details.

Items that are difficult to obtain in Peru include: your personal medical supplies, a strong money belt, sunscreen, good books in English and any electronic equipment you use. Bring your camera and plenty of film, as Peruvian stocks are expensive and often outdated.

GETTING ACQUAINTED

CLIMATE

Peru has wet and dry seasons, although on the coastal desert strip it is, not surprisingly, always dry weather. However, Lima suffers a bizarre weather condition prevailing from April to November called the "garua", a damp cold mist which obliterates the sun and sours everyone's mood. August is the worst month for this with temperatures around 55°F-62°F (13°C-17°C). The rest of the year, Lima enjoys sunshine and moderate temperature from 69°F-79°F (20°C-26°C).

Towns like Nazca on the western slopes of the Andes are dry and hot all year round, but the central Andes do experience distinct wet and dry seasons. The best time to visit the highlands – and for most people, that means the best time to visit Peru generally – is between May and September when views of the mountains are crystal clear. Although the days are clear, nights can be bitterly cold and temperatures fall to 0°C. The rest of the year, weather is warmer but wetter, and the Andes are often obscured.

In the Amazon basin, the wet season lasts from January to April, when landslides and flooding is a constant problem. During the dry season, May to October, it might not rain for weeks at a time (although there might be short showers every day). Daytime temperatures average from 81°F-90°F (23°C-32°C), with nighttime lows averaging 69°F-79°F (20°C-26°C). However unexpected cold fronts called "friajes", which come up from the south are unique to the southern rainforests, and can bring a few days of wind and rain with spring-like daytime temperatures of 55°F-65°F (13°C-18°C) and night lows of 50°F (10°C).

TIME ZONES

Lima is five hours behind Greenwich Mean Time and therefore coincides with Eastern Standard Time in the U.S.

WEIGHTS & MEASURES

Peru uses the metric system for all weights and measures. Translating the Spanish term is fairly obvious. i.e. kilometros, litros etc.

Converting to imperial is not as obvious. Here's a table to help.

To Convert:	Multiply By:
centimeters to inches	0.3937
meters to yards	1.094
kilometers to miles	0.6214
liters to US gallons	0.264
grams to ounces	0.03527
kilograms to pounds	2.205

ELECTRICTY

Peru uses 220 volts, 60 cycles AC, except Arequipa which is on 50 cycles. The major hotels provide 110 volt outlets in bathrooms for the use of shavers only.

BUSINESS HOURS

Most stores are open from 10 a.m. to 8 p.m. Monday to Friday with a break for a couple of hours between 1 p.m. and 4 p.m.

Banks are open only in the mornings during summer (January to March). For the rest of the year there is also afternoon trading between 4 p.m. and 6 p.m. although the hours often change. The *casas de cambio* (exchange houses) are open from 9 a.m. to 6 p.m., while the money changers are on the footpaths nearly 24 hours a day. These are generally quite safe and are preferred by Peruvians themselves for their convenience, but keep your wits about you.

The central post office in Lima is open from 8 a.m. to 6 p.m., Monday to Saturday and from 8 a.m. to 12 p.m. on Sundays. The Peruvian Telephone Company Office on the Plaza San Martín in Lima is open from 9 a.m. to 9 p.m. Monday to Saturday, but can take a lot of waiting before your call goes through.

The Tourist Information Office and the South American Explorers Club are open from around 9 a.m. to 5 p.m., Monday to Friday. Many of the embassies are only open in the mornings. There is very little open on Sundays.

FESTIVALS & HOLIDAYS

January 1 – New Year's Day (national holiday).

January 15-20 – Lima Foundation Week. Official celebrations of the founding of Lima by the Spaniards on January 18, 1535.

January 24-31 – National Contest of La Mariners - Trujillo.
Annual competitions for this traditional dance.

February 1-15 – Cruz de Chalpon - Chiclayo. Handicraft and commercial fair in the nearby prilgrimage center of Motupe.

February 8-14 – Virgen de la Candelaria - Puno.
"La Mamita Candicha", the patron of Puno, is honored with continual demonstrations of rich folklore. Thousands participate in the parades, dances, fireworks and music of this important religious event.

February (Every Sunday) – Carnival in Iquitos.
Colorful masquerades and dancing the typical "La Pandilla" takes place throughout the city.

February 24-27 – Carnival in Puno and Cajamarca.
Carnival is especially celebrated in these two cities with "La Pandilla" dancing and traditional festivities.

March 1-5 – The Vendimia Festival - Ica.
The grape harvest of the Ica Valley is celebrated with parades, dances and happy revelry involving the region's most important product, wine.

March/April – Holy Week
Amongst the nationwide commemorations is the spectacular procession in Cuzco in honor of the patron saint "El senor de los Temblores". (Held on Holy Monday and Thursday.) The people of Tarma make carpets of flowers to cover the streets for their evening processions. Holy Week is solemnly commemorated in many other highland towns. (Half day holiday on Holy Thursday, full day holiday on Good Friday).

April (Third Week) – National Contest of Paso Horses - Lima.
This exhibition and contest in Mamacona, 30 km south of Lima, has the participation of breeders from the most important regions of Peru.

May 1 – Labor Day

May 2 – Cruz Velacuy - Cuzco.
The crosses in all the churches of Cuzco are veiled and festivities take place.

May-2-4 – "Las Alasitas" Fair - Puno.
Important selling exhibition of miniature handicrafts.

June – Corpus Christi - Cuzco.
One of the most beautiful displays of religious folklore, the Procession of the Consecrated Host takes place in the gold monstrance of the Cathedral.

June (First Week) – Mountaineering Week in the Andes - Huaráz.
The Callejon de Huaylas and the Cordillera Blanca provide the majestic settings for the National and International Ski Championships, as well as many other adventurous activities.

June 24 – Inti Raymi, or Festival of the Sun - Cuzco.
This ancient festival is staged at the Sacsayhuaman Fortress overlooking Cuzco and involves authentic Inca rituals, parades, folk dances and contests.

June 29 – St Peter's Day (full day holiday).

July 15-17 – Feast of the Virgen del Carmen - Cuzco.
Festivities are held throughout the highlands, especially colorful in Paucartambo, 256 km from Cuzco.

July 28 & 29 – Peru's Independence (public holidays).

August 13-19 – Arequipa Week
This is the most important annual event for this attractive city. Festivities include folkloric dances, handicraft markets and a fireworks display on the 15th.

August 30 – St Rose of Lima Day (full day holiday).

September 18 – Unu Urgo Festival - Cuzco.
The Urgo ceremony is conducted with Andean music, dancing and parades in the towns of Urco and Calca near Cuzco.

October 7-20 – Lord of Luren - Ica.
Thousands of pilgrims pay homage to the patron of Ica, with the main procession on the 17th.

October 8 – Battle of Angamos (national holiday).

October 18, 19 & 28 – Lord of the Miracles - Lima.
A massive procession in honor of Lima's patron saint takes place on the 18th.

November – Bullfighting Season.
An internatinal competition is held at Rimac, Lima, in the oldest bullring in America.

November 1 – All Saint's Day (national holiday).

November 1-7 – Puno Jubilee Week.
Puno celebrates its founding by Spaniards, followed by a fascinating reenactment of the emergence of the legendary founders of the Inca Empire, Manco Capac and Mama Ocllo, from the waters of Lake Titicaca. This week sees the best of Puno's folkloric festivities.

November 29 – Zana Week - Chiclayo.
One week of celebrations for the founding of Zana include folklore shows, sporting events and exhibitions of Paso Horses.

December 8 – Immaculate Conception (full day holiday).

December 24 – Festival of Santuranticuy - Cuzco.
Native Andean toy fair.

December 24 & 25 – Christmas (half day national holiday on 24th, full day on 25th).

COMMUNICATIONS

NEWSPAPERS

The English newspaper, the *Lima Times* is published every Friday. It is a concise and welcome source of news and information including cultural events in Lima. The major morning newspapers in Lima are *El Commercio* and *Expreso*.

POSTAL SERVICES

The main post office in Lima is beside the Government Palace on the northwest corner of the Plaza de Armas. Here you can collect your mail at the Poste Restante (in Spanish, *Lista de Correos*) and, after overcoming a bit of "red tape", send certified packages overseas. There are branch offices in other districts of Lima:

Airport office
8 a.m.-6 p.m. Mon-Sat

San Isidro office
Libertadores 325, San Isidro

Miraflores office
Libertadores 325, San Isidro

Miraflores office
Petit Thouars 5201
Tel: 45-0697
8 a.m.-7.30 p.m. Mon-Fri

American Express clients can have mail received at: Amex, c/-Lima Tours, Belen 1040, Lima. Bring your passport as identification for this, as well as for the *lista de correos* at the post office. Members of the South American Explorers Club can also have mail held for them at: Casilla 3714, Lima 100, Peru.

TELEPHONE/TELEGRAM/TELEX

Long distance and international calls can be placed either through your hotel desk or by dialing 108 for the international operator with whom collect and trunk calls can be arranged. Peru has recently incorporated direct dialing so check if the service is available in your area. There is a cheaper, more chaotic method at the Peruvian Telephone Company Office located on the Plaza San Martín in Lima. Other cities in Peru are serviced by Entel Offices.

Local telephone calls are made with tokens called "fichas RIN", sold by many street vendors.

There is a telegram and telex office on the corner of Lampa and Emancipacion in downtown Lima.

EMERGENCIES

SECURITY & CRIME

As Peru's urban centers have swelled, so has petty crime. Pickpockets and thieves – including senior citizens and children – have become more and more common in Lima and Cuzco. It is recommended that tourists do not wear costly jewelry and that their watches, if worn, be covered by a shirt or sweater sleeve. Thieves have become amazingly adept at slitting open shoulder bags, camera cases and knapsacks; keep an eye on your belongings. Officials also warn against dealing with anyone calling your hotel room or approaching you in the hotel lobby or on the street, allegedly representing a travel agency or specialty shop. Carry your passport at all times.

A special security service for tourists has been created by the Civil Guard. These tourism police are recognizable by the white braid they wear across the shoulder of their uniforms and can be found all over Lima, especially in the downtown area. In Cuzco, all police have tourism police training. The tourist police office in Lima is Avenida Salaverry 1156, Tel: 714-313.

There has been much publicity of late about terrorism in Peru, although tourists are extremely unlikely to come into contact with political violence. The only area where tourists should definitely avoid is the remote Andean city of Ayacucho: this is easily done by taking the inexpensive flight between Lima and Cuzco rather than the grueling, 40-hour bus trip. Also, at present, traveling without guides into the coca-growing region around Tingo Maria in the Amazon basin should be avoided. For more specific inquiries, contact your embassy or the South American Explorer's Club in Lima (Av. Portugal 146, Breña, Lima, Tel: 31-4480).

POLICE -The Policia de Turismo cover everything pertaining to tourists, are very helpful and have English speakers on duty. Tel: 23-7225/24-6571. They are located at Salaverry 1156, Jesus Maria.

MEDICAL SERVICES

Good hotels will have reliable doctors on call. The following clinics have 24-hour emergency service and an English speaking staff member on duty:

Clinica Anglo-Americana
Av. Salazar, San Isidro
Tel: 40-3570

Clinica Internacional
Washington 1475, Lima
Tel: 28-8060

Clinica San Borja
Av. del Aire 333, San Borja
Tel: 41-3141

Clinica Ricardo Palma
Av. Javier Prado Este 1066, San Isidro
Tel: 41-6064

One dentist who has been highly recommended is Dr Gerardo Aste. He also speaks English. Tel: 41-7502 Antero Aspillaga 415, of. 101, San Isidro.

GETTING AROUND

ORIENTATION

Lima, the "City of Kings", is Peru's gateway and jumping off point for the rest of the country (although Cuzco and Iquitos have now begun promoting their international airports and direct flights from other countries are planned). If your time is limited, Lima has the facilities to fully organise your itinerary so you can fly directly to any major destination with your reservations or tour confirmed. Machu Picchu and the Sacred Valley might be the one essential destination for many tourists, while others take months to appreciate the diversity of cultures between the coastal regions, the Andes and the Amazon.

Lima itself is divided into districts, each with its own distinctive character. Downtown Lima – with its grandiose plazas, mansions and the magnificent Gran Hotel Bolivar – is the oldest, although its streets are now crowded out with street vendors and decidedly chaotic. Many Limeños and visitors prefer to stay in the more glitzy, plastic and international suburbs of Miraflores and San Isidro, where the homes have better security. Their new shopping complexes and landscaped gardens make this a complete contrast. Barranco is a beach suburb with a growing reputation for bohemian lifestyles. Cafes and restaurants have live jazz and creole music while the crumbling old mansions give the streets a relaxed ambience.

MAPS

The South American Explorer's Club at Av. Portugal 146 (Breña), Lima, is an excellent source for maps, guidebooks and information. For further geographical and aerial maps try the:

Instituto Geographico Nacional
1190 Av. Aramburu, Surquillo
Tel: 45-1939
8 a.m.-12.30 p.m. & 1.30 p.m.-3.30 p.m.
Mon-Fri

FROM THE AIRPORT

Getting to and from Lima airport is easiest in the care of your hotel shuttle or tour organiser. Otherwise there are plenty of taxis but, as ever, be prepared to bargain (about US$2.50 is average). Alternatively, Transhotel is a 24-hour shuttle service to and from the airport. They will pick up passengers from any part of town with the fare according to distance.

Transhotel
Ticardo Palma 280
Tel: 46-9872
Airport Tel: 51-8011

For Cuzco and other cities, taxis into town are very cheap – always agree on a price before you leave.

DOMESTIC TRAVEL

BY AIR

The two major domestic airlines, Aeroperu and Faucett provide daily services to most cities. There is little qualitative or price difference although Aeroperu flies more often to more destinations.

Aeroperu
Plaza San Martín
Tel: 31-7626 (domestic), 32-2995 (international); &
Pardo 601, Miraflores
Tel: 47-8900
Reservations: 47-8255

Faucett
Inca Garcilaso de la Vega 865, Lima
Tel: 33-6364

Aerocondor
Juan de Arona 781, San Isidro
Tel: 42-5663/41-1354
For flights over the Nazca Lines and charter service over the Callejón de Huaylas.

Aerochasqui
Av. Nicolas de Pierda 611 of. 301, Lima
Tel: 27-5471/27-5758
For flights to Trujillo.

It's best to book in person at the reservations office, or through a good travel agent who will confirm your tickets. Don't feel shy about confirming more than once, as tales of travelers being bumped off flights are legion: it is necessary to confirm your confirmed ticket 72 hours in advance and then reconfirm 24 hours ahead of the departure date, otherwise you might simply disappear from the airline computer. Both airlines are sadly unreliable in meeting their flight schedules. Times are often changed and, in the case of remote destinations, occasionally cancelled due to lack of interest. You often won't find out until you're at the airport.

For domestic flights there is a Security Tax of US$5 plus US$2 Municipal Tax at all airports except Lima.

BY LAND

Most travelers prefer to fly between major destinations, but overland travel in Peru is not always as problematic as often imagined. For example, the coastal Pan-American highway is fully paved and worked by regular, comfortable buses. Unfortunately, highways in the Andes are generally unpaved and the buses range from reasonable to backbreaking – although still popular with young backpackers. The journeys are dirt cheap, colorful and you get to see some amazing scenery, if you have the time and inclination.

Important note: At present, traveling by bus between Lima and Cuzco (via Nazca) is extremely dangerous for foreigners due to Sendero Luminoso guerilla activity near Ayacucho. Incidents where buses have been stopped and foreigners killed have been reported. While traveling by bus is quite safe in other parts of Peru, it cannot be stressed strongly enough that you should fly between Lima and Cuzco – and, since the bus journey is a gruelling 40-hour trip, the US$75 flight (which takes only half an hour and ranks amongst the most spectacular in the world) should seem even more attractive.

Train journeys, however, are very popular with all types of travelers. Rail services run Cuzco-Puno and Puno-Arequipa as well as Lima to Huancayo (the highest rail journey on earth). Relatively comfortable and well serviced "first-class" carriages are available (book through Lima Tours or other agencies), as well as very cheap seats. The trips provide valuable glimpses of rural life and views of magnificent landscapes. The journey Puno-Cuzco has become a particularly popular leg in recent years.

For the Lima-Huancayo journey, the Central Line Ticket Office in Lima is located at Desamparados Station. Tickets are sold from 7 a.m.-12 p.m. and 1.30 p.m.-4 p.m. Mon-Fri, and 7 a.m.-11 a.m. on Saturdays. Tel: 27-6620.

A modern train, the *Autovagen*, departs from Cuzco early for Machu Picchu and returns in the afternoon. Travel agents in Cuzco sell all-inclusive day tickets for the trip. There are much cheaper, slower trains for budget travelers.

Bus companies have morning and evening departures to most cities. Two reliable companies are:

Tepsa
P. de la Republica 129, Lima
Tel: 32-1233

Ormeno
Carlos Zavala 177, Lima
Tel: 27-5679

Comfortable buses for the 8-hour ride to Huaráz can be booked at:

Empresa Transportes Rodriquez
Lima: Av. Roosevelt 354
Tel: 28-0506
Huaráz: Av. Tarapaca 662
Tel: 72-1353

Expreso Ancash
Lima: Av. Zavala 177
Tel: 25-5679
Huaráz: Av. Raimondi 861
Tel: 72-1111

Colectivos (shared taxis) are commonly used for traveling south to Ica, Nazca and Paracas. Contact:

Comite 3
Montivideo 561, Lima
Tel: 28-1423

Comite 4
Leticia 591, La Victoria
Tel: 28-8608

Boats can be taken from the beautiful bay of Paracas to the Balletas Islands, home of sea lions, Humboldt penguins and various sea birds.

From Puno, tranquil excursions by boat across Lake Titicaca arrive at the island of Uros, Taquile and Amantani, or a more luxurious cruise is by hydrofoil all the way to Bolivia.

In the Amazon Jungle, motorized canoe down the winding muddy river is the only way to travel.

PRIVATE TRANSPORT

Certain regions are better appreciated with your own mode of transport, such as the Callejón de Huaylas, a 200-km long valley nicknamed the "Peruvian Switzerland" for its glaciers, lakes and snowy peaks. The town of Huaráz is a 6-hour drive from Lima on good surface roads. For quality car rental:

National Car Rental
Av. Espana 449, Lima
Tel: 23-2526
8.30 a.m.-5.30 p.m. Mon-Fri & 8.30 a.m.-12.30 p.m. Sat

Also at:
Diez Canseco 319 of. 13, Miraflores
Tel: 44-2333
8 a.m.-8 p.m. Mon-Sat & 9 a.m.-1 p.m. Sun

Airport Office open 24 hours.

Budget
La Paz 522, Miraflores
Tel: 44-4546
8.30 a.m.-7.30 p.m. Mon-Sat

Also at:
Corpac 514, San Isidro
Tel: 41-1129
8.30 a.m.-7.30 p.m. Mon-Sat

Airport office open 24 hours
Tel: 52-8706

PUBLIC TRANSPORT

Lima's public buses can only really be recommended for a one-time cultural experience. Flagging one down is a feat in itself – then you must survive the jostling crowds and pickpockets. There are thousands of privately-run minibuses stopping and starting every few seconds, but why bother when a taxi from downtown Lima to Miraflores is no more than US$2?

TAXI

Taxi in Peru have no meters – you simply bargain on a rate, preferably before even getting in. In many Andean cities you may prefer to walk, but in Lima taxis are often essential and very cheap: a typical fare in from the colonial downtown to Miraflores for US$2. Note that your hotel will arrange taxis for you if you ask. This is more expensive, but very secure. If you don't speak much Spanish and don't fancy bargaining on the street, this can be the best option.

Downtown Lima is definitely best explored by walking. Here amongst throngs of street vendors and money changers you can walk from the government palace to museums to colonial mansions, all in a distance of several blocks. Sit for a while in the Plaza de Armas or San Martín and gain true insights into the Limeño character.

For the more energetic walker, trekking is one of Peru's great attractions. Not all excursions require a high level of expertise. A very famous trek is the Inca Trail to Macchu Pichu. Taking 3 or 4 days, an organised group will include hired carriers who set up camp and cook ahead of your arrival. (See the feature on "Trekking in the Andes" for more information.) Tour operators can arrange shorter and less tiring walking tours.

WHERE TO STAY

Throughout Peru, a government chain called ENTUR PERU owns standard to deluxe category tourist hotels and inns.

Reservations at any **Hotel de Turista** (as they are all called) can be made through a travel agent or by contacting:

ENTUR PERU
Javier Prado Oeste 1358
San Isidro, Lima
Tel: 72-1928

LIMA

DOWNTOWN AREA

Gran Hotel Bolívar *****
Plaza San Martín
Tel: 27-6400
Tlx: 25201 PE CP HBOLI
Fax: 338626 Cable BOLIVARCO

This is the doyen of Peruvian hotels. Even newly-elected Peruvian presidents traditionally occupy one of the Bolívar's 272 graciously maintained rooms on victory night. The stately three room suites overlooking the Plaza San Martín are particularly good value – ask to see one. Even those who are not staying at the Bolívar should make a visit. Tea and cakes at 5 p.m. in the domed vestibule is a luxurious treat, while the grand salon has a competitively priced lunch menu. Dinner comes with a traditional floor show. Ask for a Catedral in the lounge bar and you'll receive the best *pisco sour* in Lima. Like all good hotels, airport shuttle and money exchange service is provided.

Hotel Crillon *****
Colmena 589
Tel: 28-3290 to 28-3295
Tlx: 25274 PE
Fax: 280682
The hotel's Sky Room, comprising a restaurant, cocktail bar and nightclub, stages the best folkloric show in Lima. Round trip transfer from your hotel is included. Office and Shuttle Service – Tel: 46-6498.

Sheraton Lima Hotel & Towers *****
Paseo de la República 170
Tel: 32-9050/32-8676
Tlx: 20286
Fax: 314622
This more recent deluxe style hotel boasts of 500 guest rooms, 3 restaurants, 2 bars and a swimming pool within its complex.

Hotel Residencial San Francisco ***
Jr. Ancash 340
Tel: 28-3643
Very close to the Plaza de Armas and yet quietly situated, here is a great value budget hotel if you decide on the downtown area. The friendly and helpful management keeps the hotel secure, immaculate and efficiently run.

Renacimiento
Parque Hernan Velarde 52-54
Tel: 31-8461
Secluded colonial style hotel ten minutes' walk from the center.

MIRAFLORES

The newer suburb of Miraflores is the commercial center of Lima and is home to the more affluent Peruvians. Here you will find the fashionable boutiques, restaurants and businesses.

Miraflores Cesar's Hotel***
La Paz & Diez Canseco
Tel: 44-1212
Tlx: 25202 CP MIRAF
The most luxurious hotel in Miraflores.

Jose Antonio Hotel **
Av. 28 de Julio 398
Tel: 45-6870/45-7743

Hostal El Patio *
Diez Canseco 341
Tel: 44-2107/44-4884
Includes breakfast in the tariff. English and French spoken.

SAN ISIDRO

The more residential "garden" suburb of Lima.

El Country Club **
Los Eucaliptos 550
Tel: 40-4060

Hostal Residencial Callacocha *
Andres Reyes 100
Tel: 42-3900/42-4160

**Residencial Los Petirrojos **
Av. Los Petirrojos 230
Tel: 41-6044
(Av. Javier Prado Este, 9th block)
Offers clean spacious rooms with breakfast included.

THE SOUTH COAST

PISCO

Hotel Paracas *
Rivera del Mar, Paracas-Pisco
Tel: 2220
Reservations in Lima: 46-5079/46-4865
Bungalows on the beach, tennis courts, swimming pool and excursions to the Peninsula can be arranged.

Las Dunas – Centro Vacacional *
Km. 300 Panamericana Sur, Ica
Tel: 23-1031
Reservations in Lima: 42-4180/42-3092
Tlx: 21162 PE
A holiday resort, complete with horse riding and private airstrip for Nazca flights.

NAZCA

Hostal de la Borda *
Panamericana Sur Km. 447, Nasca
Reservations in Lima: 42-6391/40-8430
Located near the airfield, the hotel is a renovated hacienda with garden, swimming pools, hot showers and friendly service.

AREQUIPA

El Portal Hotel *
Portal de flores 116, Arequipa
Tel: 21-5530
Reservations in Lima: 40-6447/40-6155
On the Plaza de Armas, with excellent views and roof top swimming pool.

Hostal La Casa de Mi Abuela *
Jerusalem 606, Arequipa
Tel: 22-4582
Receives rave reviews from all visitors. Behind the huge stone wall is an idyllic garden setting. Breakfast can be taken on the patio or roof terrace. English is spoken and the management is very friendly. A popular spot so reserve well in advance.

PUNO (LAKE TITICACA)

Hotel Isla Esteves ***
Isla Esteves, Puno
Tel: 724
Tlx: 54785 ENTURPUN
Reservations in Lima: 42-8626/42/8633
Tlx: 21588 ENTURLIMA
One of the government owned tourist hotels. Built on a nearby island, a known site of the Tiwanaku period, it is connected to the mainland by a causeway 5 km northeast of Puno. Deluxe services include a discotheque, bar and good restaurant.

Hostal Don Miguel *
Av. La Torre 545, Puno
Tel: 177
Reservations in Lima: 35-1371/35-2873

Tel: 54770 HDMPUNO
Fax: 35-1371

CUZCO

Don't be daunted by the number of hotels in Cuzco. The competition is high and so is the quality.

Hotel Libertador Cuzco ***
San Augstin 400, Cuzco
Tel: 23-1961
Tlx: 52043 LIBCUS
Fax: 084 23-3152
Reservations in Lima: 42-0166/42-1995
The best of the five stars.

Hotel El Dorado Inn ***
Av. El Sol 395, Cuzco
Tel: 23-1135/23-3112
Reservations in Lima: 27-6400
Tlx: 52039 DORADO
Adds a sauna to the list of services.

Hotel Marques de Picoaga **
Santa Teresa 344, Cuzco
Tel: 22-7251/22-7691
Reservations in Lima: 28-6314/27-9501
Tlx: 52041 HOCUSA

Hostal Royal Inka I *
Plaza Regocijo 299, Cuzco
Tel: 22-2284/23-1067
Reservations in Cuzco: 23-4221
Tlx: 52620 INKA
Attractively situated on the upper plaza, with good service, though not as new or as expensive as Royal Inka II.
Same reservations number for both hotels.

Hotel San Augustin *
Maruri & San Augutin 390, Cuzco
Tel: 23-1001
Tlx: 52224 HASAGUST
Reservations in Lima: 23-6006/28-7656

Hostal Loreto **
Pasaje Loreto (the famous Inca walled laneway), Cuzco
Very popular with budget travelers, several of the rooms have original Inca walls. Ask for an electric heater.

Hotel de las Marquesas **
Garcilaso 256, Cuzco
Tel: 23-2512
Another economical option. Colonial ambience is created by a charming inner courtyard.

MACHU PICCHU

Hotel de Turistas de Machu Picchu
Tel: 31
Tlx: 52438 ENTURHTM
Reservations in Lima: 42-8626/42-8633
Tlx: 21558 ENTURLIMA
The one and only hotel right next door to the ruins.

URUBAMBA VALLEY

Hostal Alhambra III - Plaza
Plaza Manco II 123, Yucay
Tel: 22-4976
Reservations in Lima: 44-1199/47-8776
Tlx: 21618 HOTDIPLO
Situated in the pretty village of Yucay, just 4 km from the town of Urubumba, the hotel was once a beautiful hacienda. It now includes a small museum and as well as a quality restaurant.

EL Albergue
(beside Railway Station 1 km from center of town, Ollantaytambo)
The more adventurous travelers might choose this charming rustic-style hostel managed by a friendly north American family. Trekking groups are accommodated during the June to September season and guided trips arranged. They can be contacted through the Ollantaytambo telephone operator.

HUARÁZ

Hostal Andino *
Jr. Cochachin 357, Huaráz
Tel: 72-1662
Fax: (044) 72-2830
Reservations in Lima: 45-9230/72-1501
For the best views of the mountains.

Hostal Colomba *
Jr. Francisco de Zela 210, Huaráz
Tel: 72-1501
Friendly, family run bungalows within pleasant garden.

Edward's Inn **
Av. Bolognesi 121, Huaráz
Tel: 72-2692
Very popular with trekkers. Edward knows a lot about the region.

El Tumi *
Jr. San Martin 1121, Huaráz
Tel: 72-1784
A comfortable place for budget travelers.

TRUJILLO

Hotel El Golf ****
Mz. J-1 Urbanizacion El Golf, Trujillo
P.O. Box 329
Tel: (044) 24-2592
Fax: (044) 23-2515
Luxury hotel including swimming pools, private parking lot and several suites with direct dial telephones.

Hotel de Turistas de Trujillo ***
Jr. Independencia 485, Plaza de Armas, Trujillo
Tel: 23-2741/23-5741
Tlx: 43016 ENTURTRU
Reservations in Lima: 42-8626/42-8633
Tlx: 21588 ENTURLIMA
Good value accommodation with an excellent buffet lunch on Sundays.

Hostería El Sol ***
Vallecito de Coina, Coina
Reservations in Trujillo:
Los Brillantes 224
Tel: 23-1933
Coina is a village 132 km east of Trujillo, set at 1,500 meters in the Sierra Alto Chicama. The late German Dr Kaufmann gave prominence to the area by building a hospital for the Indians and the Hosteria de Sol. Now managed by Dr Kaufmann's family, the location provides glorious views of the Sierra and full board is offered.

CAJAMARCA

Hostal Laguna Seca ***
Av. Manco Capac, Banos del Inca
Tel: 05
Reservations in Lima: 46-3270
Six km from Cajamarca, you can enjoy hot thermal baths in the privacy of your room at this rennovated hacienda.

Hotel de Turistas de Cajamarca ***
Jr. Lima 773, Cajamarca
Tel: 2470
Reservations in Lima: 42-8626/42-8633
Tlx: 21588 ENTURLIMA
Well located in the center of town and very comfortable.

CHICLAYO

Garza Hotel
Av. Bolognesi 756, Chiclayo
Tel: 22-8172/23-8968
Fax: 22-8171

Hotel de Turistas de Chiclayo
Av. Salaverry (no number)
Tel: 23-4911
A short distance from the town center. Includes a swimming pool, car park and car hire services.

IQUITOS (NORTHERN AMAZON)

Hotel Amazonas Plaza *****
Abelardo Quinones Km. 2, Iquitos
Tel: 23-5731/23-1091
Tlx: 91055
Reservations in Lima: 44-1199/44-1990
Tlx: HOTDIPLO
Iquitos' top class hotel, 3 km out of town.

Acosta II
Ricardo Palma 252
Tel: 23-2904

Acosta I
Esq. Huallaga & Araujo
Tel: 23-5974
Not quite as prestigious as Acosta II although includes a swimming pool and a very good restaurant.

Lodges

Amazon Village
Rio Mommon
Reservations in Lima:
Alcanfores 285, Miraflores
Tel: 44-1199/47-8776
Tlx: 21618 HOTDIPLO
Excursions to the Amazon jungle are made from this location on the River Mommon, weather conditions permitting.
Bungalows are clean and well-ventilated

and good food is served. For the more comfort-conscious traveler.

Amazon Lodge & Safaris
Putumayo 165, Iquitos
Tel: 23-3023
Reservations in Lima:
Carmino Real 1106, San Isidro
Tel: 41-9194
Tlx: 21371
Day trips available on the powerful "Amazon Explorer" launch as well as two day/one night stays.

Explorama Lodge & Explornapo Camp
Av. La Marina 340 - Casilla 446, Iquitos
Tel: 23-5471/23-3481
Tlx: 91014
Fax: 23-4968
Reservations in Lima: 24-4764
Also offers two day packages with charges of US$40 for each additional day. Managed by the well-organised Explorama Tours, the Explornapo Camp is better situated than the above two lodges for sighting fauna. It offers a good balance of comfort and penetration of the jungle for those who wish to experience the Amazon with a fairly structured itinerary.

For the more adventurous traveler:

Tamshiyacu Lodge
Reservations:
Wilderness Expeditions
310 Washington Ave SW
Roanoke Va. 24016 USA
Tel: (703) 342-5630
Organised trips include Yarapa River Lodge, Tambo Safari Inn Camp and wilderness expeditions.

Selva Lodge & Yarapa Lodge
Reservations:
Amazon Selva Tours
Putumayo 133
Experienced guides and great food.

Yarapa River Camp
Reservations:
Amazonia Expeditions
Putumayo 139
Strongly conservationist.

MADE DE DIOS REGION (SOUTHERN AMAZON BASIN)

MANU BIOSPHERE RESERVE

Manu Lodge
c/- Manu Nature Tours
Avenida Sol 627-B
Oficina 401, Cuzco
Tel/Fax: (084) 23-4793
15 km from Puerto Maldonado on the Madre de Dios River.

Albergue Cuzco Amazonico ***
Reservations in Lima:
Tel: 46-2775/46-9777
Fax: 45-5598
Tlx: 21475 PELATI

Also at:
Procuradores 48, Cuzco
Tel: 5047

TAMBOPATA-CANDAMO RESERVE

Explorer's Inn ***
c/- Peruvian Safaris
Garcilazo de la Vega 1334
P.O. Box 10088, Lima
Tel: (14) 31-3047
Reservations at:
Plaza San Francisco 168, Cuzco
Tel: 23-5342; or
Fitzcarrald 136, Puerto Maldonado
Although not quite as comfortable as the Albergue Cuzco Amazonico, there is a better chance for observing wildlife from this location i.e. a further 2 hours' boat travel away from Puerto Maldonado on the Tambopata River.

Also in this area:
Tambopata Macaw Lodge
c/- Tambopata Tours
Avenida Sol 627-B
Oficina 202, Cuzco

FOOD DIGEST

Peru's *criolla* cuisine evolved through the blending of native and European cultures. A *la criolla* is the term used to describe slightly spiced dishes such as *sopa a la criolla*, a wholesome soup containing beef, noodles, milk and vegetables.

Throughout the extensive coastal region, seafood plays a dominant role in the creole diet. The most famous Peruvian dish, *ceviche*, is raw fish or shrimp marinated in lemon juice and traditionally accompanied by corn and sweet potato. Other South American countries have their own version of *ceviche* but many foreigners consider Peru's to be the best. *Corvina* is sea bass, most simply cooked *a la plancha*, while scallops, *conchitas* and mussels, *choros* might be served *a lo mancho*, in a shellfish sauce. *Chupe de Camarones* is a thick and tasty soup, of salt or freshwater shrimp.

A popular appetizer is *palta a la jardinera*, avocado stuffed with a cold vegetable salad or *a la reyna*, chicken salad. *Choclo* is corn on the cob, often sold by street vendors at lunchtime. Other Peruvian "fast food" includes *anticuchos*, shish kebabs of marinated beef heart; and *picarones*, sweet lumps of deep fried batter served with molasses. For *almuerzo* or lunch, the main meal of the day, one of four courses might be *lomo saltado*, a stir-fried beef dish, or *aji de gallina*, chicken in a creamy spiced sauce.

The most traditional of Andean foods is *cuy*, guinea pig, which is roasted and served with a peanut sauce. Another specialty of the Sierra is *Pachamanca*, an assortment of meats and vegetables cooked over heated stones in pits within the ground. Succulent freshwater trout is plentiful in the mountain rivers.

Peruvian sweets might be *suspiro* or *manjar blanco*, both made from sweetened condensed milk, or the ever popular ice-cream and cakes. There are many weird and wonderful fruits available in Lima, notably *chirimoya*, custard apple, *lucuma*, a nut-like fruit, delicious with ice-cream, and *tuna*, which is actually the flesh from a type of cactus.

In towns, many Peruvians drink the soft drink *chicha morada*, made with purple maize (different from the *chicha de jora,* the traditional home made alcoholic brew known throughout the Andes). The lime green *Inca Cola* is more popular than it's northern namesake, as well as *Orange Crush, Sprite* and *Seven-up.* The *jugos*, juices, are a delightful alternative to sodas and there are many fruits available. Instant Nescafe is often served up even in good restaurants, although real coffee can be found at a price. Tea drinkers would be advised to order their beverage without milk, to avoid receiving some peculiar concoctions.

The inexpensive beers are of high quality. Try Cusqueña, Cristal or Arequipena. Peruvian vines can't compete with Chilean excellence, but for a price, Tabernero, Tacama, Ocucaje and Vista Alegre are the reliable names. The Peruvian *Pisco Sour* is, however, a strong contender. Try the famous, potent *cathedral* at the Gran Hotel Bolívar in Lima.

Although Lima offers a huge choice of restaurants in the city area, the following are the most reliable, providing high quality food and service:

International Cuisine

Pabellon de Caza
Alonzo de Molina 1100, Monterrico
Tel: 37-9533
12 p.m.-3 p.m. & 7 p.m.-1 a.m. Mon-Sat
Brunch on Sun 10.30 a.m.-4 p.m.
Located only a short stroll from the Gold Museum, containing a luxuriant garden and elegant decor.

Carlin
La Paz 646, Miraflores
Tel: 44-4134
12 p.m.-4 p.m. & 7 p.m.-12 a.m. daily

A cozy international style restaurant popular with foreign residents and tourists.

Los Condes de San Isidro
Paz Soldan 290, San Isidro
Tel: 22-2557
12 p.m.-3 p.m. & 7 p.m.-12 a.m. daily
Set in a spectacular San Isidro mansion.

El Alamo
Cnr of La Paz and Diez Canseco, Miraflores
12.30 p.m.-3 p.m. & 7 p.m.-12 a.m. Mon-Sat
A cozy spot for imported wines and cheeses. Specializing in fondues.

Seafood Restaurants

La Rosa Nautica
Espigon No. 4
Coasta Verde, Miraflores
Tel: 47-0057
12.30 p.m.-2 a.m. daily
Lima's most famous seafood restaurant prestigiously located at the end of an ocean boardwalk.

La Costa Verde
Barrangquito Beach, Barranco
Tel: 67-8218
12 p.m.-12 a.m. daily
Romantic at night under a thatched roof and right on the beach.

Criolla Cuisine

Las Trece Monedas (The Thirteen Coins)
Jr. Ancash 536, Lima
Tel: 27-6547
12 p.m.-4 p.m. & 7 p.m.-11.30 p.m. Mon-Sat
Formal presentation within a beautiful 18th-century colonial mansion, including courtyard and antique coach.

Manos Morenos
Av. Conquistadores 887, San Isidro
Tel: 42-6271
12 p.m.-3.30 p.m. & 6 p.m.-12 a.m. Tues-Sun
Criollo Breakfast: Sat & Sun 8.30 a.m.-11 a.m.
The best "criollo" fare Lima has to offer, specializing in *anticuchos* (shish kebab of marinated beef heart).

French Cuisine

L'Eau Vive
Ucayali 370, Lima
Tel: 27-5612
12 p.m.-2.45 p.m. & 8.15 p.m.-10.15 p.m. Mon-Sat
Fine provincial dishes prepared and served by a French order of nuns. The skylit inner courtyard is one of Lima's most pleasurable settings for luncheon – the perfect place to take a break from sightseeing.
(Ave Maria is sung nightly at 10 p.m. and dinner guests are invited to join in).

Italian

Valentino
Manuel Banon 215, San Isidro
Tel: 41-6174
12 p.m.-3 p.m. & 7.30 p.m.-12 a.m. Mon-Sat
Great Italian food at Lima's best international restaurant.

La Trattoria
Manuel Bonilla 106, Miraflores
Tel: 46-7002
1 p.m.-3.30 p.m. & 8 p.m.-12 a.m. Mon-Sat
Authentic Italian fare.

Japanese

Matsuei
Canada 236, La Victoria
Tel: 72-2282
12 p.m.-3 p.m. & 7 p.m.-11 p.m. Mon-Sat; 7 p.m.-11 p.m. Sun
Excellent quality Japanese food.

Steak

La Carreta
Rivera Navarrete 740, San Isidro
Tel: 40-5424
12 p.m.-8.30 p.m. daily
For typically excellent Argentine beef.

The Steak House
La Paz 642, Mezzanine – "El Suche", Miraflores
Tel: 44-3110
12 p.m.-3 p.m. & 7 p.m.-12 a.m.
Charming setting that has good steaks and salads.

Pizza

Las Cuatro Estaciones
Vcayali (near cnr Jiron de la Union), Lima
One of the very few great pizza restaurants
of South America, also serving exotic local
fruit juices. Wholesome and highly recommended for all travelers.

La Pizzeria
Benavides 322, Miraflores
Tel: 46-7793
9.30 a.m.-12 a.m. daily
Nighttime haunt of trendy Miraflores crowd.

"Tex-Mex"

Villa Taxco
Libertad 435 (F. Gerdes), Miraflores
For Reservations: 47-5264
12 p.m.-11.30 p.m. Mon-Thurs
The show "Mariachis" on Fridays & Saturdays starts at 9.30 p.m. Authentic Mexican
dishes including Tampiquena Steak, Burritos
and Fajitas. Mexican decor throughout with
banquet rooms available.

Cafes

La Tiendecita Blanca – Cafe Suisse
Av. Larco 111, Miraflores
Tel: 45-9797
Boasts of 30 different kinds of chocolates,
excellent ice-cream and desserts. Popular
with shoppers but also serves lunch and
dinner.

AREQUIPA

This attractive city has always maintained a
reputation for style and affluence. There are
several good restaurants around the Plaza de
Armas and cafes can be found in the first
block of San Francisco.

La Rueda – Argentine Grill
Mercaders 315
Tel: 21-9330
Barbequed meats and good wine in a cozy
ranch style restaurant.

Le Paris
Mercaders 228
French cuisine and other international dishes.

El Fogón
Santa Marta 112
Tel: 21-4594
Specializes in barbequed chicken.

Sol de Mayo
Jerusalem 207 (Yanahuara district)
Good lunch time menu of Peruvian specialties
such as *rocoto relleno*, stuffed hot peppers,
or *ocopa*, potatoes in a spicy sauce with
melted cheese. Include a visit to the Mirador
de Yanahuara as part of your day's itinerary.

CUZCO

While in Cuzco, sample the succulent pink
trout, prepared in many of the Peruvian and
international style restaurants. Cuzquenos
have also mastered the art of pizza baking
and there is always a new establishment to be
found within the plaza's portals. Good restaurants will also provide exciting Andean
music.

Pizzeria La Mamma
Portal Escribanos 177, Plaza Regocijo
Just one of the many restaurants which serves
mouth-watering garlic bread and fresh mixed
salads as well as pizzas.

El Trujo
Plaz Regocijo 247
Catering to most of the large tour groups,
this nightly dinner and show is the most
elaborate in Cuzco and very good value.

Trattoria Adriano
Sol 105, cnr Mantas
Friendly service and excellent pink trout.
Try it simply grilled and with a squeeze of
lemon.

Le Petit Montmarte
Garcilaso 270
Fine French cuisine.

Quinta Zarate
Calle Tortera Paccha
One of the many "quintas", or inns, in the
suburbs. The specialty here is roast *cuy*,
guinea pig.

El Ayllu
Portal de Carnes 203 (beside Cathedral)
A must to visit for breakfast of ham and egg,

toast and fruit juice, or homemade fruit yo-ghurt, cakes, teas and good coffee. Continuous opera musak and cosmopolitan clientele gives this place its unique character.

Meson de Espaderos
Espaderos 105
A quaint wooden balcony provides perfect dining views of the Plaza. The mixed grill, *asado*, is excellent and huge.

Cuzzo's best two hotels, the El Dorado Inn and the Libertador have excellent restaurants, with high prices set in US$.

Cafes around the plaza serve *mate de coca*, chocolate mud cake and hot milk with rum on chilly Cuzco nights.

HUARÁZ

Samuel's
Jr. Jose de la Mar 626
Good breakfasts.

Chalet Suisse
Hostal Andino
Jr. Cochachin 357
Fancy international meals.

La Familia
Av. Luzuriage 431
Wide selection of wholesome foods.

Pizzeria Ticino
Av. Luzuriaga 651

Creperie Patrick
Av. Luzuriaga 424

TRUJILLO

De Marco
Francisco Pizarro 725
Tel: 23-4251
Peruvian and international cuisine. Popular for ice-creams and desserts.

There is a concentration of restaurants near the market and a number of vegetarian places on Bolívar.

THINGS TO DO

GENERAL

Lima Tours is the main tour organiser in Peru, having branches in every tourist region. They offer tours to every part of the country mentioned in this book – for example, to Cuzco and Machu Picchu of three days and two nights duration for around US$150 plus airfare; or to Arequipa, the Amazon, the north or Lake Titicaca.

Lima Tours also keeps up-to-date on new events and offer theme trips: for example, they offer tours to the new Sipán archaeological dig; and have exclusive rights on visits to some colonial houses in Lima (even including evening dinners in 17th-century mansions etc.). It's worth dropping by their modern offices in Calle Belem and asking for one of their brochures:

Lima Tours
Belen 1040
Tel: 27-6624
8.30 a.m.-5.15 p.m. Mon-Fri & 8.30 a.m.-3 p.m. Sat & Sun

Also at:
4 Pardo 392, Miraflores
Tel: 43-1948; and
Juan de Arona 883, San Isidro
Tel: 72-3559

LIMA

Lima possesses a wealth of tourist attractions in the form of historical landmarks, such as colonial houses and churches, as well excellent museums. Tours can also be taken to nearby archaeological sights located on the central and southern highways leading way from Lima.

The independant traveler can take quite a while seeing all there is to offer or join a city tour if time is limited.

Many travel agencies and tour operators are located on Colmena, the northwest side of Plaza San Martín. For daily sightseeing tours of the city, night excursions including dinner and show, or day trips beyond Lima, the largest and most organized tour company is Vista Peru, providing pick-up from all major hotels, English speaking guides and deluxe motorcoaches. All reservations and enquiries can be made through:

Lima Tours
Belen 1040
Tel: 27-6624
8.30 a.m.-5.15 p.m. Mon-Fri & 8.30 a.m.-3 p.m. Sat-Sun

Also at:
Pardo 392, Miraflores
Tel: 43-1948; and
Juan de Arona 883, San Isidro
Tel: 72-3559

Reservations for tours or adventure travel throughout Peru can usually be made in Lima. Direct flights from Lima over the Nazca lines can be booked through:

Aero Condor
Hotel Sheraton
Tel: 32-9050 ext. 117

Apart from Lima tours, recommended specialist adventure travel companies for river running, trekking and jungle expeditions include:

Expediciones Mayuc
Conquistadores 199, San Isidro
Tel: 225-988

Explorandes
Bolognesi 159, Miraflores
Tel: 45-0532

PISCO

Located 235 km south of Lima, Pisco is noted for the wildlife of the Balletas Islands and Paracas Peninsula, as well as the archaeological site of Paracas Necropolis. Boat tours to the Balletas Islands are reserved through the Hostal Pisco and the more expensive Hotel Paracas, which also has tours to the Paracas Peninsula (see "Hotel" section).

ICA

Ica is an oasis surrounded by sand dunes, famous for wine and *pisco*. Tourists visit the distilleries and wineries, particularly Tacama and Ocucaje, as well as the attractive colonial churches and museums. Best time to come is in February, for the grape harvest and Vintage festival.

NAZCA

For flights over the Nazca lines in light aircraft, reservations with Aero Condor can be made at either Condor's Nest (across from the airport), at their office opposite the Hotel de Turistas, or at the Hotel Nazca.

The Hotel Nazca will organise ground level viewing of the lines for those who don't want to fly. The Nazca Lines-Mirador Tour includes the observation tower 20 km north of Nazca.

AREQUIPA

Most attractions in Arequipa are accessible on foot and easily appreciated as an independent traveler, although if you don't have much time, city tours are available to include the Santa Catalina Monastery and other points of interest. Day tours into the mountainous terrain include the Colca Canyon, climbing the volcano – El Misti, viewing the petroglyphs at El Toro and so on.

Lima Tours offer the most comfortable visits. Contact:

Lima Tours
Santa Catalina 120
Tel: 22-4210

An interesting option is with Holley's Unusual Excursions. The Englishman Anthony Holley knows the surrounding area inside out and runs four-wheel drive excursions of six people. For information write c/- Casilla 77, Arequipa or in Arequipa phone: 22-4452/21-2525. Again, Mayuc Expediciones handles kayak and rafting expeditions in the Colca Canyon. In Arequipa they're located at Apartado 5 96.

Some travelers prefer to drive themselves. National Car Rental in Arequipa rents VW's and Toyota Jeeps at reasonable rates.

PUNO (LAKE TITICACA)

Tours can be taken around the lake, to the ruins at Sillustani, Chucuito and the town of Juli. One reliable tour operator is:

Turpuno
Jr. Lambayeque 175
Tel: 35-2001
Tlx: 54792
Fax: 35-1431

Many travelers take the short boat ride across Lake Titicaca to the Floating Islands of the Uros, or to the tranquil islands of Taquile or Amantaní. Simply stroll to the dock area where boats leave every hour.

Hydrofoils to the Island of the Sun, the village of Copacabana and to Bolivia, including lunch, can be booked through Transturin:

In Puno: Jiron Tacna 201
Tel: 737.

In Cuzco: Portal de Panes 109, Of. 1, Plaza de Armas
Tel: 22-2332

Crillon Tours also operates an all-inclusive bus-hydrofoil-bus journey to La Paz, Bolivia. Expensive but delightful.

CUZCO

The first thing to do is to purchase a "Visitors Ticket", a combination entry pass to all the historic buildings of note. US$10 includes fourteen different sites, many of them "a must", but each site can only be visited once.

Tour operators in Cuzco fall into two categories: those offering standard tours of Cuzco and surrounding ruins or market villages, and those operating adventure tours such as trekking, climbing, river running and jungle expeditions. Recommended for tours are:

Lima Tours
Av. Sol 567
Tel: 22-8431/22-1266/22-3791

Receptour (Hotel Libertador)
San Agustin 400
Tel: 22-3981

Lima Tours offers structured trekking trips (including a "Full Moon on the Inca Trail" trek) and can arrange visits to the Amazon from Cuzco.

There are many other adventure travel companies to choose from. The following also handle jungle expeditions into the Manu National Park from Puerto Maldonado and take reservations for jungle lodges.

Expediciones Mayuc
Procuradores 354
Tel: 23-2666

Explorandes
Urb. Magisterio N-17
Tel: 22-6599

Expediciones Manu
Procuradores 372
Tel: (084) 22-6671
For the Manu Biosphere Reserve.

Manu & Tambopata Nature Tours
Av. Sol 627-B Of. 401
Tel: 23-4793

Cuzco Maldonado Tour
Portal de Panes 109
Tel: 22-2332

Other specialist adventure companies with guides and equipment for rent are:

Peruvian Andean Treks
Pardo 705
Tel: 22-5701
Mountaineering specialists.

Dalfi
Plateros 352
Tel: 22-2300
Trips on the Machu Picchu Inca Trail organized and equipment rented.

APU Expediciones
Portal de Carnes 236, Plaza de Armas
Tel: 23-5408
Recommended for river running.

HUARÁZ

For tours to Chavin and other day trips:

Huaráz Chavin Tours
Av. Luzuriaga 740, Huaráz-Ancash
Tel: 72-1922

Milla Tours
Av. Luzuriaga 515, Huaráz-Ancash
Tel: 72-1742

Pablo Tours
Av. Luzuriaga 501, Huaráz-Ancash
Tel: 72-1145

Equipment rental for trekking and climbing:

Andean Sport Tours
Av. Luzuriaga 571, Huaráz-Ancash
Tel: 72-1612

TRUJILLO

For tours to the five major archaeological
sites:

Trujillo Tours
Jr. Gamarra 440-448
Tel: 23-3069/23-3091
Fax: (044) 25-7518

CHICLAYO

Important new archaeological sites such as
Sipan can be reached with Lima Tours or the
following:

Indiana Tours
M.M. Izaga 774
Tel: 24-0833

CAJAMARCA

Tours of the city include numerous colonial
churches, thermal baths at Banos del Inca
and the Ventaillas de Otuzco. Contact:

Intertours
Jr. Lima (main square)
Tel: 92-2777

Cumbemayo Tours
Jr. Amalia Puga 635
Tel: 92-2938

IQUITOS

There are many interesting sights apart from
jungle expeditions. Most tour operators can
be found along Calle Putumayo between the
plaza and the river.

Explorama Tours
Av. La Marina 340-Casilla 446, Iquitos
Tel: 23-5471/23-3481
Tlx: 91014
Fax: 23-4968
Reservations in Lima:
Camana 851 Of. 1501, Lima
Tel: 24-4764

CULTURE PLUS

MUSEUMS

LIMA

Museo de la Nación
Javier Prado Este 2466, San Borja
Tel: 37-7822/37-7776
9 a.m.-6 p.m. Tues-Fri; 10 a.m.-6 p.m. Sat-
Sun
Entrance US$3.00
Lima is justly proud of its newest museum,
a large modern structure containing many
floors of meticulously prepared exhibitions.
They include impressive models of new and
established archaeological sites as well as a
spacious mannequin showroom displaying
Peru's magnificent folkloric costumes.
Worth at least one long visit.

Museo de Oro del Peru (Gold Museum)
Alonso de Molina 100, Monterrico
Tel: 35-2917
12 p.m.-7 p.m. daily
Entrance US$5.00
There are actually two private museums at
this outer suburb address. Apart from Peru's
unique collection of Pre-Inca and Inca gold,
there is an astonishingly complete Arms

Museum which includes a number of highly decorative uniforms.

Museo Rafael Larco Herrera
Bolívar 1515, Pueblo Libre
Tel: 61-1312
9 a.m.-1 p.m. & 3 p.m.-6 p.m. Mon-Sat; 9 a.m.-1 p.m. Sun
Entrance US$4.00
Private collection of over 400,000 well-preserved ceramics, pre-Columbian art and artifacts. Famous erotic "huacos" ceramics from the Moche culture are housed in a separate room beside the gift shop.

Museo Nacional de Antropologia y Arqueologia
Plaza Bolivar, Pueblo Libre
Tel: 63-5070
10 a.m.-6 p.m. daily
Entrance US$4.00
Highly comprehensive exhibitions depicting the prehistory of Peru from the earliest archaeological sites to the arrival of the Spaniards. All the major Peruvian cultures are well represented.

Museo Nacional de la Republica
(the National Museum of History)
Plaza Bolívar (next door to the Archaeological Museum), Pueblo Libre
Tel: 63-2009
9 a.m.-6 p.m. daily
Entrance US$4.00
Both San Martín and Bolívar had lived in this building, now containing the furnishings and artifacts from colonial, republican and independent Peru. A must for those interested in the Peruvian revolution.

Museo Pedro de Osma
Pedro de Osma 501, Barranco
Tel: 67-0915/670019
11 a.m.-1 p.m. & 4 p.m.-6 p.m.
Admission by appointment only.
Treasured collection of Viceregal painting, sculpture and silver.

Museo de Arte
Paseo de Colon 125, Lima
Tel: 23-4732
9 a.m.-5 p.m. Tues-Sun
Entrance US$1.00
Grand building containing four centuries of Peruvian artworks, including modern painting. Also houses pre-Columbian artifacts and colonial furniture.

Amano Museum
Retiro 160 (off 11th of Angamos), Miraflores
Tel: 41-2909
Admission by appointment only, guided tours in small groups at: 2 p.m., 3 p.m., 4 p.m. & 5 p.m. Mon-Fri
Particularly beautiful is the textile collection from the lesser known Chancay culture.

Museo del Banco Central de Reserva
Ucayali 291, Lima
Tel: 27-6250
10 a.m.-5 p.m. Mon-Sat; 10 a.m.-1 p.m. Sun
A welcome relief from the hoards of money changers in this part of town, the bank offers a collection of looted pre-Columbian artifacts recently returned to Peru, paintings from the Viceroyalty to the present and also numismatics.

Museum of the Iquisition
Junin 548 (right side of the Plaza Bolívar as you face the Congress), Lima
9 a.m.-7 p.m. Mon-Fri; 9 a.m.-4.30 p.m. Sat
Admission free
Explicit representations of torture methods in the Dungeon of this, the headquarters of the Inquisition for all Spanish America from 1570-1820.

Museo de Historia Natural
Arenales 1256, Jesus Maria
Tel: 71-0117
9 a.m.-3.30 p.m. Mon-Fri; 9 a.m.-1 p.m. Sat
Collection of Peruvian flora and fauna.

Museo de Ciencias de la Salud
(Health Sciences Museum)
Junin 270, Lima
Tel: 27-0190
10 a.m.-4 p.m. Wed-Sun
Entrance US$1.00
Details pre-Columbian medical practices with English translations. The museum also arranges pre-Columbian banquets for organized groups.

Museo Etnografico de la Selva
Avenida Tacna (first block)
Within the grounds of the Santuario de Santa Rosa de Lima
9.30 a.m.-1 p.m. & 3.30 p.m.-7 p.m. daily

Dominican missionaries have collected jungle Indian artifacts from south-eastern Peru.

Numismatic Museum
Banco Wiese, 2nd Floor
Cuzco 245, Lima
Tel: 27-5060 ext. 553
9 a.m.-1 p.m. Mon-Fri
Admission free
Peruvian coin collection from Colonial times to the present.

PARACAS

J C Tello Museum
Information Center, Paracas Peninsula

ICA

Regional Museum
Ayabaca, Ica
(1.5 km from Plaza de Armas)
Best collection in the region of Indian artifacts, including preserved mummies and beautiful Nazca ceramics.

AREQUIPA

Santa Catalina Convent
Av. Santa Catalina 301
Take a few hours at least to explore this tranquil complex, one of the most fascinating visits in Peru.

Casa Ricketts
San Francisco (near Moral)

Casa Moral
Cnr Moral & Bolivar

Goyeneche Palace
La Merced (two blocks away from plaza)

PUNO

Carlos Dreyer Museum
Cnr Deusta & Lemos
9 a.m.-7 p.m. Mon-Fri

CUZCO

A bewildering number of museums and historic sights. Independent travelers can visit them separately with a US$10 Visitor's Ticket, available from several of the major attractions. Hours are listed on the ticket and attractions explained in the Cuzco section of this book.

HUARÁZ

Archaeological Museum of Ancash
Plaza de Armas, Huaráz-Ancash

TRUJILLO

Trujillo Archaeological Museum
Jr. Pizarro 349

Cassinelli Museum
Av. Mansiche (near Av. Espana)

Casa de la Emancipacion
Jr. Pizarro 610 cnr Gamarra

Casa de Mayorazgo
Jr. Pizarro 314

Casa Urquiaga & Casa Bracamonte
Plaza de Armas

Palacio Iturregui
Jr. Pizarro 688

CAJAMARCA

Rescue Room
Jr. Amalia Puga 750

Teatro Municipal
Av. Amazonas

Cerro Apolonia
Jr. 2 de Mayo (three blocks from plaza)

IQUITOS

The Iron House
Putumayo & Raymondi
(cnr of the Plaza de Armas)
Supposedly designed by Eiffel and imported piece-by-piece during rubber boom days.

ANTIQUE & ART GALLERIES

LIMA

The best establishments are located in San Isidro, Miraflores and Barranco.

Banco Continental
Tarata 201, Miraflores
Tel: 44-0011
2 p.m.-8.30 p.m. Mon-Fri; 6 p.m.-8 p.m. Sat

Borkas
Las Camelias 851, San Isidro
Tel: 40-8415
10.30 a.m.-8 p.m. Mon-Fri; 5 p.m.-8 p.m. Sat

Camino Brent
Burgos 170, San Isidro
4 p.m.-8 p.m. Mon-Sat

Cosmos
Pasaje los Pinos 173, Miraflores
5 p.m.-9 p.m. Mon-Sat

El Taller
Los Manzanos 353, San Isidro
Tel: 22-0351

Equus
Colon 501, Miraflores
Tel: 45-6592
5 p.m.-9 p.m. Mon-Sat

Forum
Larco 1150, Miraflores
11 a.m.-1 p.m. & 5 p.m.-9 p.m. Mon-Fri

Sanchez Galeria de Arte Colonial
Jose Granda 460, San Isidro
Tel: 22-5970

Porta 725
Porta 725, Miraflores
Tel: 47-6158
11 a.m.-1 p.m. & 4 p.m.-8 p.m. Mon-Sat

Peruvian North American Cultural Institute
Arequipa 4798, Miraflores
Tel: 46-0381

Also at:
Cuzco 446, Lima
Tel: 28-3530

Praxis
San Martin 689, Barranco
Tel: 67-2845
5 p.m.-9 p.m. Mon-Sat

"715"
Benavides 216, Miraflores
Tel: 47-2687
4 p.m.-8 p.m. Mon-Sat

Sol
Las Lias 150, Lince
Tel: 71-1029
5 p.m.-9 p.m. Mon-Sat

Trapecio
Larco 143, Miraflores
Tel: 44-0842
5 p.m.-9 p.m. Mon-Sat

Galeria Artesanal Chiwake
Av. Arequipa 4005, Miraflores
Tel: 40-2173

CONCERTS

In Lima, the Philharmonic Society presents celebrated international orchestras and soloists. For information:

Porta 170, Of. 301, Miraflores
Open Mon/Wed/Fri 10 a.m.-12 p.m.
Tel: 45-7395

THEATER & MUSIC

Teatro Municipal
Ica 300, Lima
Symphony, opera, plays and ballet.

The English troupe – "The Good Companions", which is set up by the British Council, performs different plays each month. These are advertised in the English-language weekly, the *Lima Times*, available at all major hotels. Tel: 47-9760 for information.

Other theater venues in Lima:

Teatro Segura
Huancavelica

Teatro Arequipa
Av. Arequipa

NIGHTLIFE

LIVE MUSIC

LIMA

In Lima the traveler encounters two types of live music: Folkorica and Criolla. The former is typical of the Andean highlands, while the coastal Criolla style is more popular in Lima.

The best places to see live Peruvian music are "Peñas" – lively nightclubs with colorful performances and enthusiastic audience dancing.

Peña Hatuchay
Trujillo 228, Rimac (across the bridge from the center of town)
The best night out for budget-conscious travelers, and anyone else for that matter who is willing to get into the informal spirit of the evening. An instantly welcoming interior and a great variety show.

Barranco is Lima's "bohemian" suburb of cafes, bars and live music. A couple of venues offer regular shows:

Karamanduka
Sanchez Carrion 135, Barranco
Tel: 47-3237
Open for lunch and dinner with music every night.

El Buho Pub
Sucre 315
Creole music.

Los Balcones
Grau (in front of Municipal Park)
For Creole and Negroide music.

La Estacion de Barranco
Pedro de Osma 112

Taberna 1900
Grau 268

For jazz and contemporary music try:

La Casona de Barranco
Grau 329

La Casa de Edith Barr
Ignacio Merino 250, Miraflores
Tel: 41-0612
A more prestigious ambience presenting creole music

CUZCO

Cuzco has some of the best peñas in South America, with a range of Andean styles (some of the bands are internationally well-known). They're mostly around the plaza and easy to find because the music blares out of their windows. Two peñas sharing the same staircase on the south-western side of the plaza are probably the best place to start.

Several restaurants around the plaza (such as the Roma and El Truco) also have live music – just stroll around and listen for the playing. Alternatively, many of the larger hotels also stage folkloric shows.

HUARÁZ

El Tambo
Jose de la Mar 776, Huaráz

Tasco Bar
Jr. Lucar y Torre 556, Huaráz

Taberna Imantata
Av. Luzuriaga 407, Huaráz

NIGHTCLUBS

LIMA

Satchmo Jazz Bar
538 La Paz, Miraflores
Tel: 44-1753
Sophisticated New Orleans style jazz and surroundings.

Casablanca
117 P. Fierro, San Isidro
Tel: 40-7751

Lions Club
Madrid 338 (by the Plaza Bolognesi)
Features live jazz most evenings.

BARS

LIMA

Brenchley Arms
Atahualpa 174
Typical English Pub with wholesome fare
and dart board.

Johann Sebastian Bar
Schell 369
Relaxing venue with classical background
music.

CUZCO

A favorite hangout for gingos in Cuzco is the
Cross Keys Pub, run by British-born ornithologist Barry Walker (who, incidentally,
wrote the section on "Wildlife of the Sierra"
in this book) and his Peruvian wife. It's very
friendly and relaxed – you can even buy
English gin and Australian rum if you so
desire (although the South American versions are cheaper and almost as good). It's
also on the south-western side of the plaza.

DISCOS

LIMA

Arizona Colt
(below El Pacifico cinema, Miraflores)
La Miel, Jose Pardo 120

Faces
Centro Comercial
Camino Real, Level A 68-72
(intersection of Camino Real & Choque-
huanca in San Isidro)

SHOPPING

WHAT TO BUY

In Lima as well as the many regional market
places, the best quality and value lies in
handcrafted products (see chapter on
Artesanías). This particularly applies to gold,
silver and copper work, as well as Peru's rich
textile goods – such as alpaca garments and
woven tapestries. Many tourists also take
home reproductions of pre-Columbian ceramics, with gourds being a great favorite.

Visitors to the jungle may have the opportunity to purchase traditional handicrafts,
including adornments (dance necklaces),
utensils (baskets, food bowls, hunting bags),
and weapons (bows, arrows, spears). However, visitors should never be tempted to buy
skins, live animals, or arrows decorated with
colorful parrot feathers. This trade is often
illegal and has direct negative consequences
in destroying wildlife populations.

The harvesting of wild Brazil-nuts is a
major economy of the jungle and is not
destructive to the forest. Fresh Brazil-nuts
are richer in flavor than processed nuts as
they still contain many of their natural oils.

Apart from artesanías, quality shopping
goods can only be found in the commercial
streets of Miraflores and San Isidro, where
suppliers for international brands keep a
limited stock at very high prices. For bargains
in electronics, you would do better to cross
the southern border into northern Chile and
its Duty Free Zona Franca complexes.

This is true also for camera supplies, as
well as any photo developing. Peruvian
standards will often disappoint you, so save
your exposed film to be developed when you
get home.

If you are looking for books in English,
however, there are several possibilities. The
South American Explorers Club has a good
library for all things South American and
relevant guide books are on sales. Members

of the club can utilize the free book exchange of paperbacks. There is a chain of ABC bookstores in Lima providing newspapers, magazines, guide books and "coffee table" books in English, French and German. Keep in mind these items will be more expensive than at home. The English language newspaper, *The Lima Times*, also advertises books about Peru which can be obtained from their office in Miraflores at Carabya 928, 3rd Floor. For paperback fiction try: Libreria El Pacifico, under the cinema "El Pacifico" in Miraflores. There is also a book exchange for used paperbacks at Ocona 211, two blocks from the Plaza San Martín, if you can ignore the money changers.

SHOPPING AREAS

Each region has its own distinctive crafts, however, if your time is limited, you'll find that many cultures are well represented in Lima. There are a number of shops within an attractive courtyard at "1900" Belen 1030, as well as at Belen 1066, just down from the Plaza San Martín. Two other recognized centers of quality merchandise are at El Alamo, 5th block of La Paz, Miraflores and El Suche, the 6th block of La Paz in Miraflores.

Outdoor markets offer the best bargains although the quality varies and one needs to be wary of pickpockets. The best outdoor market, known as the Mercado Indio, takes place on Avenida La Marina from blocks 6 to 10. A relaxed artists' market with varying quality canvasses is on Parque Kennedy in the heart of Miraflores. Here are some other reliable sources for artesanía:

Artesanías del Peru
Av. Jorge Basadre 610, San Isidro

In Arequipa: Av. General Moran 120

In Iquitos: Putomayo 128

In Cuzco: There are many outlets facing the main plaza and quite a few more near the major hotels.

In Lima:

Poco a Poco S.A.
Av. Nicolas de Pierola 712, Of. 14, Lima

Also at:
Juan de Arona 425-431, San Isidro

For alpaca, leather and fur products in Lima:

Royal Alpaca
La Pasz 646, store 14-15
El Suche commercial center, Miraflores
9.30 a.m.-9.30 p.m. Mon-Sat; 11 a.m.-7 p.m. Sun

Alpaca 111 S.A. (English spoken)
Av. Larco 859, Miraflores
Tel: 47-7163

Also at:
Camino Real Shopping Center
Level A, Shop 32-33, San Isidro

In Arequipa:

Alpaca 111
Jerusalem 115
Tel: 21-2347

Also in Arequipa:
El Zaguan
Santa Catalina 120A
Tel: 22-3950

In Cuzco: 4 Ruinas 472
Tel: 23-6322

For gold objects try *in Lima*:

Casa Welsch
Jiron Union 498

Cabuchon
Libertadores 532, San Isidro

Wako
Jr de la Union 841, Lima
10 a.m.-1.30 p.m. and 3 p.m.-7.30 p.m. Mon-Sat

Ceramics and tapestries are the specialty of El Artesano, Jr Diez Canseco 498, Miraflores, Lima.

The major hotels often house exclusive jewelry and artezanía stores such as H. Stern Jewelers, with outlets at the Hotel Gran Bolivar, the Lima Sheraton, Miraflores Cesar's Hotel, the Gold Museum and the International Airport.

For clothing printed with Peruvian designs in Lima:

Silvania Prints
Colmena 714 (between the Gran Bolivar and the Hotel Crillon)

Also at:
Conquistadores 905, San Isidro

Club Peru
Conquistadores 946, San Isidro

SPORTS

Lima Tours can arrange visits to El Pueblo Inn, a country club 11 km east of Lima, specifically for sporting activities such as tennis, golf, horse riding and swimming. Another agency to try is:

Sudex Agency
Carabaya 933, Miraflores
Tel: 28-6054

Ask about other 18 hole golf courses at Country Club de Villa, Granja Azul and La Planicie.

For ten-pin bowling and pool playing, go to the Brunswick Bowl, Balta 135, Miraflores.

Volleyball and polo have a large following in Peru and cricket is played at the Lima Cricket Club.

A great variety of sports are available to tourists outside Lima. Horse riding is popular in the Sierra, where horses can easily be hired. Fly fishing in Andean lakes and streams is a rewarding pastime and there is excellent deep-sea fishing off Ancon, north of Lima.

SPECTATOR

The main spectator sports in South-American countries are football, horse racing and, to a lesser extent, bullfighting.

Association football matches take place at the National Stadium, Paseo de le Republica in downtown Lima, which seats 45,000.

Horse racing takes place most weekends and some summer evenings at the Monterrico Racetrack at the junction of the Pan-American Highway South with Avnida Javier Prado. Take your passport to join the members stand.

The two bullfighting seasons in Lima are October-November and a short one in March. The prestigious bullfighting ring is at Acho in Rimac, where famous international matadors make guest appearances. However, the regular proceedings are often a little sordid, with the bullfighters little more than incompetent butchers and the audience, drunk on beer, throwing bottles and howling in derision. Still, a cultural experience.

FURTHER READING

GENERAL

Galeano, Eduardo. *The Open Veins of Latin America*. Monthly Review Press. A vivid account of the region's history from a left-wing perspective.

Hemming, John. *The Conquest of the Incas*. Penguin, 1983. The best modern account of the fall of the Inca empire. Extremely readable style, brings the history of Peru to life. Hemming has also written a coffee table book called *Monuments of the Incas* with black and white photography by Edward Ranney. Both are classic introductions to understanding Peru.

Reid, Michael. *Peru: Paths to Poverty*. Latin American Bureau, 1985. Probably the most cogent and readable interpretation of Peru's modern history.

Wright, Ronald. *Cut Stones and Crossroads*. Viking Press, 1984 (also in Penguin). Subtitled "A Journey in the Two Worlds of Peru", this is considered the best travel book on the country in recent years. Wright captures the many ups and downs of travel in Peru, with some stimulating insights. Worth reading despite a certain snobbishness in outlook.

The novels of Peru's high-profile writer Mario Vargas Llosa are another interesting insight into the country's psyche. *Aunt Julia and the Scriptwriter* (the basis for the recent US film "Tune in Tomorrow") and *The Time of the Hero* are probably the most readable. *The Green House* is set in Peru's Amazon basin.

For a collection of shots by Peru's most famous photographer (and one of Latin America's greats), look for *Martin Chambi: Photographs of Peru 1920-1950*, published by the Banco de la República.

ARCHAEOLOGY & PRE-INCA CULTURES

"Long Before the Inca." *Natural History* 2: 66-82. (1989)

Donnan, Christopher B. (ed.) *Early Ceremonial Architecture in the Andes*. Dumbarton Oaks Research Library and Collection, 1985.

"Masterworks of Art Reveal a Remarkable Pre-Inca World." *National Geographic* 177/6: 16-33. (1990)

Hadingham, Evan. *Lines to the Mountain Gods: Nazca and the Mysteries of Peru*. Random House, 1987.

Isbell, William H. and Katharina J. Schreiber. "Was Wari a State?" *American Antiquity* 43/4: 372-389. (1976)

Keatings, Richard W. (ed.) *Peruvian Prehistory*. Cambridge University Press, 1988.

Kolata, Alan L. "Tiwanaku and its Hinterland." *Archaeology* 40/1: 36-41. (1987)

Moseley, Michael E. and Carol J. Mackey. "Chan Chan: Peru's Ancient City of Kings." *National Geographic* 143/3: 318-344. (1973)

Moseley, Michael E. and Luis Watanabe. "The Adobe Sculptures of Huaca de los Reyes." *Archaeology* 27: 154-161. (1974)

Pozorski, Shelia and Thomas Pozorski. "Recent Excavations at Pampa de las Llamas-Moxeke – a Complex Initial Period Site in Peru." *Journal of Field Archaeology* 13/4: 381-401. (1986)

Pozorski, Thomas and Shelia Pozorski. "An Early Stone Carving from Pampa de las Llamas-Moxeke, Casma Valley, Peru." *Journal of Field Archaeology* 15/3: 114-119. (1988)

Quilter, Jeffrey. "Architecture and Chronology at El Paraíso, Peru." *Journal of Field Archaeology* 12: 279-297. (1985)

Reinhard, Johan. *The Nazca Lines: A New Perspective on their Origins and Meaning*. 4th edition. Editorial Los Pinos, 1988.

INCA SOCIETY

Brundage, Burr Cartwright. *Lords of Cuzco*. Norman, Oklahoma, 1967.

Brundage, Burr Cartwright. *Empire of the Incas*. Norman, Oklahoma, 1963. This and the above are two highly tendentious but well written and researched accounts.

Garcilaso De La Vega, Inca. *Comentarios Reales de los Incas*. Buenos Aires, 1943. Classic 16th-century accounts by mestizo chronicler (in Spanish).

Gaspairini, Garziano and Louise Margolies. *Inca Architecture*. Bloomington, 1980. The most complete book on the subject.

Guaman Poma De Ayala, Felipe. *Nueva Cronica y Buen Gobierno*. Mexico City, 1988. Hard-to-read 16th-century chronicle, with classic illustrations (in Spanish).

Hyslop, John. *The Inka road system*. New York, 1984. Firsthand account of the author's investigations.

Kendall, Ann. *Everyday Life of the Incas*. London, 1973. Some useful background information.

Rostworowski de Diez Canseco, Maria. *Historia del Tahuantinsuyu*. Lima, 1988. Modern, non-imperialist view of the Incas (in Spanish).

Rowe, John H. *The Incas* (Section of the Handbook of South American Indians). Washington, 1946. A study that set the groove in Inca-ology for three decades. Nowadays its conclusions about Inca history and social organization are challenged by some scholars.

Urbano, Henrique. *Wiracocha y Ayar*. Cuzco, 1981. Summary of Inca origin myths (in Spanish).

Urton, Gary. *At the Crossroads of the Earth*

and the Sky. Austin, 1981. A scholarly, well-written and absorbing account of the cosmology of the modern Quechua people, by a field anthropologist. Soon to be reprinted in paperback.

Von Hagen, Victor W. *Realm of the Incas*. New York, 1957. Still one of the better accounts of Inca daily life.

COLONIAL HISTORY

Descola, Jean. *Daily Life in Colonial Peru*. Trans. by Michael Hern. George Allen & Unwin, 1968.

Dobyns, Henry E. and Paul L. Doughty. *Peru: A Cultural History*. Oxford University Press, 1976.

Kubler, George. "The Quechua in the Colonial World." *Handbook of South American Indians*. Julian H. Steward (ed.) Vol 2: 331-410. Smithsonian Institution, 1946.

Lothrop, Samuel K. *Inca Treasure as Depicted by Spanish Historians*. The Southwest Museum, 1938.

Spalding, Karen. *Huarochiri: An Andean Society under Inca and Spanish Rule*. Standford University Press, 1984.

Wachtel, Nathan. *Vision of the Vanquished: The Spanish Conquest through Indian Eyes*. The Harvester Press, 1977.

MACHU PICCHU

Angles, Victor. *Machu Picchu – Enigmatica Ciudad Inka*. 2nd edition. Lima, 1987. Account of the author's studies and Inca Trail explorations (in Spanish).

Bingham, Hiram. *Lost City of the Incas*. New York, 1972. Classic account of Bingham's explorations. Outdated theories, but a great read.

Bingham, Hiram. *Machu Picchu, an Inca Citadel*. New York, 1979. More details of Bingham's discoveries.

Fejos, Paul. *Archaeological Explorations in the Cordillera Vilcabamba*. New York, 1944. Hard to find but fascinating record of the first systematic survey of the Inca Trail.

Lumbreras, Luis G. *Arqueologia de la America Andina*. Lima, 1981. A search for connections in Andean culture (in Spanish).

Savoy, Gene. *Antisuyo*. New York, 1970. Fascinating book, long out of print, by a man with an incredible nose for lost cities.

OTHER "LOST CITIES"

Hagen, Victor W. von. *The Golden Man: The Quest for El Dorado*. Glasgow, 1974.

Hemming, John. *The Search for El Dorado*. London, 1978.

Iwaki Ordóñez, Rubén. *Operacion Paititi*. Cuzco, 1975.

Levillier, Roberto. *El Paititi, El Dorado, y las Amzonas*. Buenos Aires, 1976.

Pérez de Tudela y Bueso, Juan. *Mirabilis in altis*. Madrid, 1983.

Polentini Wester, Juan Carlos. *Por las rutas del Paititi*. Lima, 1979.

ANDEAN WILDLIFE

Pearson, Oliver P. *Mammals in the Highlands of Southern Peru*. Museum of Comparative Zoology, Harvard.

Grimwood, I.R. *The Distribution and Status of some Peruvian Mammals*. New York Zoological Society, Special Publication 21, 1968.

AMAZON JUNGLE

GENERAL

Tropical Nature – by Adrian Forsyth and Ken Myiata. An excellent introduction to life and death in a New World rainforest.

Jungles – by Ayensu. A good overall account of the world's rainforests.

The Cloud Forest – Peter Matthiesson's account of travel on the Amazon and through the cloud forest of Peru.

Lizzie – Edited by Tony Morrison. The true story of a young, turn-of-the-century Englishwoman's trip up the Amazon and over the Fitzcarrald pass into Manu, based on her letters.

WILDLIFE

Castner, James L. *Rainforests: A Guide to Tourist and Research Facilities at Selected Tropical Forest Sites*. Feline Press.

Forsyth, Adrian and Ken Miyata. *Tropical Nature*. Charles Scribner's Sons. Entertaining and well written account of rainforest ecology.

Hilty, Steve. *A Guide to the Birds of Colombia*. Princeton Press. The most useful bird identification guidebook.

Myers, Norman. *The Primary Source – Tropical Forests and Our Future.*

Parker, T. *An Annotated Checklist of Peruvian Birds.*

AMAZON INDIANS

At Play in the Fields of the Lord – Peter Mattiesson's novel of uncontacted tribes and missionaries set in the department of Madre de Dios, Peru.

Keep the River on the Right – the true account of a Fulbright scholar who lived with an uncontacted tribe in southeast Peru.

The Wizard of the Upper Amazon – Ralph Lamb's true account of a boy captured by Indians in northern Peru and his apprenticeship as a shaman.

Shabono – by Florinada Donner. Although this novel is set in Brazil and not Peru, it is one of the best accounts of what it is like to live with an Amazonian tribe, written by an anthropologist who threw away her notes and "went native".

Farewell to Eden – Matthew Huxley's account of the Amahuaca Indians in southeast Peru.

People of the Sacred Waterfall – Michael Harner's celebrated ethnography of the head-shrinking Jivaro Indians in northeast Peru.

The Conquest of the Incas – The classic account of the Spanish conquest by the British historian John Hemming. The last few chapters deal with the Inca jungle capital Vilcabamba and its discovery.

Location of Peruvian Amazon Indian agencies:

COICA
Jiron Almagro 614, Lima 11, Peru
Tel: 63-1983

CAAP
Avenida Gonzales Prada 626, Magdalena del Mar (Lima), Peru
Tel: 61-5223.
Has small but good Amazon library.

CIPA
666 Avenida Ricardo Palma, Miraflores (Lima), Peru
Tel: 46-4823

Name of Peruvian Amazon Indian artesanal store in Lima:

Antisuyo
Jiron Tacna 460, Miraflores
Tel: 47-2557

USEFUL ADDRESSES

EMBASSIES & CONSULATES

Argentina
Pablo Bermudez 143, 2nd Floor, Jesus Maria
Tel: 24-5984/23-8172
8 a.m.-1 p.m.

Austria
Av. Central 643, San Isidro
Tel: 42-8851
9 a.m.-12 p.m.

Bolivia
Los Castanos 235, San Isidro
Tel: 22-8231
9 a.m.-1 p.m.

Britain
Washington Building, 12th Floor
Plaza Washington, Lima
Tel: 33-5032/28-3830
10 a.m.-3 p.m. Mon-Thur, 10 a.m.-1 p.m. Fri

Canada
(also representing Australian and New Sealand citizens)
Libertad 130, Miraflores
Tel: 44-4015/46-3890
8.30 a.m.-11 p.m.

Chile
Javier Prado Oeste 790, San Isidro
Tel: 40-7965
8.45 a.m.-12.30 p.m.

Colombia
Natalio Sanchez 125, 4th Floor, Lima
Tel: 31-2074/40-7835

Denmark
Bernardo Monteagudo 201, San Isidro
Tel: 62-1090
9 a.m.-1 p.m.

Ecuador
Las Palmeras 356, San Isidro
Tel: 22-8138
9 a.m.-1 p.m.

Finland
Los Eucaliptos 291, 7th Floor, San Isidro
Tel: 70-3750
8.30 a.m.-4 p.m.

France
Arequipa 3415, San Isidro
Tel: 70-4968
9 a.m.-12 p.m. (Visas 9 a.m.-11 a.m.)

West Germany
Arequipa 4210, Miraflores
Tel: 45-9997
9 a.m.-12 p.m.

Ireland
Carlos Povias Osores 410, San Isidro
Tel: 23-0808

Israel
Washington Building, 6th Floor
Plaza Washington, Lima
Tel: 33-4431
9 a.m.-12 p.m.

Italy
Gregorio Escobedo 298, Jesus Maria
Tel: 63-2727
9 a.m.-12 p.m.

Japan
San Felipe 356, Jesus Maria
Tel: 63-0000
9 a.m.-11 a.m.; 3 p.m.-6 p.m. Mon-Fri

The Netherlands
Av. Principal 190, San Borja
Tel: 75-1548/72-8635
9 a.m.-12 p.m.

Norway
Canaval Moreyra 595, San Isidro
Tel: 40-4080
9.30 a.m.-1.30 p.m.

Spain
Jorge Basadre 498, San Isidro
Tel: 70-5600/31-0420
9 a.m.-12 p.m.

Switzerland
Av. Salaverry 3240, San Isidro
Tel: 62-4090
9 a.m.-12 p.m.

United States
Grimaldo del Solar 346, Miraflores
Tel: 44-3621
8.15 a.m.-11 a.m. Mon-Fri (except Wed)
USA Embassy office on the 1400 block of
Garcilaso de le Vega and Av. Espana in the
city center. Tel: 28-6000

U.S.S.R.
Salaverry 3516, San Isidro
Tel: 61-6473
10 a.m.-1.30 p.m.

Venezuela
Av. Salaverry 3005, San Isidro
Tel: 41-5948
9 a.m.-12 p.m.

AIRLINE OFFICES

Aerocondor
Juan de Arona 781, San Isidro
Tel: 42-5663/41-1354

Aerochasqui
Av. Nicolas de Pierola 611, Of. 301, Lima
Tel: 27-5471/27-5758

Aeroflot
Paseo de le Republica 144, Lima
Tel: 32-1377

Aerolines Argentinas
Av. Jose Pardo 805, 3rd Floor, Miraflores
Tel: 44-0810/45-8845

Aeroperu
Plaza San Martín
Tel: 31-7626 (domestic)
32-2995 (international); or

Pardo 601, Miraflores
Tel: 47-8900
Reservations: 47-8255

Air France
Juan de Arona 830, San Isidro
Tel: 70-4870/70-4702

Air Panama
Av. Arequipa 4036, Miraflores
Tel: 72-5277

Alitalia
Camino Real 497, San Isidro
Tel: 42-8507

American Airlines
Francia 597, Miraflores
Tel: 47-9798

Avianca
Blvd Los Olivos, Paz Soldan 225, San Isidro
Tel: 70-4435

British Airways
Camino Real 348, 12th Floor, San Isidro
Tel: 47-1774

Canadian Airlines
Paseo de la Republica 126, Lima
Tel: 31-9293

Cubana
Paseo de la Republica 126, Lima
Tel: 31-9812

Ecuatoriana
Jose Pardo 231, Miraflores
Tel: 47-2454

Faucett
Inca Garcilaso de la Vega 865, Lima
Tel: 33-6364

Iberia
Nicolas de Pierola 820, Lima
Tel: 28-3833

KLM
Jose Pardo 805, 6th Floor, Miraflores
Tel: 47-1277

Lan Chile
Jose Pardo 805, 5th Floor, Miraflores
Tel: 47-6682

Lloyd Aereo Boliviano
Jose Pardo 805, Of. 201, Miraflores
Tel: 47-3292

Lufthansa
Centro Camino Real, Torre de Pilar
(8th Floor), San Isidro
Tel: 42-4455

Varig
Nicolas de Pierola 616, Lima
Tel: 24-6060

Viasa
Jose Pardo 805, 4th Floor, Miraflores
Tel: 47-8666

TOURIST INFORMATION OFFICES (FOPTUR)

Lima
Jiron de la Union 1066, (2nd Floor of
the Tambo de Oro restaurant), Belen, Lima
Tel: 32-3559
8 a.m.-7 p.m. Mon-Fri

Also worth visiting is the South American
Explorers Club for up-to-date information:

Av. Republica de Portugal 146, Lima
Tel: 31-4480
9.30 a.m.-5 p.m. Mon-Fri
or write to : Casilla 3714, Lima 100, Peru

Ica
Cajamarca 179
7.30 a.m.-3 p.m. Mon-Fri

Nazca
The Hotel Nazca on Av. Lima is the main
source of local information.

Cuzco
Portal Belen 115, Plaza de Armas
Tel: 23-7364
8 a.m.-5.30 p.m. Mon-Fri; 8.30 a.m.-12.30
p.m. Sat
Airport office open until 12 p.m. daily.

Puno
Jr. Arequipa 314
Tel: 35-3804
8 a.m.-12.30 p.m. & 2.15 p.m.-5.30 p.m.
Mon-Fri

Arequipa
La Merced 117
8.30 a.m.-12.30 p.m. & 2.30 p.m.-3.30 p.m.
Mon-Fri
Airport office open daily.

Huaráz
Av. Luzuriaga 459
Tel: 721521
8.30 a.m.-12.30 p.m. & 2.30 p.m.-3.30 p.m.
Mon-Fri

Casa de Guias (Guide House)
Parque Ginebra 28G, Apartado 123
Huaráz-Ancash
Tel: 721333

FOPTUR - Tourist Office
Plaza de Armas/Post Office Buidling
Huaráz-Ancash
Tel: 721031

Trujillo
Independencia 628
Tel: 24-1936
Airport Office

Cajamarca
Direccion de Turismo
conjunto Belen (also comprising the colonia
church and hospital of Belen)

Chiclayo
Elias Aguirre 830-832, Of. 202
Tel: 22-7776

Art/Photo Credits

Photography by

INDEX

A

acculturation, 115
acllas, 53
adobe
  city, 23, 300
  friezes, 36
agricultural cycle in the Andes, 101
Aguirre, Wrath of God (1972), 259
Almagro, Diego de, 59, 62, 66, 188, 195
Alianza Popular Rvolucionaria Americana (APRA), 77, 79-81, 177, 297
almuerzo (lunch), 102
Alva, Walter, 44, 48
alpacas, 29
Amazon
  birdlife, 276-278
  commercial riverboat, 269
  hardwood trees, 113
  Indians, 111, 114
  jungle, 113, 259-274
  jungle lodges, 268
  jungle survival, 270
  population, 264
  river, 26, 111
  tribes, 114, 115
  village, 114
ancient civilizations, 35, 36, 49, 287
Andean
  climate, 101
  festivals, 105
  hospitality, 104
  musical tradition, 106, 108
  popular music, 108
  tradition, 89
Andes, 26, 29, 131
Antis, 111, 219
Antisuyo, 111
Apurimac River, 191
apus, 52
aqueducts, 29, 135
Arequipa, 30, 247-253
Artesanias del Peru, 118
Antesanias Huamanqaqa, 118
astronomy, 187
Atahualpa, 52, 59, 60, 62, 179, 187, 303-304
Ayacucho, 39
Ayala, Felipe Waman Puma de, 108
ayllus, 51, 53
Aymara, 52, 90
Aztec empire, 59

B

Balta, Jose President, 76
bankruptcy of Peru, 76
Basque immigrants, 76
Batab Grande, 40
Battle of Ayacucho, 74
Belaunde Fernando (1963-68), 77, 78
Bible, 60
Bingham, Hiram, 43, 188, 213-214, 219
Bolívar, Simón, 74, 160, 297
Bonaparte, Napoleon, 73
Bondy, Sebastian Salazar, 159
Bruning Gold Museum (Lambayeque), 44, 45
Bujanda, Don Baltasar Jaime Martinez de Companon, 73

C

Cabinet of Natural History and of Antiquities, 73
Cahuachi, 38
Cajamarca, 60, 303, 305, 308, 311-312
Callao, 160, 161, 168
Callejon de Conchucos, 37
Callejón de Huaylas, 37, 285-293
Cameloid fiber, 37
capitalism, 96
Casma valley, 36
Catac, 289
ceramics
  Moche, 43
  contemporary, 120, 121
Chalcuchima, 62
Chan Chan, 40, 300-301
Charles III, 73
Charles V, 62, 73
Chavín, 37-38
Chavín de Huantar (temple complex), 291-293
Chicha, 102
Chiclayo, 39-40, 49
Chillon Valley, 40
Chimu, 40
Chincha, 102
Chincha guano islands, 75
Chinese immigrants and labour, 26, 75, 91
Chosen women, 194
Christianity
  Inca times, 67
  Catholicism, 26, 96, 99, 103, 104, 173, 176, 178, 185, 194, 195, 280
  colonial times, 70-71
  missionaries, 113, 114, 115
Club de la Banca y Comercio, 92
Club Nacional, 91-92
Coca leaf, 30, 70, 80, 280
cocaine industry, 265, 280
Colca canyon, 191
colonial Peru, 69-71
Columbus, Christopher, 210
communications, 29
condors, 29, 143, 320
conquest of the Incas, 60
conservation of wildlife in Peru, 265, 266
Copacabana, 238
Coricancha, 52-53, 63
Cortes, Hanando, 59

crafts of Peru, 117-121, 241
Croix, Viceroy Teodoro de, 73
Cuzco, 26, 51, 54, 63, 111, 185-209

D – E

deepest canyon, 26
desert coast of Peru, 26, 317-328
diseases, 115
Dobyns, Henry E., 74
Doughty, Paul L., 74
Earthly Paradise, 210
Easter Island: A Mystery Solved, 49
economy, 80, 81
eco-tourism, 266
education, 97
El Condor Pasa, 106
El Dorado
    see Legend of El Dorado
Elias Domingo, 322
El Niño, 29, 39, 40, 78
El Purgatorio, 48
El Rayo, 48
El Triunfo, 190, 192
encomienda system, 63, 69
ethnic cultures, 26
eucalyptus, 136, 178
European diseases, 111
European immigrants, 91
exploring Peru, 151
extraterrestrials, 57

F

Ferdinand VII, 73
fertilizers, 29
fishing vacations, 306-307
folk art, 94
food
    contemporary Peruvian cuisine, 123-127
    grains, 29, 36, 100, 101
    guinea pig, 132, 142
    potatoes, 36, 100-101
    tropical fruits, 100
    vegetables, 100
freak showers, 29
Fujimori, Alberto, 81, 97, 171
FUNAI, 114

G

Galleries
    see museums
Garcia, Alan, 79-80, 81
Garden of Eden, 212
geoglyphs, 38
Gibbs, Anthony and Sons, 75
glaciers, 135, 136
Gondwandaland, 259
Government Palace (Lima), 161
grave robbing, 44
guano, 75
Guzman, Abimael, 79

H

Hemmingway, Earnest, 306-307, 312
Herzog, Werner, 259
Heyerdahl, Thor, 47-48, 302
Hospital Albert Schweitzer, 271
hot springs, 288, 309
Huacas, 52, 159
Huaca de los Reyes, 36
Huallaga Valley, 280-281
Huancayo, 177
Huancavelica, 37
Huaqueros, 44, 106
Huaráz, 286
Huaricoto, 36
Huasear, 59-63
Huascaran, 136, 139, 286
Huaylas, culture, 285
Huayna-Capac, 56-59
Humbolt current, 29
hunting, 52

I

Incas
    administrator, 54, 55
    agriculture, 54, 131
    chosen women, 53
    expansion, 55, 56
    festivals, 53, 55
    Incas' bathing spot, 309
    Inca Kola, 200
    Inca legends, 186
    Inca throne, 198
    Inca trail, 134, 141
    inventions, 57
    military, 56
    rebellions, 64, 71, 73, 197
    religion, 52
    society, 35, 51-52, 323
    writing, 57
independence of Peru, 74
Iquitos, 267
irrigation systems, 26-29
Isle of Amantani, 242-243

J

Japanese immigrants and community, 26, 91
Jauja, 159, 178, 179
jijipapas, 120, 301
Julio C. Tello site museum, 321
jungle 26-30
Karwa, 37
Kon-titi, 47
Kon-titi Museum, 48
Koricancha, 193
Kosok, Paul, 325

L

Lake Titicaca, 26, 39, 231-237
Lambayeque, 40, 44
lapis lazuli, 39

legend of El Dorado, 111, 212
Limab, 30, 63, 64, 71, 74, 95, 159-168, 177
llamas, 29, 36, 100, 137
Llosa, Mario Vargas, 80, 81, 97, 171
Lopez, Joaquin Don, 94
Lord of Sípan, 43-44, 302

M

Machu Picchu, 43, 135, 188, 200, 214, 219-226
Madre de Dios and Mayu rivers, 112, 273, 274
Mama Ocllo, 185
Manco Capac, 51, 64, 67, 111, 185, 188, 190, 197,
    202, 231
Maoist Sendero Luminoso guerilla movement, 79,
    80, 115, 172, 173
Mar, Jose de la, 75
marinera dance, 297, 301-302
Martin, Jose de San, 74, 75, 160
mass communication, 93
mate, 102, 177
Meiggs, Henry, 76, 176, 178
Melville, Herman, 159
Mercado Artesanal, 117
mestizos, 26, 72, 91
micro-climate, 100, 159
migrants, 95, 101
mines, 69, 70, 71, 77
mit'a, 54, 70, 75
Moche, people, 38, 39, 43, 44, 45, 47, 48
modernization, 95
mote, 102
mountain retreat, 286
Mount Huascaran, 26
Moxeke, 36
Museums
    Archaeological Museum (Huaráz), 287
    Archaeological Museum (Trujillo), 300
    Bruning Gold Museum (Lambayeque), 44, 45
    Cassinelli Museum (Trujillo), 300
    Ethnographic and Archaeological Museum
        (Cajamarca), 305
    Gold Museum (Lima), 167
    Julio C. Tello Site Museum (Paracas), 321
    Military Museum (Callao), 168
    Museo Ferroviario (Tacna), 328
    Museo Regional (Ica), 323
    Museum of Anthropology and Archaeology
        (Lima), 166, 293
    Museum of the Inquisition (Lima), 167
    Museum of Religious Art (Cuzeo), 195
    National Museum (Lima), 166
    Rafael Larco Herrera Museum (Lima), 167
    Religious Art Museum (Cajamarca), 305
    Rosa de Ocopa Monastery (Ocopa), 178

N

National Geographic Society, 44, 302
National Parks and Reserves
    Huascaran National Park, 289
    Manu National Park, 30, 263, 272
    Manu Biosphere Reserve, 276
    Tambopata Wildlife Reserve, 30
    Tambopata-Candamo Reserve, 277
natural disasters, 286

Nazca, 38, 39, 324
Nazca lines, 325, 329
Nikei, 91
nitrates, 29
northern desert, 29

O – P

Ollantay, 186
Ollantaytambo, 56, 65, 201
Orellana, Francisco, 111, 112
Orton, James, 237
outdoor pursuits, 285
Pachacamac, 172-173
Pachacutec Yupanqui, 185, 186, 317
Panaca, 51, 53
Paititi, 214-215
Paracas Bay, 37, 320
Parachuti, 56
Paseo de Aguas, 72
Pierola, Nicholas de, 76
Pitluga, Phyllis, 329
Piura, 303
Pizarro
    Diego, 65
    Ferdinand, 66
    Francisco, 26, 29, 59-67, 90, 111, 131, 159, 162,
        178, 286, 297
    Gonzalo, 111, 195
    Hernando, 60, 64, 131, 168
    Pedro, 65
Poor Man's Galápagos, 320
Potosi (Bolivia), 69
Prado, Mariano, 76
pre-Columbian history, 44, 69, 73, 106, 131, 167,
    168, 173, 317, 321
pre-Inca history, 43, 159, 285, 287, 317
public education, 94
puna, 100-101
Pyramids of the Sun and Moon, 40

Q

Quechua, 26, 51-52, 75, 90, 99, 104, 109
quinine, 261
Quito, 56, 111
Radio Tawantinsuyu, 102
railway to Huancayo, 176-179
rainforest, 26, 30, 263
rebellion, 73
reducciones, 101
Reiche, Maria, 325-326, 329
republicanism, 74
republics, 73
retablo, 94, 121
roads, 93
Roman Catholic Church
    see Christianity
rubber
    trees, 112
    boom, 112, 261-262
    market, 113
    seeds, 262

S

sacred valley of the Incas, 191
Sacsayhuaman, 64, 65, 187, 197, 198
Saenz, Manuela, 160
San Francisco Monastery (Lima), 163, 164
Santa Catalina convent, 249-250
Savoy, Gene, 111
sculpture, 39
seven viceral intendencies, 73-74
Shining Path Militants,
    see Maoists Sendoro Liminoso movement
Sierra, 29-30
Simon, Paul and Garfunkel Art (1960s), 106
Sípan
    see Lord of Sípan
soroche, 133, 137-138, 176, 177
Soto, Hernando de, 61
South American Explorers Club, 132
southern coast, 29
Spanish
    conquistadors, 26, 43, 59, 64
    invasion and conquest, 56, 59-67, 125, 131, 140,
        178, 187
    cruelty, 67
    music, 107
subsistence agriculture and pastoralism, 100
Summer Institute of Linguistics, 114, 271
syncretism, 104

T

Tacaynamu, 40
tapadas, 72
Taqujle, 119, 236
Tarapaca, 76
Tawan tinsuyo, 185, 189
Tello, Julio C., 43
Tello Obelisk, 37, 293
Temple of the Sun, 192, 222
terrace farms, 29
Tihuananaco, 39-40
Titu Cusi, 67
Takapu, 52
Toledo, Francisco de, 69, 101
Topa Inca, 185
Torre, Victor Raul Haya de la, 77, 177, 297
Trago, 103
transportation, 29
trekking in the Andes, 131-139

trial marriage, 104
Tristan, Flora, 72
tropical fruits, 100
Trujillo (Peru), 297
Trujillo Valley, 36, 297-305
Tucume, 40, 47, 302
Tumbez, 59
Tupac Amaru, 67
Tupac Amaru II, 71, 189
Tupac Inca Yupanqui, 201

U – V

Ugarte, Jose de la Torre, 322
Uhle, Max, 43
Urco Inca, 186
Uros islands, 236
Urubamba valley, 191-196, 201
Valverde, Vincente de, 60, 61, 62, 66
Vega, Garcilasco de la, 159
Velasco, General Juan Alvarado, 77, 93
vicuña fibers, 119-120
Vilcambamba, 66, 67, 219
Villa El Salvador, 172-173
village life in the Andes, 99
Villegas, Michaela, 72
Viracocha Inca, 185
Vitcos, 66, 67
volcanic activity, 30

W – Y

Wari, 39-40
War of the Pacific, 29, 160
war with Chile, 76
water, 36
wayno, 102, 108-109
weaving, 38, 119-120
wheel invention, 57
Wickham, Henry, 262
wildlife, 30, 140-143, 320
wild vicuña, 135
women in Peruvian society, 96
wool, 119
yanakuna, 52

A
C
D
E
F
G
H
I
J
a
b
c

e
f
g
h
i
j
k
l